Easy Piano

Disney's BEAUTY AND THE BEAST
THE BROADWAY MUSICAL

Walt Disney Productions
presents

SUSAN EGAN TERRENCE MANN

in

Disney's
Beauty and the Beast

Music by
ALAN MENKEN

Lyrics by
HOWARD ASHMAN & TIM RICE

Book by
LINDA WOOLVERTON

with

BURKE MOSES GARY BEACH BETH FOWLER HEATH LAMBERTS
ELEANOR GLOCKNER STACEY LOGAN BRIAN PRESS KENNY RASKIN

JOAN BARBER ROXANE BARLOW HARRISON BEAL MICHAEL-DEMBY CAIN
KATE DOWE DAVID ELDER MERWIN FOARD GREGOREY GARRISON JACK HAYES
KIM HUBER ELMORE JAMES ALISA KLEIN ROB LOREY PATRICK LOY
BARBARA MARINEAU JOANNE McHUGH ANNA McNEELY DAN MOJICA
BILL NABEL WENDY OLIVER VINCE PESCE PAIGE PRICE SARAH SOLIE SHANNON
GORDON STANLEY LINDA TALCOTT CHUCK WAGNER WYSANDRIA WOOLSEY

and
TOM BOSLEY
as Maurice

Scenic Design
STAN MEYER

Costume Design
ANN HOULD-WARD

Lighting Design
NATASHA KATZ

Sound Design
T. RICHARD FITZGERALD

Hair Design
DAVID H. LAWRENCE

Illusions
JIM STEINMEYER
JOHN GAUGHAN

Prosthetics
JOHN DODS

General Management
DODGER PRODUCTIONS

Production Supervisor
JEREMIAH J. HARRIS

Production Stage Manager
JAMES HARKER

Press Representative
BONEAU/BRYAN-BROWN

Casting
JAY BINDER

Dance Arrangements
GLEN KELLY

Musical Coordinator
JOHN MILLER

Fight Director
RICK SORDELET

Orchestrations
DANNY TROOB

Musical Supervision & Vocal Arrangements
DAVID FRIEDMAN

Music Direction & Incidental Music Arrangements
MICHAEL KOSARIN

Choreography by
MATT WEST

Directed by
ROBERT JESS ROTH

ISBN 978-0-634-00063-8

Walt Disney Music Company
Wonderland Music Company, Inc.

DISTRIBUTED BY

7777 W. BLUEMOUND RD. P.O. BOX 13819 MILWAUKEE, WI 53213

Disney's
BEAUTY AND THE BEAST
THE BROADWAY MUSICAL

BELLE

Lyrics by HOWARD ASHMAN
Music by ALAN MENKEN

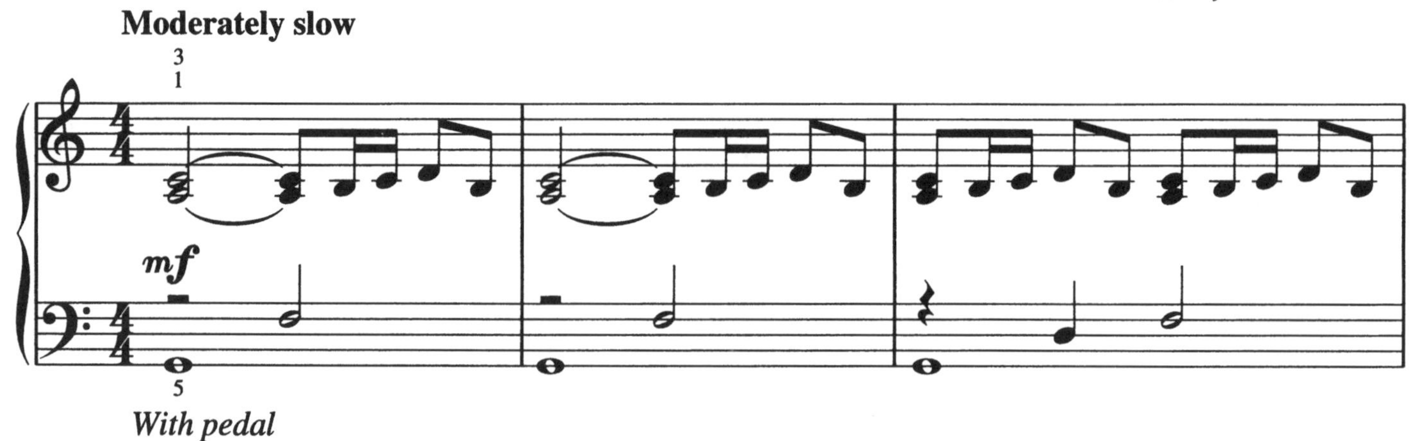
Moderately slow
mf
With pedal

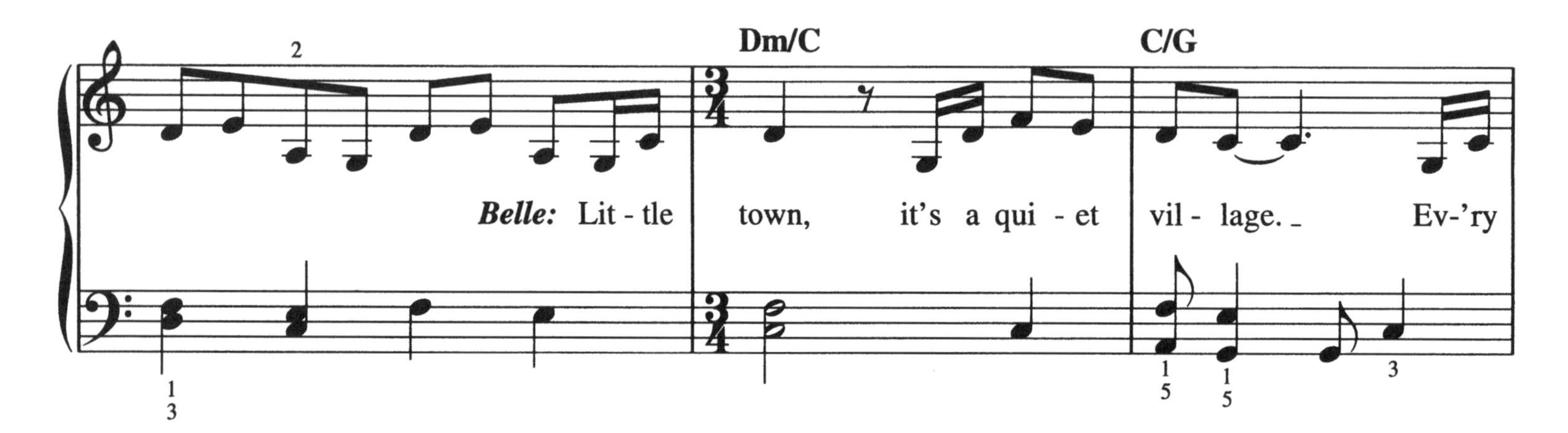
Dm/C
C/G
Belle: Lit - tle
town, it's a qui - et
vil - lage.
Ev-'ry

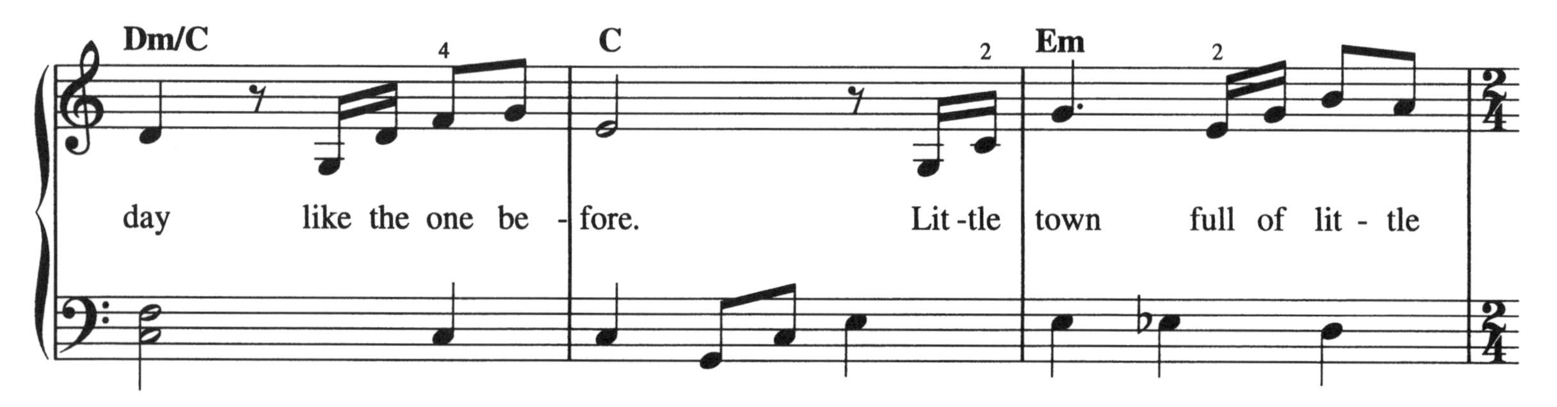
Dm/C
C
Em
day like the one be - fore.
Lit - tle
town full of lit - tle

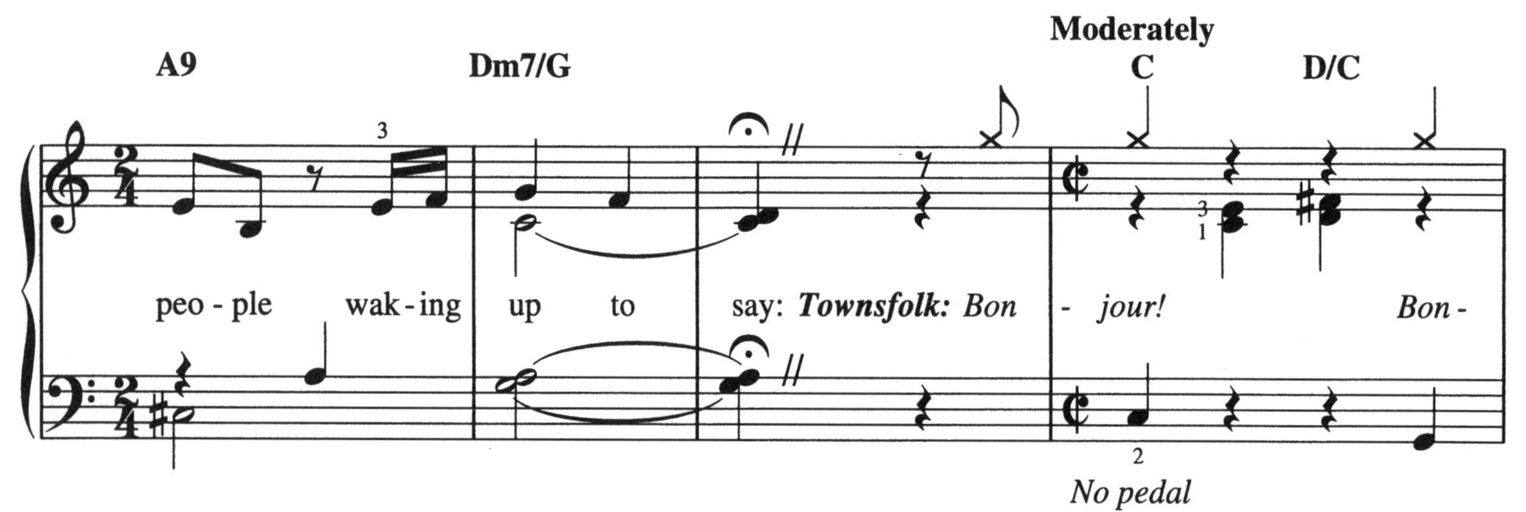
Moderately
A9
Dm7/G
C
D/C
peo - ple wak - ing up to say: Townsfolk: Bon - jour! Bon -
No pedal

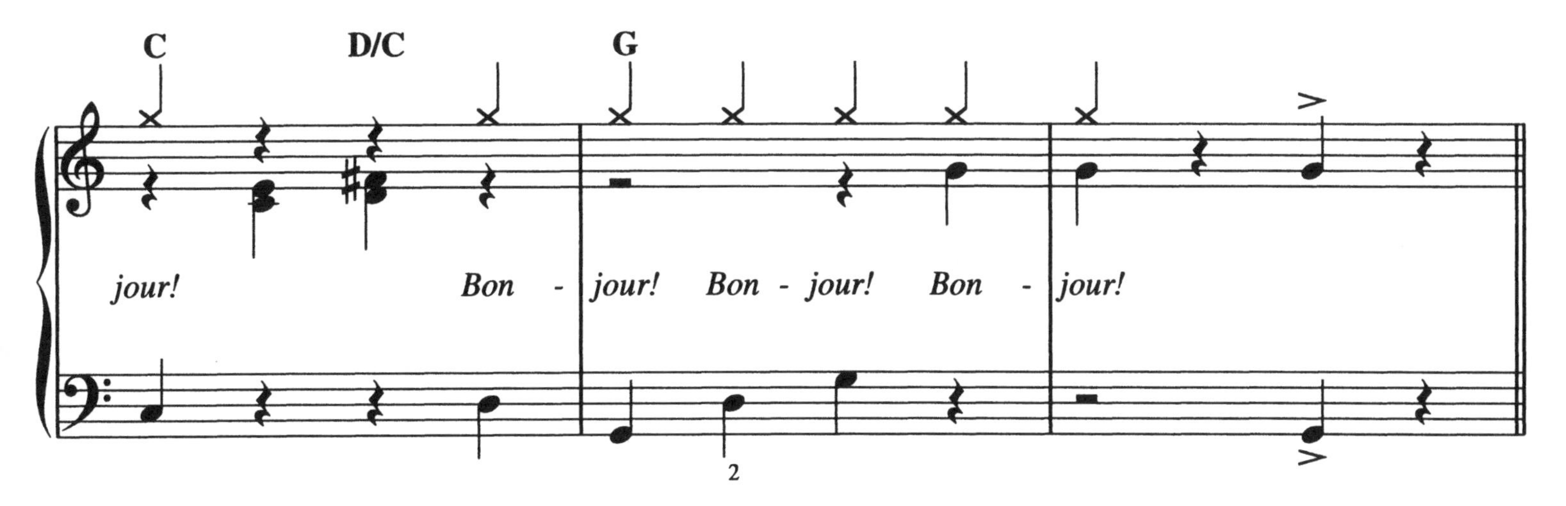
C D/C G
jour! Bon - jour! Bon - jour! Bon - jour!

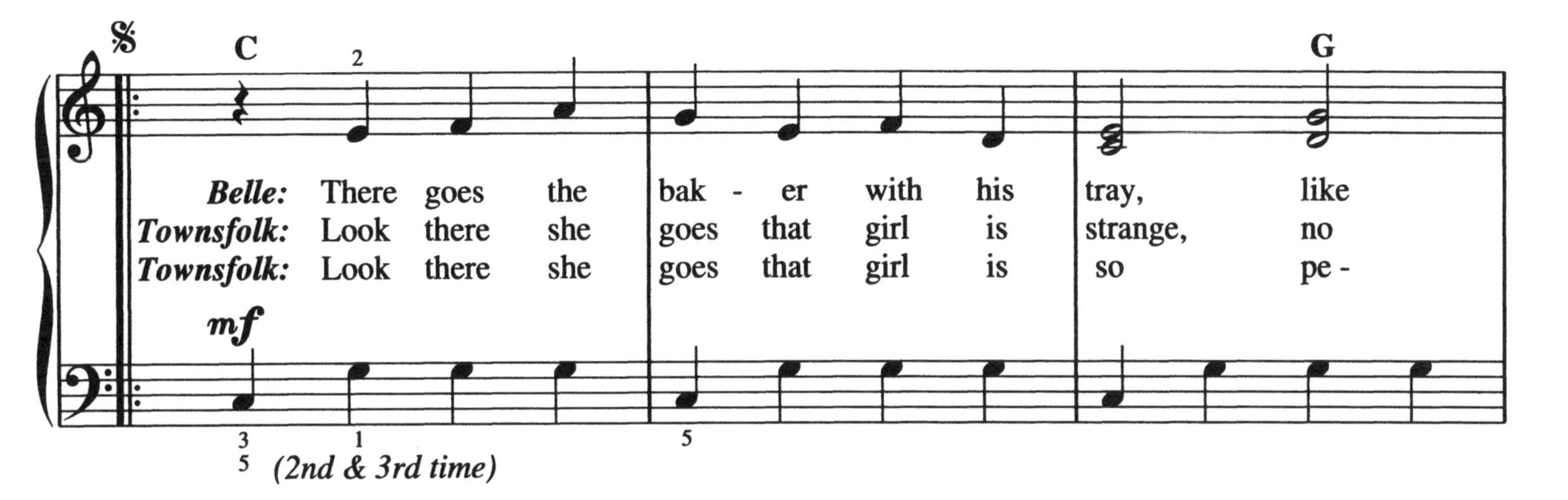
C G
Belle: There goes the bak - er with his tray, like
Townsfolk: Look there she goes that girl is strange, no
Townsfolk: Look there she goes that girl is so pe -
mf
(2nd & 3rd time)

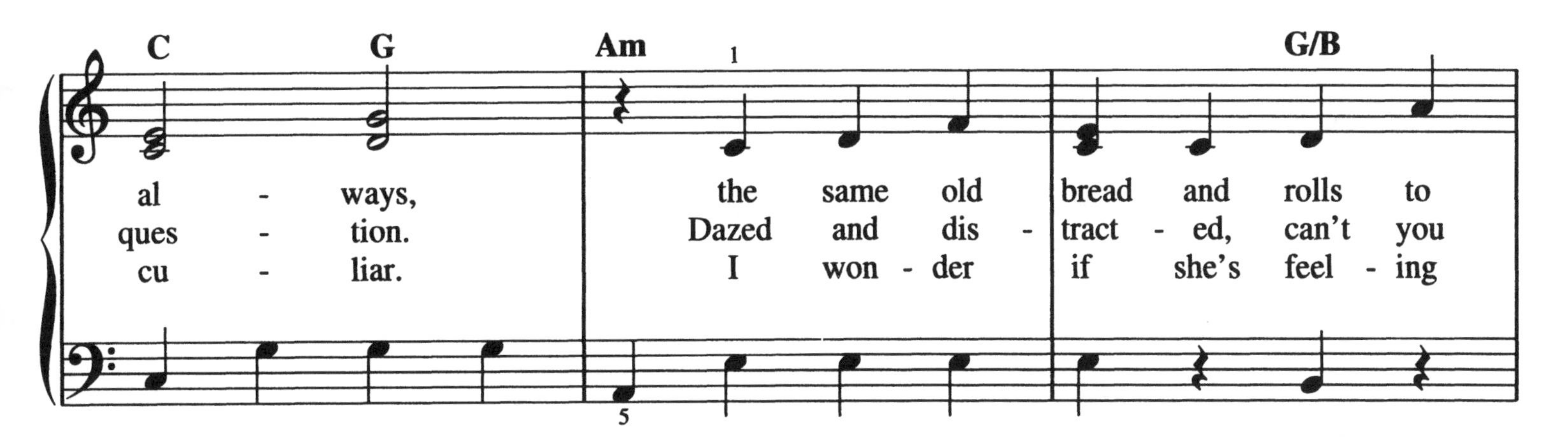
C G Am G/B
al - ways, the same old bread and rolls to
ques - tion. Dazed and dis - tract - ed, can't you
cu - liar. I won - der if she's feel - ing

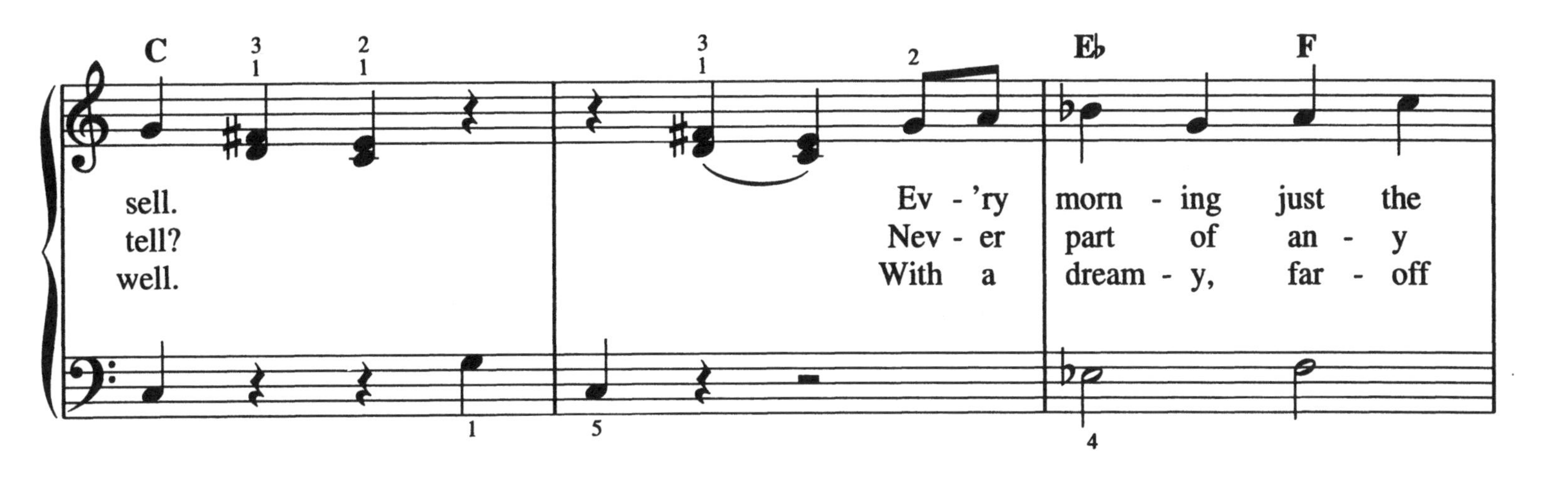
C E♭ F
sell. Ev - 'ry morn - ing just the
tell? Nev - er part of an - y
well. With a dream - y, far - off

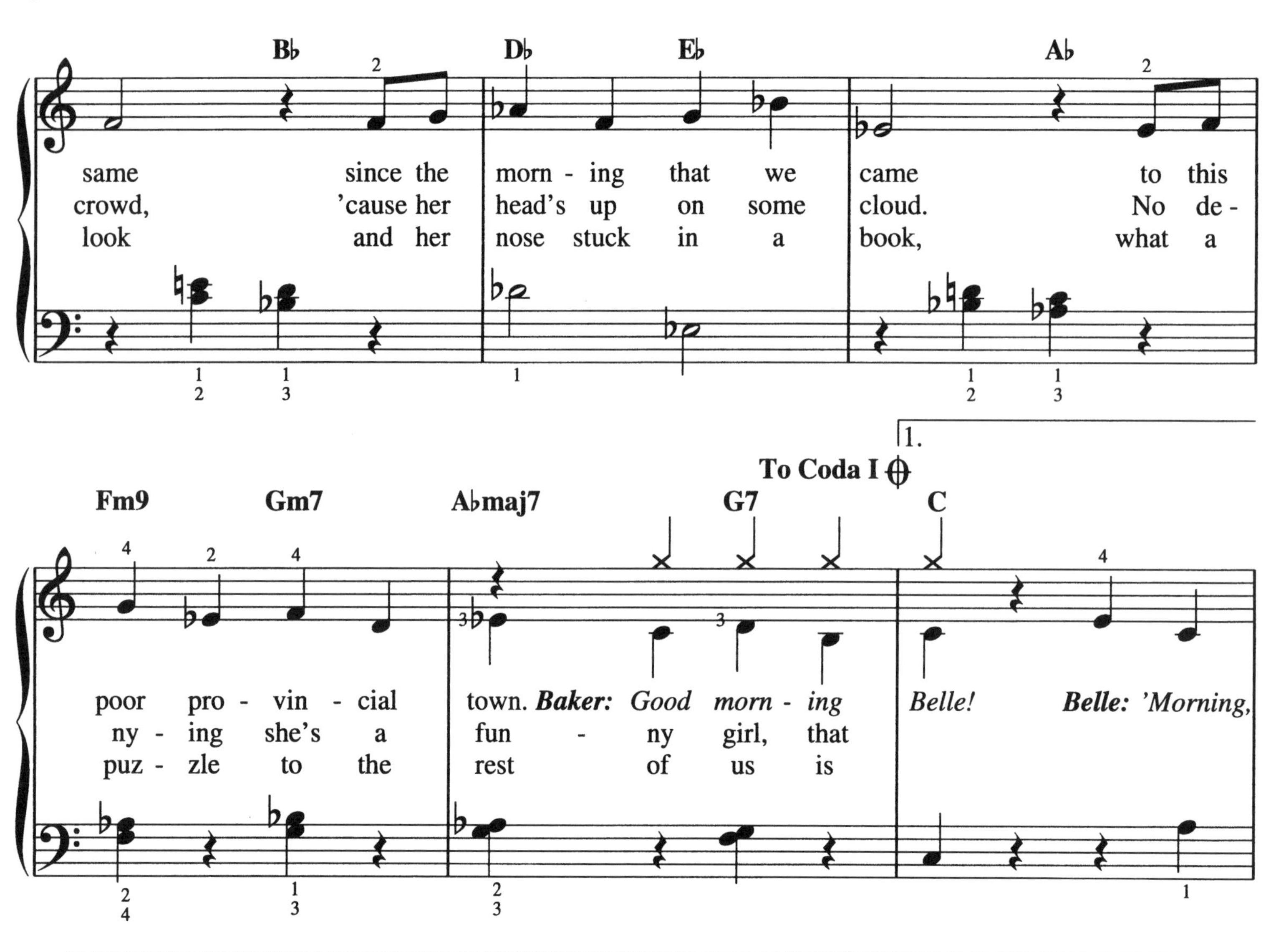
B♭
D♭
E♭
A♭
same since the morn - ing that we came to this
crowd, 'cause her head's up on some cloud. No de -
look and her nose stuck in a book, what a
1.
To Coda I
Fm9
Gm7
A♭maj7
G7
C
poor pro - vin - cial town. Baker: Good morn - ing Belle! Belle: 'Morning,
ny - ing she's a fun - ny girl, that
puz - zle to the rest of us is

Gsus
G7
C
Monsieur, Baker: Where are you off to? Belle: The bookshop. I just finished the

Gsus
G7
Cadd9
most wonderful story about a beanstalk and an ogre and a... Baker: That's nice. Ma -

2.
C
rie! The
baguettes! Hurry
up!
Belle.

F G
F G
F G/F
Man I: Bon-jour.
Woman I: Good day.
Man I: How is your

C/E
F G
F G
F G7/F
fam - 'ly?
Woman II: Bon- jour.
Man II: Good day.
Woman II: How is your

C/E
A♭ B♭
A♭ B♭
A♭
wife?
Woman III: I need
six eggs!
Man III: That's too ex-

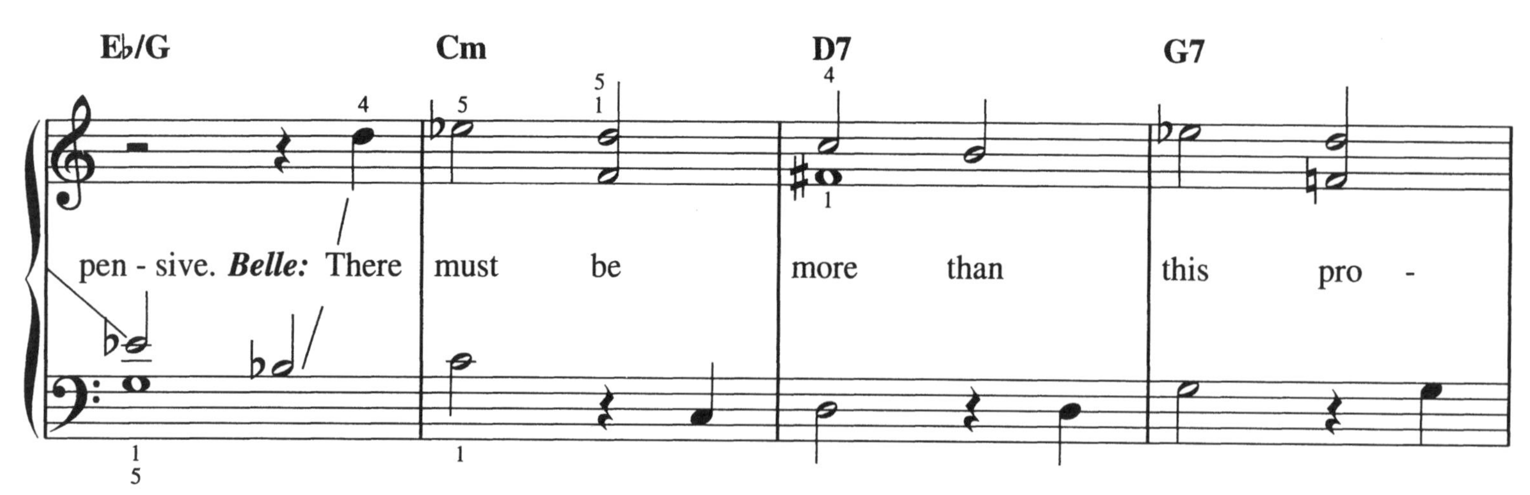
E♭/G
Cm
D7
G7
pen - sive. Belle: There
must be
more than
this pro -

C
(2) Second time
Gsus
vin - cial
life. Bookseller:
anything new? Bookseller:
mp
Ah, Belle!
Ha, ha! Not since
Belle: Good morning.
yesterday.

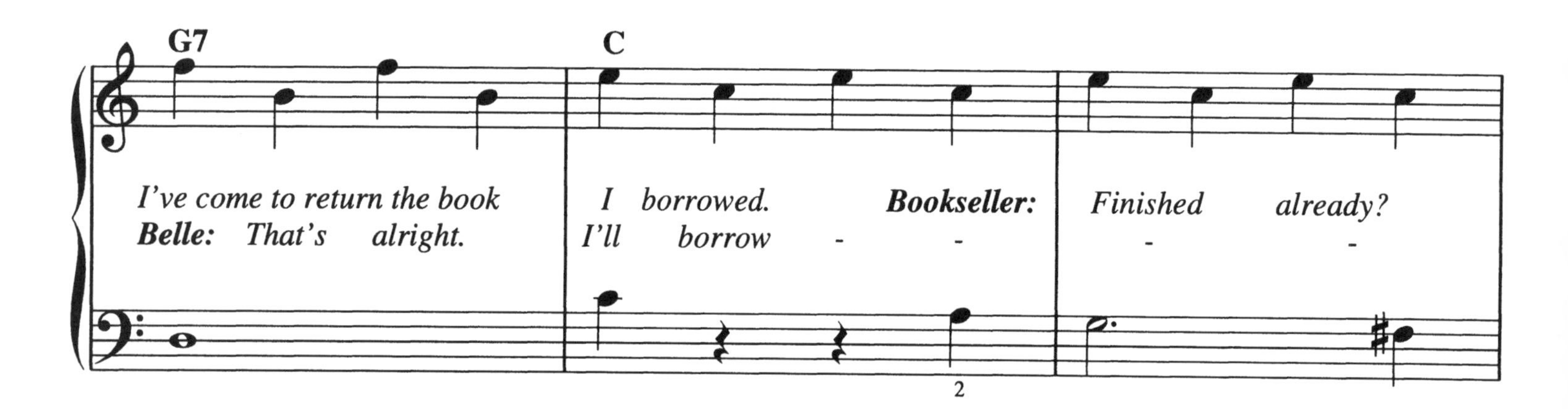
G7
C
I've come to return the book
Belle: That's alright.
I borrowed. Bookseller:
I'll borrow - -
Finished already?
- -

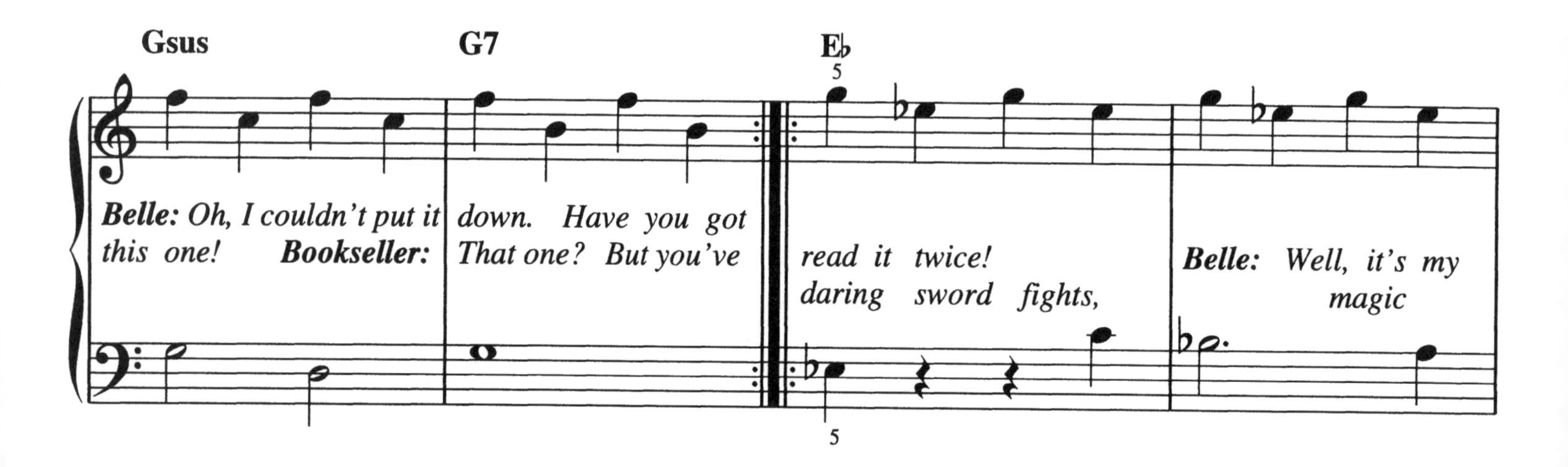
Gsus
G7
E♭
Belle: Oh, I couldn't put it
this one! Bookseller:
down. Have you got
That one? But you've
read it twice!
daring sword fights,
Belle: Well, it's my
magic

1.
B♭sus
B♭7
2.
B♭sus
B♭7
favorite!
far off places,
spells, a prince
in disguise...Bookseller:

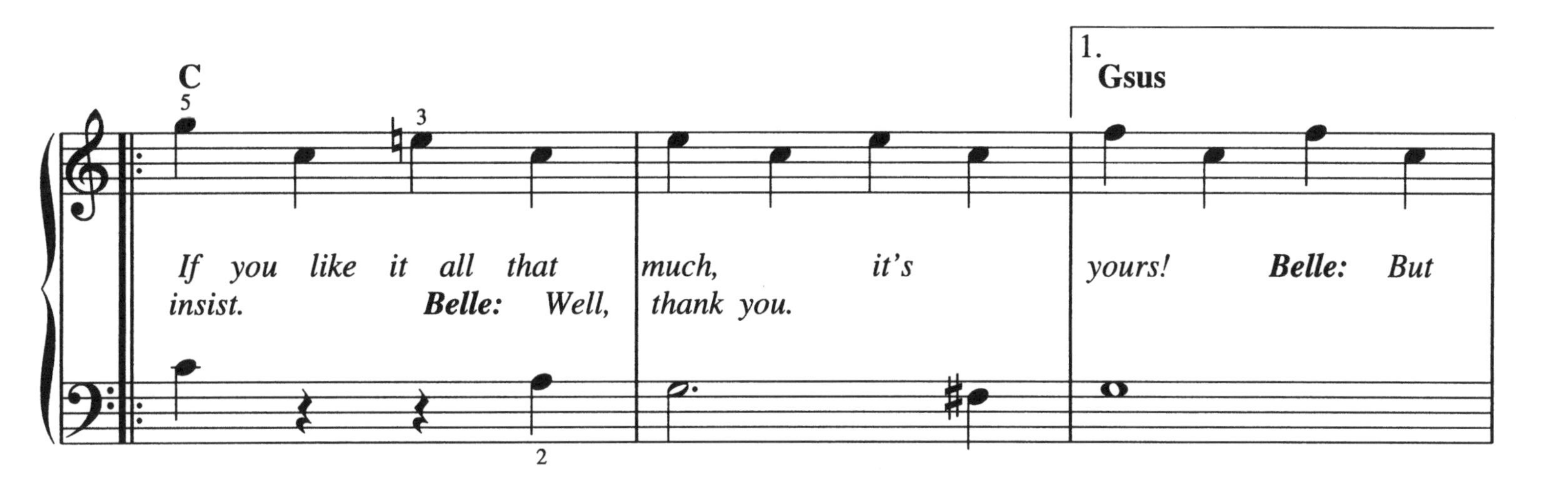
C
1.
Gsus
If you like it all that
insist. Belle: Well,
much, it's
thank you.
yours! Belle: But

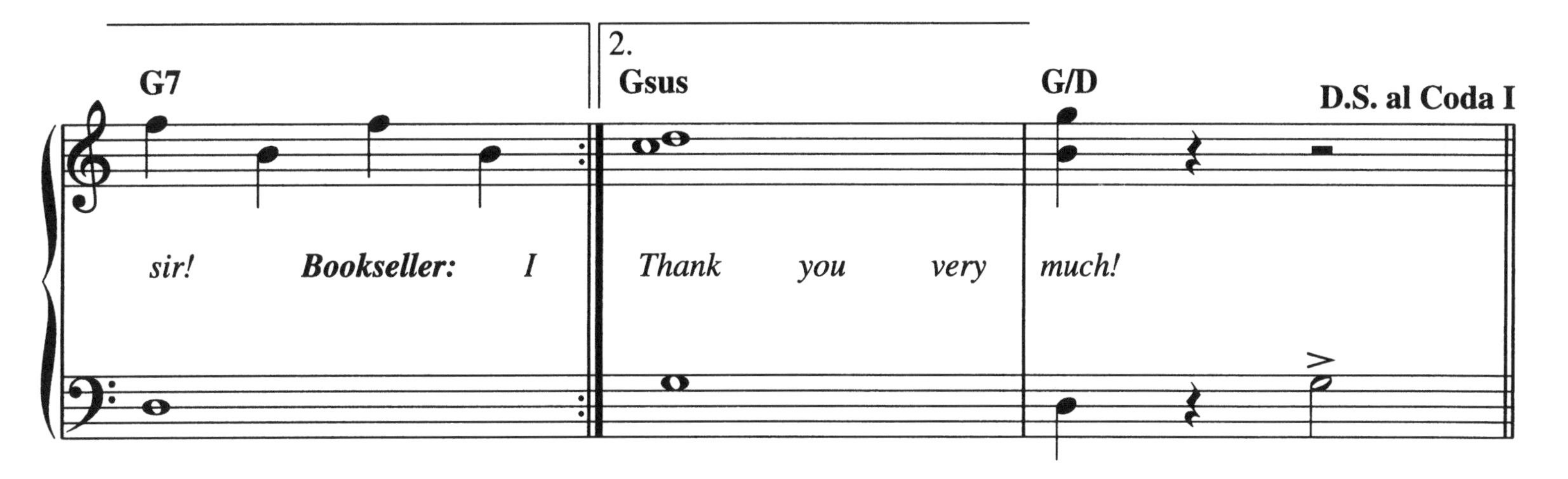
G7
2.
Gsus
G/D
D.S. al Coda I
sir! Bookseller: I
Thank you very
much!

CODA I
C
F
Belle.
Belle:
Oh,
With pedal

Am7/E Dm7 G7sus G7 Em
isn't this amazing

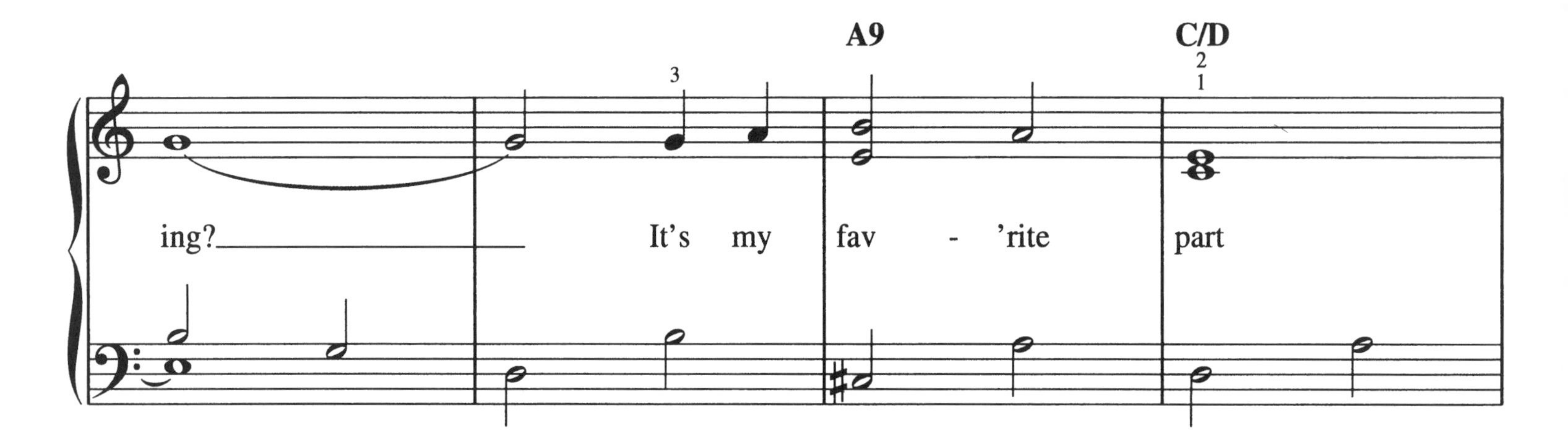
A9 C/D
ing? It's my fav'rite part

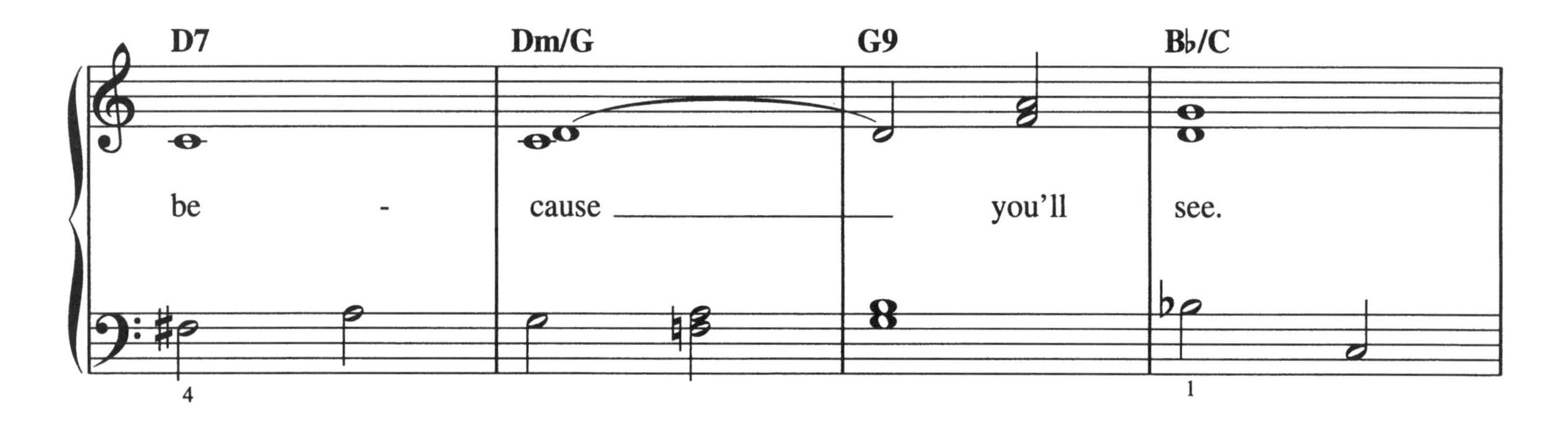
D7 Dm/G G9 B♭/C
because you'll see.

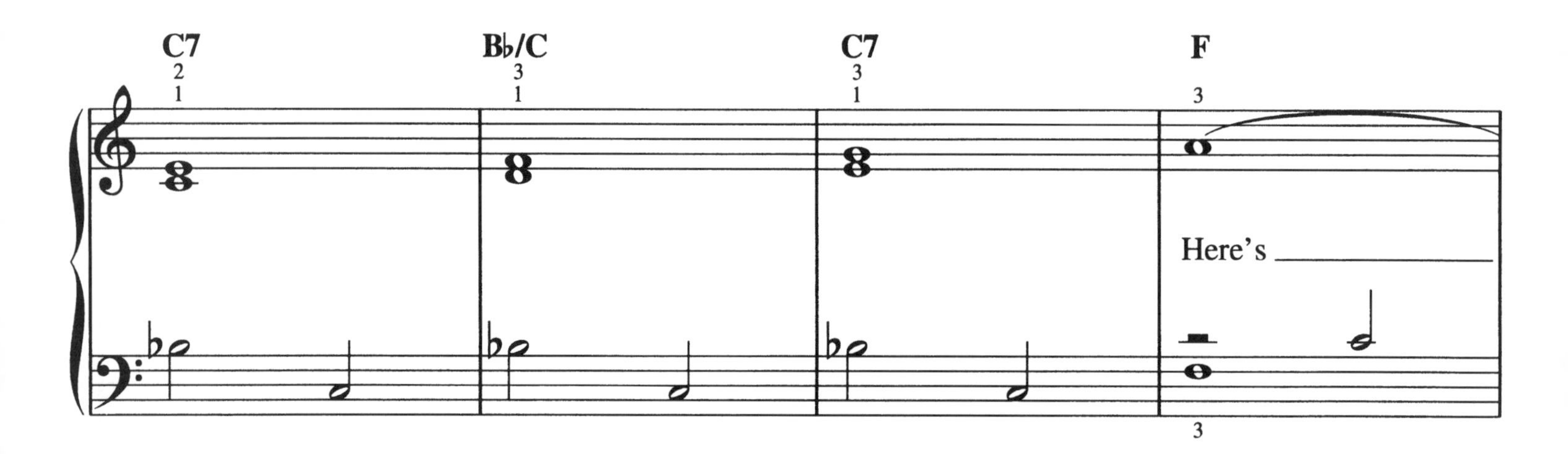
C7 B♭/C C7 F
Here's

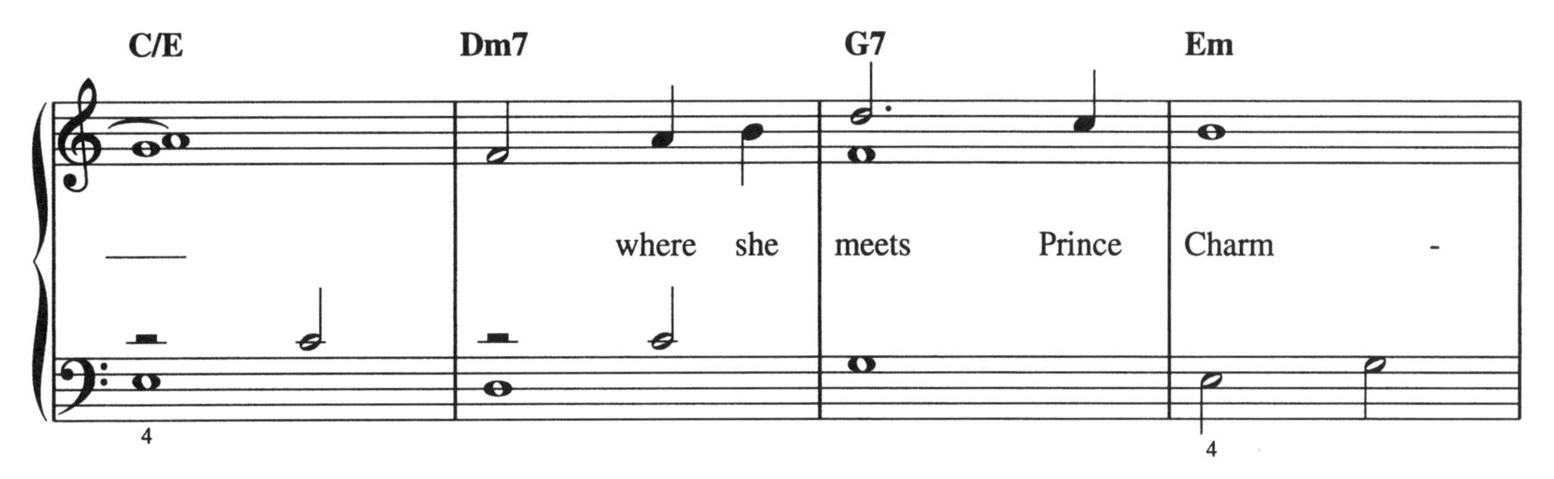
C/E
Dm7
G7
Em
where she meets Prince Charm -
4
4

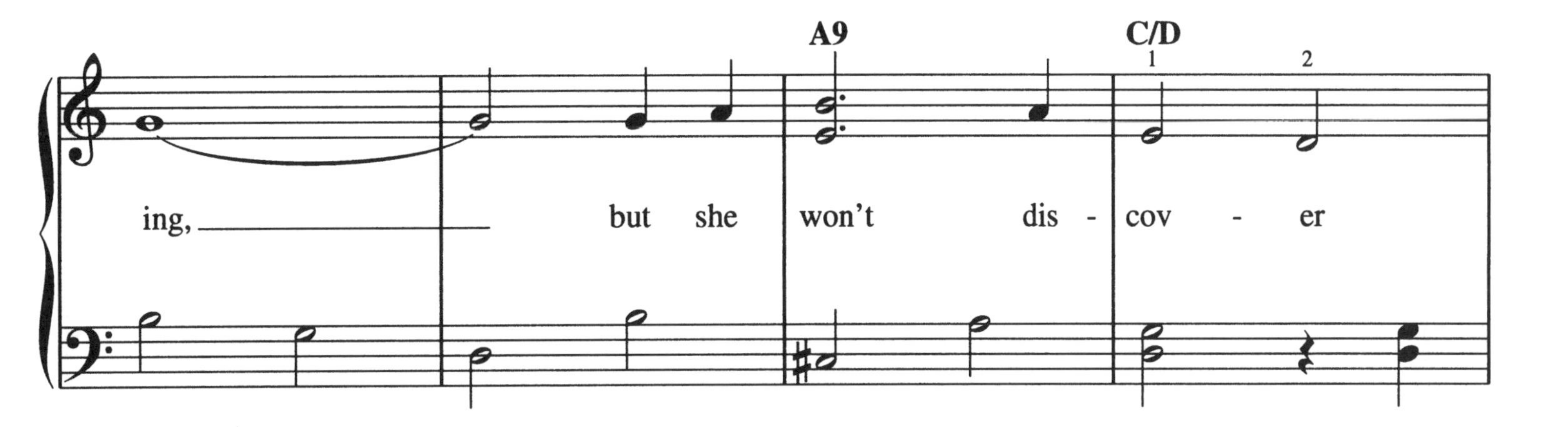
A9
C/D
1
2
ing, but she won't dis - cov - er

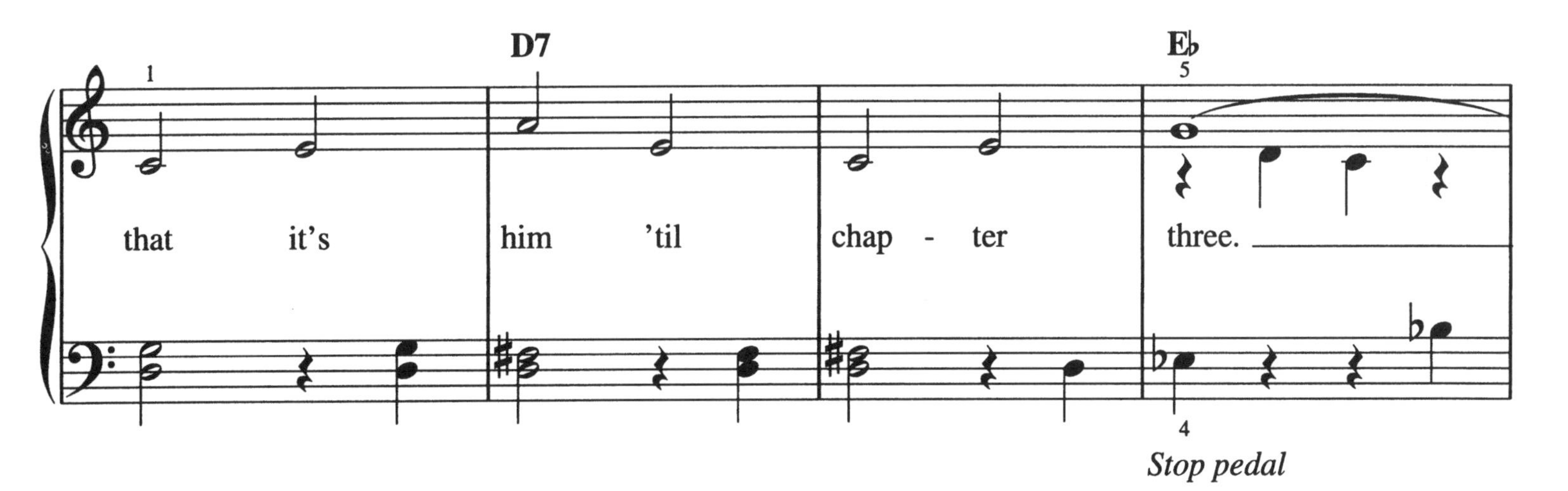
D7
E♭
1
5
that it's him 'til chap - ter three.
4
Stop pedal

Dm7
G7
C
2
Woman: Now, it's no
Townsfolk: Look there she

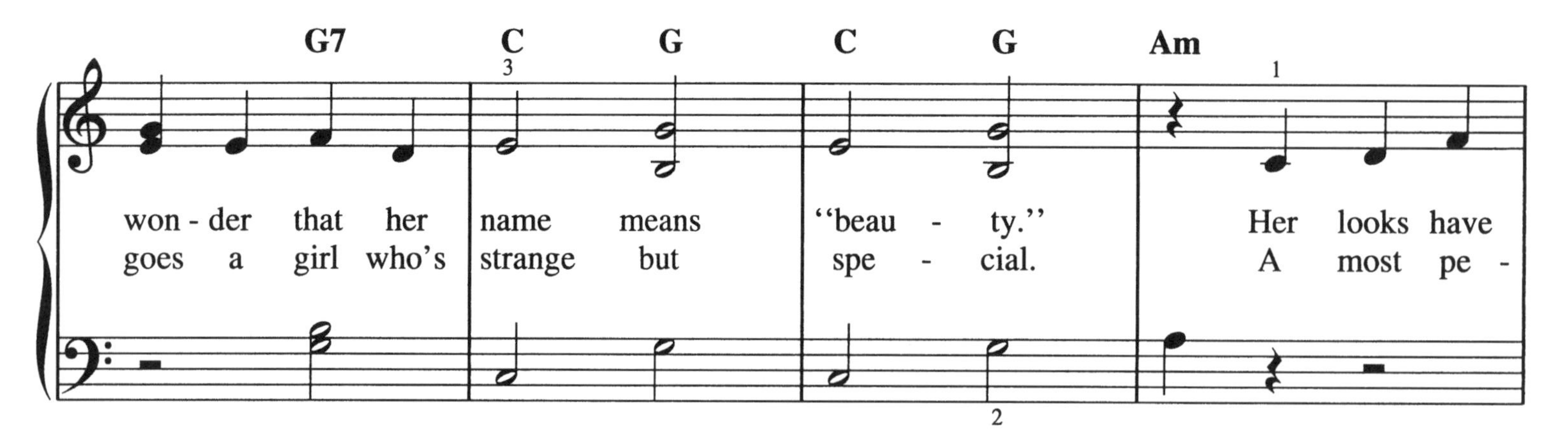
G7 C G C G Am
won - der that her name means "beau - ty." Her looks have
goes a girl who's strange but spe - cial. A most pe -

C E♭ F
got no par - al - lel. Shopkeeper: But be- hind that fair fa -
cu - liar mad - 'moi - selle. It's a pit - y and a

B♭ D♭ E♭ A♭
çade. I'm a - fraid she's rath - er odd. Ver - y
sin. She does - n't quite fit in 'cause she

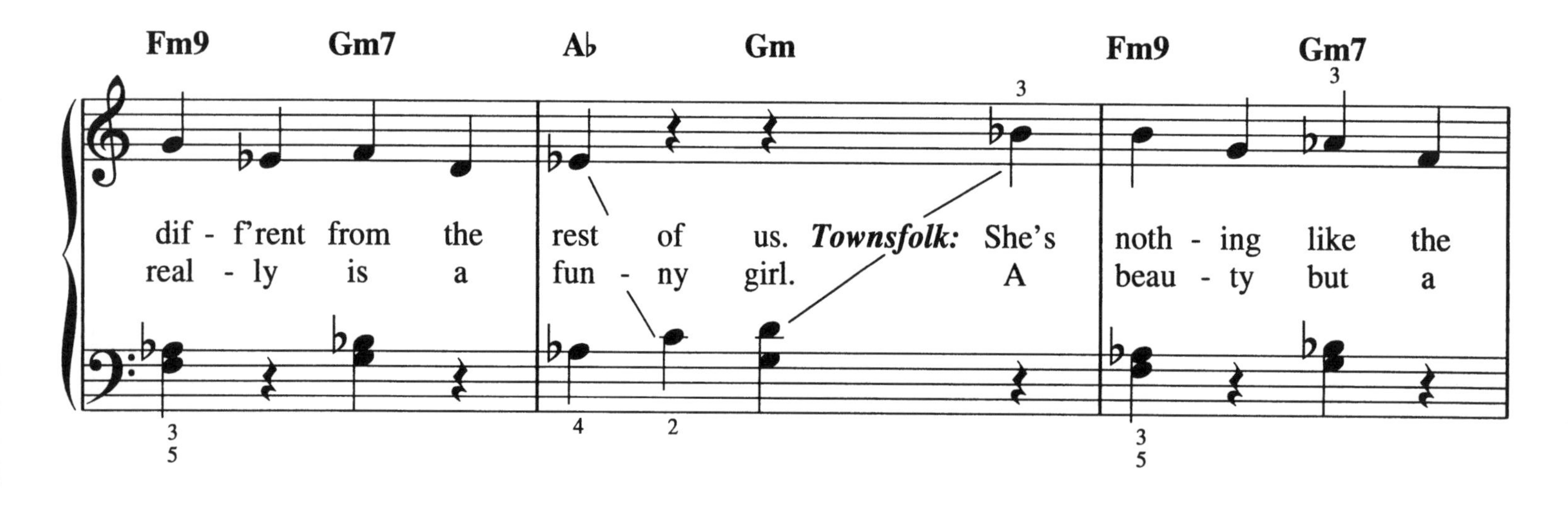
Fm9 Gm7 A♭ Gm Fm9 Gm7
dif - f'rent from the rest of us. Townsfolk: She's noth - ing like the
real - ly is a fun - ny girl. A beau - ty but a

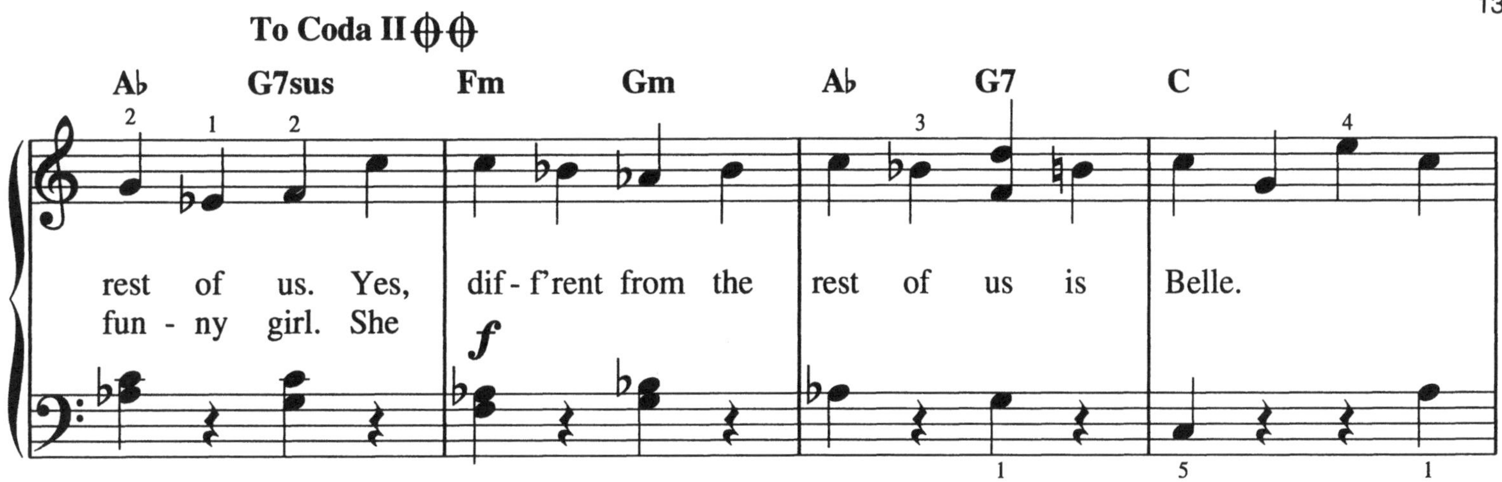
To Coda II
Ab
G7sus
Fm
Gm
Ab
G7
C
rest of us. Yes, dif - f'rent from the rest of us is Belle.
fun - ny girl. She
f

Gsus
G7
C

Gsus
G7
Pompously
Gadd9
f

Dm
Fmaj7
G
Gaston: Right from the

Dm7
G
Dm
Em
mo - ment when I
met her,
saw her,
I said she's

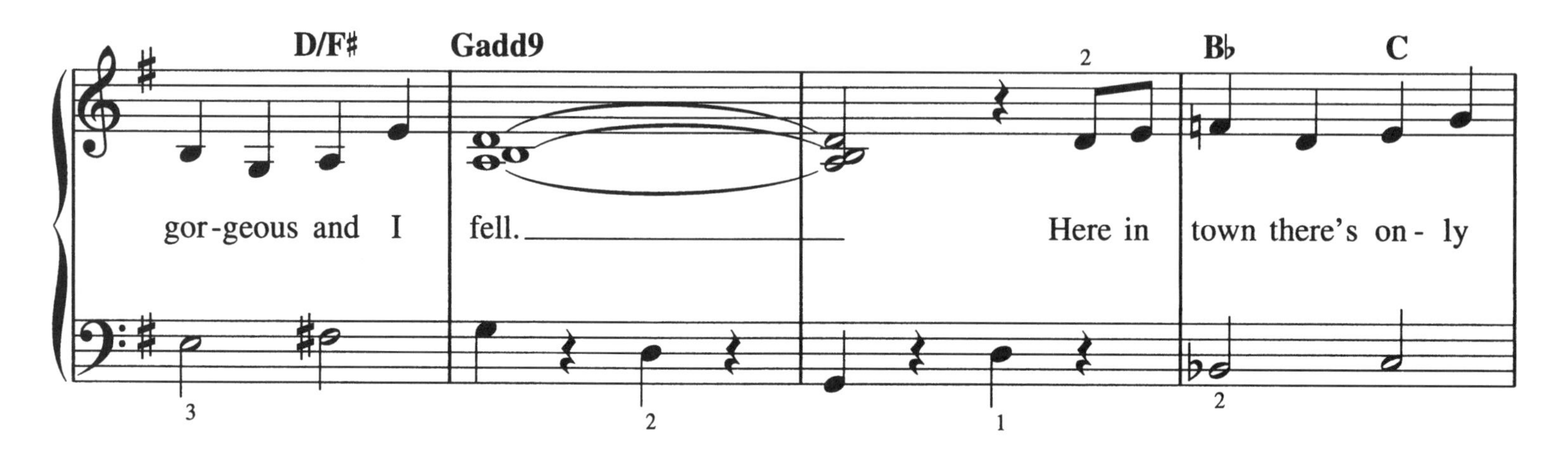
D/F♯
Gadd9
B♭
C
gor - geous and I
fell.
Here in
town there's on - ly

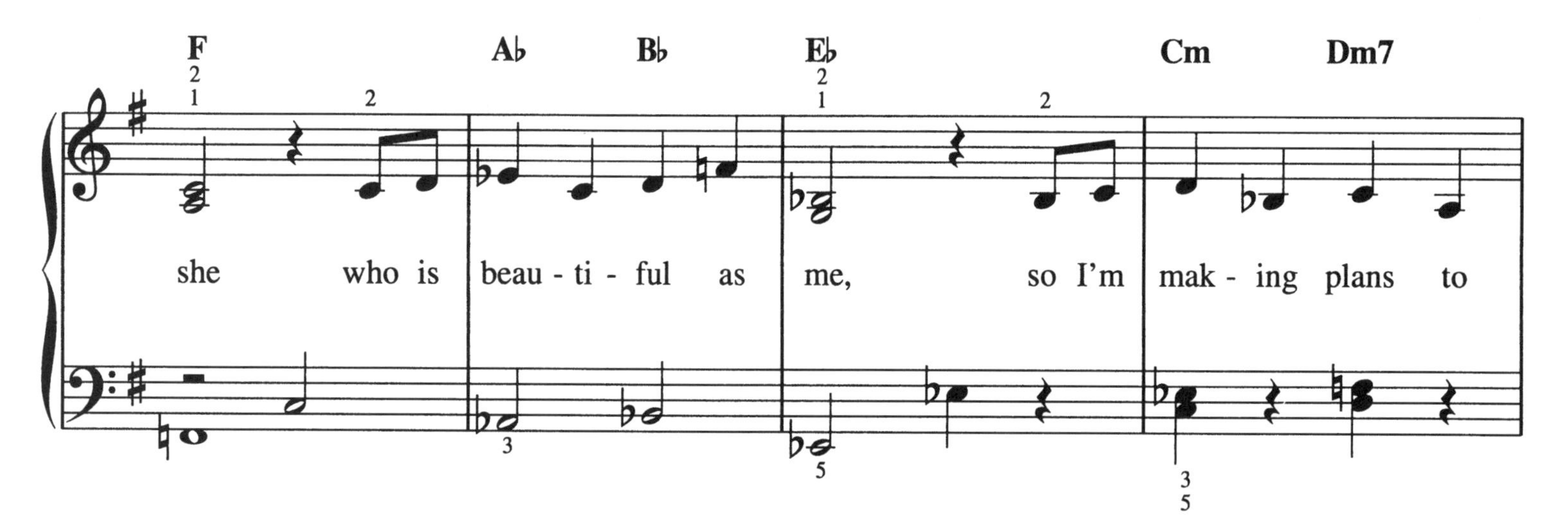
F
A♭
B♭
E♭
Cm
Dm7
she who is
beau - ti - ful as
me,
so I'm
mak - ing plans to

E♭
D
Gadd9
C
D
woo and mar -ry
Belle.
Silly girls: Look there

C D C D7 G/B C D
he goes! Is - n't he dream - y? Mon - sieur

C D C D7 G/B E♭ F
Gas - ton! Oh, he's so cute! Be still

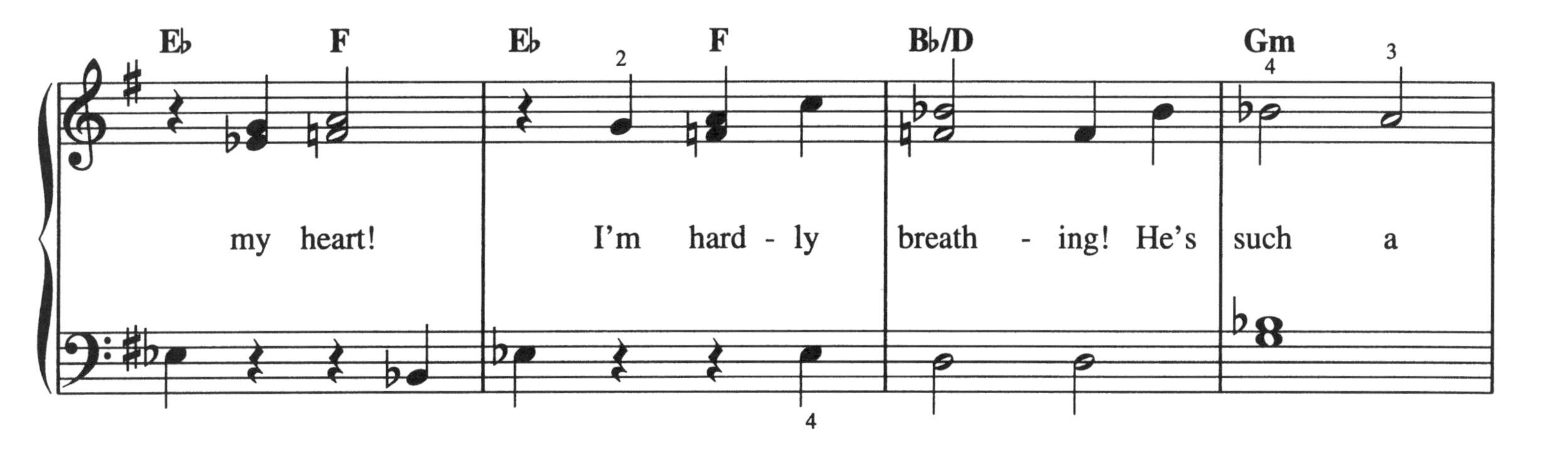
E♭ F E♭ F B♭/D Gm
my heart! I'm hard - ly breath - ing! He's such a

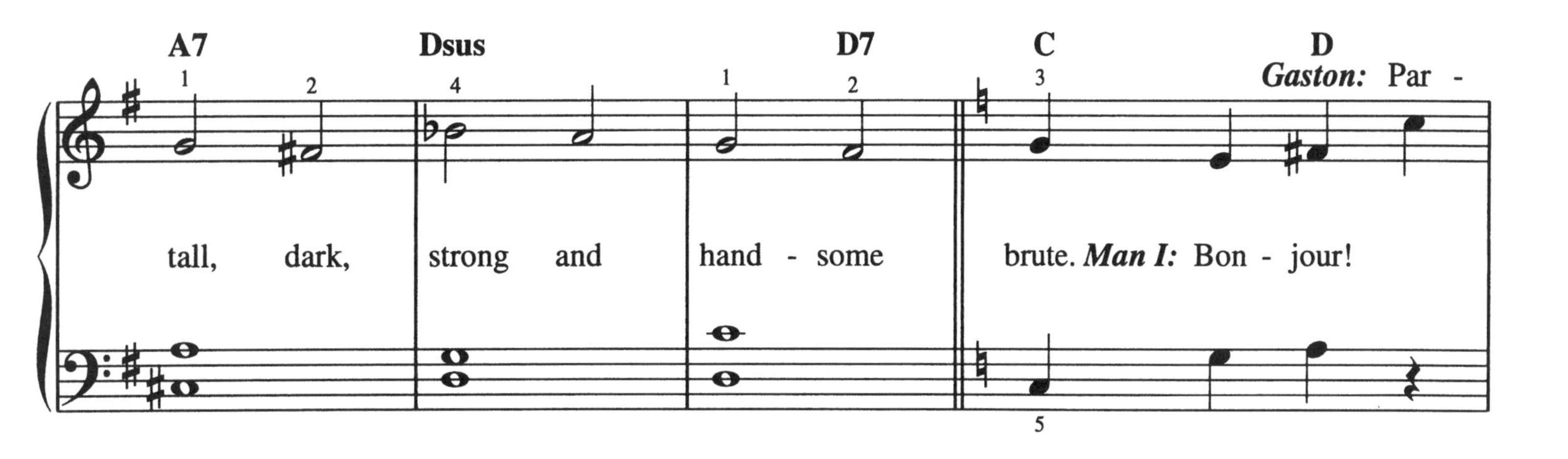
A7 Dsus D7 C D
Gaston: Par -
tall, dark, strong and hand - some brute. Man I: Bon - jour!

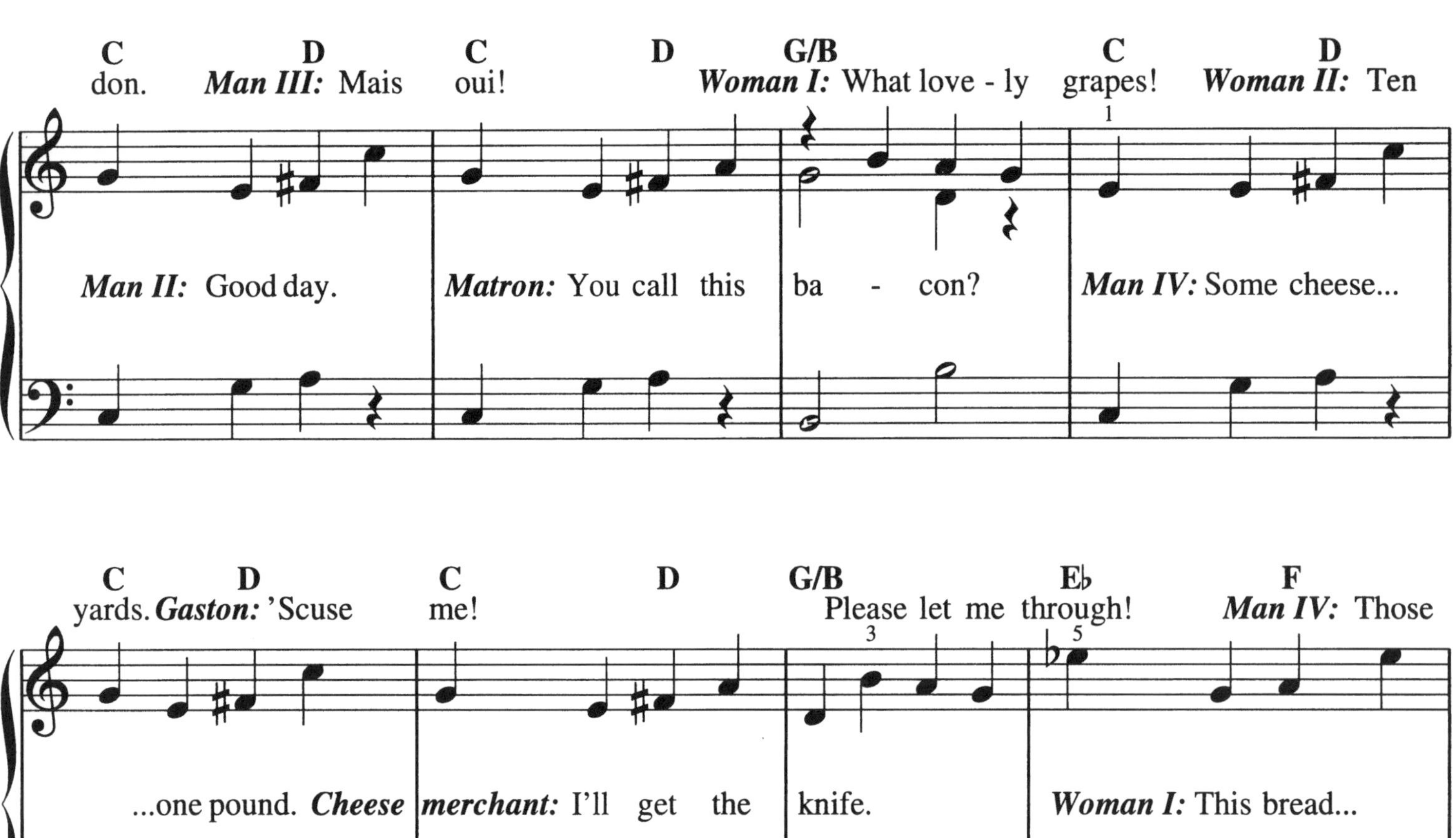
C D C D G/B C D
don. Man III: Mais oui! Woman I: What love - ly grapes! Woman II: Ten
1
Man II: Good day. Matron: You call this ba - con? Man IV: Some cheese...
C D C D G/B E♭ F
yards. Gaston: 'Scuse me! Please let me through! Man IV: Those
3 5

...one pound. Cheese merchant: I'll get the knife. Woman I: This bread...
5

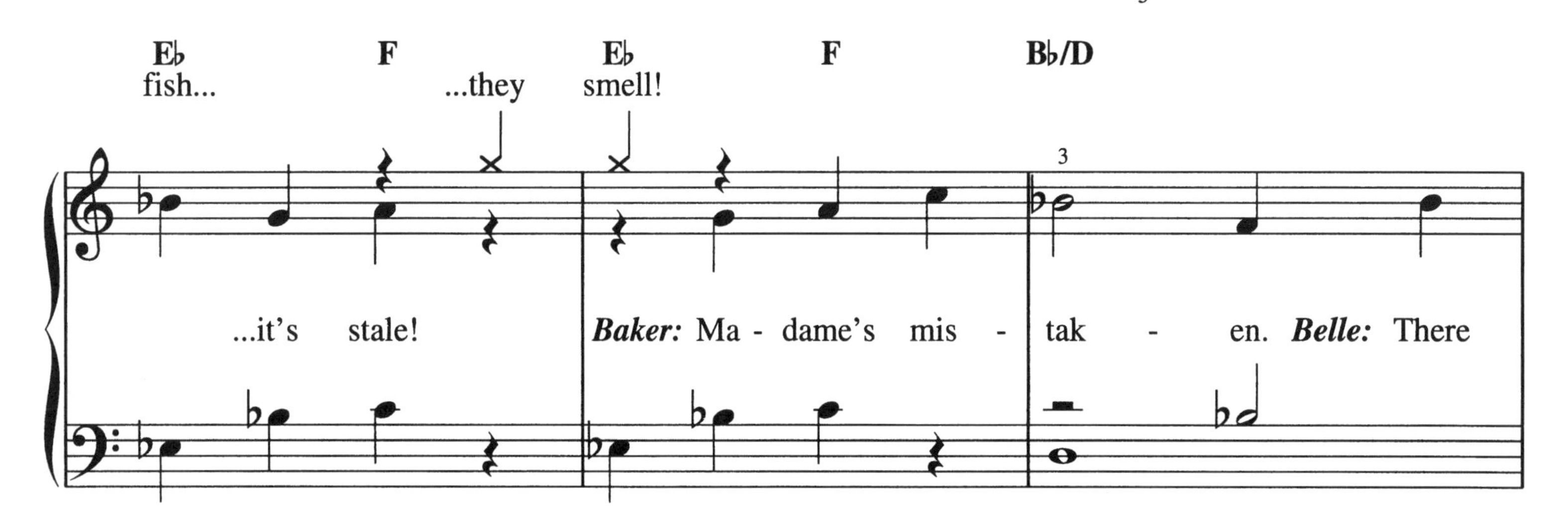
E♭ F E♭ F B♭/D
fish... ...they smell!
3
...it's stale! Baker: Ma - dame's mis - tak - en. Belle: There

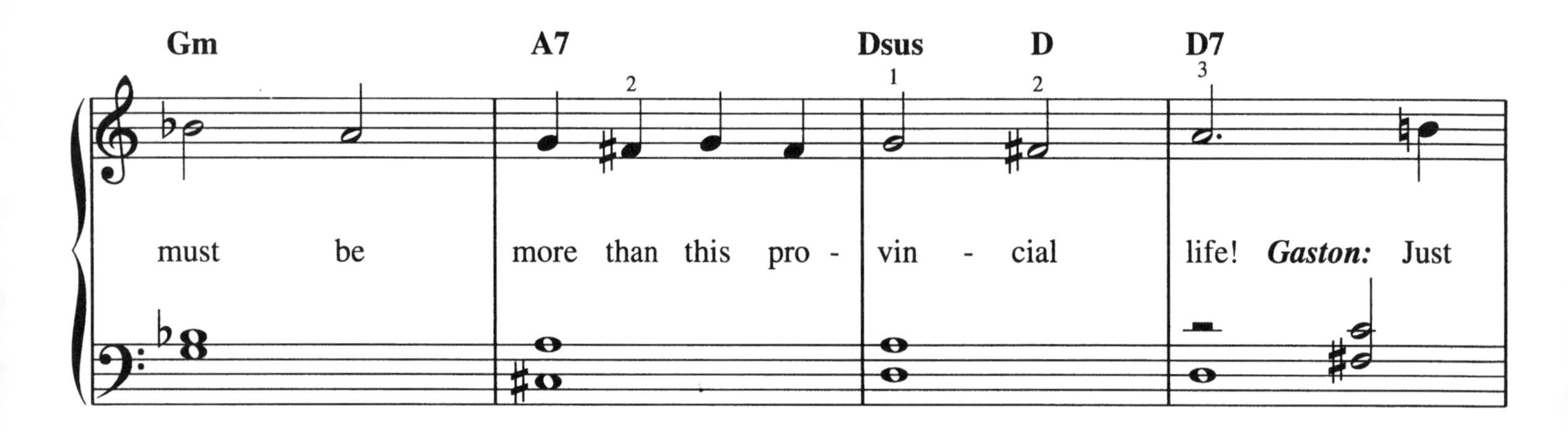
Gm A7 Dsus D D7
2 1 2 3
must be more than this pro - vin - cial life! Gaston: Just

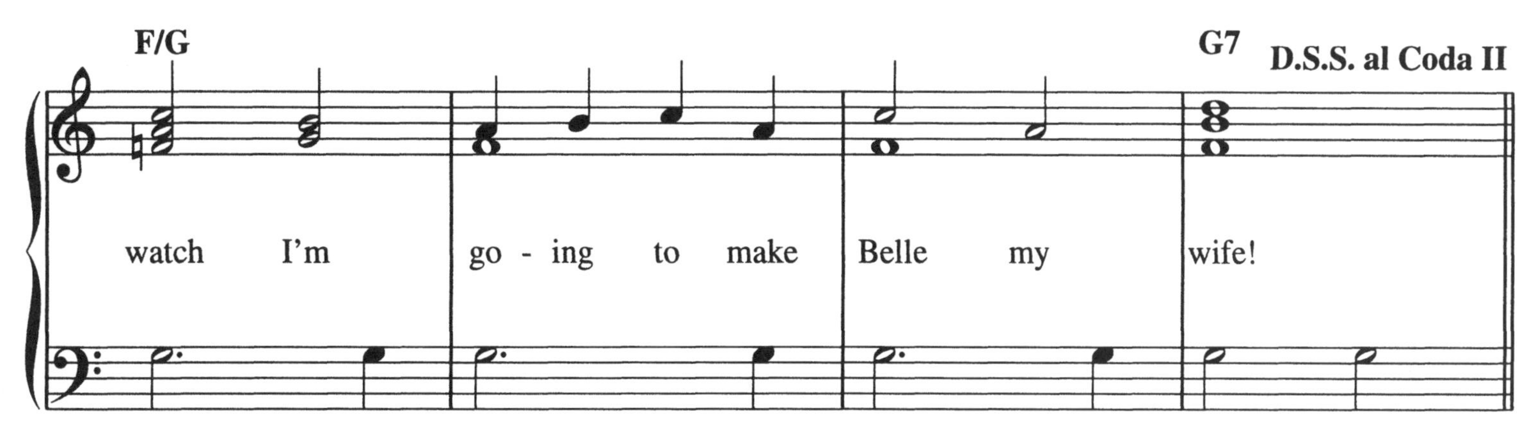
F/G
G7
D.S.S. al Coda II
watch I'm go - ing to make Belle my wife!

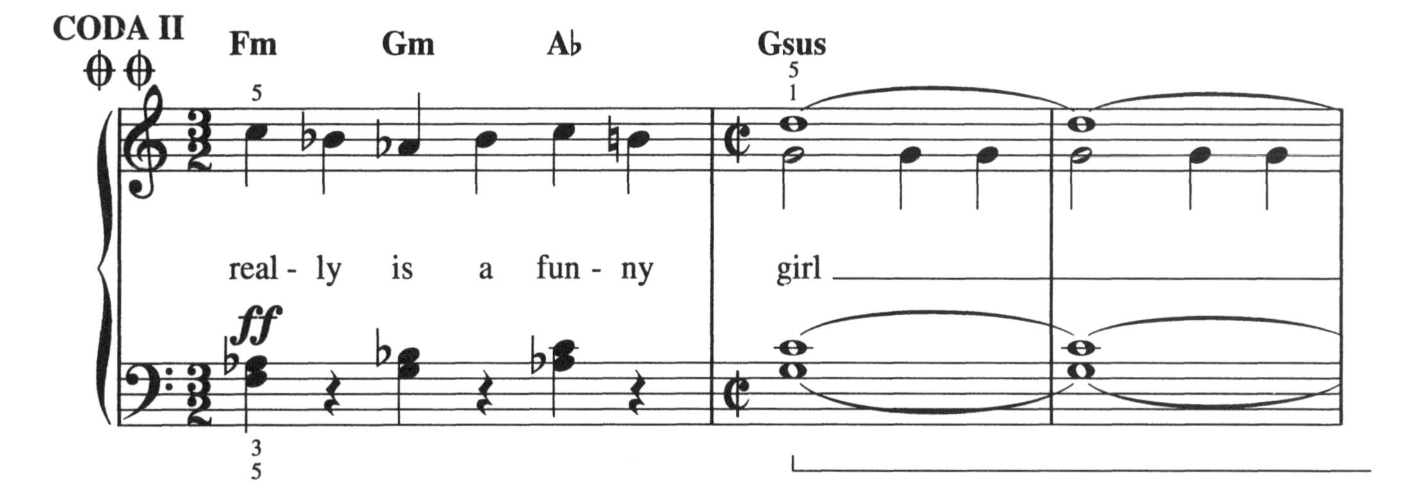
CODA II
Fm
Gm
A♭
Gsus
real - ly is a fun - ny girl
ff

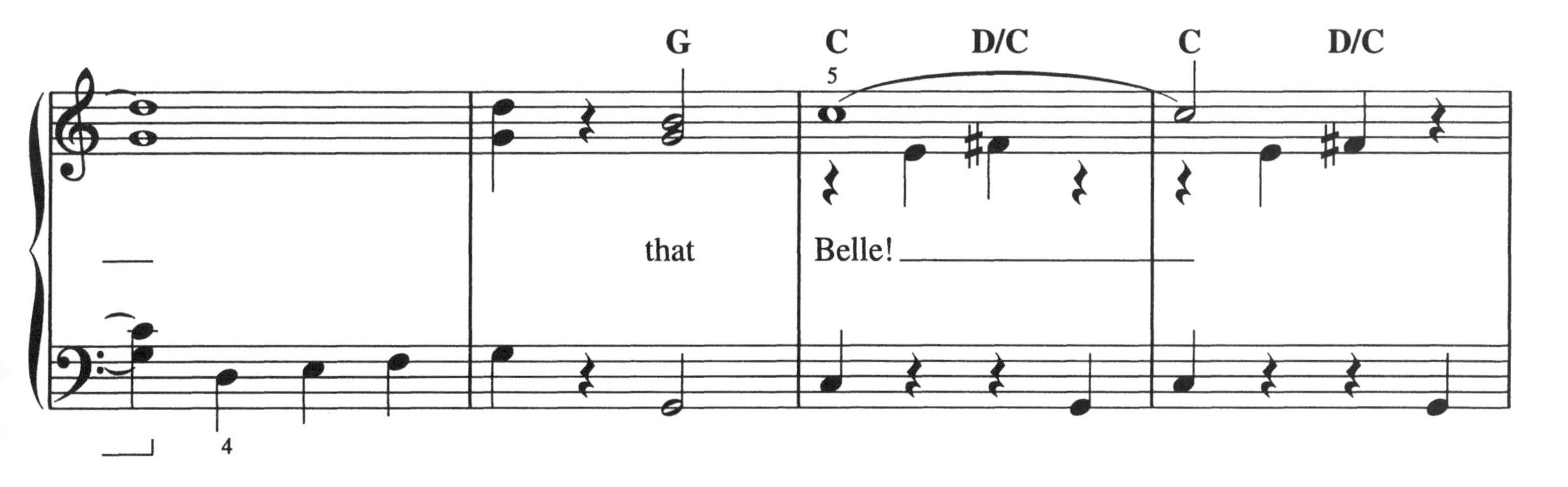
G
C
D/C
C
D/C
that Belle!

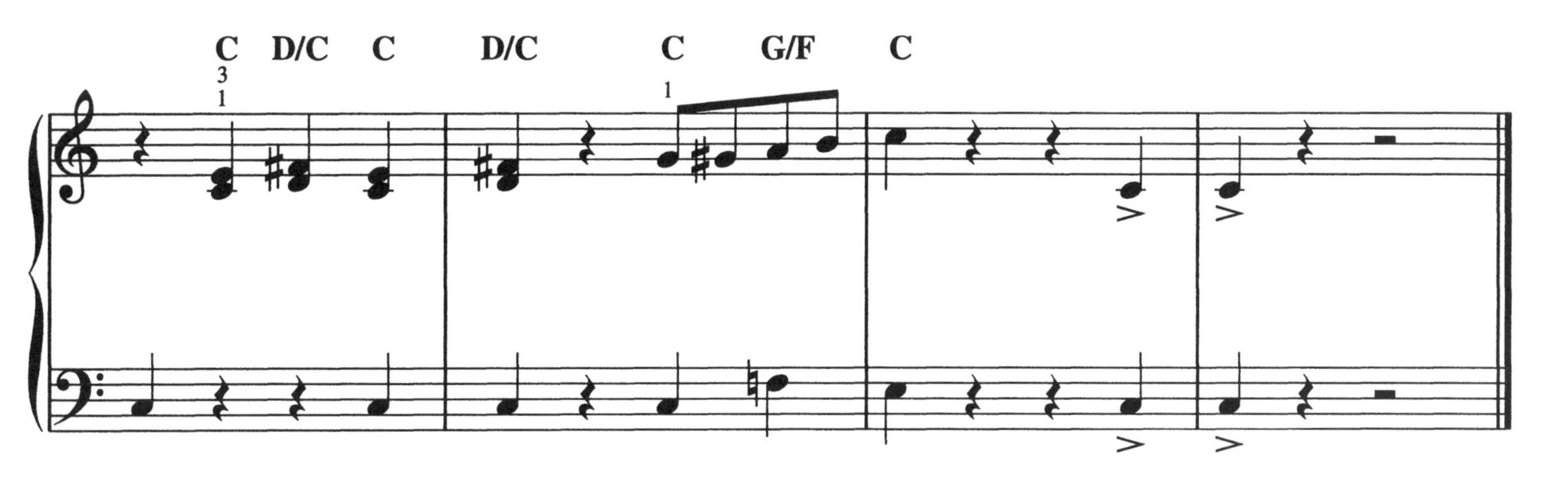
C
D/C
C
D/C
C
G/F
C

NO MATTER WHAT

Music by ALAN MENKEN
Lyrics by TIM RICE

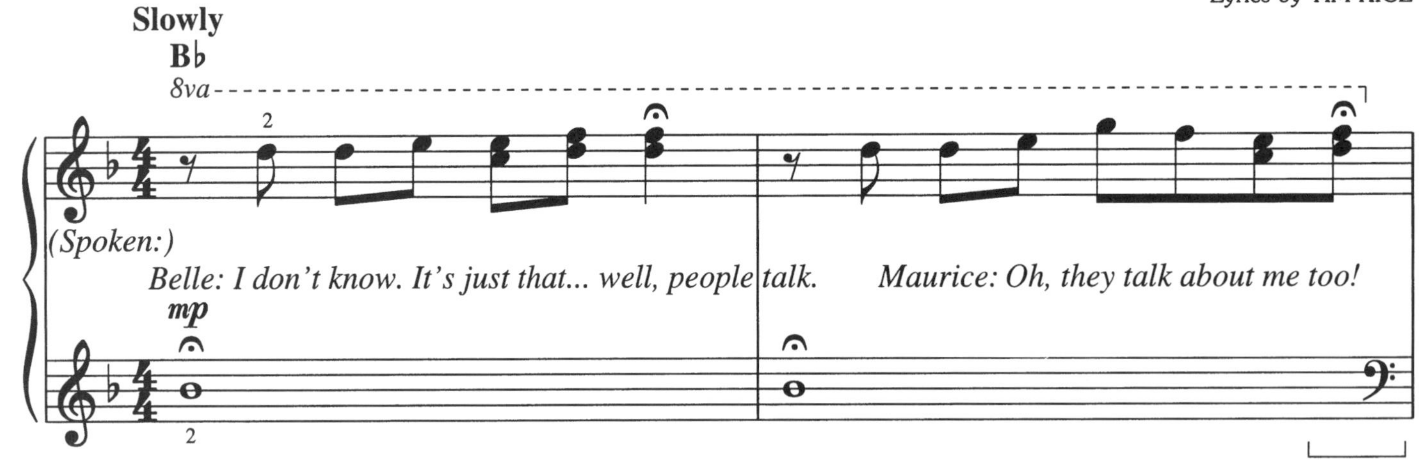

Belle: I don't know. It's just that... well, people talk.
Maurice: Oh, they talk about me too!

Moderately
loco

(Sung:) Maurice: No, I'm not odd, nor you.

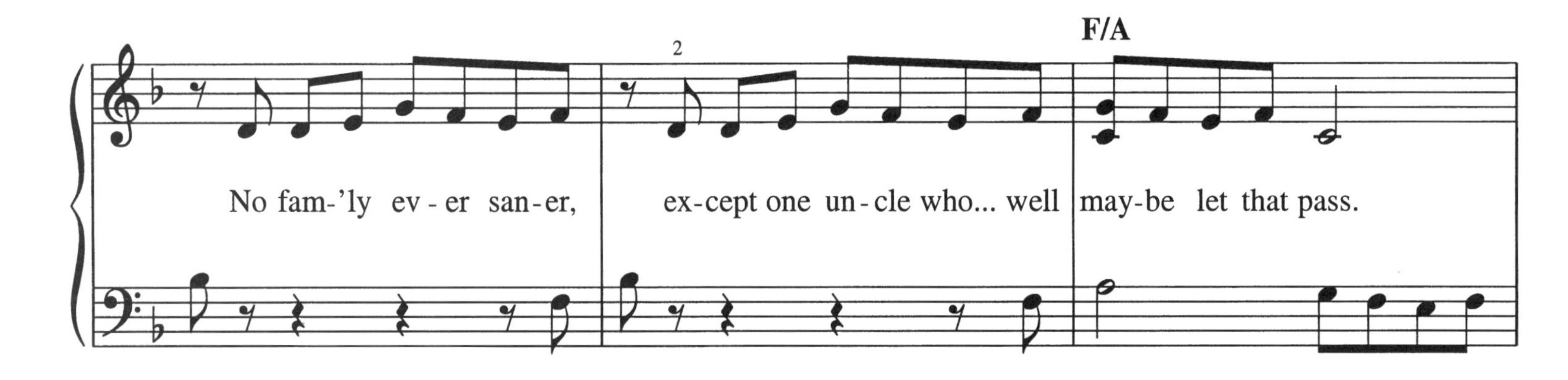

F/A
No fam-'ly ev - er san-er,
ex-cept one un-cle who... well
may-be let that pass.

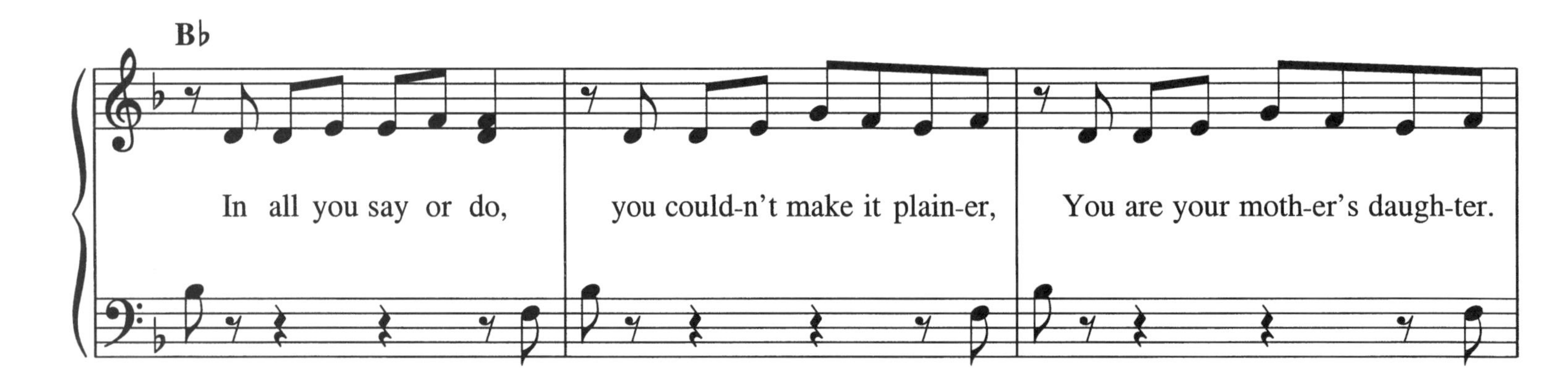

B♭
In all you say or do,
you could-n't make it plain-er,
You are your moth-er's daugh-ter.

F/A
Dm
A/C♯
There-fore you are class.
Belle: So I should just ac - cept I'm
sim - ply

Add pedal

Cm6
G/B
B♭m
F/A
not like
them? Maurice: They are the
com - mon herd.

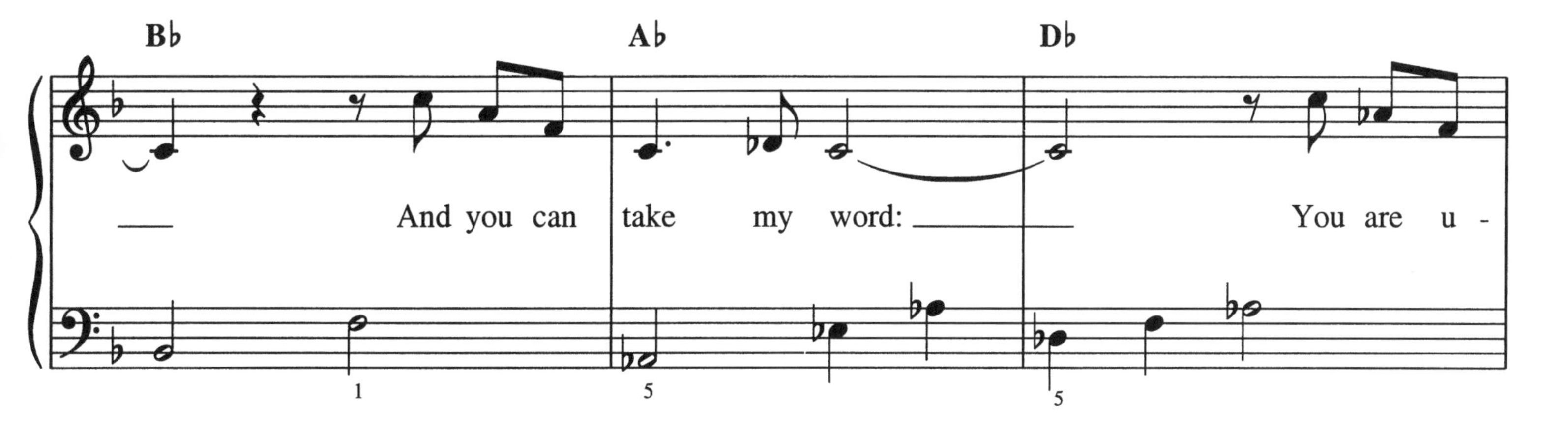
B♭
A♭
D♭
And you can
take my word:
You are u -

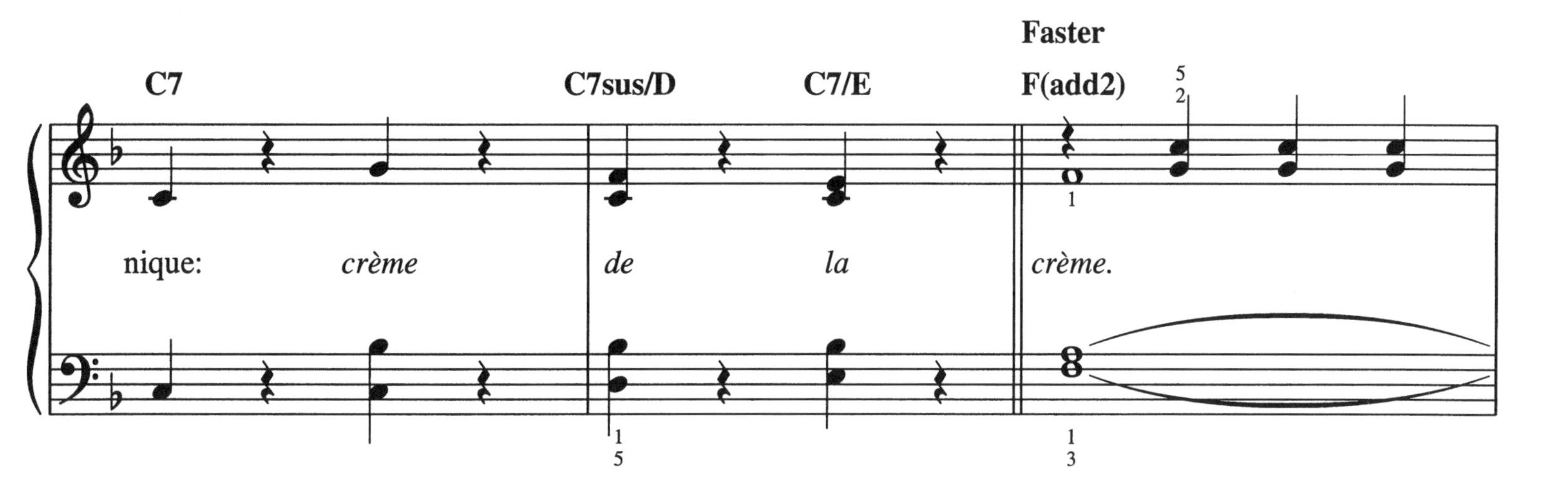
Faster
C7
C7sus/D
C7/E
F(add2)
nique: crème
de la
crème.

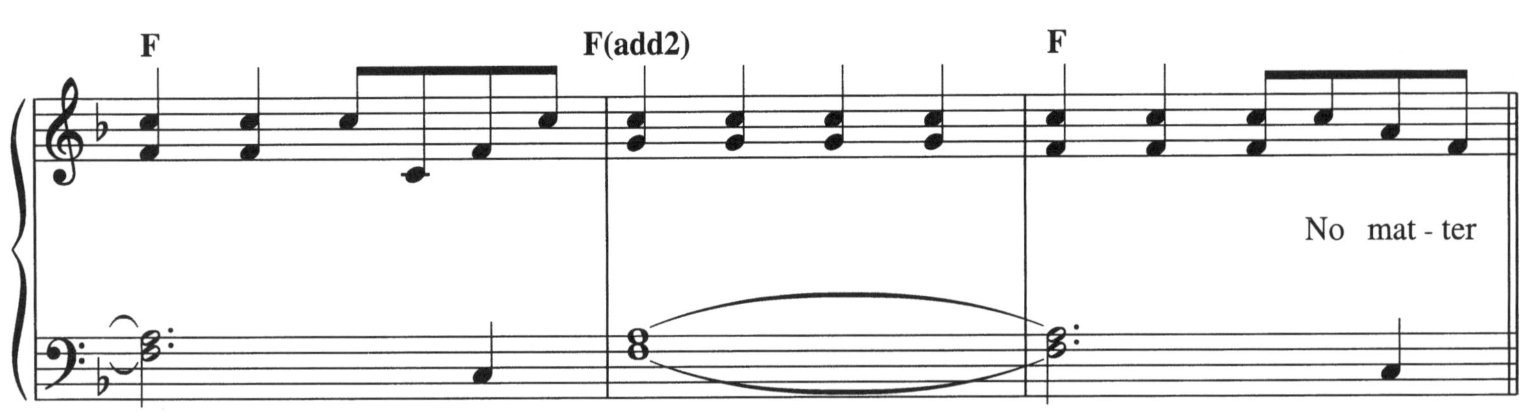
F
F(add2)
F
No mat - ter

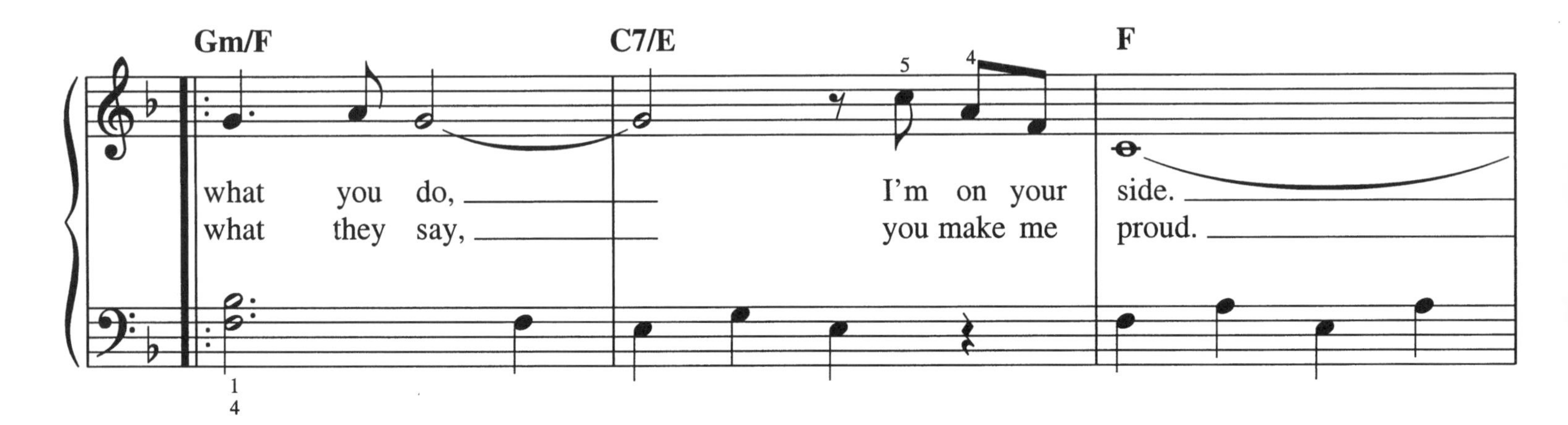
Gm/F
C7/E
F
what you do, I'm on your side.
what they say, you make me proud.

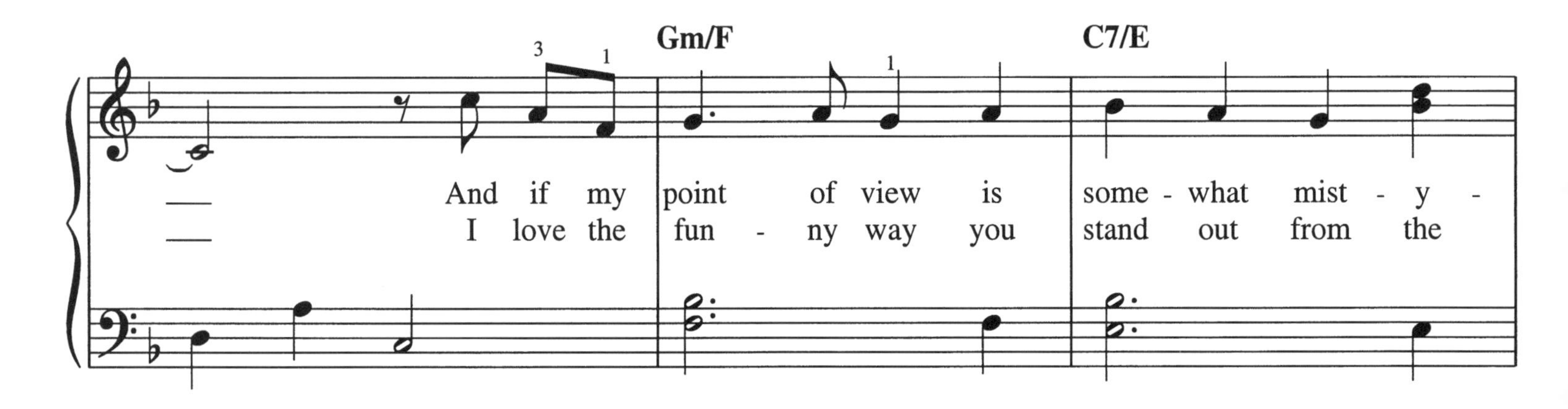
Gm/F
C7/E
And if my point of view is some - what mist - y -
I love the fun - ny way you stand out from the

F
A♭
eyed, there's noth - ing clear - er in my
crowd. Maurice: It's my in - ten - tion my in -

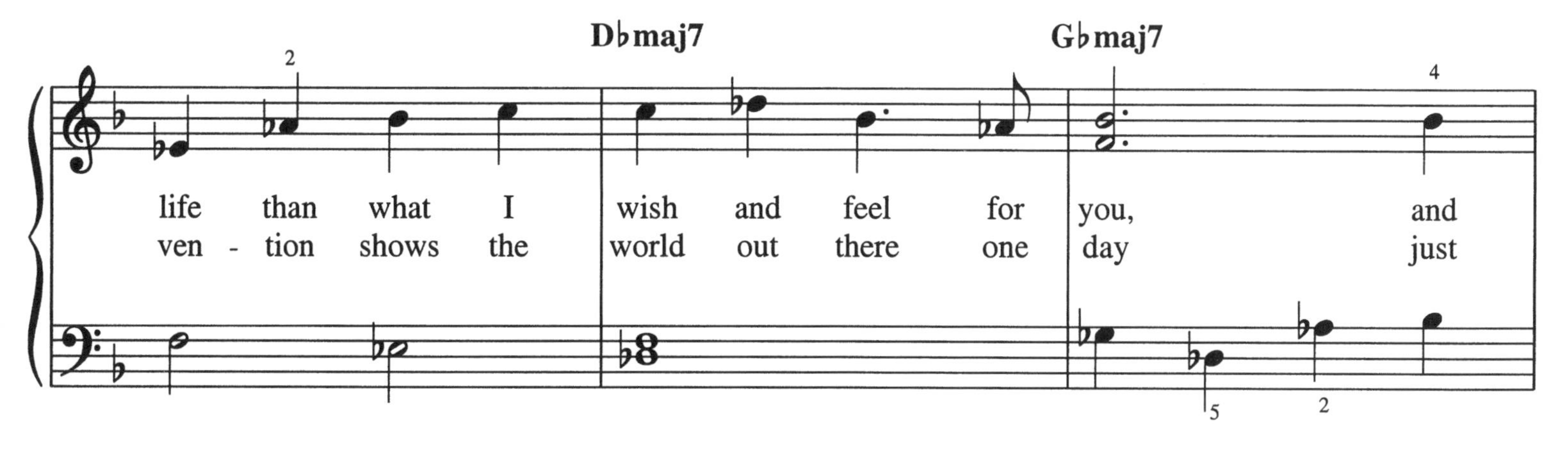
D♭maj7
G♭maj7
life than what I wish and feel for you, and
ven - tion shows the world out there one day just

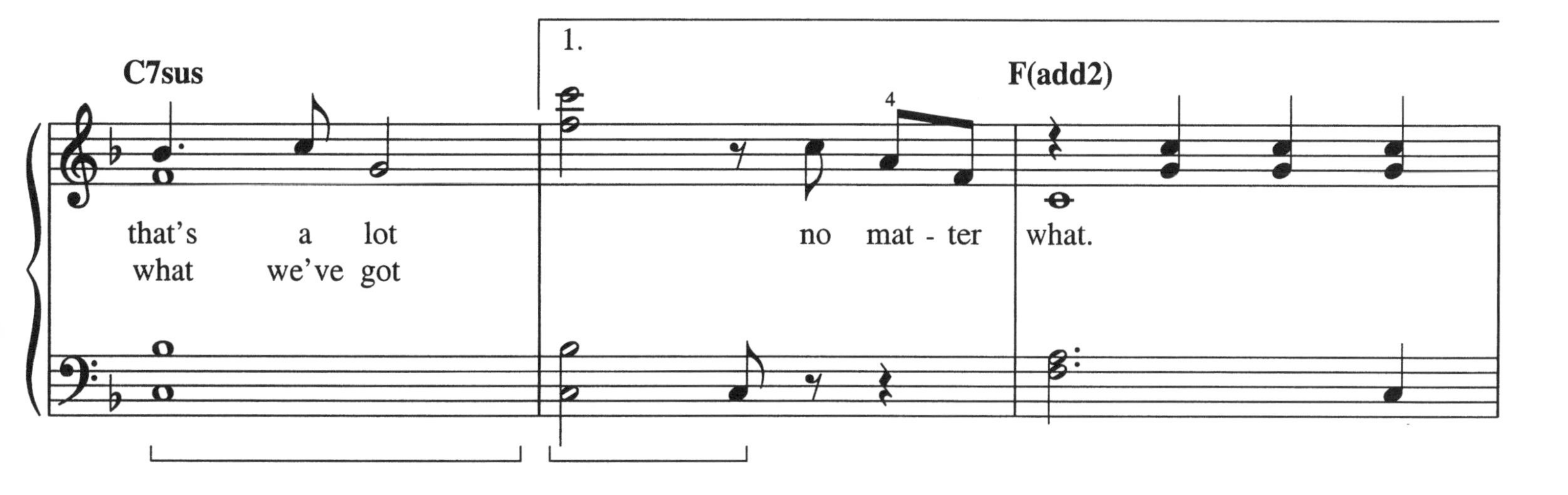
C7sus
1.
F(add2)
that's a lot no mat - ter what.
what we've got

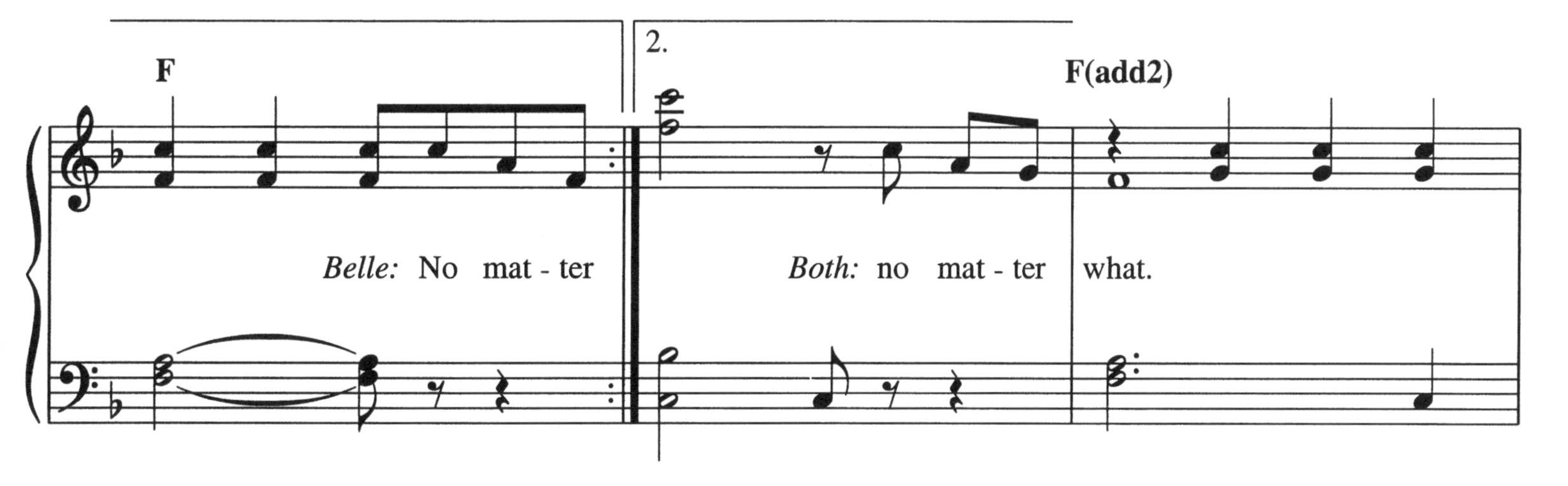
F
2.
F(add2)
Belle: No mat - ter
Both: no mat - ter what.

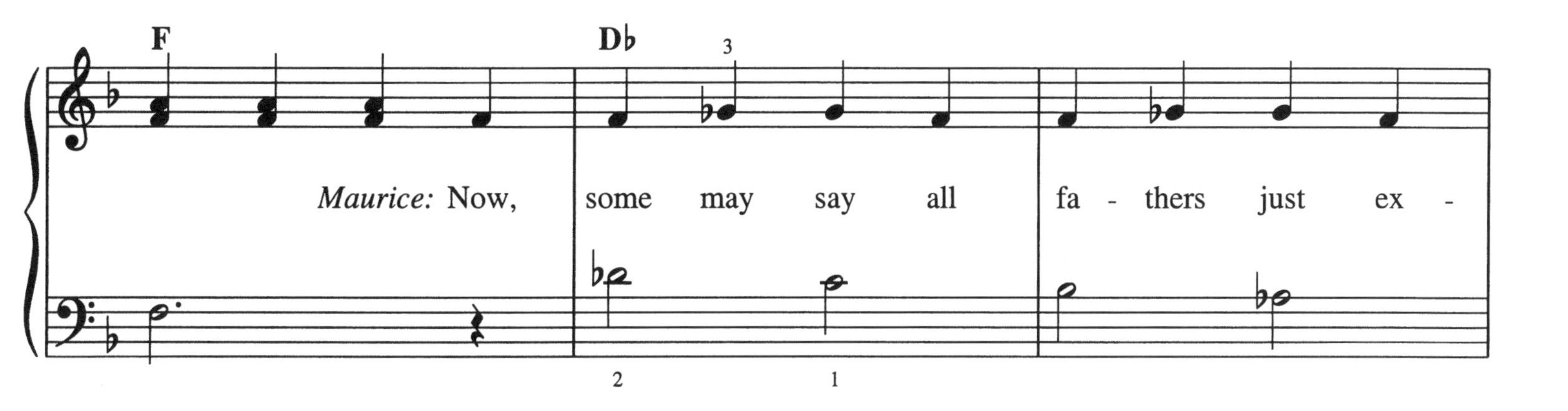
F
D♭
Maurice: Now, some may say all fa - thers just ex -

G♭
D♭/F
E♭m7
ag - ger - ate. ___ Belle: That ev - 'ry daugh - ter's great? ___
3
5

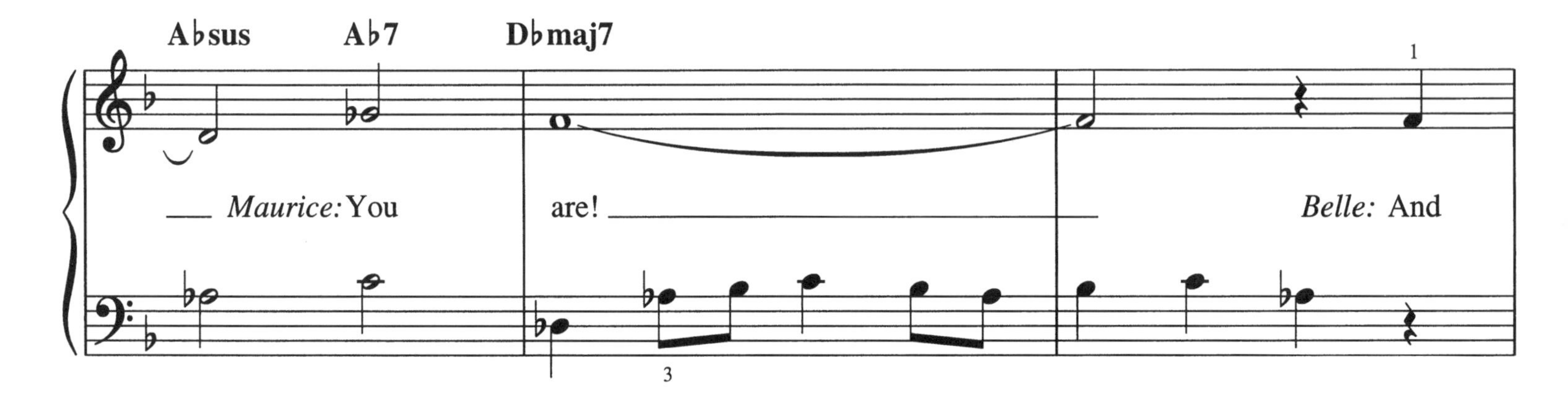
A♭sus
A♭7
D♭maj7
1
___ Maurice: You are! ___ Belle: And
3

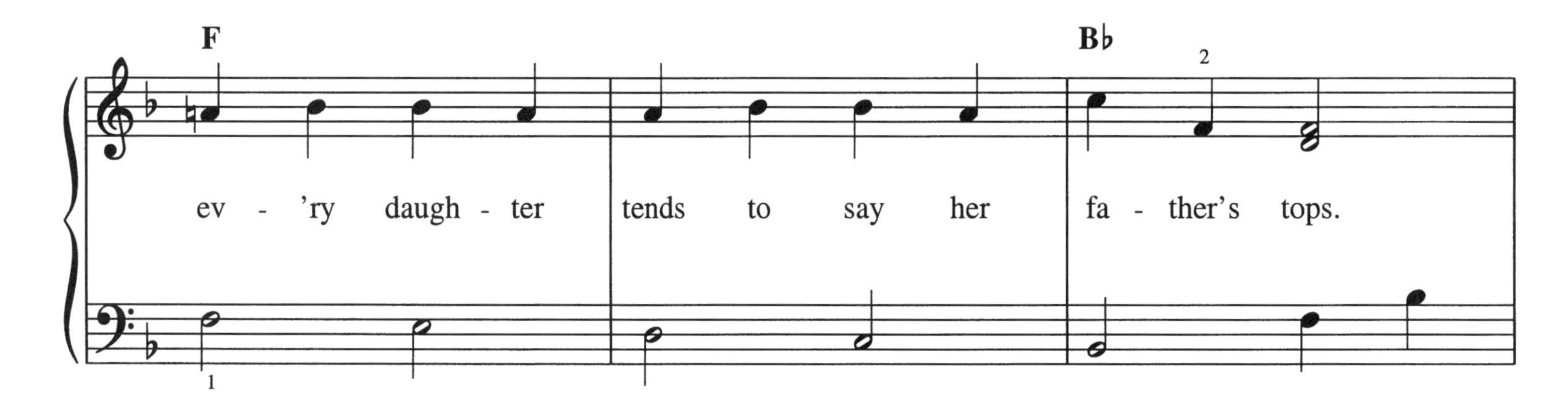
F
B♭
2
ev - 'ry daugh - ter tends to say her fa - ther's tops.
1

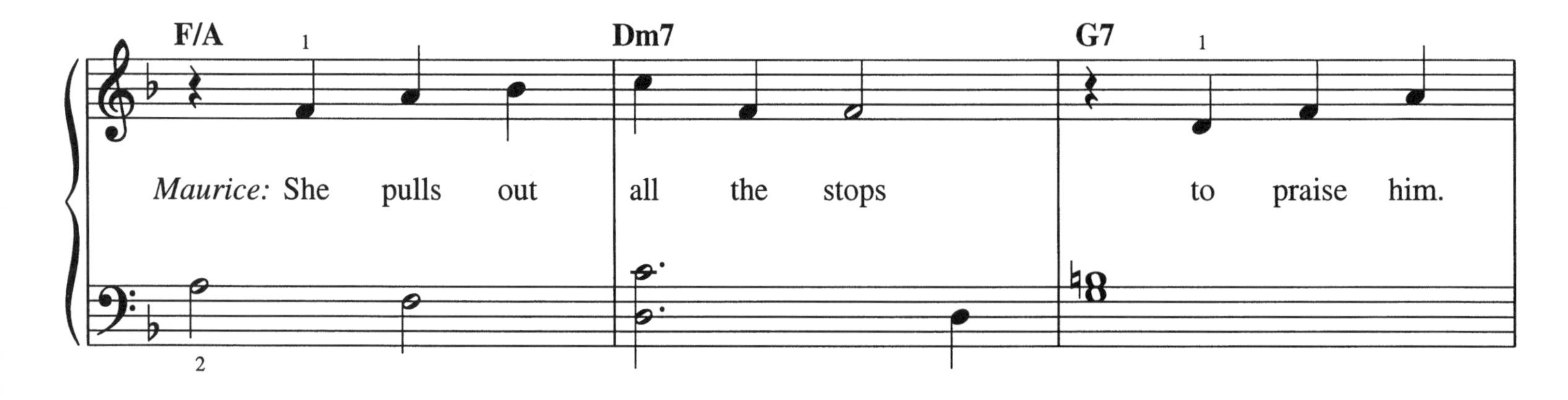
F/A
1
Dm7
G7
1
Maurice: She pulls out all the stops to praise him.
2

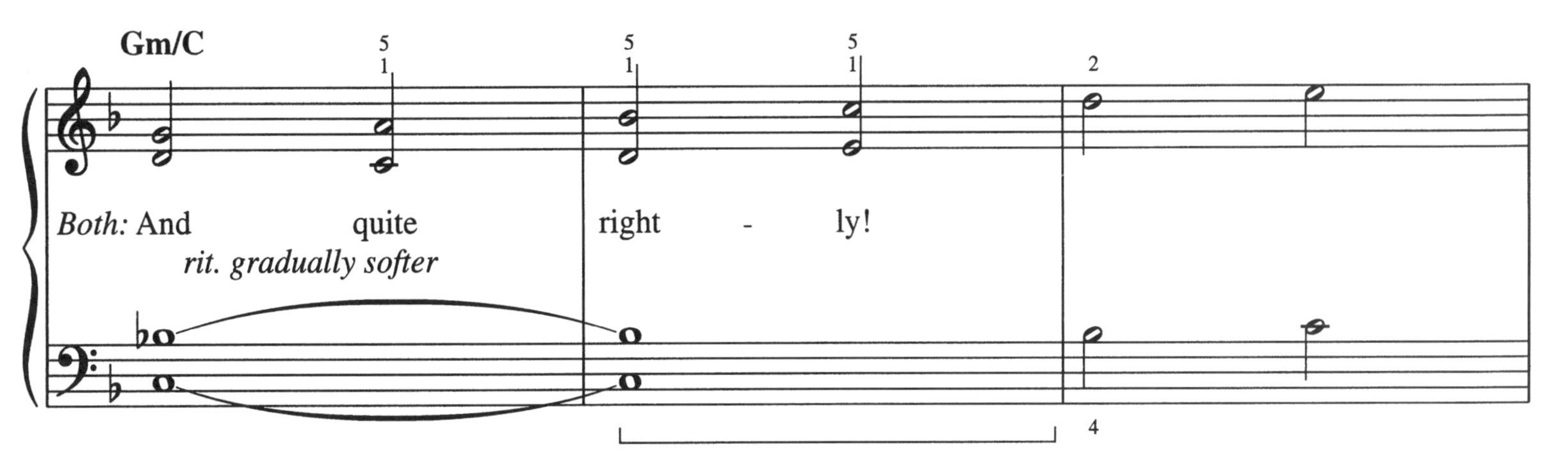
Gm/C
Both: And quite right - ly!
rit. gradually softer

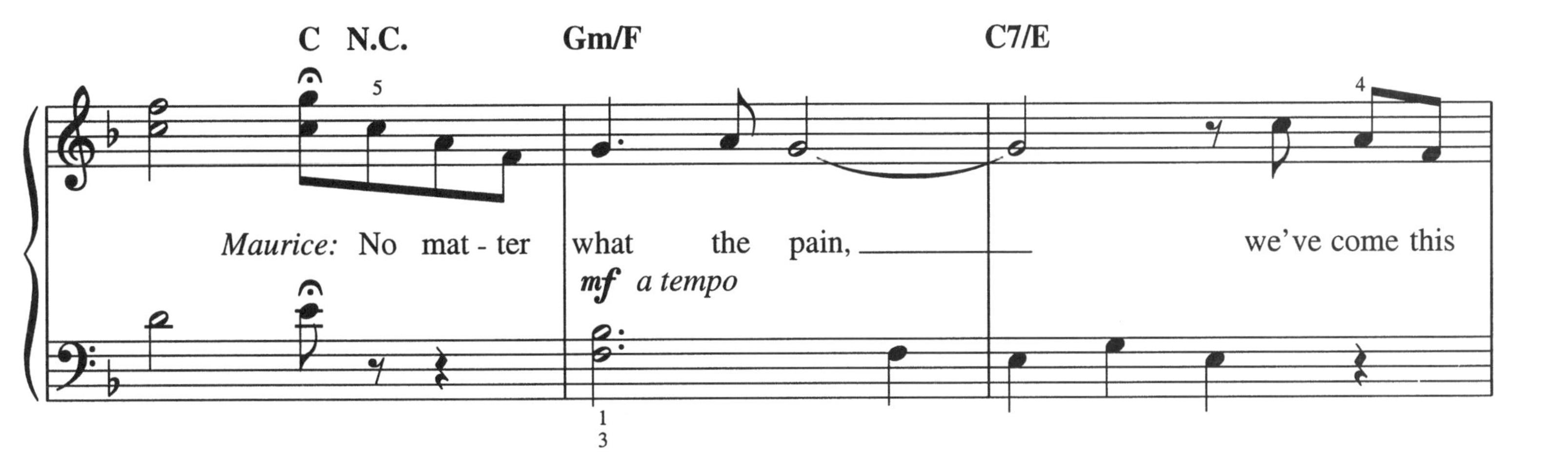
C N.C.
Gm/F
C7/E
Maurice: No mat - ter what the pain, we've come this
mf a tempo

F
Gm/F
far. I pray that you re - main ex -

C7
F
N.C.
act - ly as you are. This real - ly

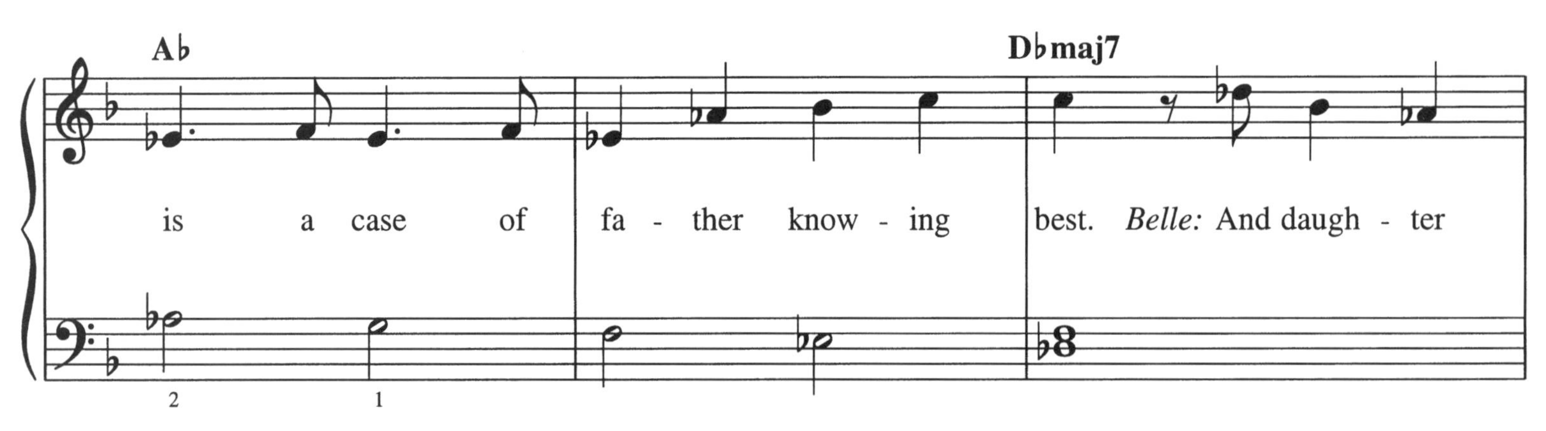
A♭
D♭maj7
is a case of fa - ther know - ing best. Belle: And daugh - ter
2 1

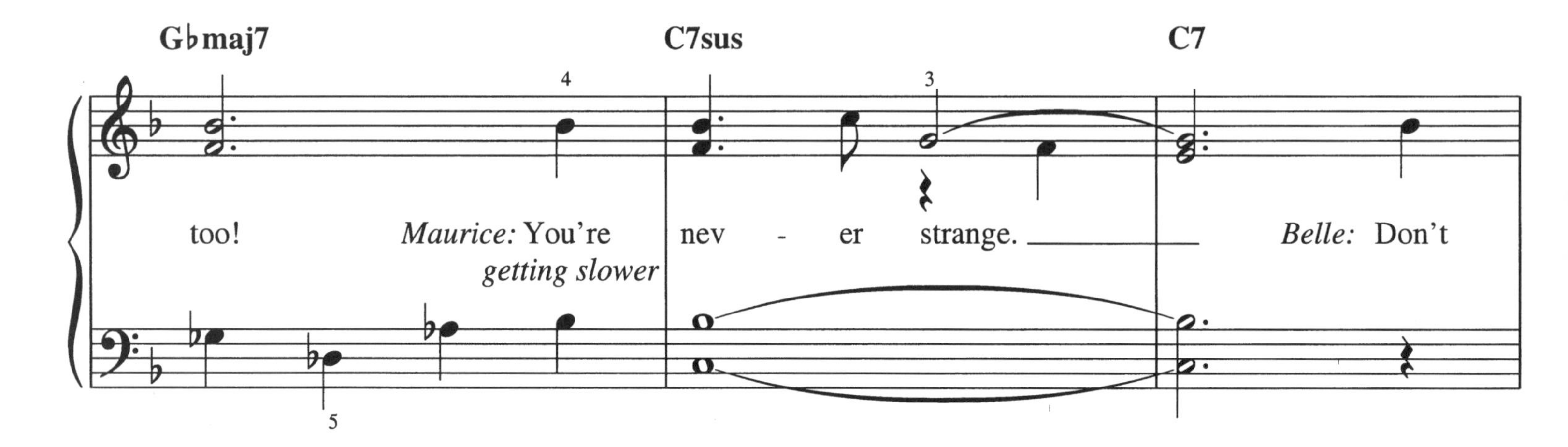
G♭maj7
C7sus
C7
4 3
too! Maurice: You're nev - er strange. Belle: Don't
getting slower
5

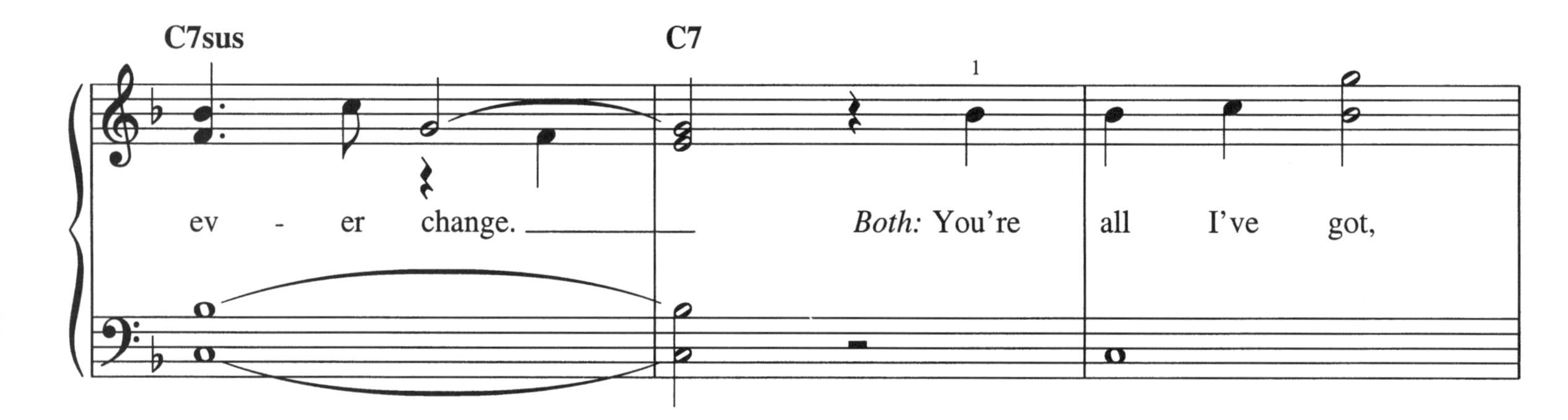
C7sus
C7
1
ev - er change. Both: You're all I've got,

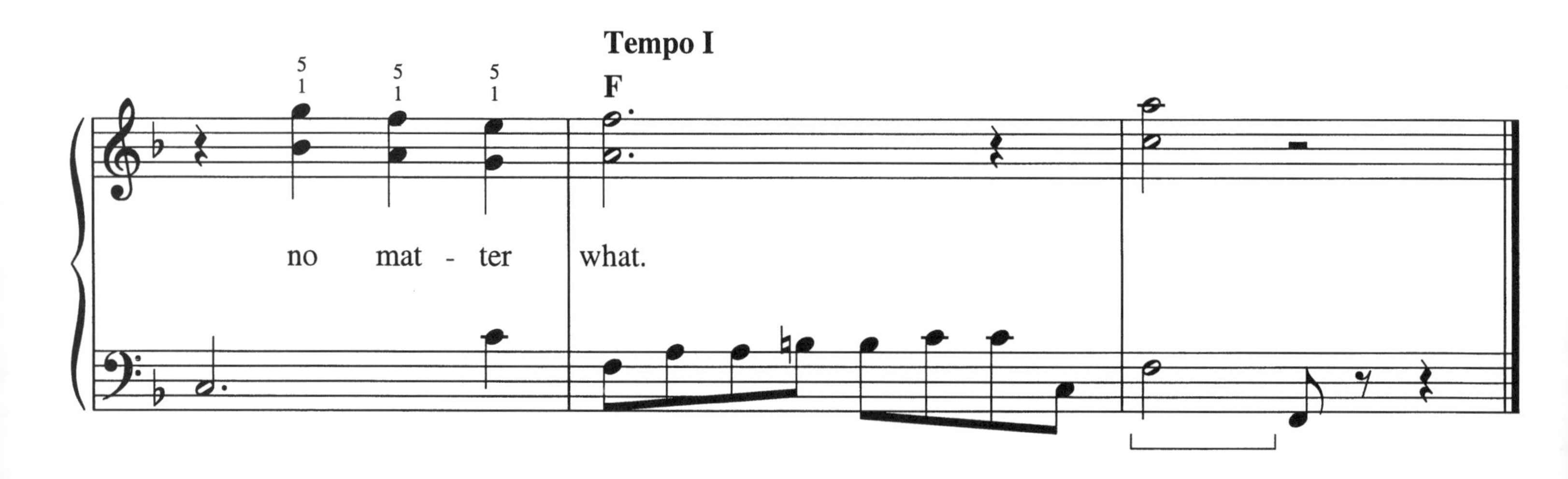
Tempo I
F
5 1 5 1 5 1
no mat - ter what.

ME

Music by ALAN MENKEN
Lyrics by TIM RICE

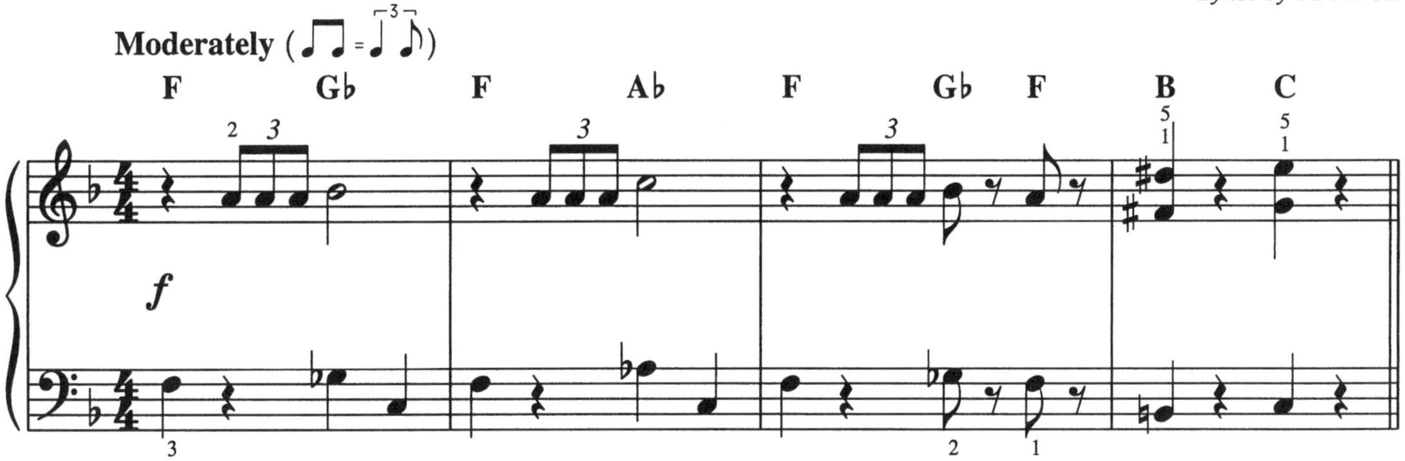

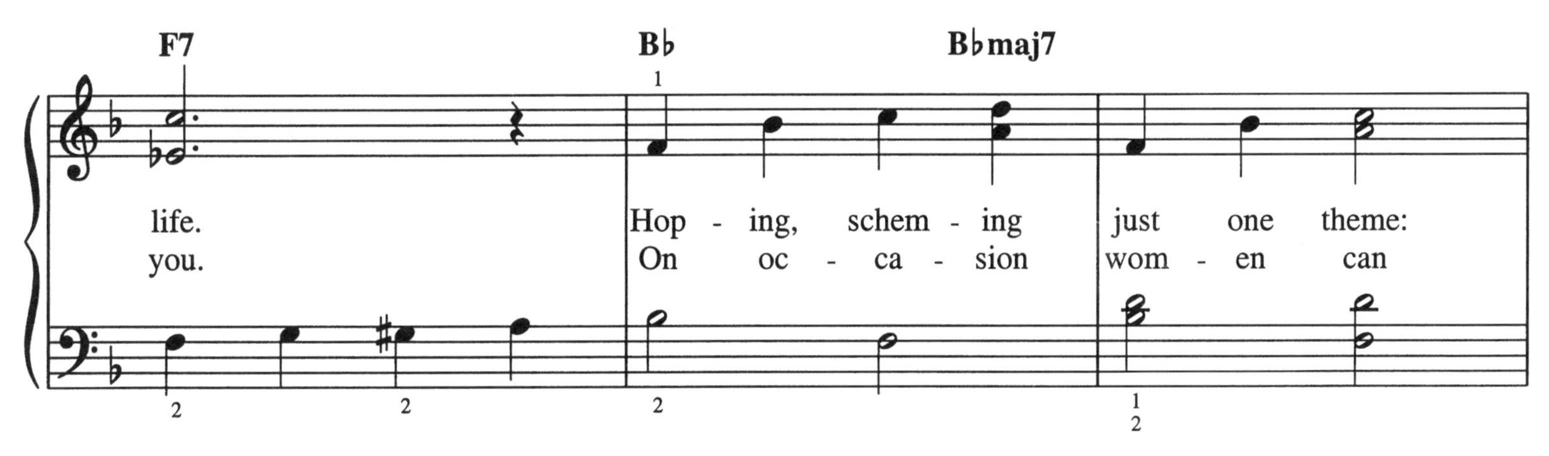

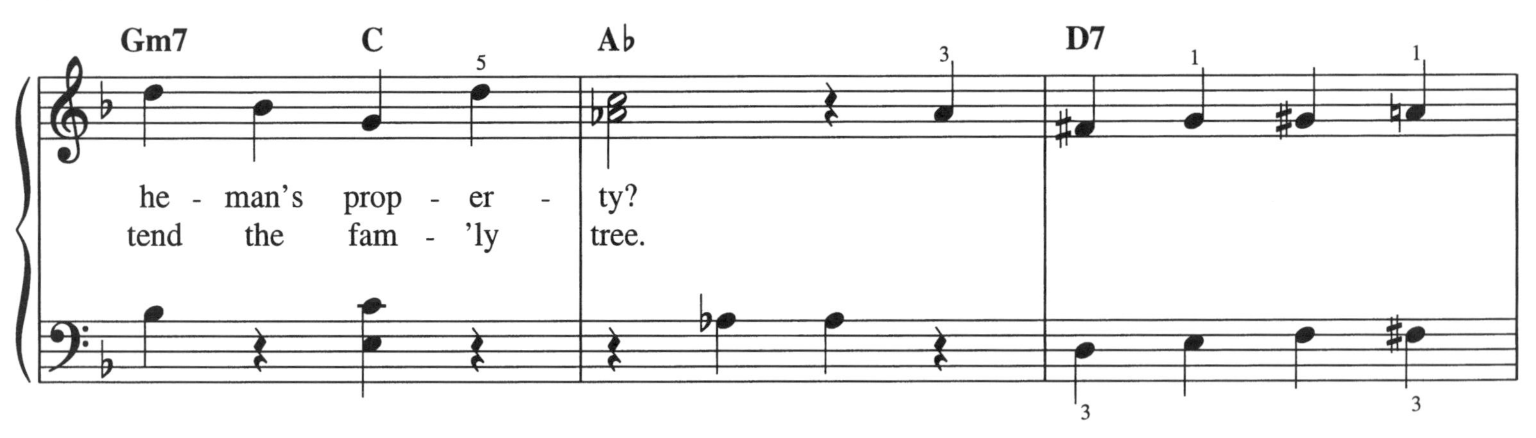
Gm7 C Ab D7
he - man's prop - er - ty?
tend the fam - 'ly tree.

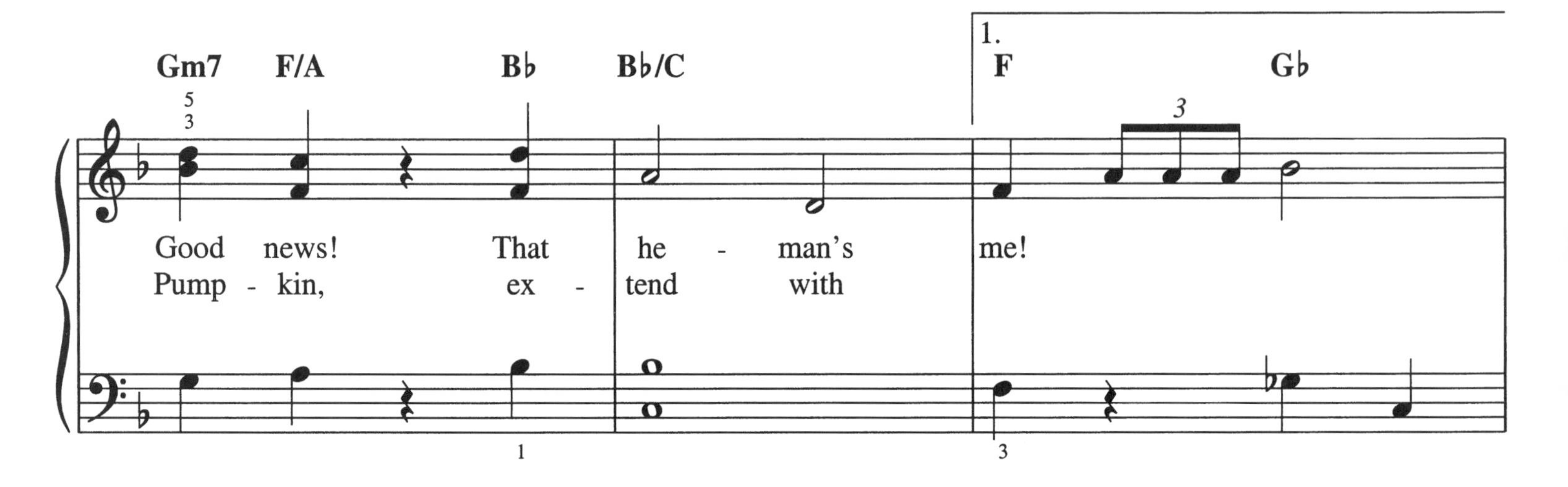
Gm7 F/A Bb Bb/C
1.
F Gb
Good news! That he - man's me!
Pump - kin, ex - tend with

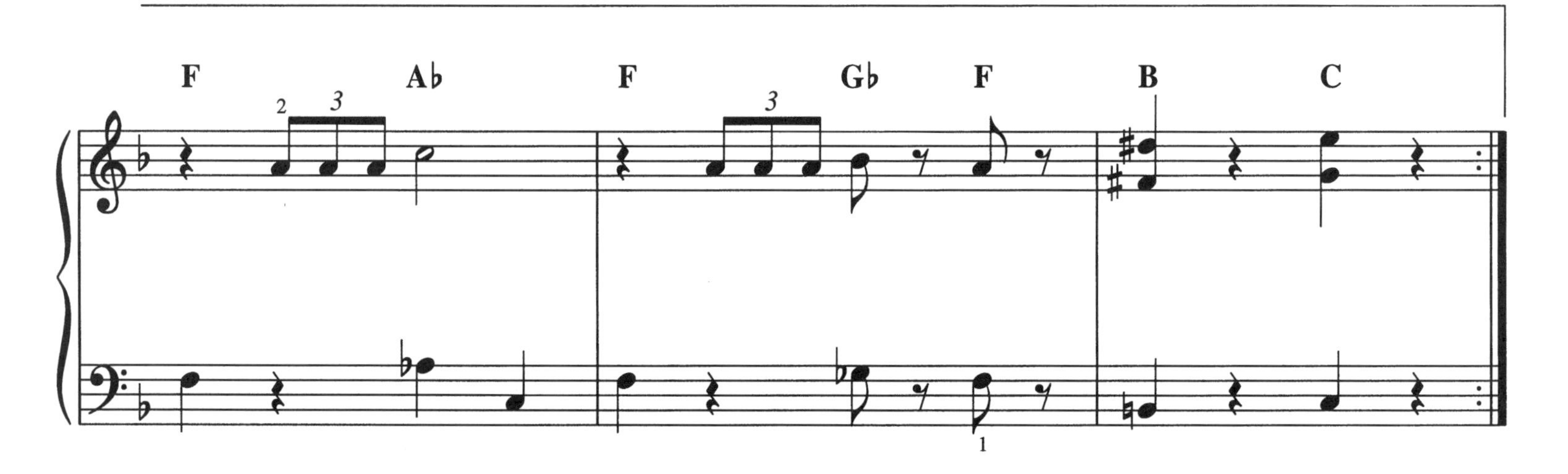
F Ab F Gb F B C

2.
F Gb F Ab C7
me! We'll be rais - ing sons ga -

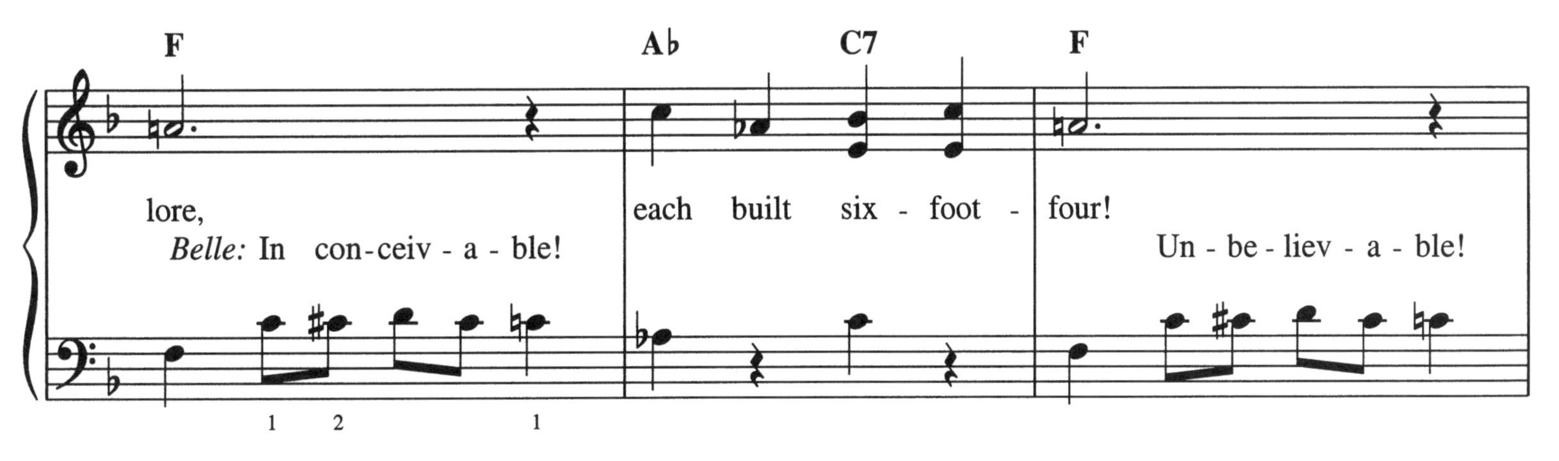
F Ab C7 F
lore, each built six - foot - four!
Belle: In con-ceiv - a - ble! Un - be - liev - a - ble!

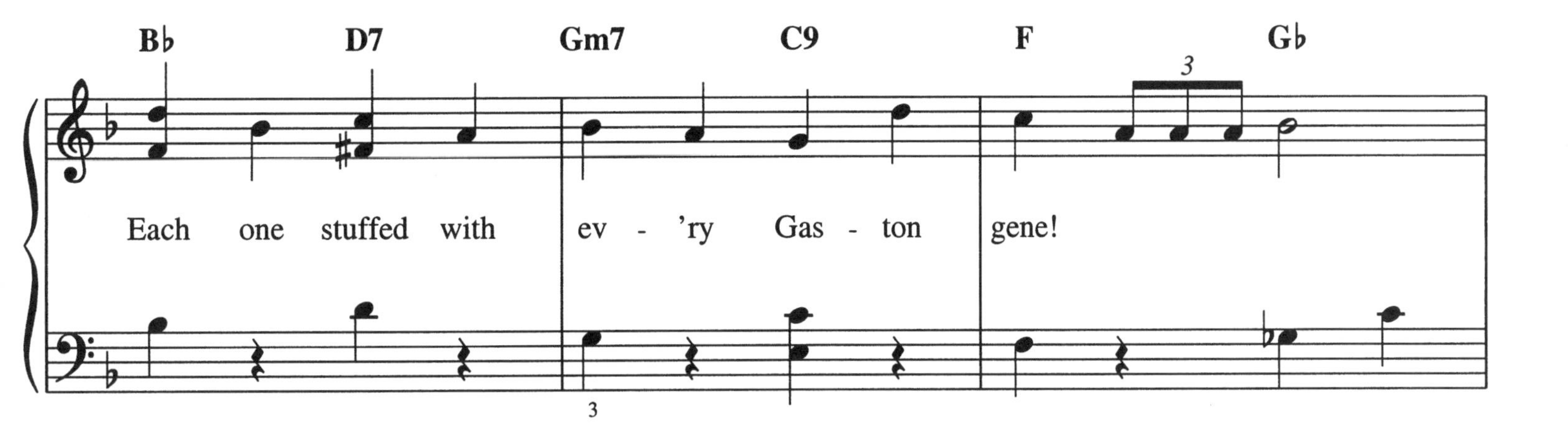
Bb D7 Gm7 C9 F Gb
Each one stuffed with ev - 'ry Gas - ton gene!

F Ab C7 F
You'll be keep - ing house with pride.
I'm not hear-ing this! Just in-cred - i - ble!

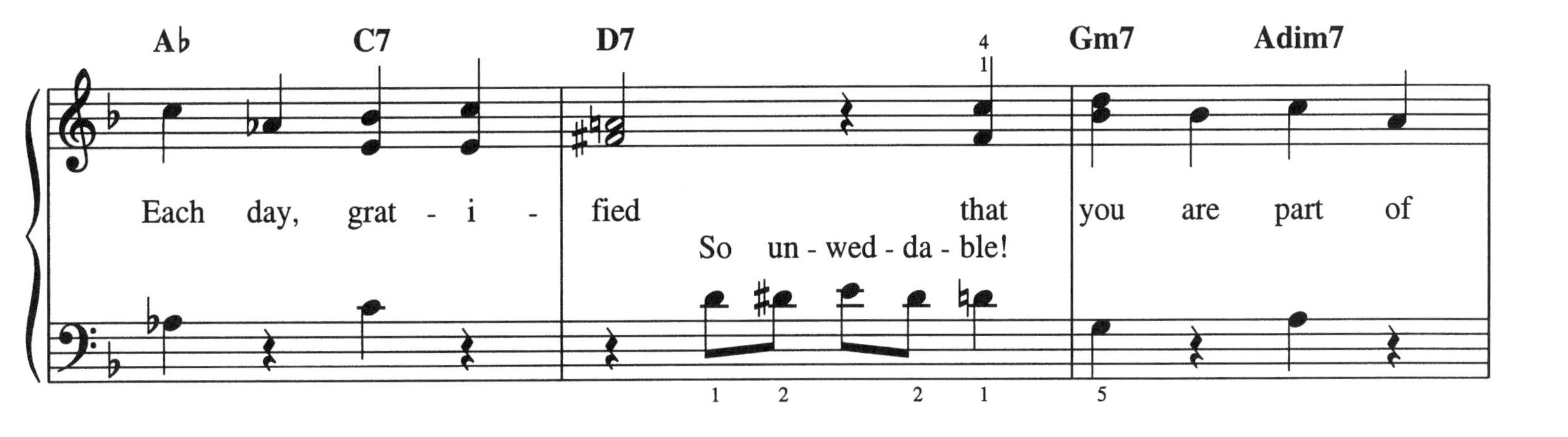
Ab C7 D7 Gm7 Adim7
Each day, grat - i - fied that you are part of
So un-wed-da-ble!

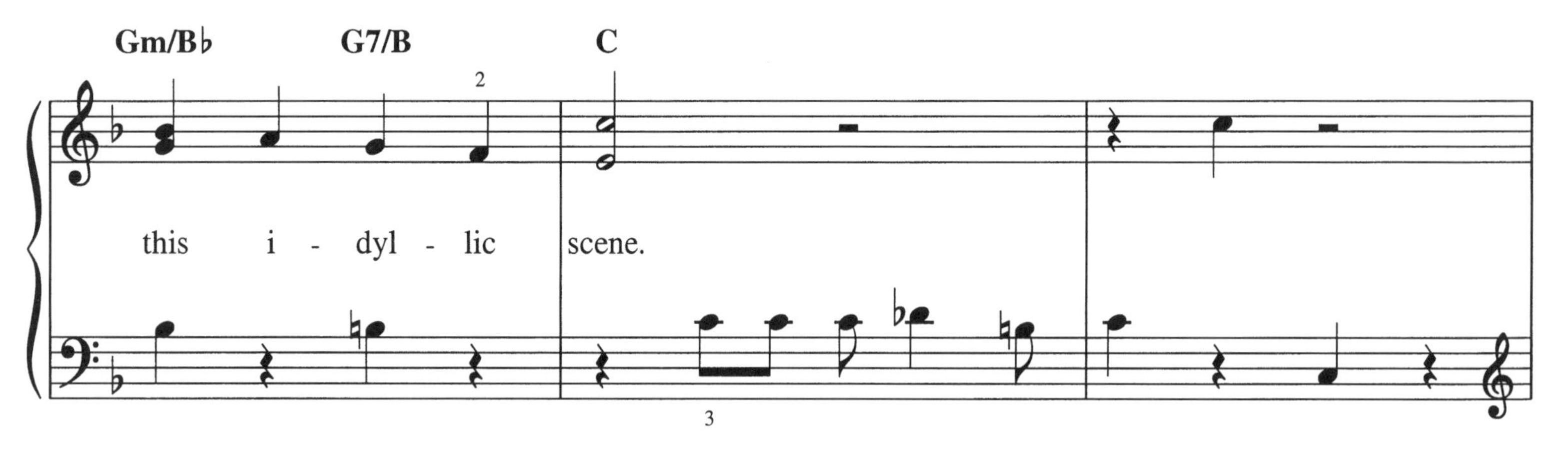
Gm/B♭
G7/B
C
this i - dyl - lic
scene.

F
F7
(Spoken:) Picture this:
A rustic lodge...
my
latest kill,

B♭ Bm7♭5

roasting over the fire... my little wife massaging my feet...

Am
C7/G
Cm
D7
while the little ones play
on the floor with the dogs, Oh, we'll have six or seven!

Gm7 F/A B♭ B♭/C F G♭
Belle: Dogs? Gaston: No Belle! Strapping boys... like me!

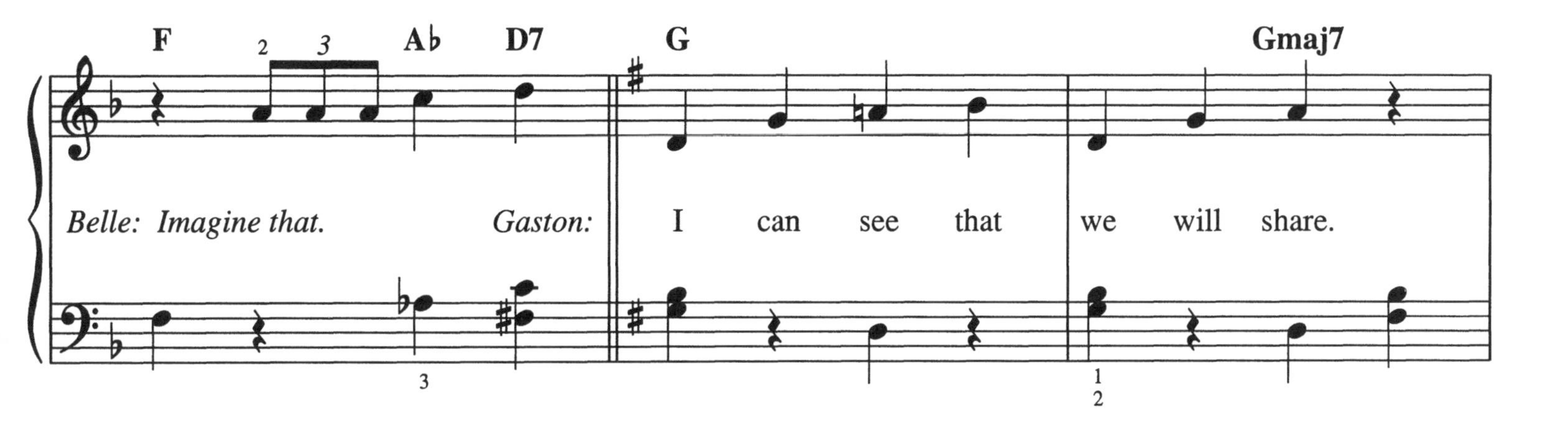

F A♭ D7 G Gmaj7
Belle: Imagine that. Gaston: I can see that we will share.

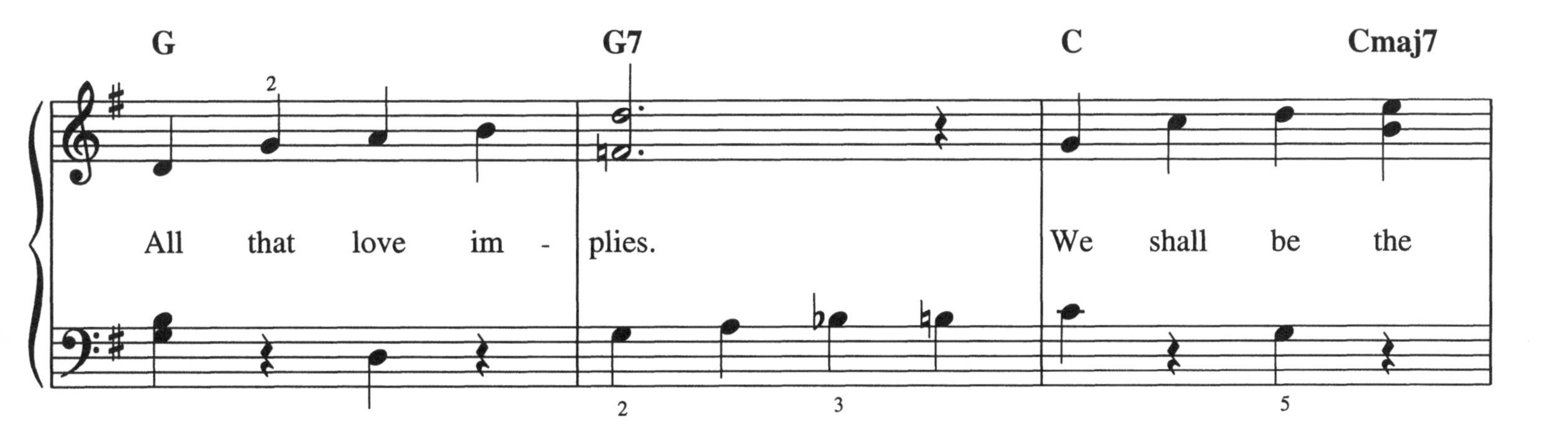

G G7 C Cmaj7
All that love im - plies. We shall be the

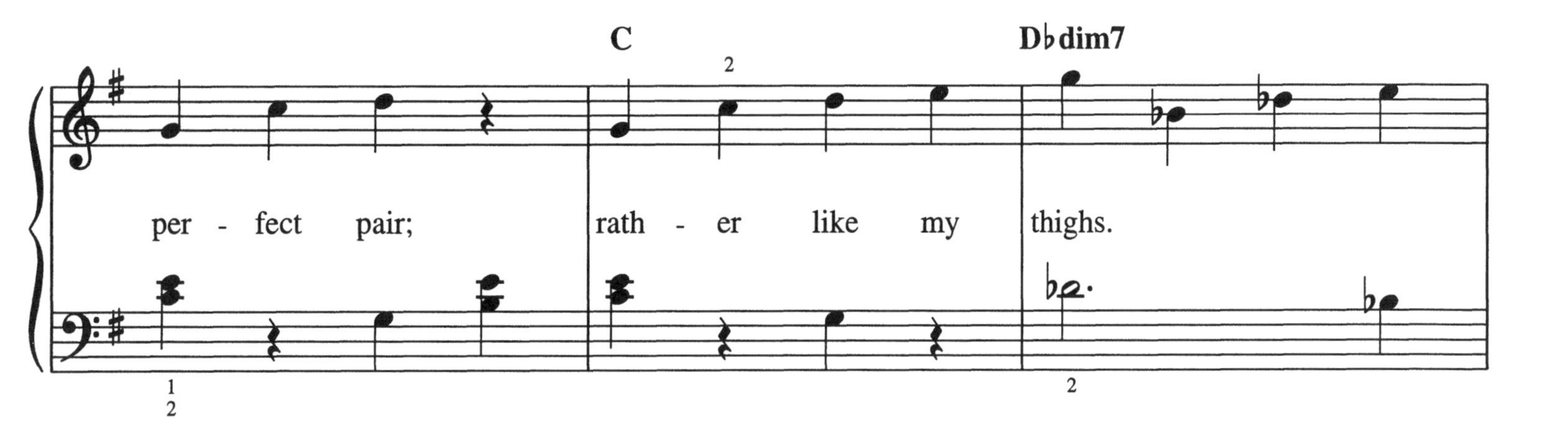

C D♭dim7
per - fect pair; rath - er like my thighs.

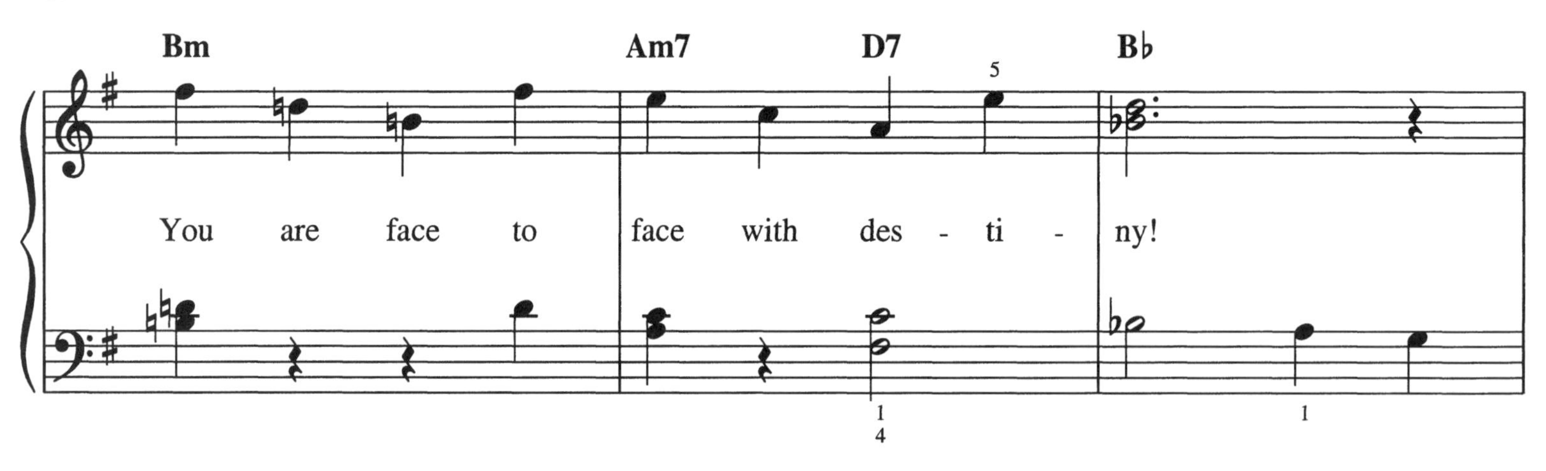
Bm
Am7
D7
B♭
You are face to face with des - ti - ny!

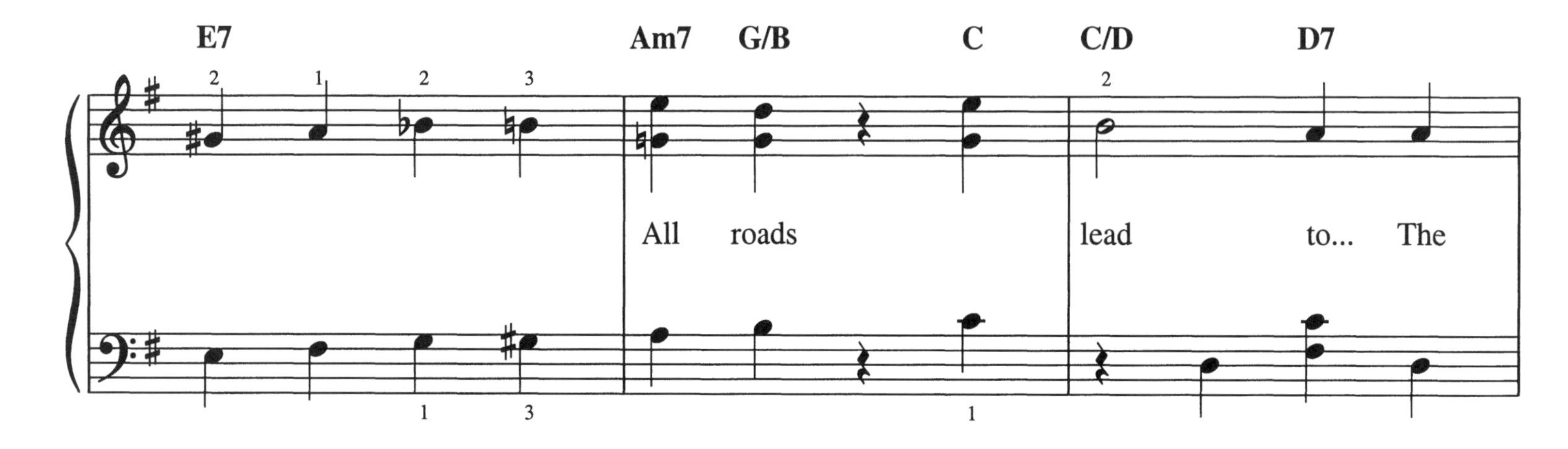
E7
Am7
G/B
C
C/D
D7
All roads lead to... The

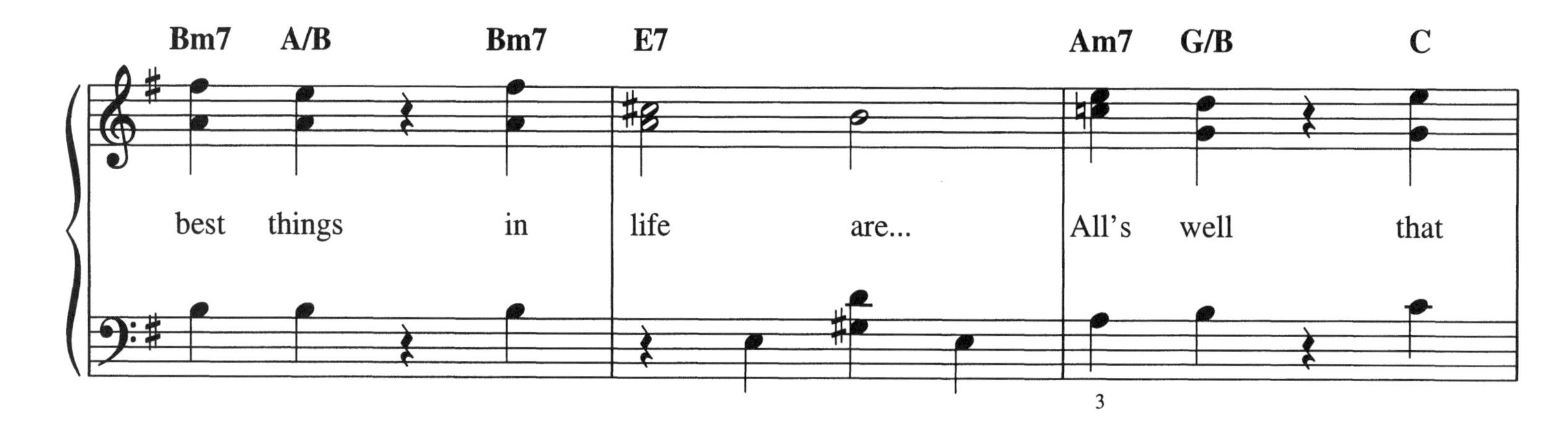
Bm7
A/B
Bm7
E7
Am7
G/B
C
best things in life are... All's well that

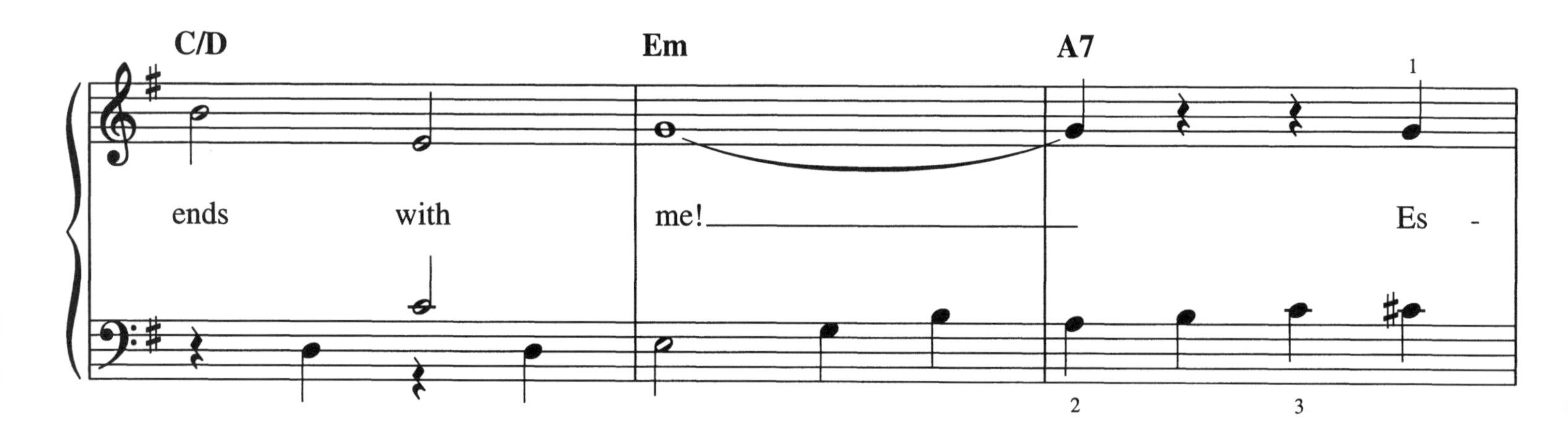
C/D
Em
A7
ends with me! Es -

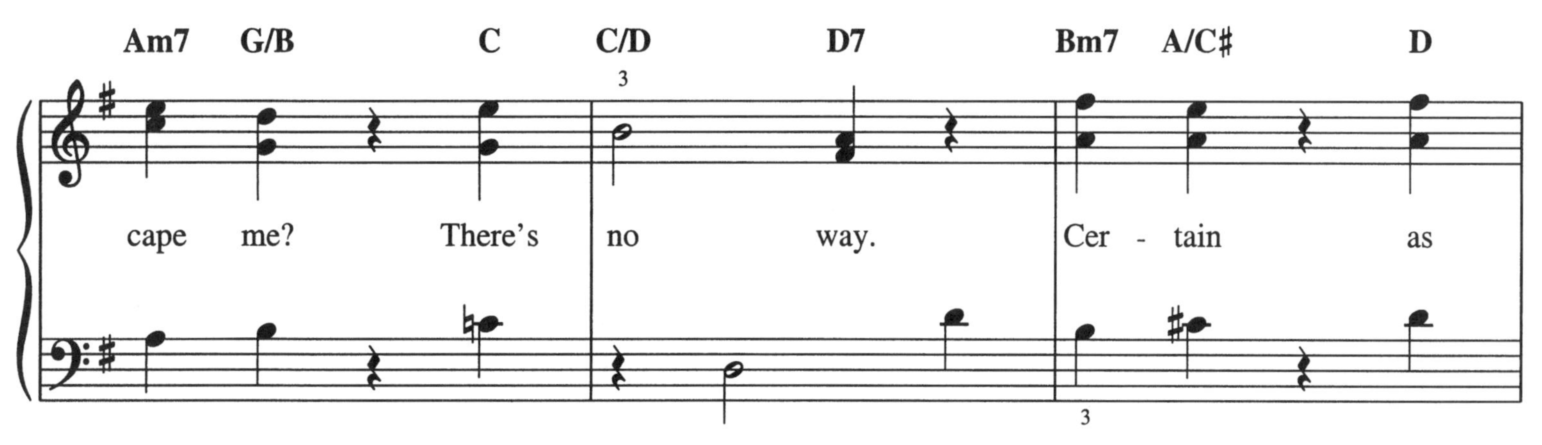
Am7 G/B C C/D D7 Bm7 A/C# D
cape me? There's no way. Cer - tain as

E7 Am7 G/B C Cmaj7/D
Do Re, Belle, when you mar -

D7sus G A♭
ry
(Spoken:) Gaston: So, Belle, what'll it be? Is it "yes", or is it... "Ohhh, yes!"
Belle: I... I just don't deserve you!
Gaston: Who does?
me!

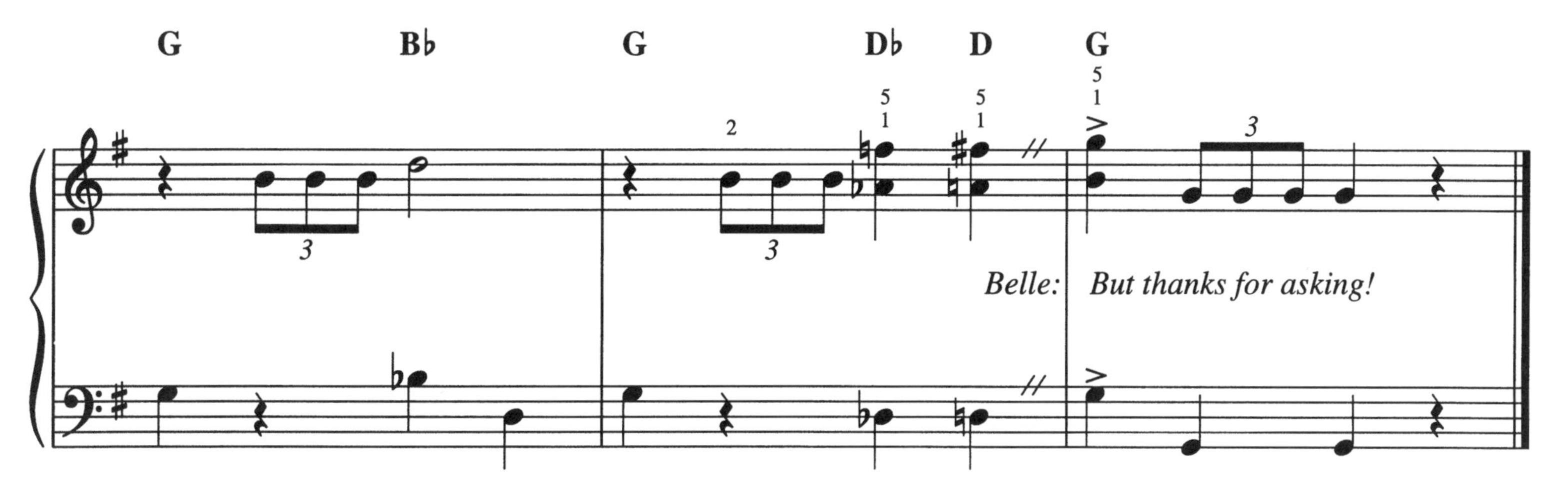
G B♭ G D♭ D G
Belle: But thanks for asking!

HOME

Music by ALAN MENKEN
Lyrics by TIM RICE

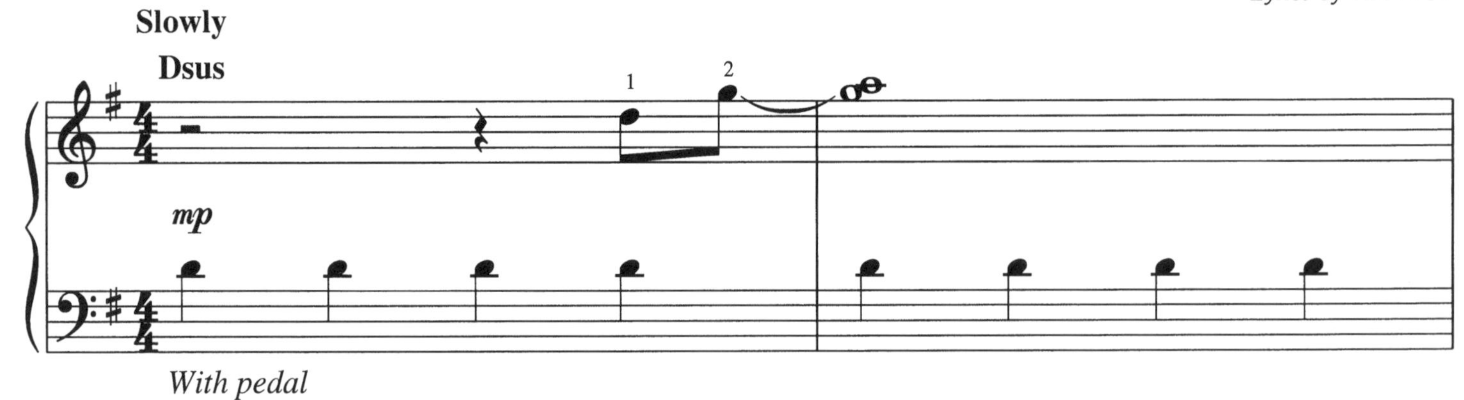

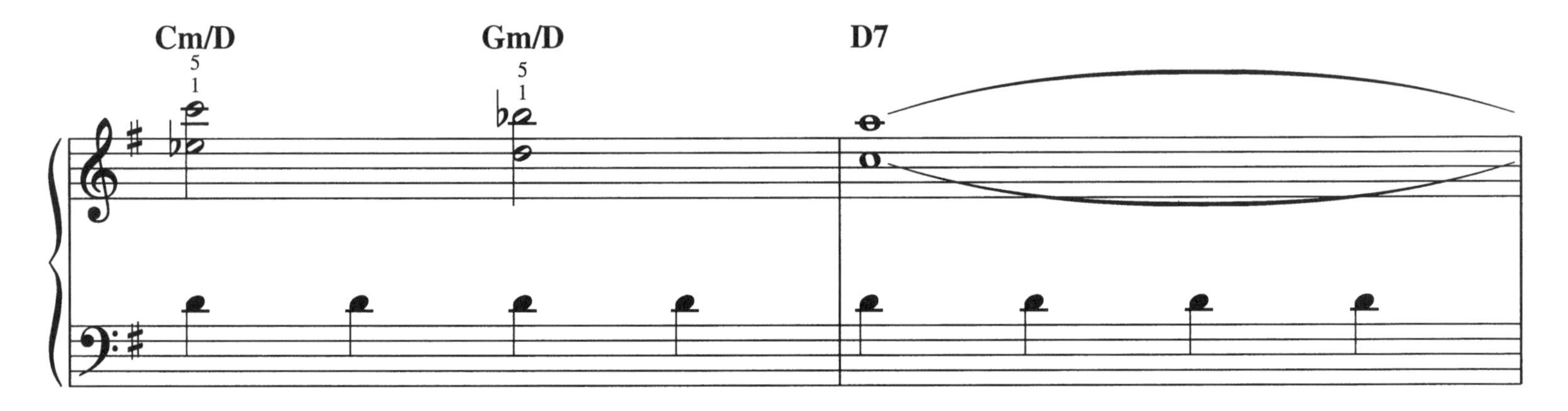

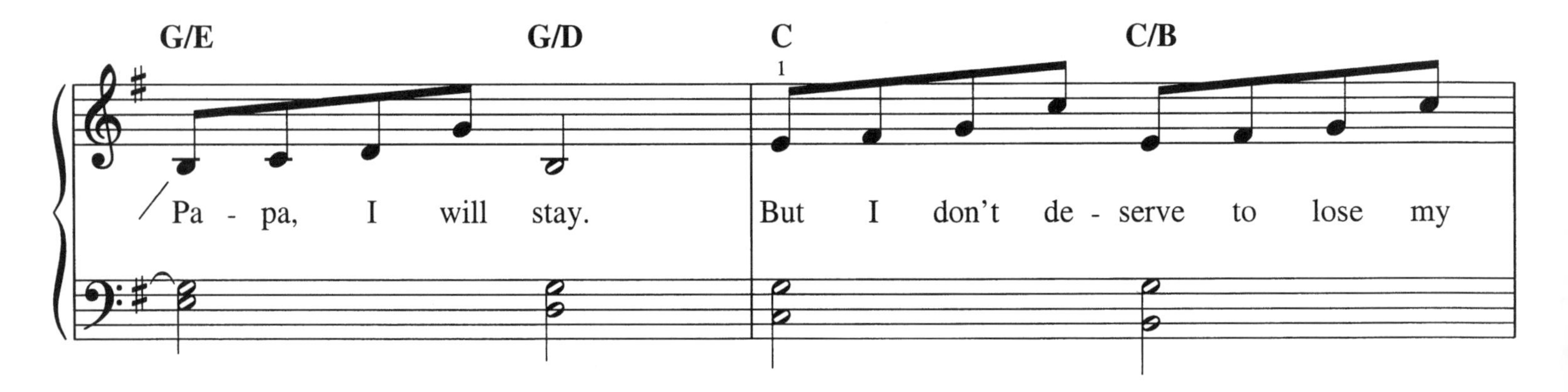

Am7
C/D
G
free - dom in this way, you mon - ster!

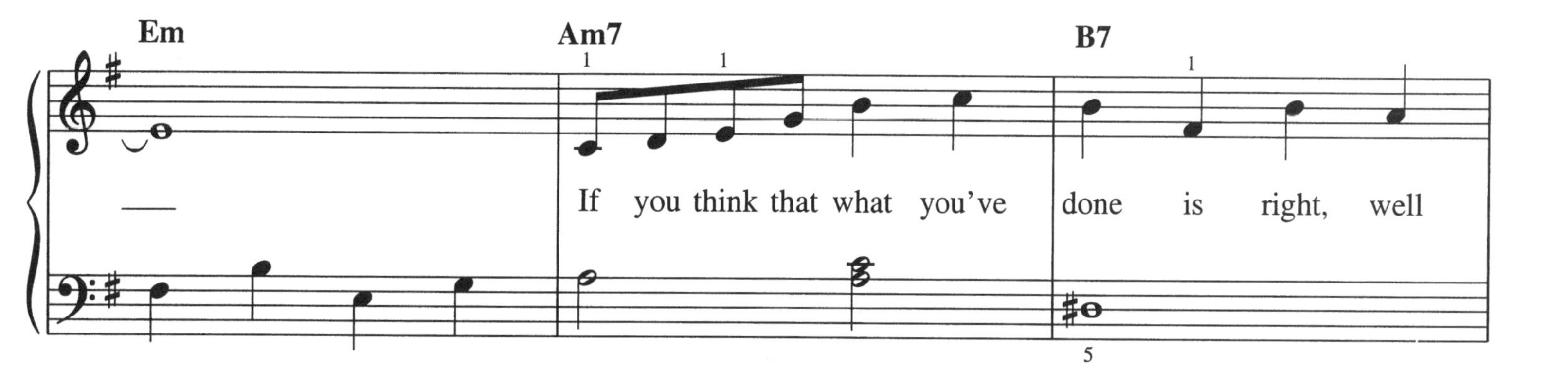
Em
Am7
B7
If you think that what you've done is right, well

Em
G7/D
C6
then you're a fool!

Bm/D
G
G/E
G/D
Think a - gain!

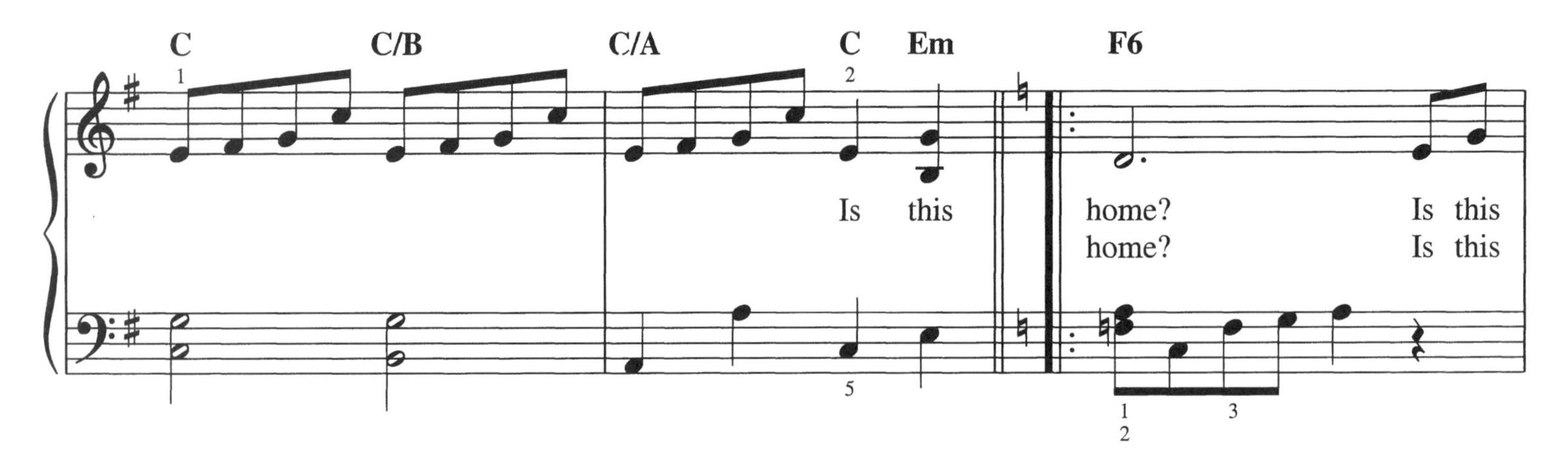
C C/B C/A C Em F6
Is this home? Is this
home? Is this

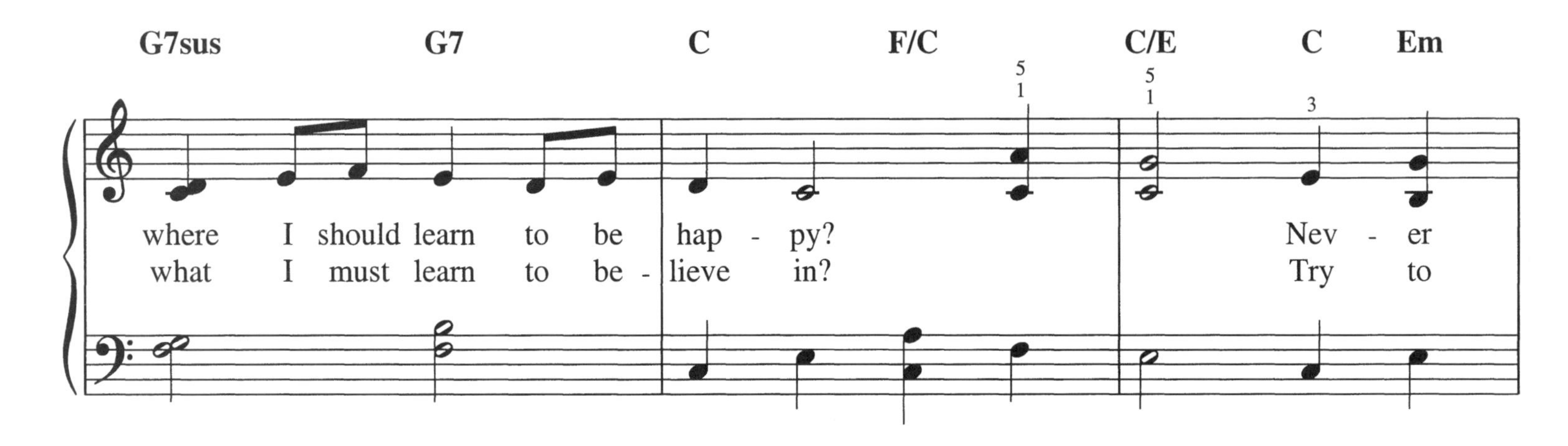
G7sus G7 C F/C C/E C Em
where I should learn to be hap - py? Nev - er
what I must learn to be - lieve in? Try to

F6 G7 C G/D
dreamed that a home could be dark and cold.
find some-thing good in this tra - gic place.

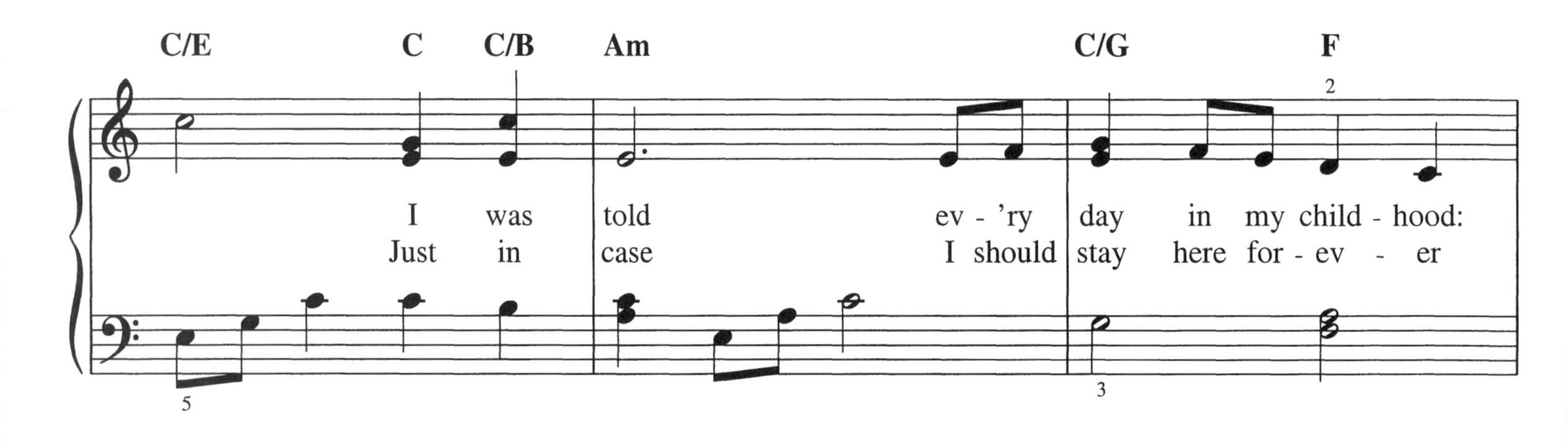
C/E C C/B Am C/G F
I was told ev - 'ry day in my child - hood:
Just in case I should stay here for - ev - er

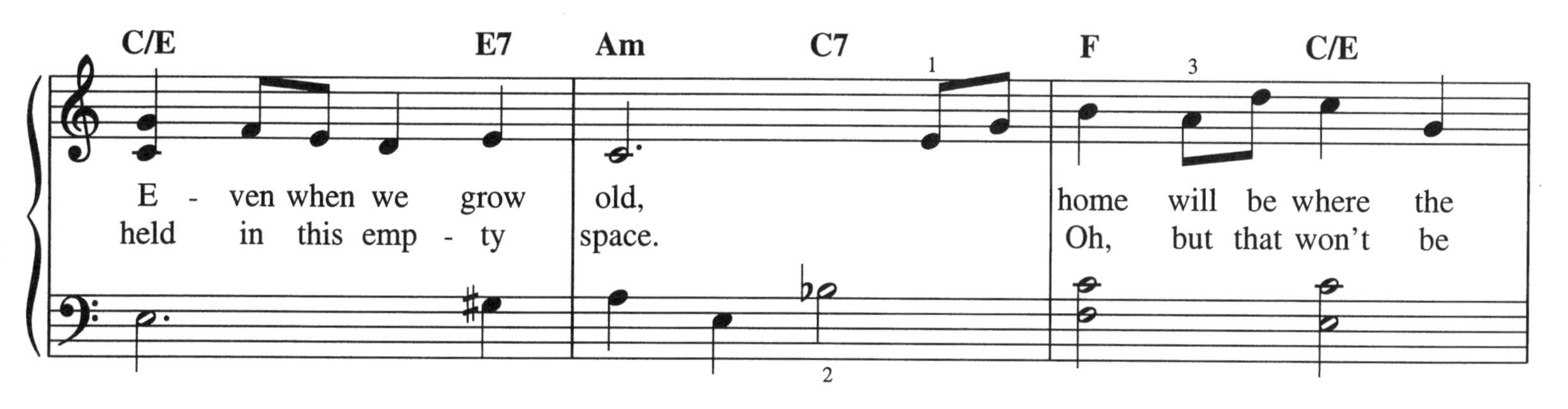
C/E E7 Am C7 F C/E
E - ven when we grow old, home will be where the
held in this emp - ty space. Oh, but that won't be

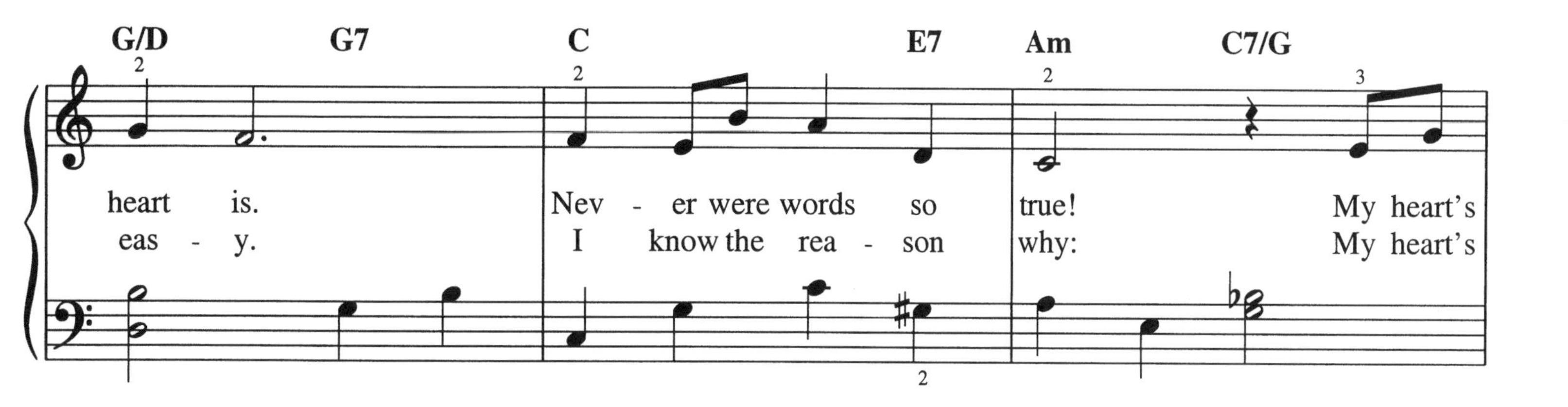
G/D G7 C E7 Am C7/G
heart is. Nev - er were words so true! My heart's
eas - y. I know the rea - son why: My heart's

1.
F6 Gsus G7 C F/C G/C
far, far a - way. Home is too.
far, far a -

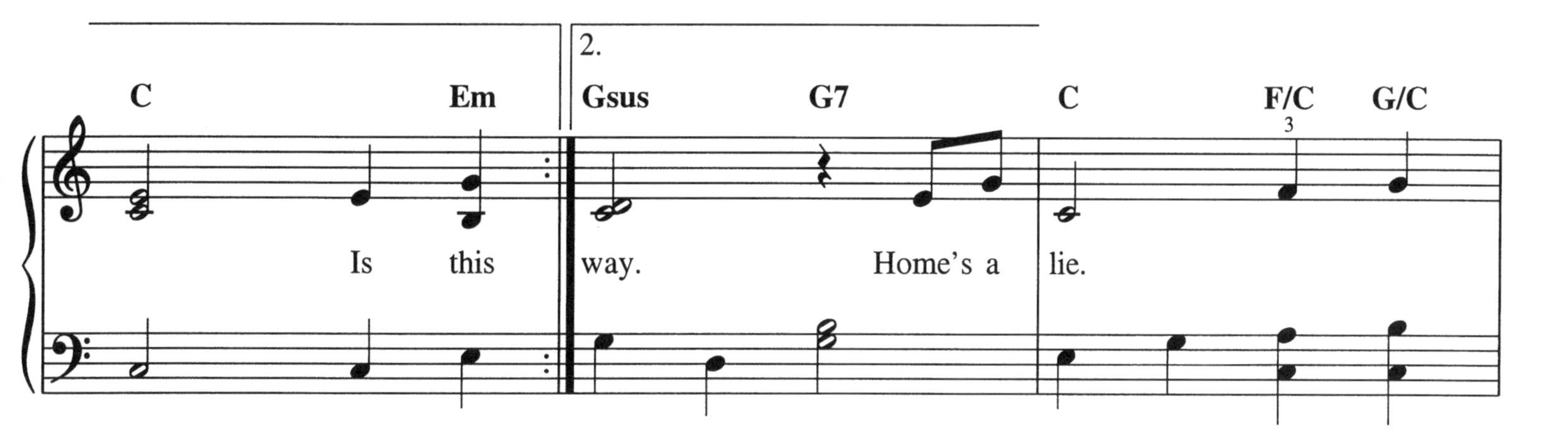
2.
C Em Gsus G7 C F/C G/C
Is this way. Home's a lie.

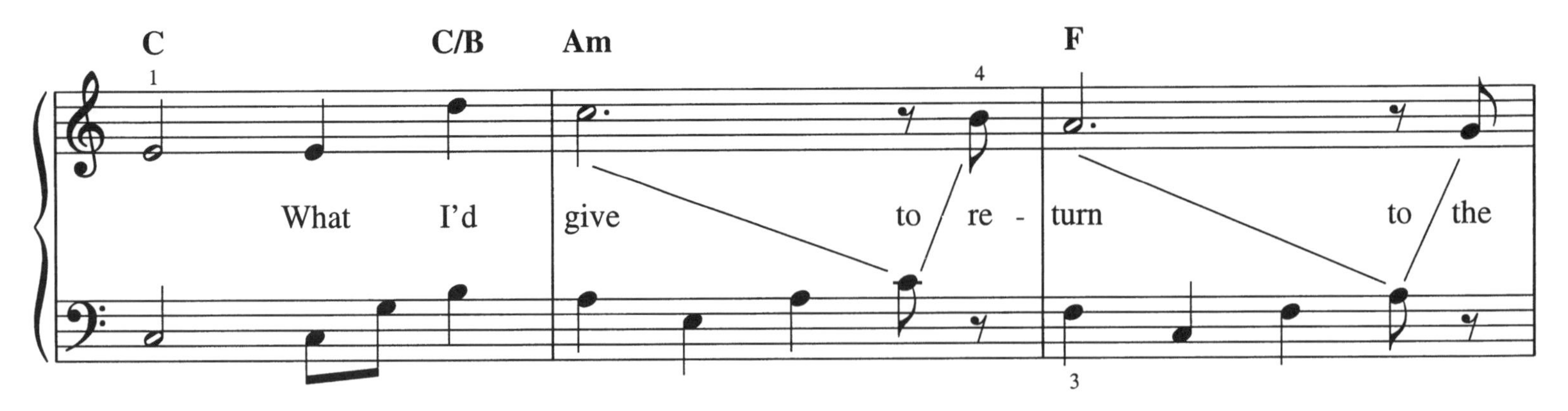
C C/B Am F
What I'd give to re - turn to the

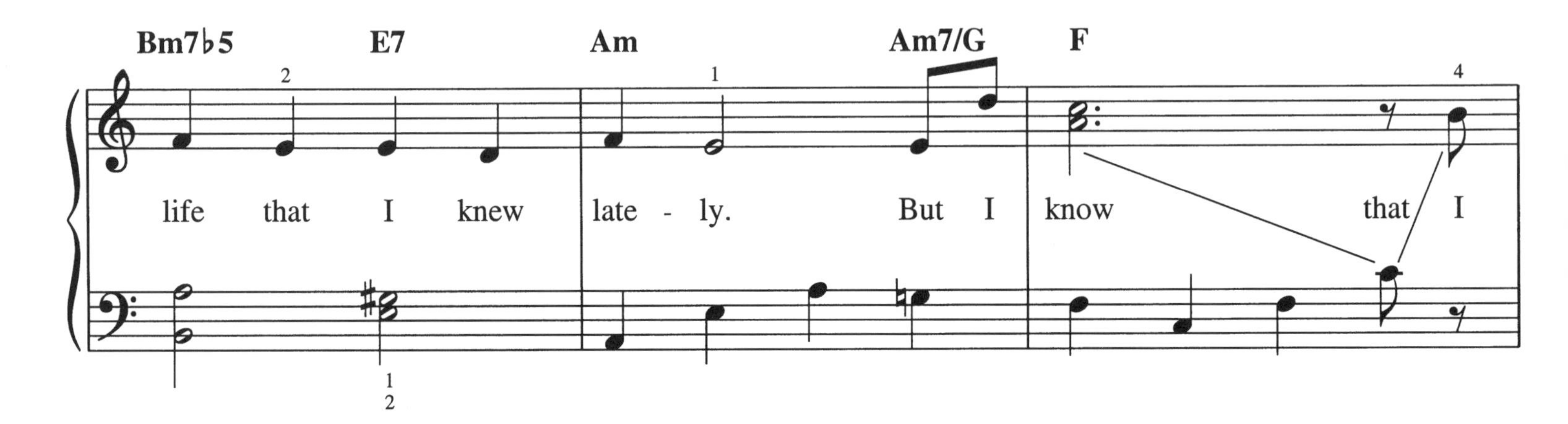
Bm7♭5 E7 Am Am7/G F
life that I knew late - ly. But I know that I

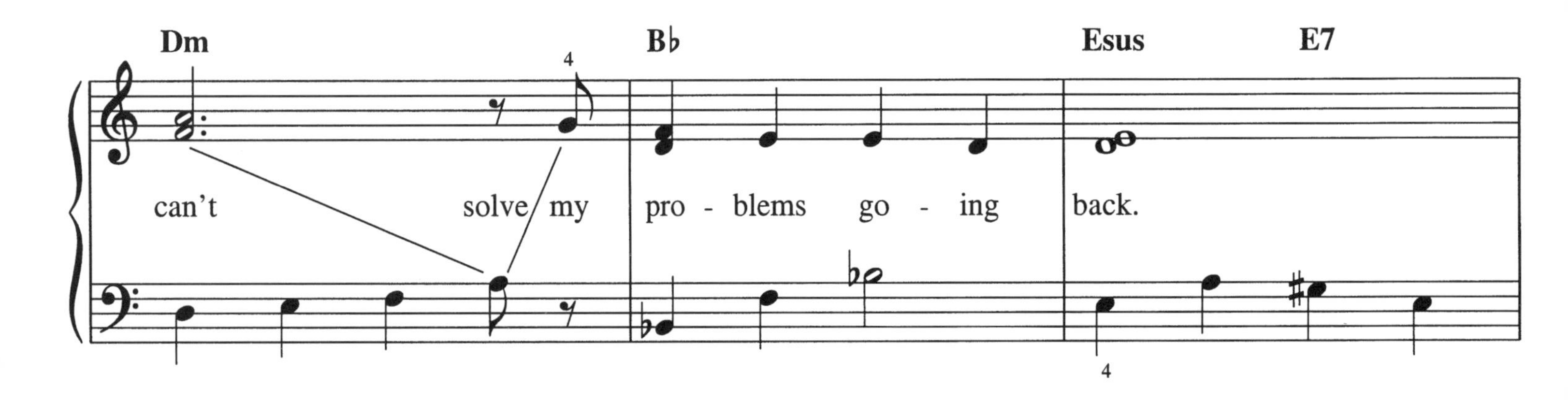
Dm B♭ Esus E7
can't solve my pro - blems go - ing back.

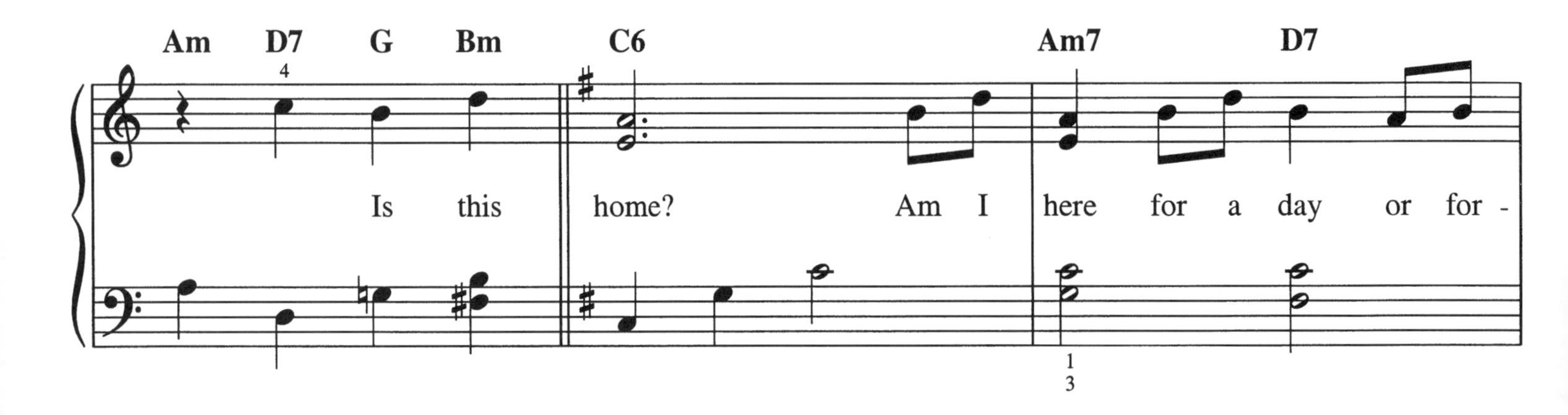
Am D7 G Bm C6 Am7 D7
Is this home? Am I here for a day or for -

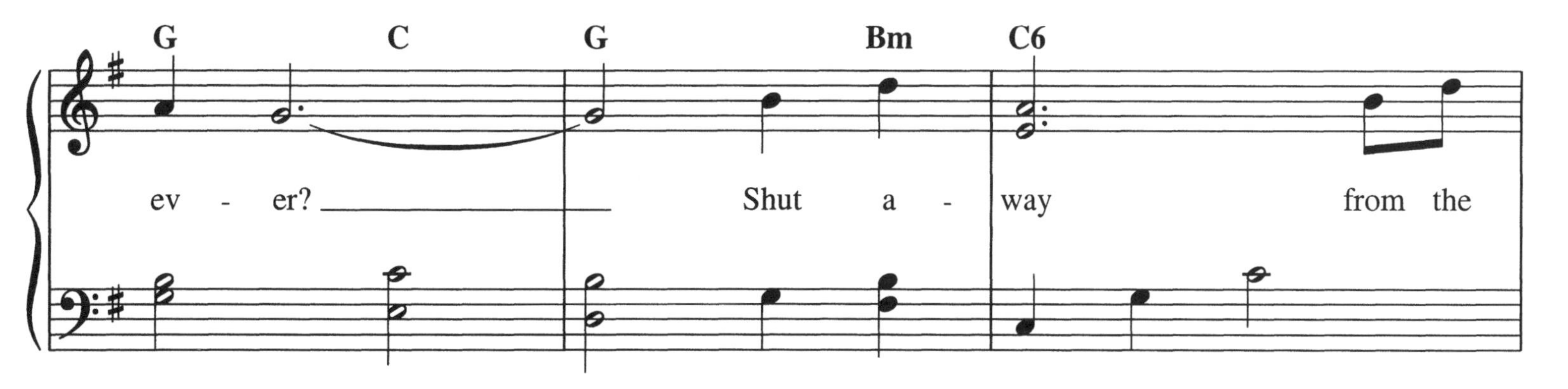
G C G Bm C6
ev - er? Shut a - way from the

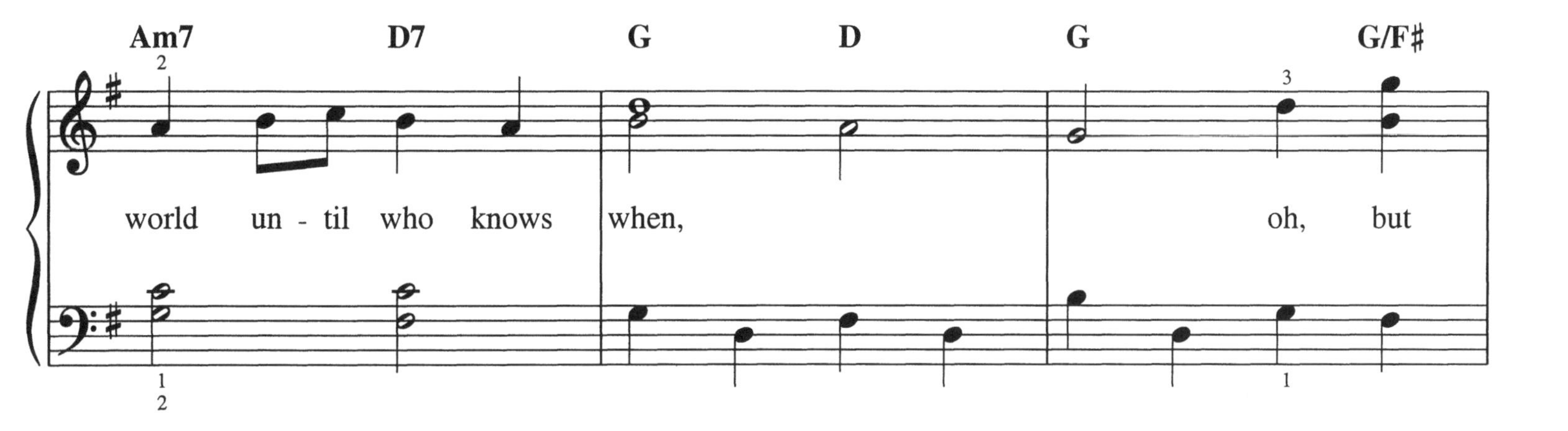
Am7 D7 G D G G/F♯
world un - til who knows when, oh, but

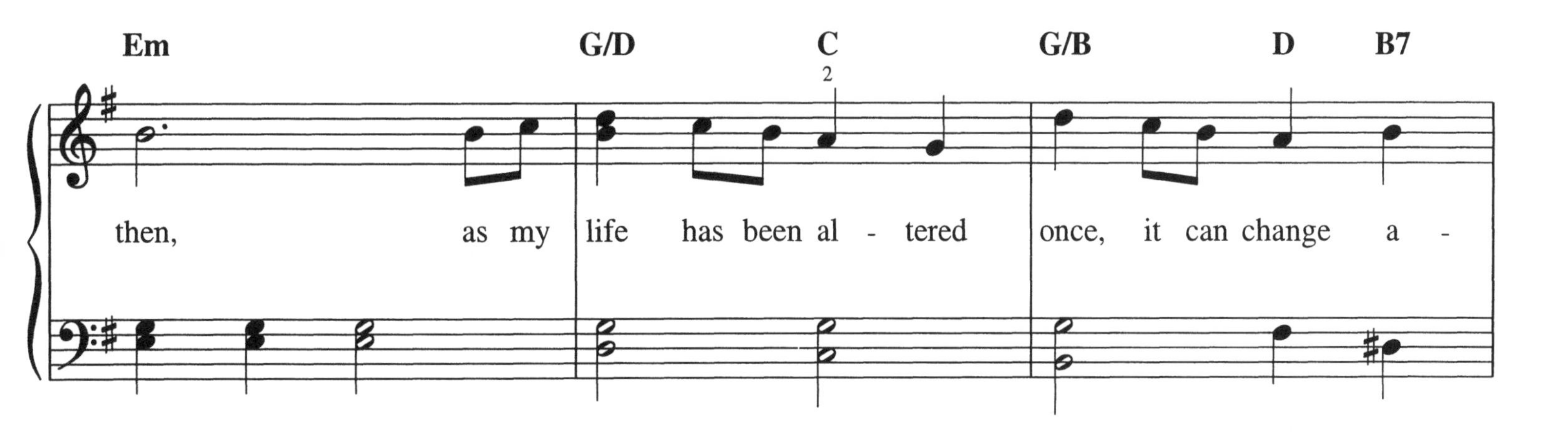
Em G/D C G/B D B7
then, as my life has been al - tered once, it can change a -

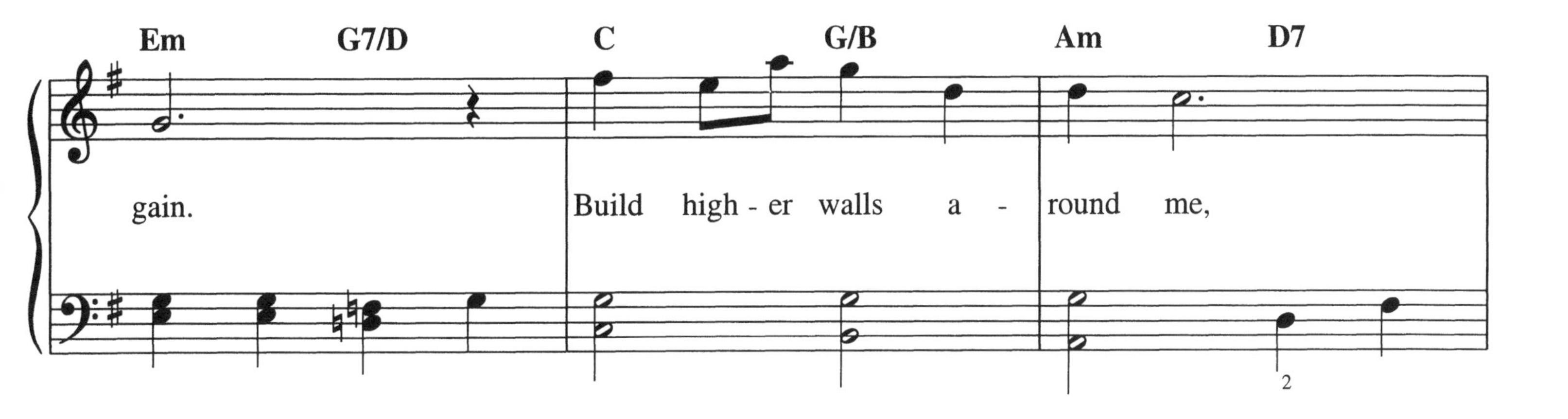
Em G7/D C G/B Am D7
gain. Build high - er walls a - round me,

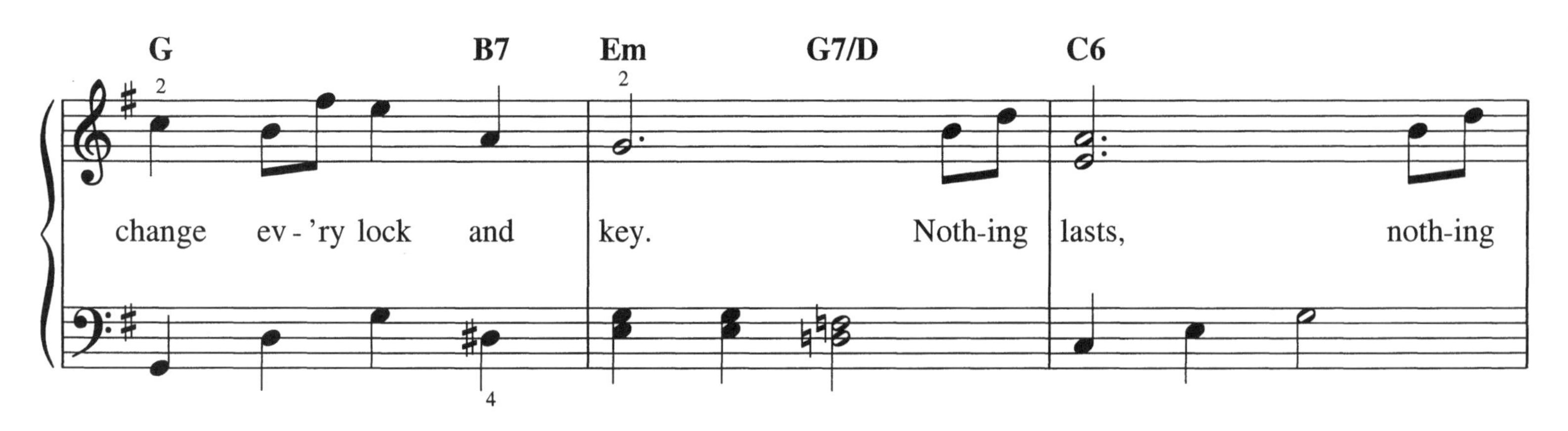
G
B7
Em
G7/D
C6
change ev - 'ry lock and key. Noth-ing lasts, noth-ing

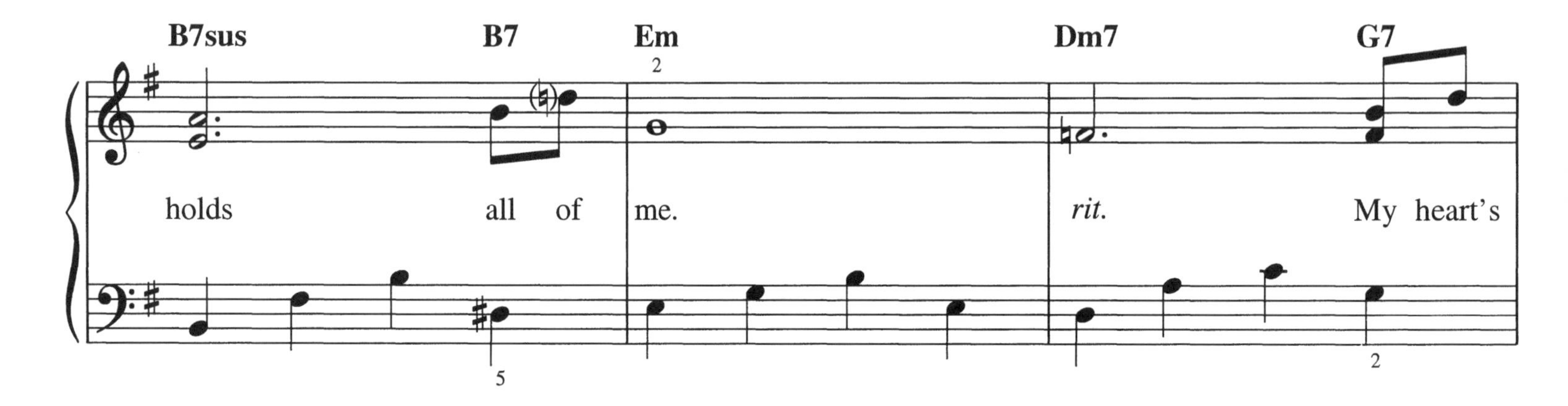
B7sus
B7
Em
Dm7
G7
holds all of me. rit. My heart's

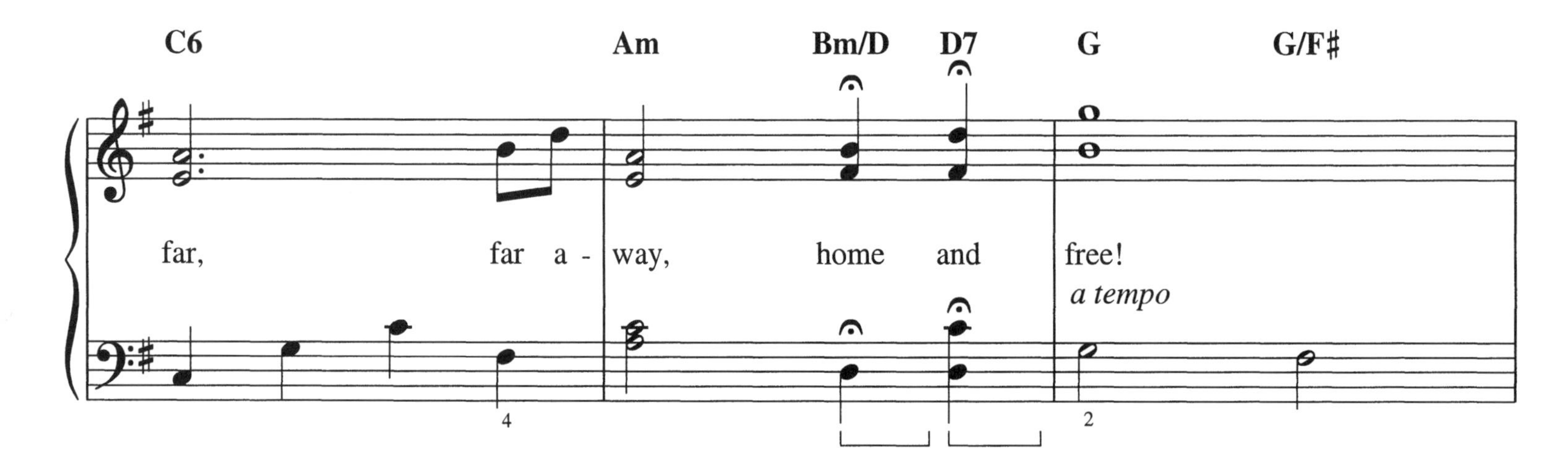
C6
Am
Bm/D
D7
G
G/F♯
far, far a - way, home and free!
a tempo

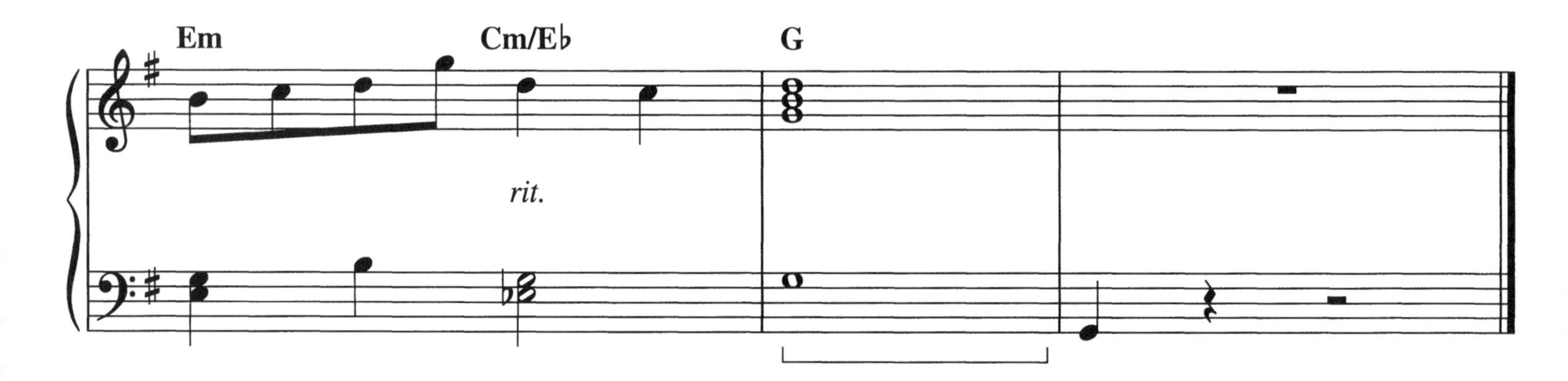
Em
Cm/E♭
G
rit.

GASTON

Lyrics by HOWARD ASHMAN
Music by ALAN MENKEN

Moderately fast waltz

C6
G7
mf
Gaston: Who does she think

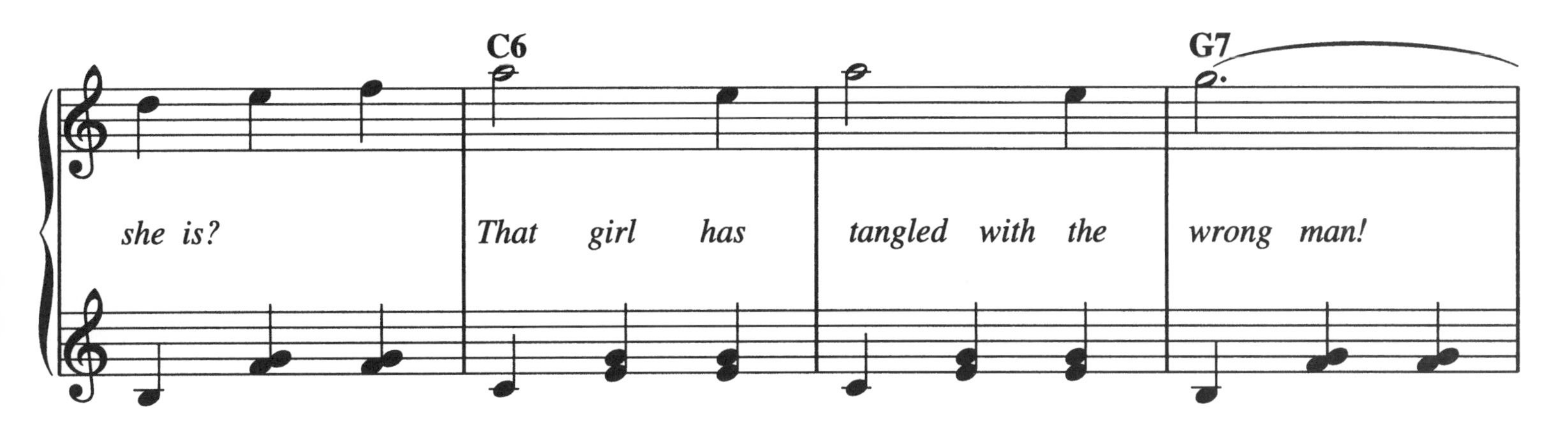
C6
G7
she is? That girl has tangled with the wrong man!

C6
G7
No one says "no" to Gaston! LeFou: Heh, Heh. Darn right.

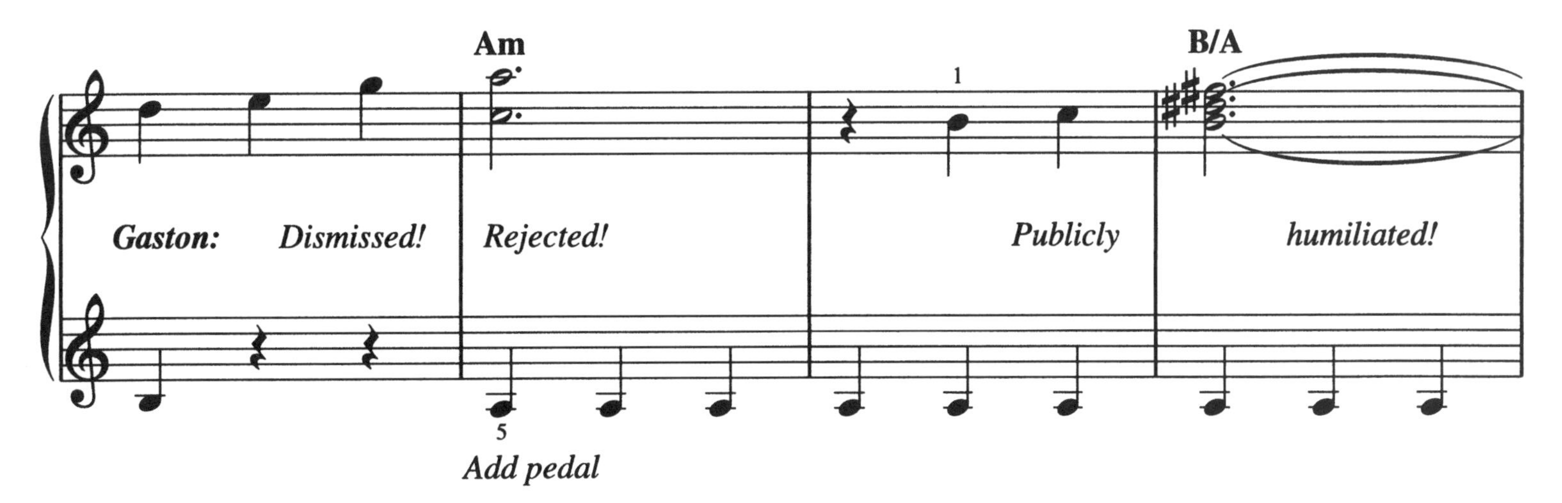
Am
B/A
Gaston: Dismissed! Rejected! Publicly humiliated!
Add pedal

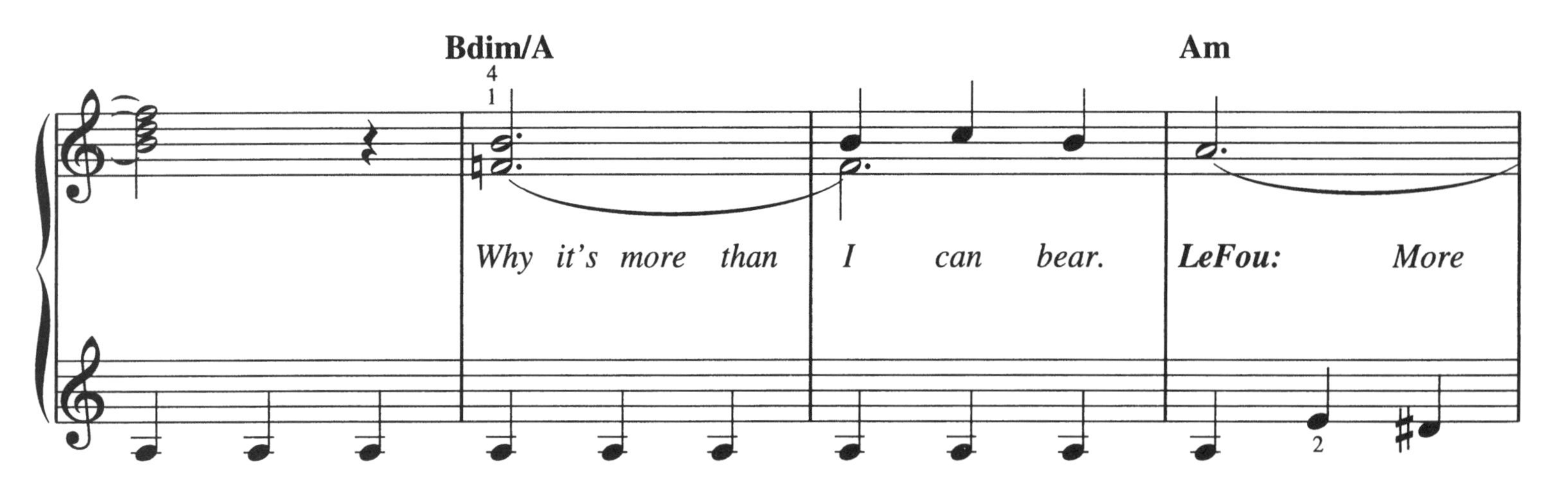
Bdim/A
Am
Why it's more than I can bear.
LeFou: More

B7/A
beer?
Gaston: What for?
Nothing helps.
I'm disgraced.

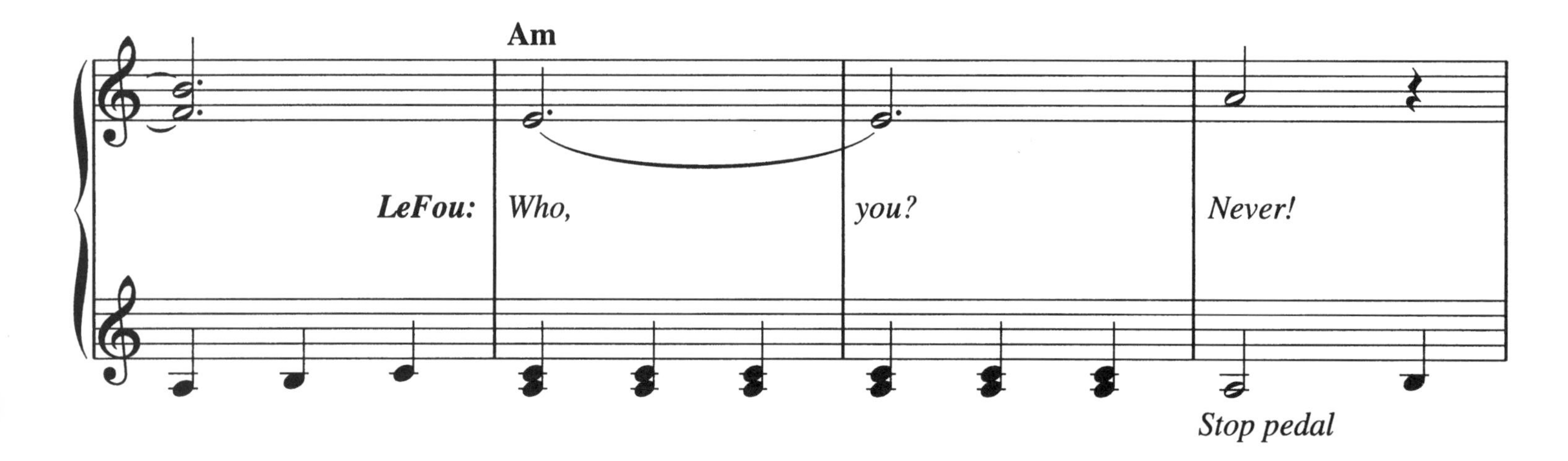
Am
LeFou: Who, you?
Never!
Stop pedal

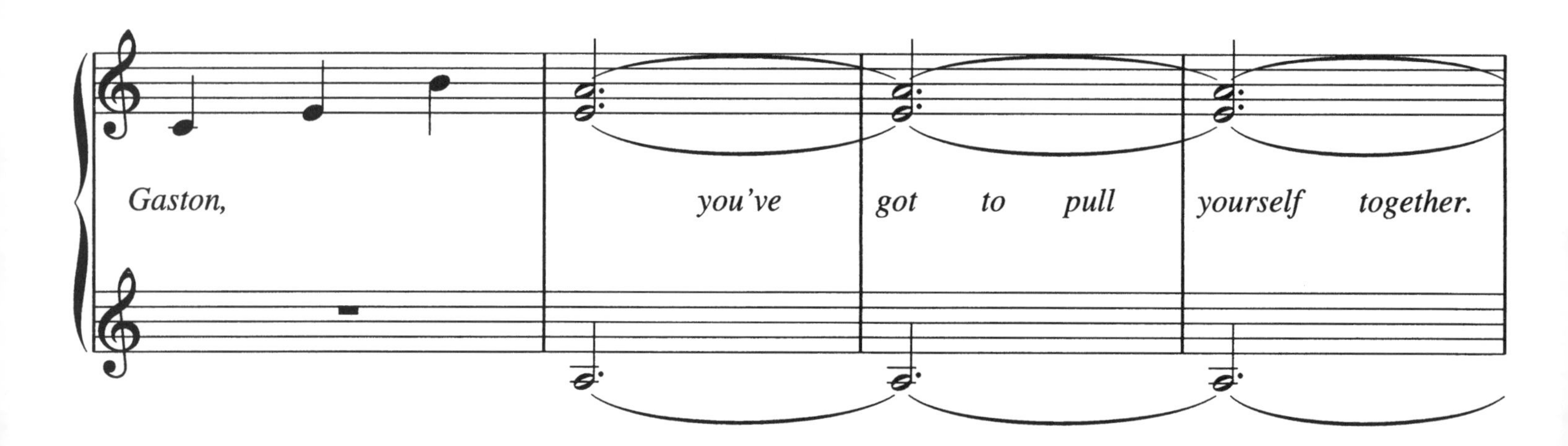
Gaston, you've got to pull yourself together.

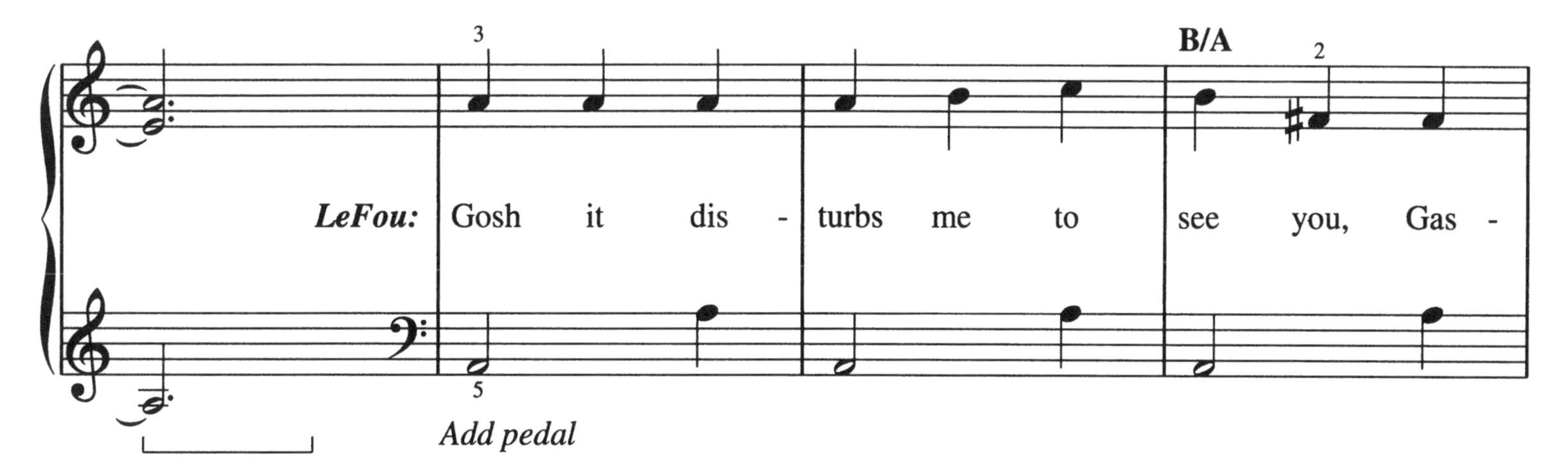
B/A
LeFou: Gosh it dis - turbs me to see you, Gas -
Add pedal

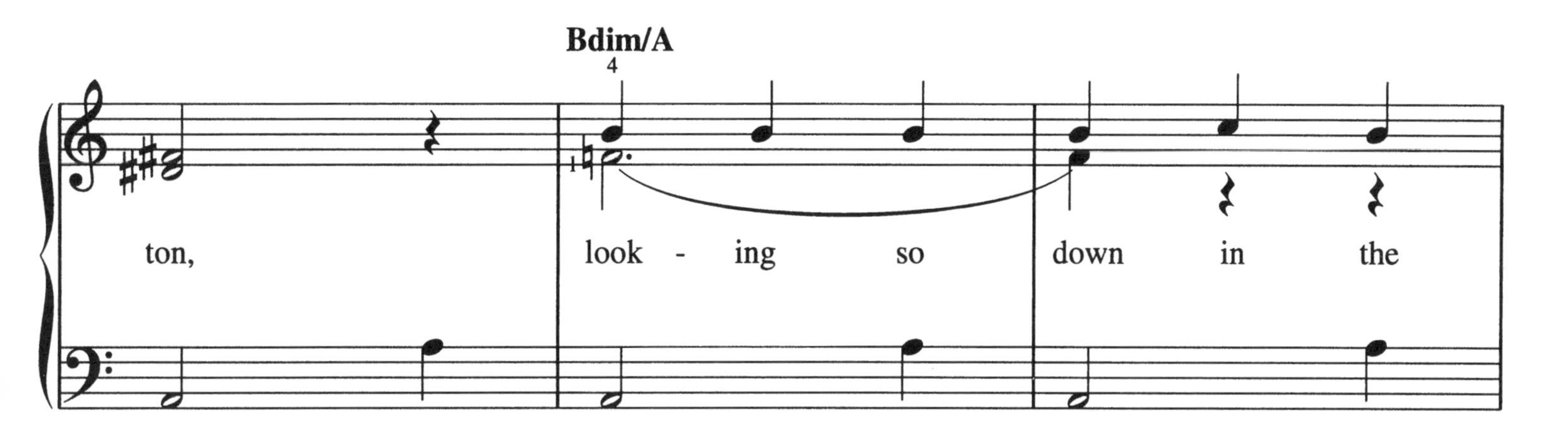
Bdim/A
ton, look - ing so down in the

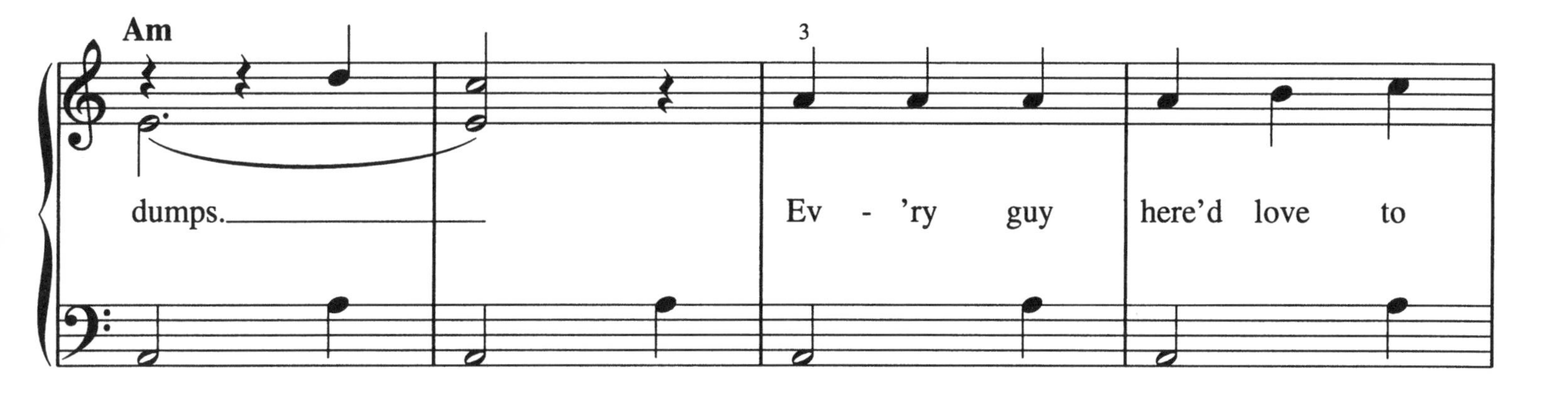
Am
dumps.
Ev - 'ry guy here'd love to

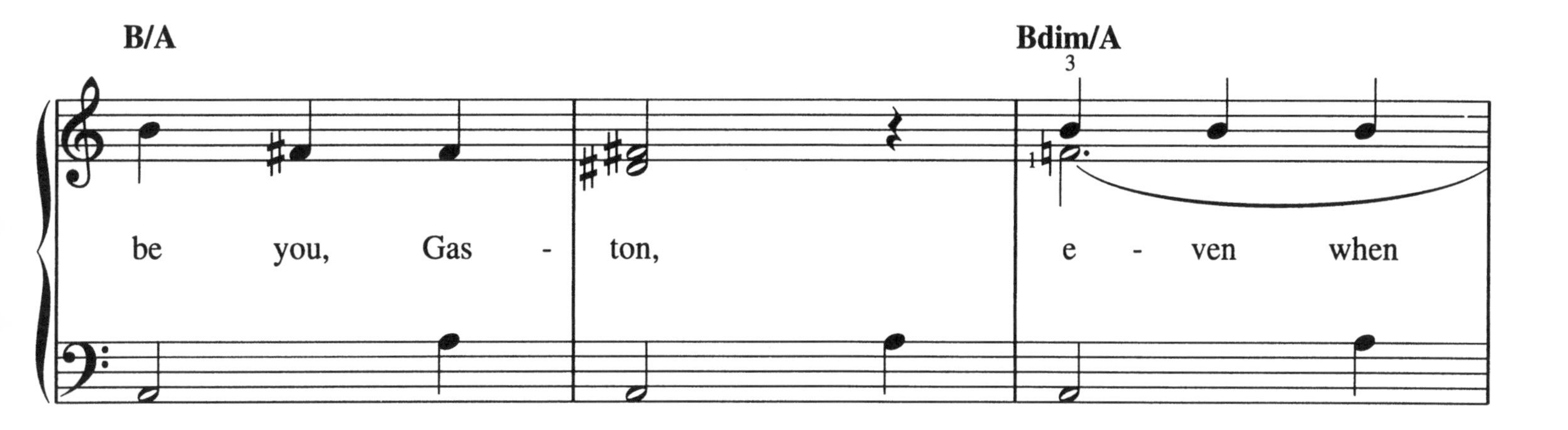
B/A
Bdim/A
be you, Gas - ton, e - ven when

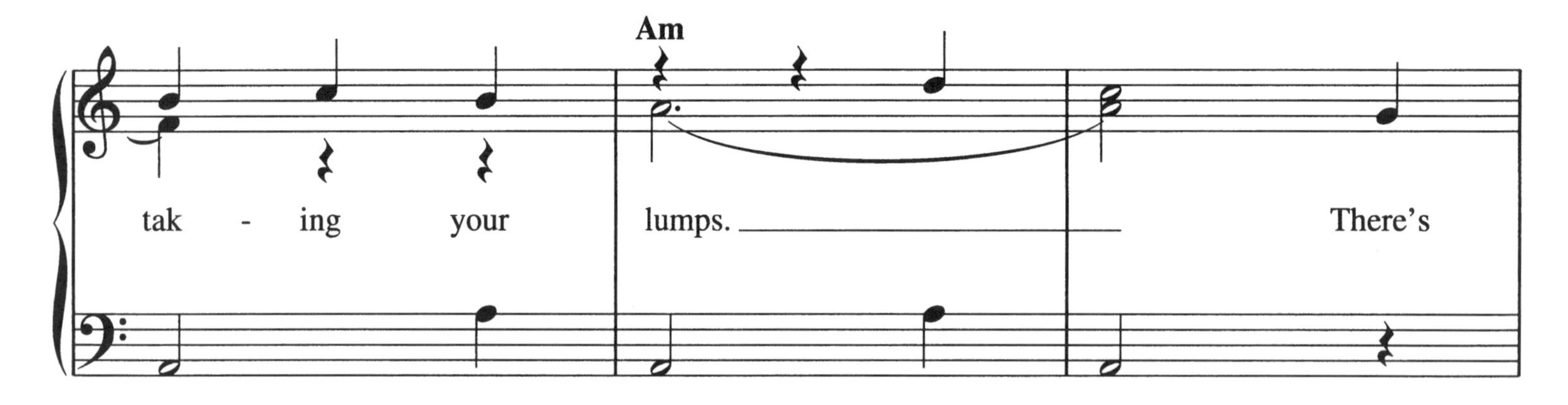
Am
tak - ing your lumps. There's

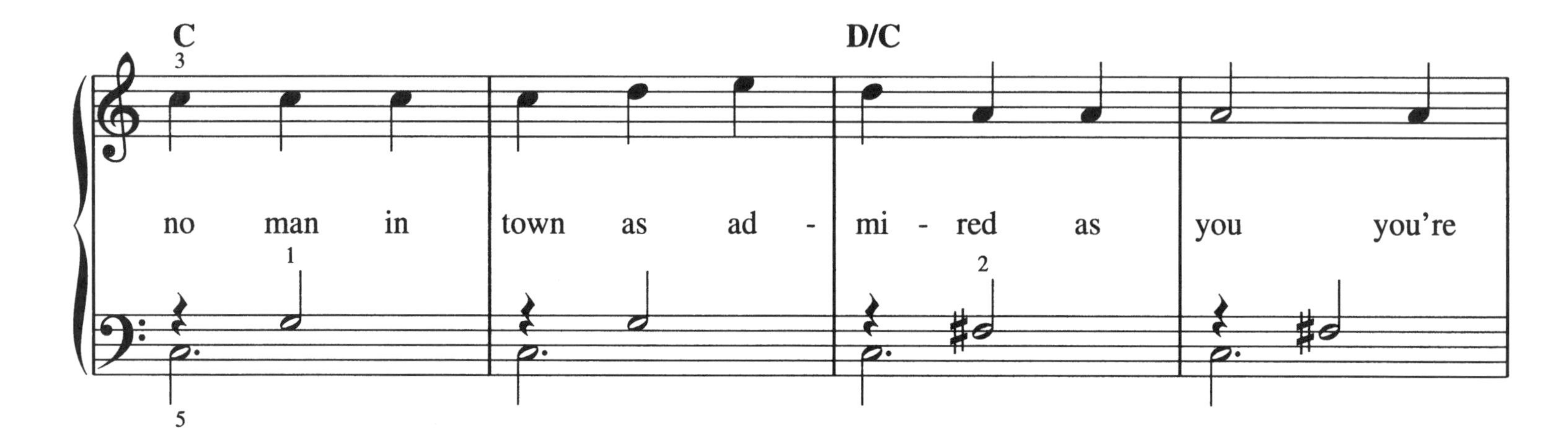
C
D/C
no man in town as ad - mi - red as you you're

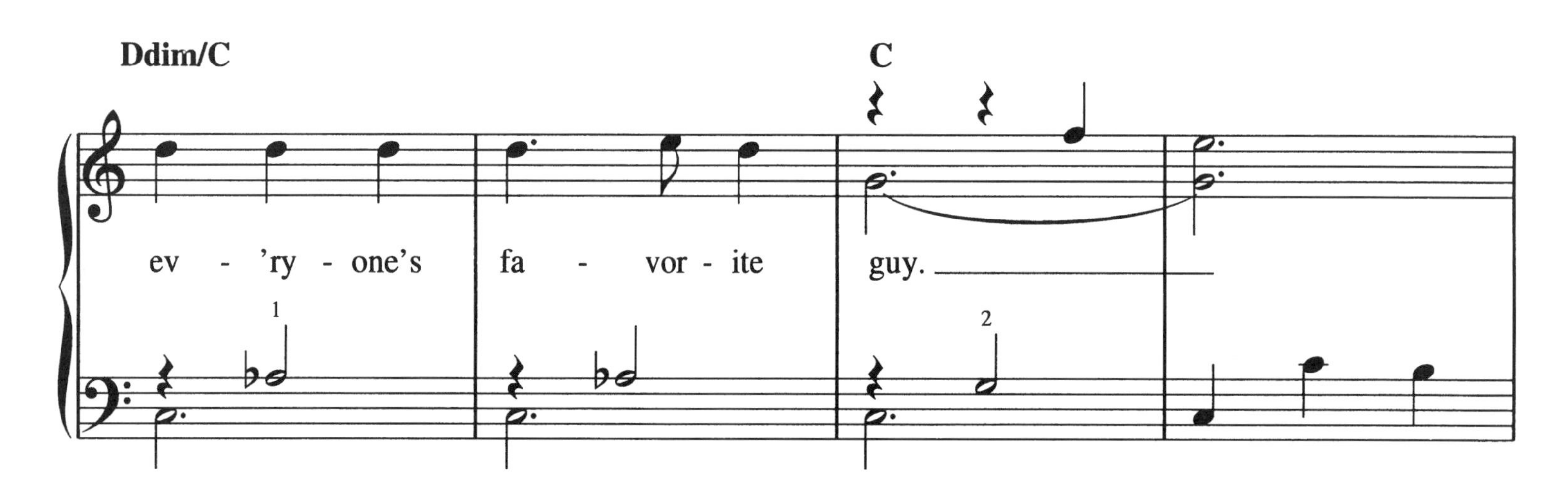
Ddim/C
C
ev - 'ry - one's fa - vor - ite guy.

Am
Am/G
D7/F#
Ev - 'ry - one's awed and in - spi - red by you, and it's

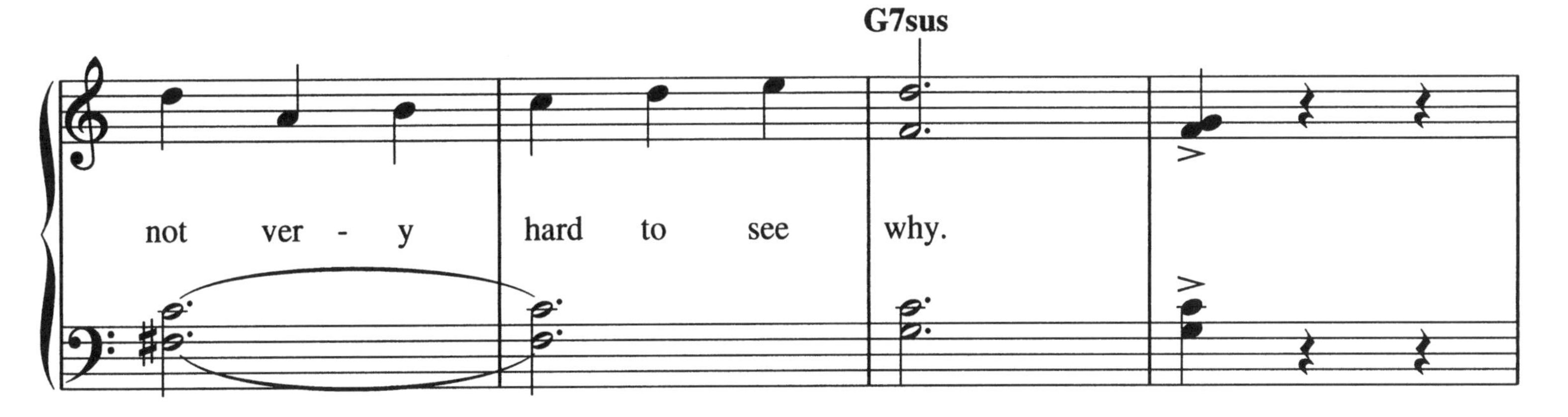
G7sus
not ver - y hard to see why.

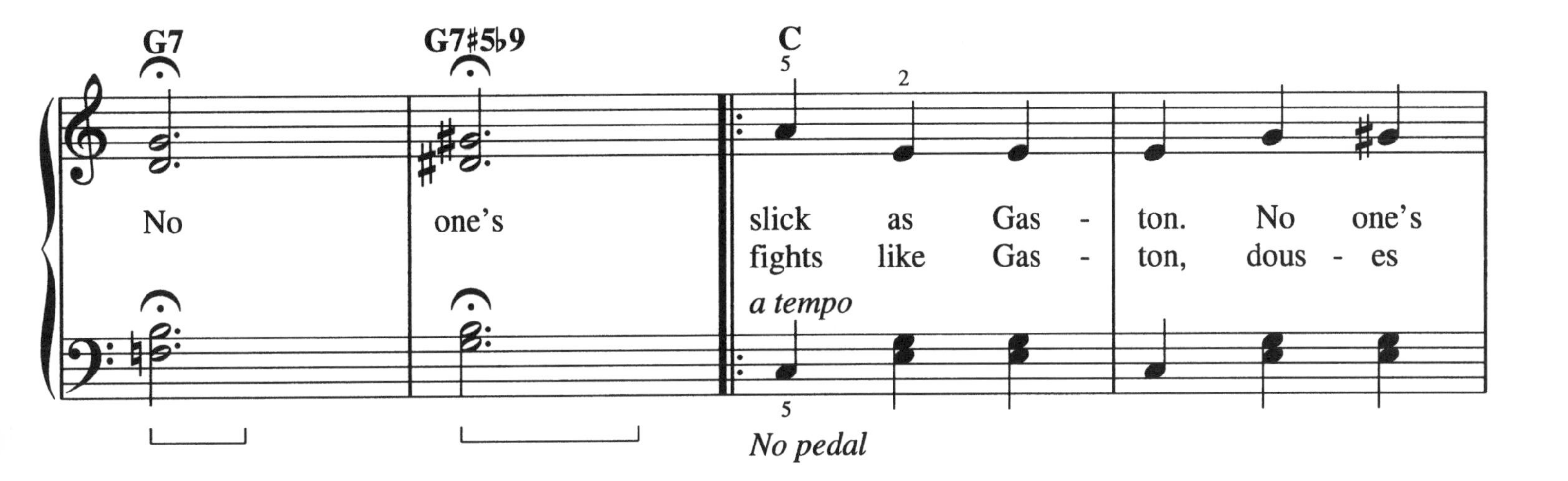
G7
G7#5♭9
C
No one's
slick as Gas - ton. No one's
fights like Gas - ton, dous - es
a tempo
No pedal

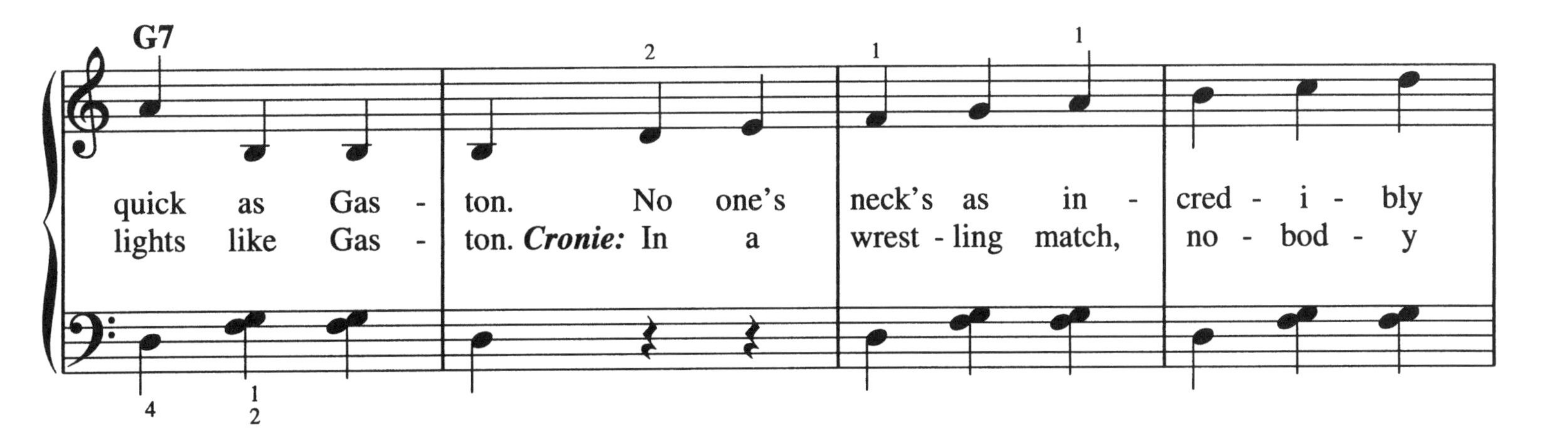
G7
quick as Gas - ton. No one's neck's as in - cred - i - bly
lights like Gas - ton. Cronie: In a wrest - ling match, no - bod - y

C
Am
thick as Gas - ton! For there's no man in town half as
bites like Gas - ton! Girls: For there's no one as bur - ly and

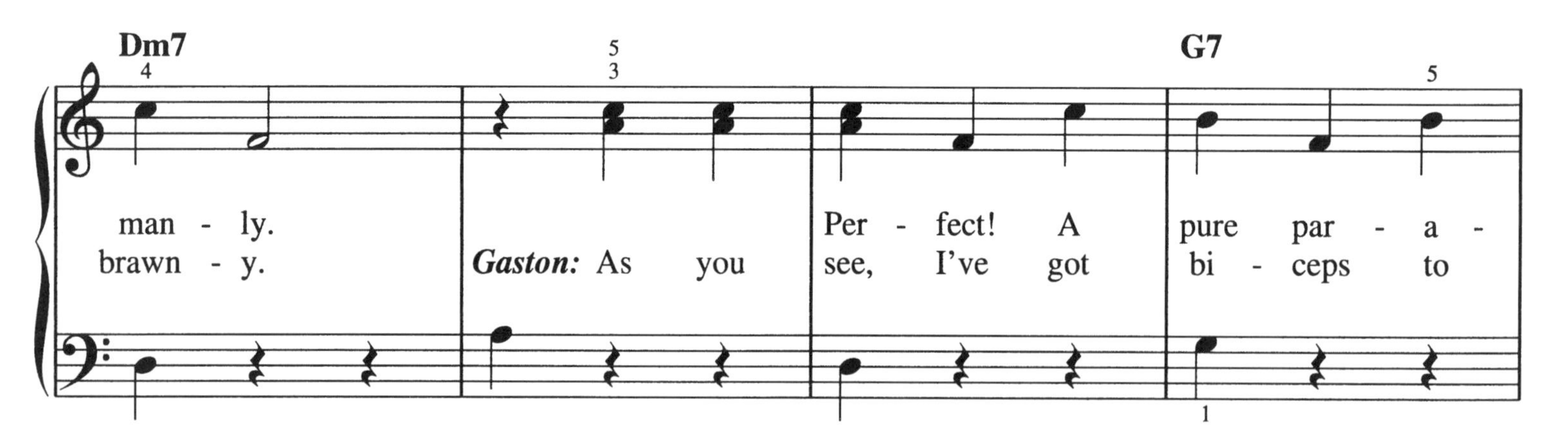
Dm7
G7
man - ly.
brawn - y.
Gaston: As you
Per - fect! A
see, I've got
pure par - a -
bi - ceps to

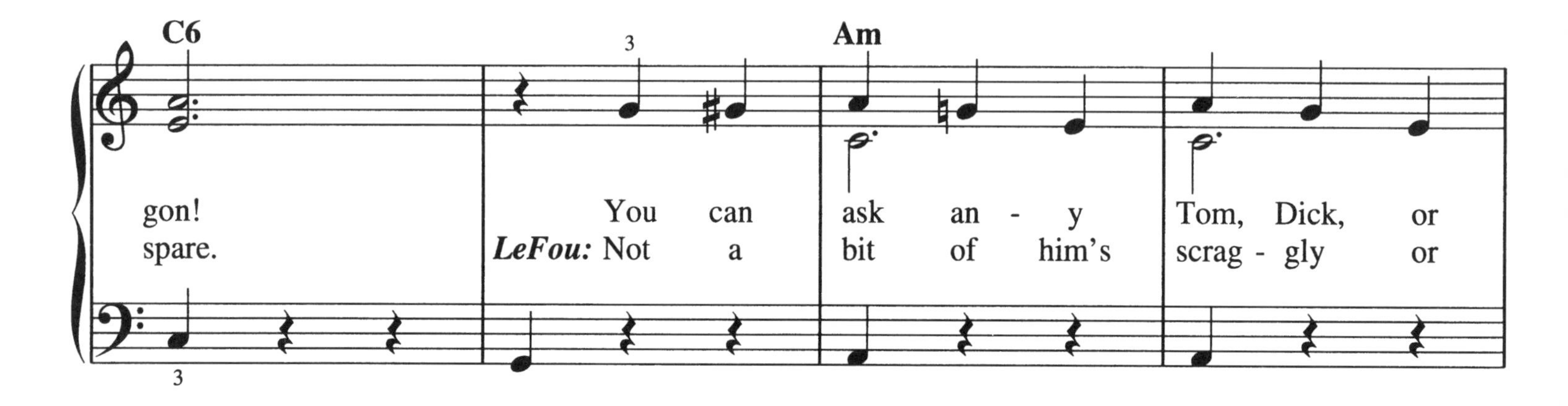
C6
Am
gon!
spare.
You can
LeFou: Not a
ask an - y
bit of him's
Tom, Dick, or
scrag - gly or

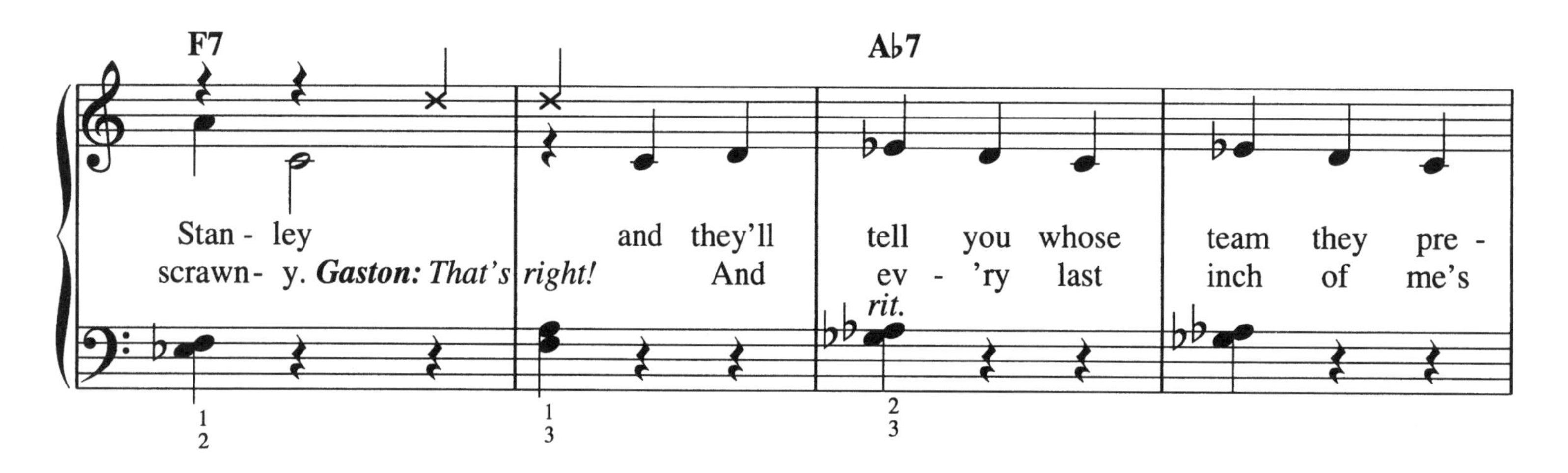
F7
A♭7
Stan - ley
scrawn- y. Gaston: That's right!
and they'll
And
tell you whose
ev - 'ry last
rit.
team they pre -
inch of me's

G7
G7♯5♭9
fer to be
cov - ered with
on! Chorus:
hair! Cronies:
Chorus:
No -
No -
No -
one's
one
one

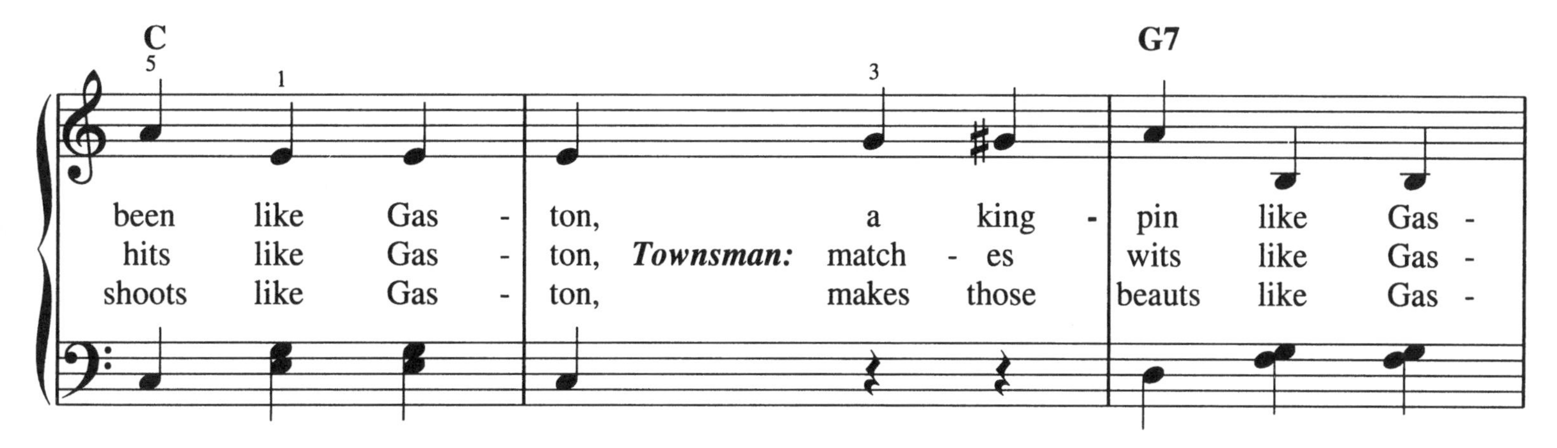
C
G7
been like Gas - ton, a king - pin like Gas -
hits like Gas - ton, Townsman: match - es wits like Gas -
shoots like Gas - ton, makes those beauts like Gas -

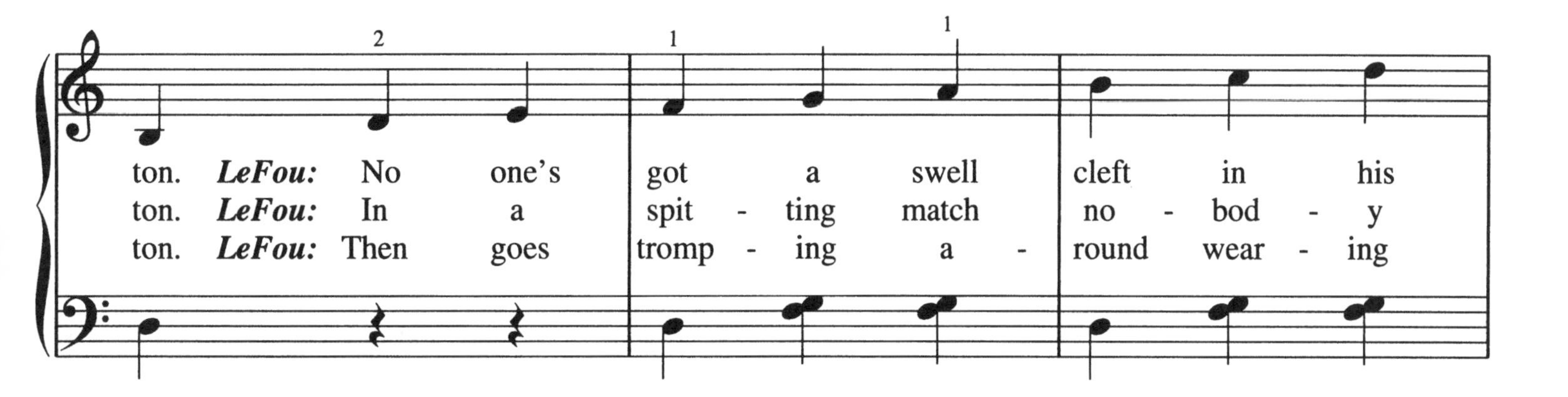
ton. LeFou: No one's got a swell cleft in his
ton. LeFou: In a spit - ting match no - bod - y
ton. LeFou: Then goes tromp - ing a - round wear - ing

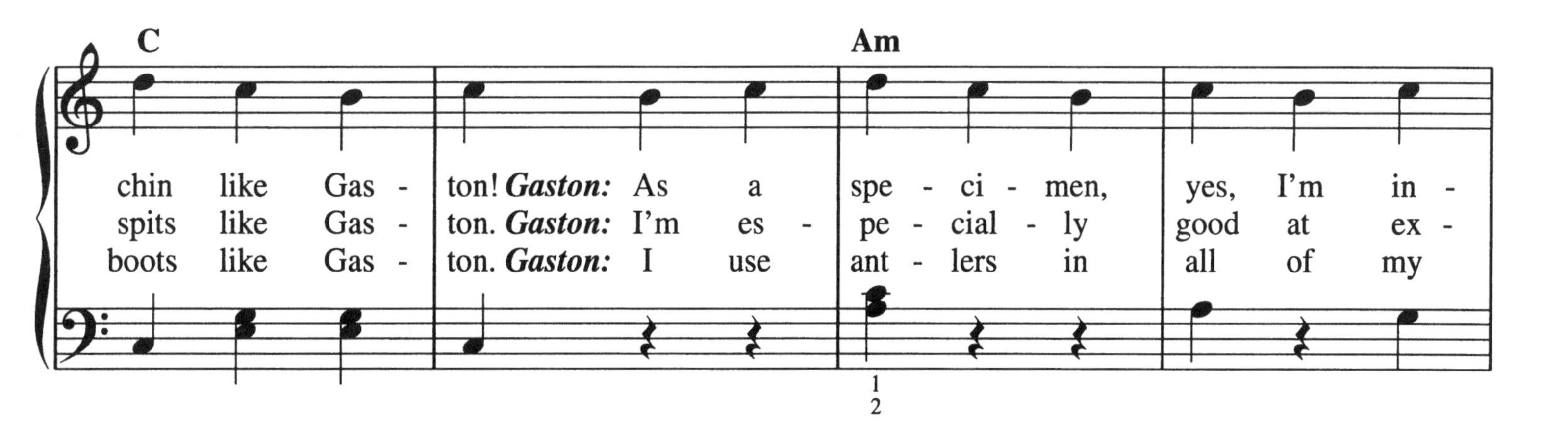
C
Am
chin like Gas - ton! Gaston: As a spe - ci - men, yes, I'm in -
spits like Gas - ton. Gaston: I'm es - pe - cial - ly good at ex -
boots like Gas - ton. Gaston: I use ant - lers in all of my

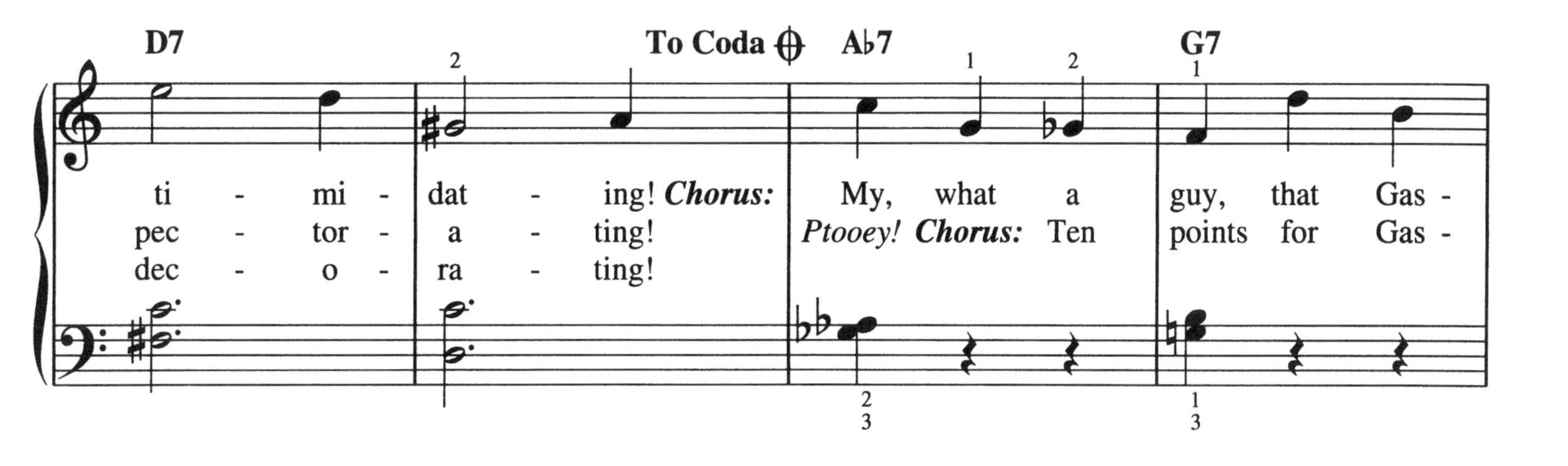
D7
To Coda
A♭7
G7
ti - mi - dat - ing! Chorus: My, what a guy, that Gas -
pec - tor - a - ting! Ptooey! Chorus: Ten points for Gas -
dec - o - ra - ting!

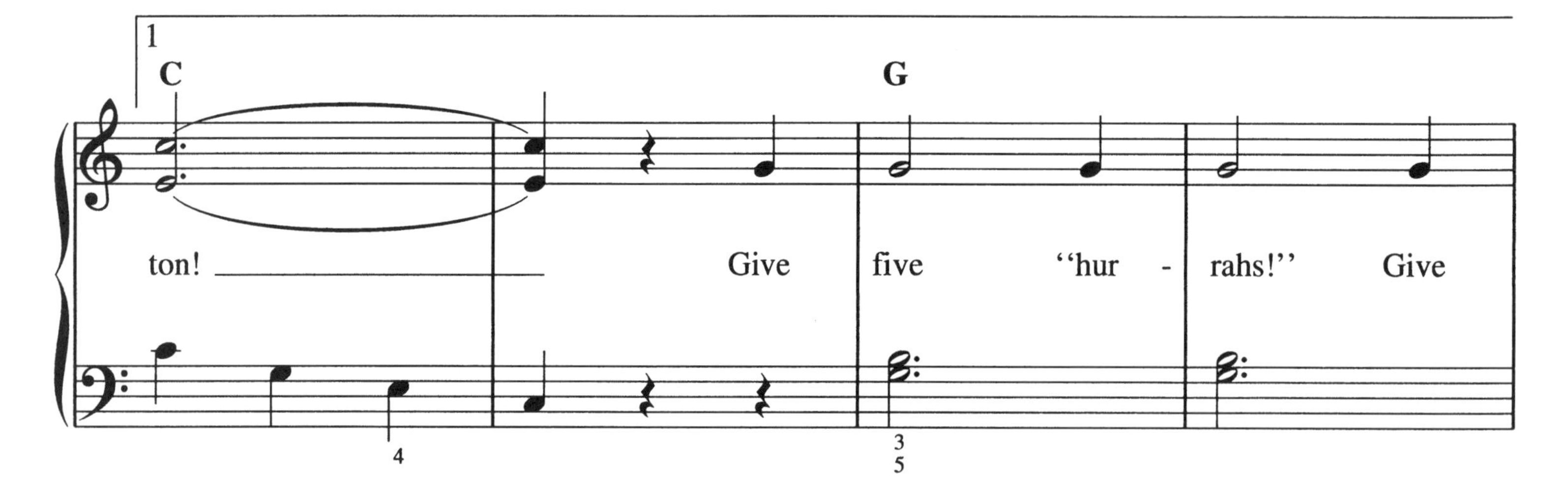
1
C G
ton! Give five "hur - rahs!" Give

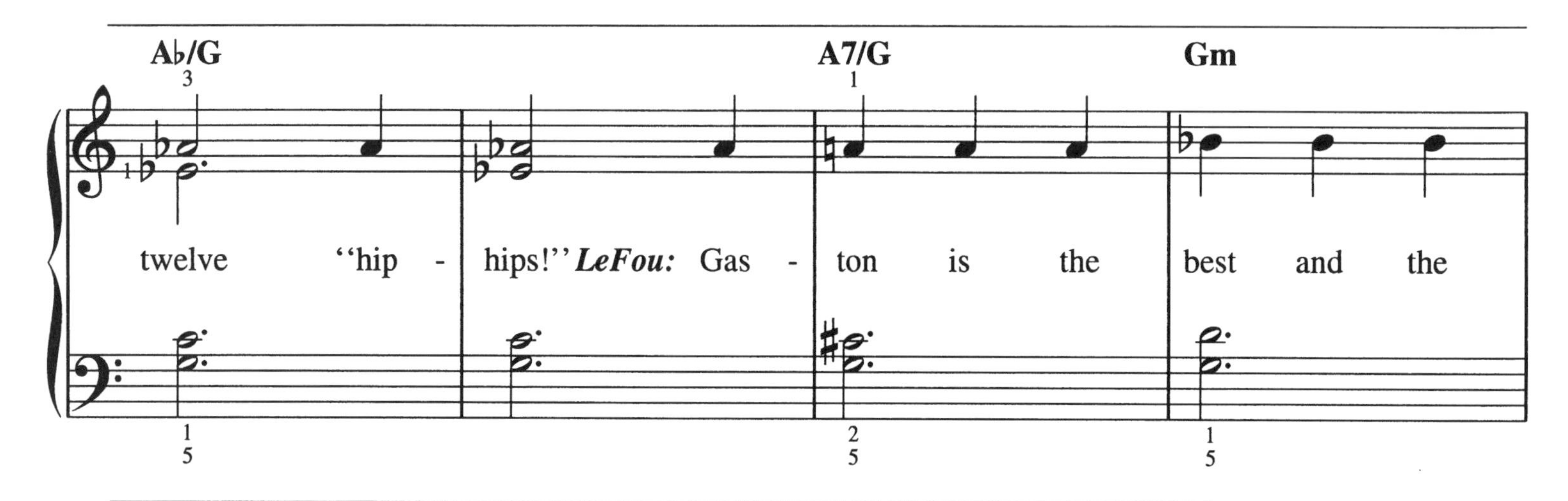
A♭/G A7/G Gm
twelve "hip - hips!" *LeFou:* Gas - ton is the best and the

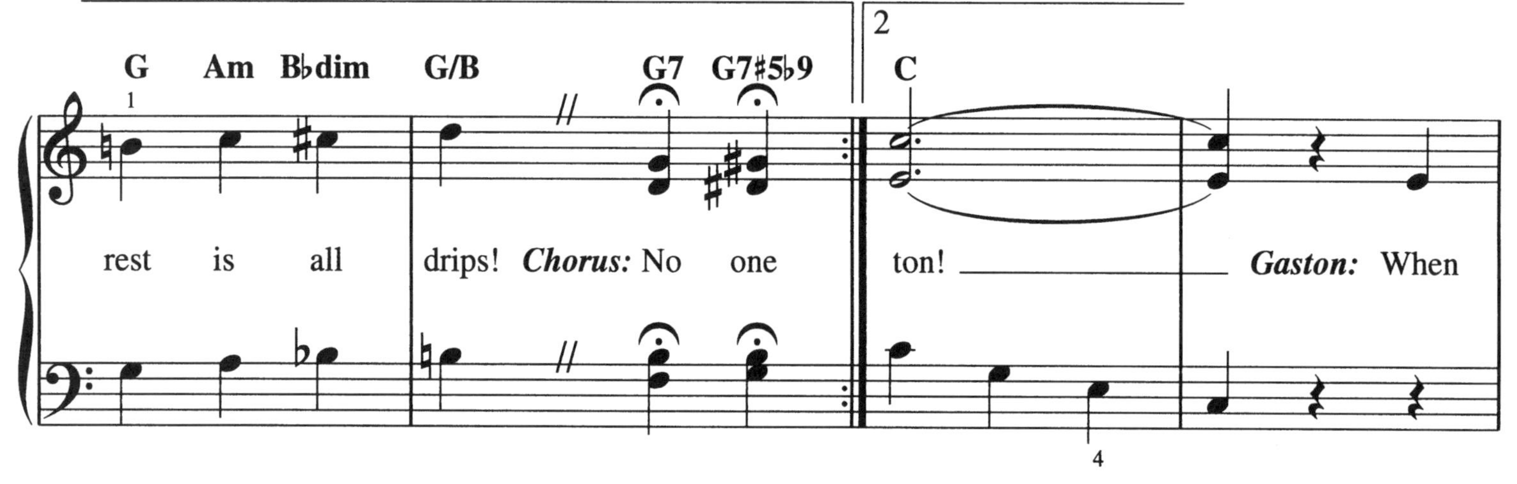
2
G Am B♭dim G/B G7 G7♯5♭9 C
rest is all drips! *Chorus:* No one ton! *Gaston:* When

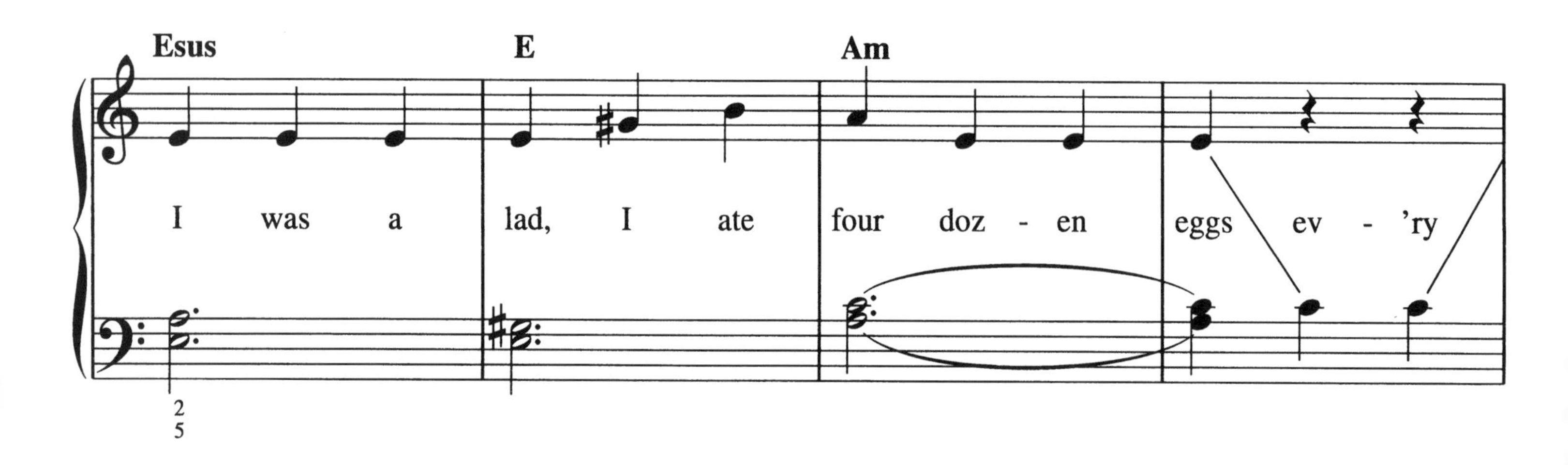
Esus E Am
I was a lad, I ate four doz - en eggs ev - 'ry

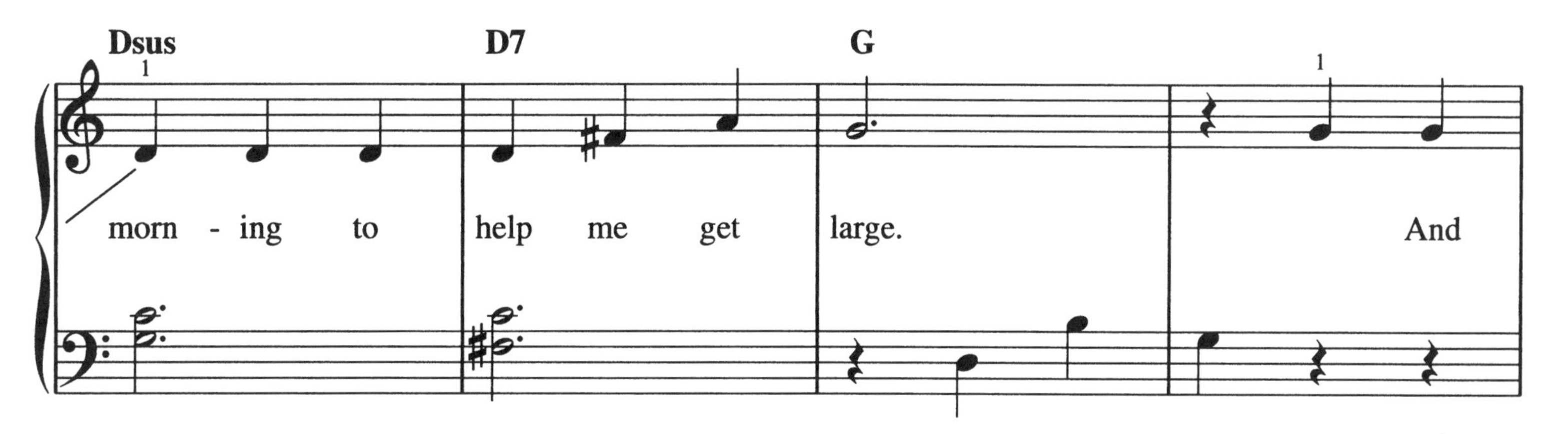
Dsus
D7
G
morn - ing to help me get large. And

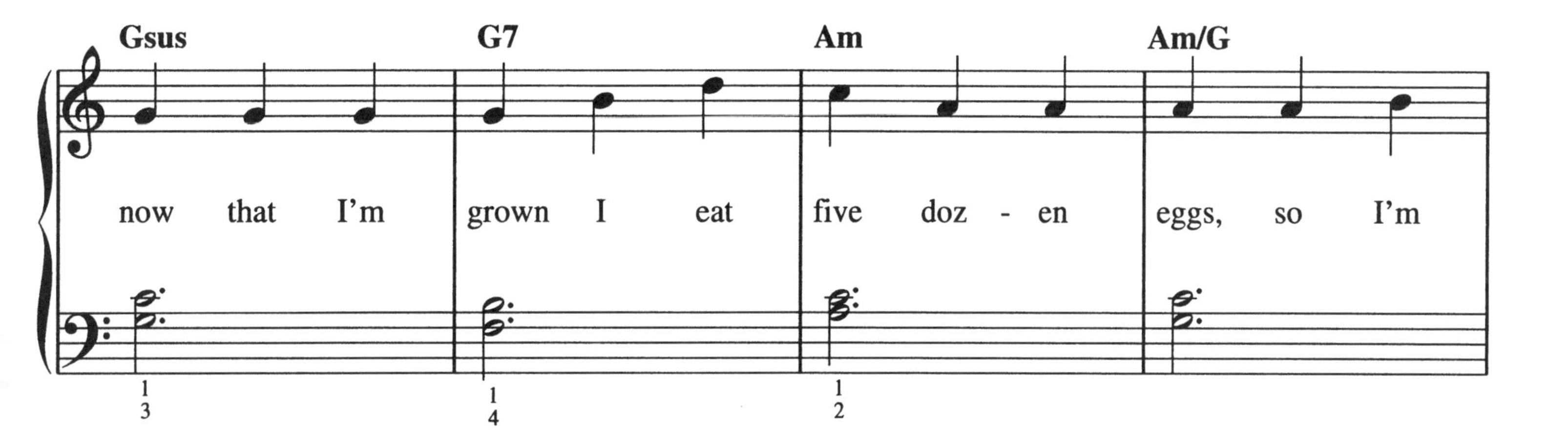
Gsus
G7
Am
Am/G
now that I'm grown I eat five doz - en eggs, so I'm

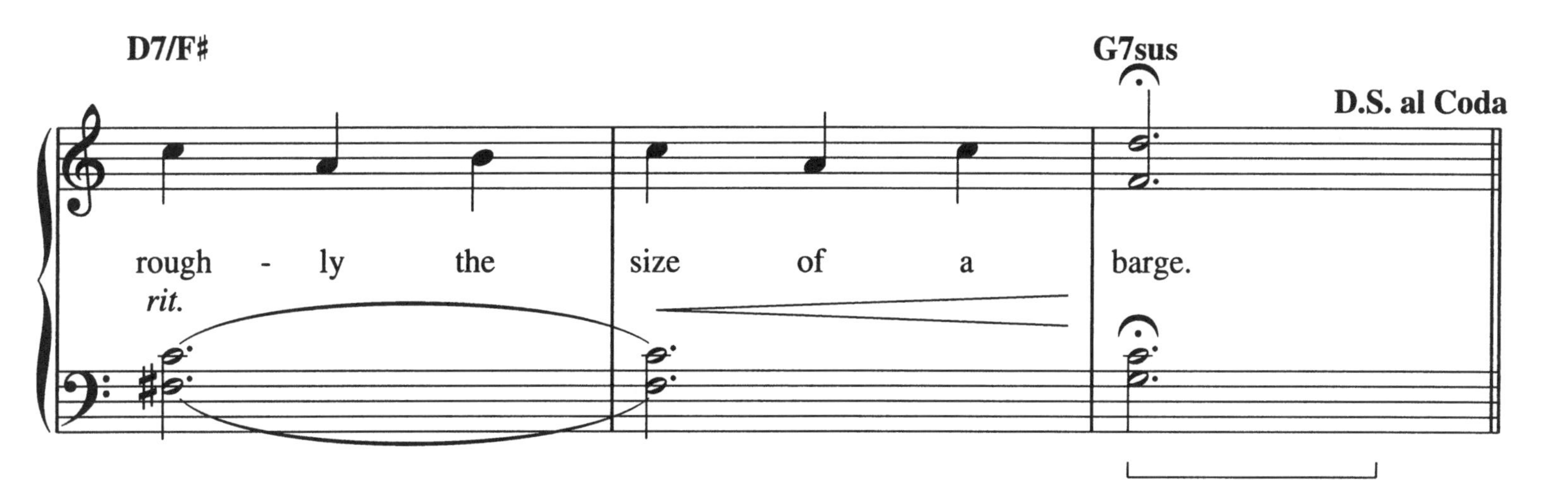
D7/F♯
G7sus
D.S. al Coda
rough - ly the size of a barge.
rit.

CODA
C/G
Chorus: Say it a - gain. Who's a

F♯m7♭5
C/G
man a - mong men? And then say it once more. Who's the

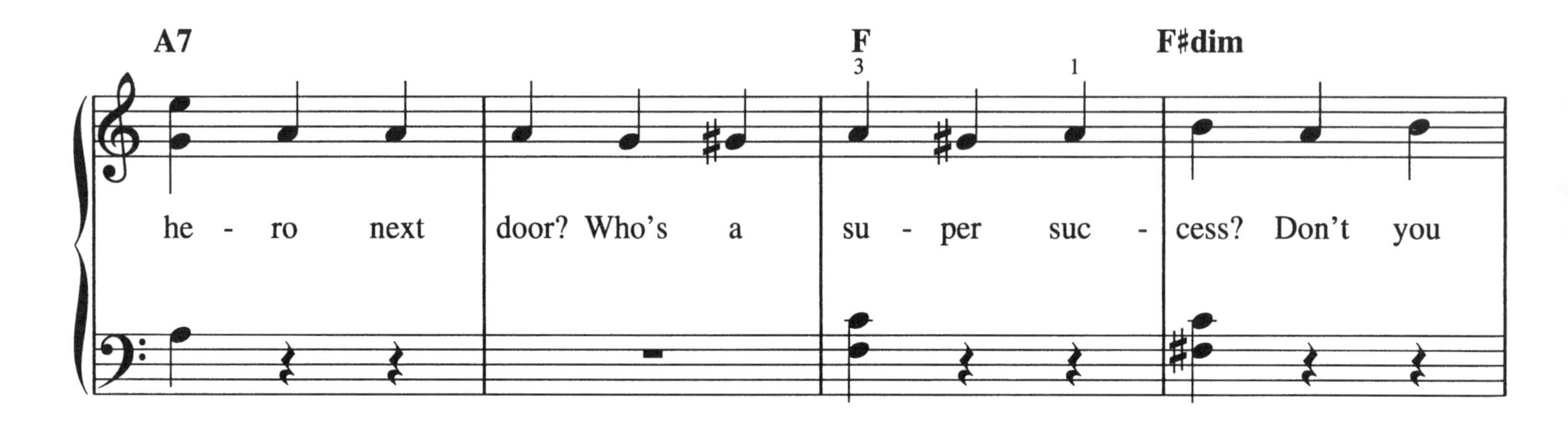
A7
F
F♯dim
he - ro next door? Who's a su - per suc - cess? Don't you

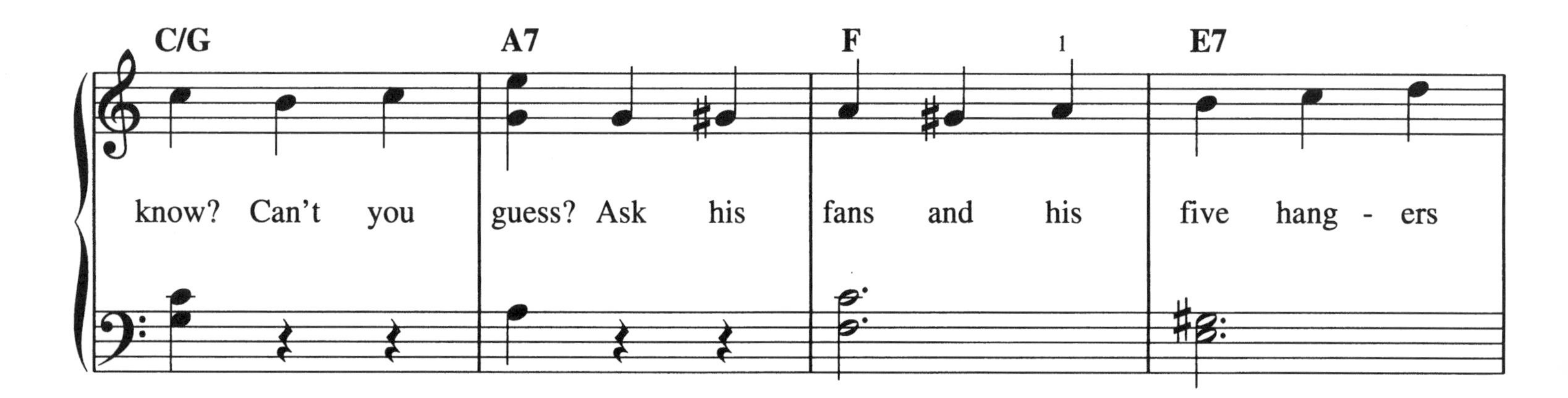
C/G
A7
F
E7
know? Can't you guess? Ask his fans and his five hang - ers

Am
C7
F
F♯dim
on. There's just one guy in town who's got

C/G
A7
N.C.
Dm7
all of it down.
LeFou: And his name's G - A -

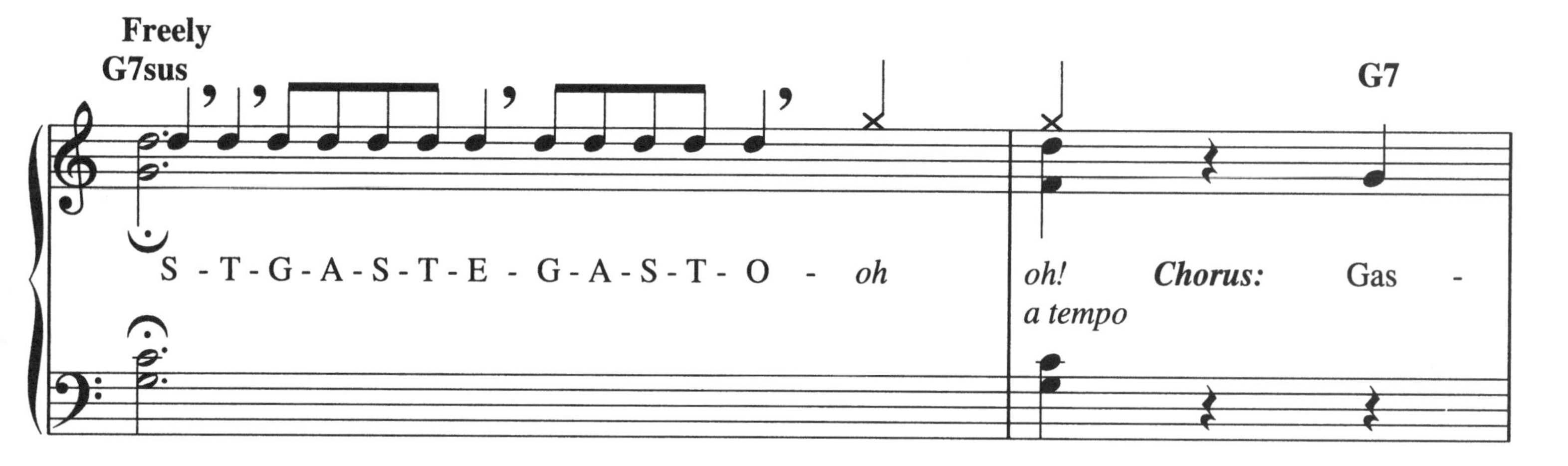
Freely
G7sus
G7
S - T - G - A - S - T - E - G - A - S - T - O - oh
oh! Chorus: Gas -
a tempo

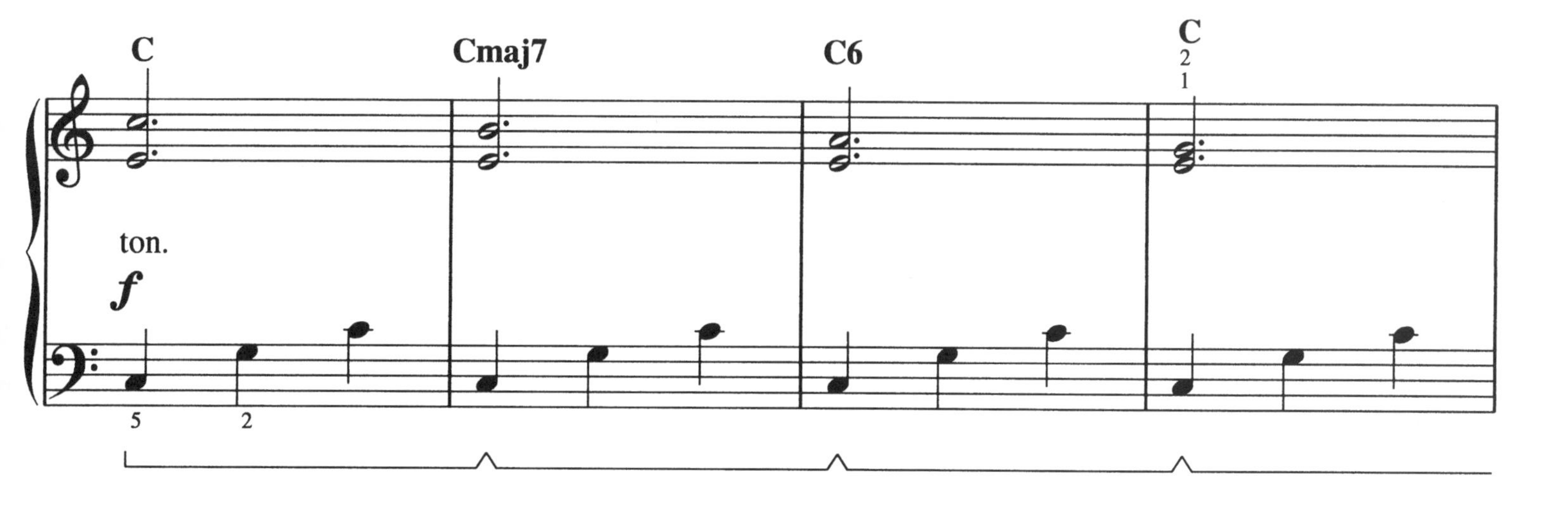
C
Cmaj7
C6
C
ton.
f

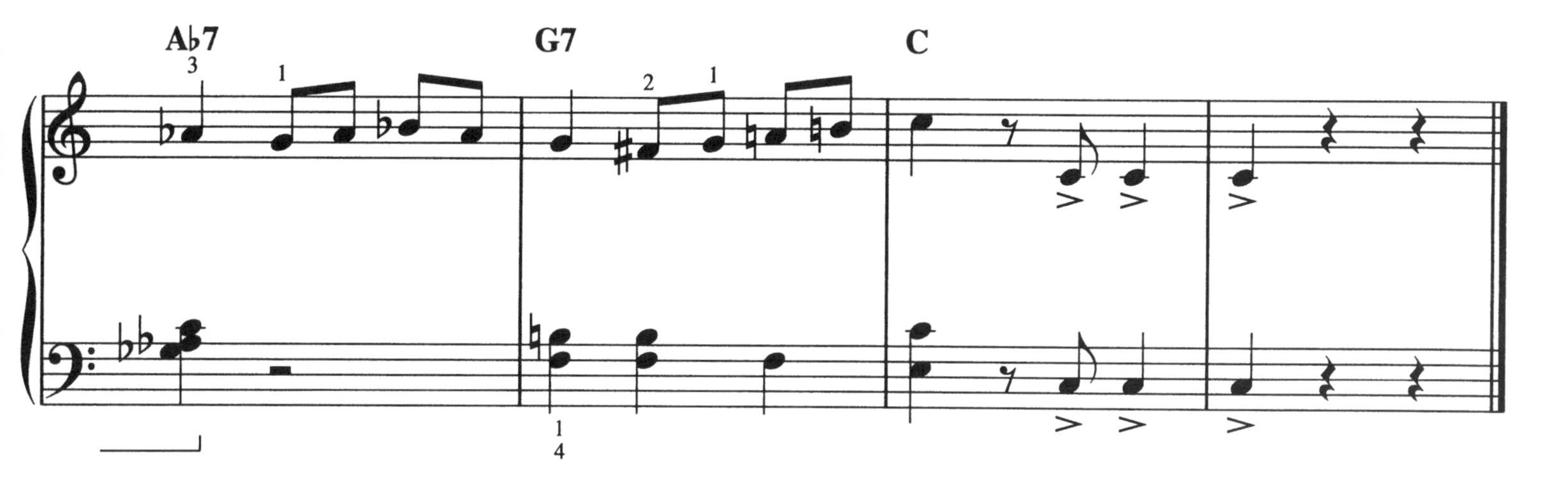
A♭7
G7
C

HOW LONG MUST THIS GO ON?

Music by ALAN MENKEN
Lyrics by TIM RICE

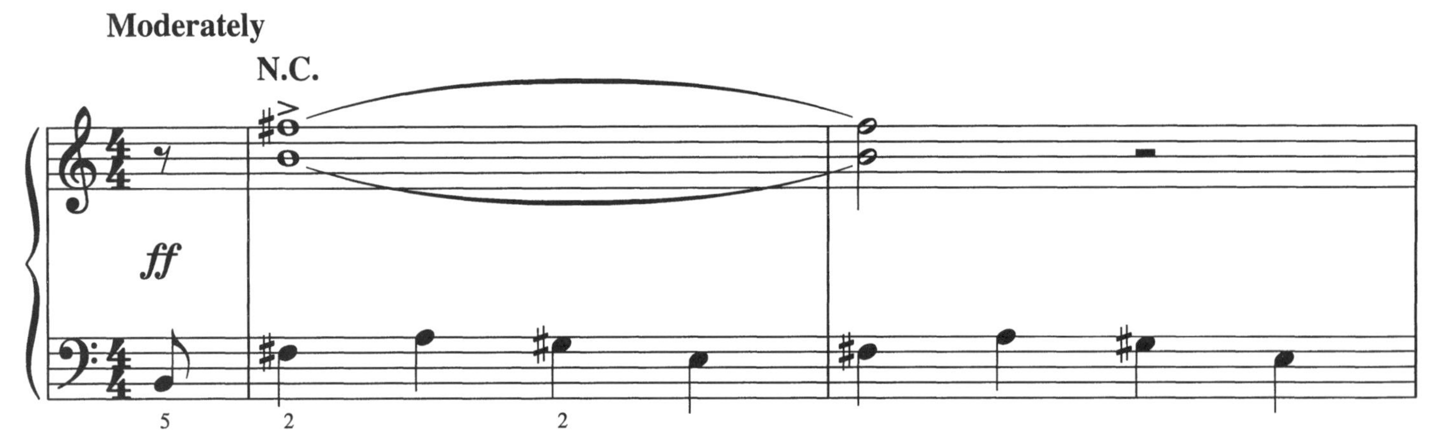

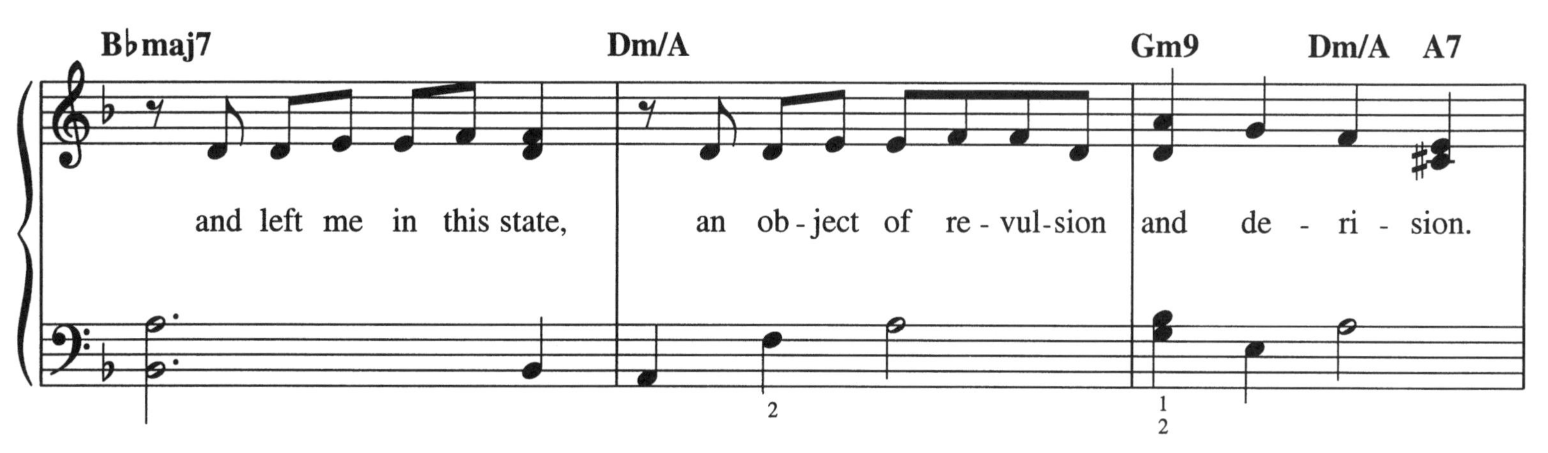
B♭maj7
Dm/A
Gm9
Dm/A
A7
and left me in this state,
an ob - ject of re - vul - sion
and de - ri - sion.

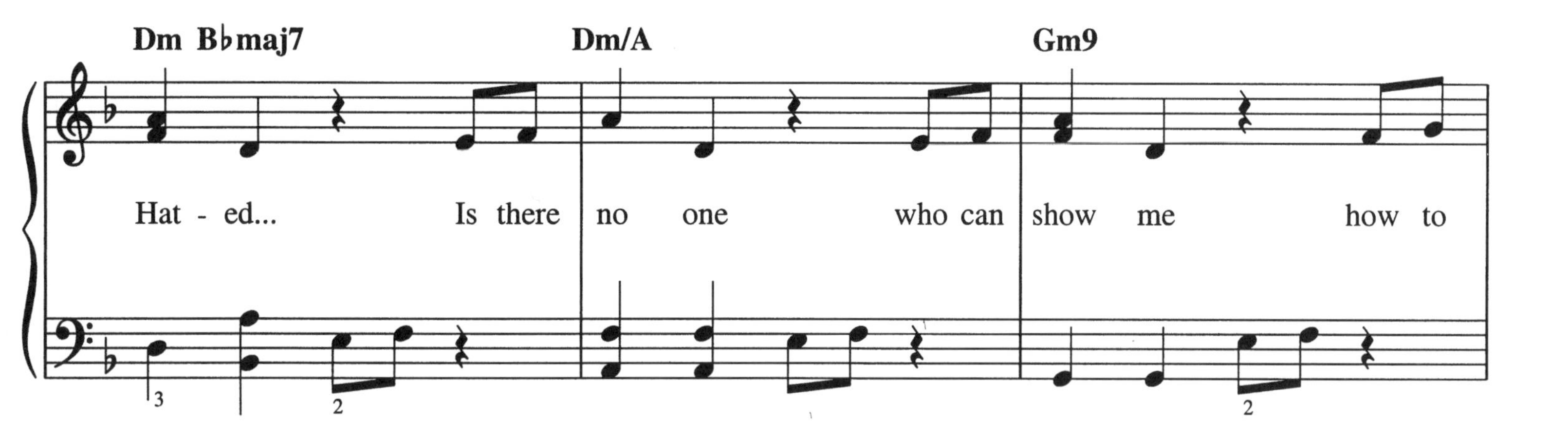
Dm
B♭maj7
Dm/A
Gm9
Hat - ed...
Is there
no one
who can
show me
how to

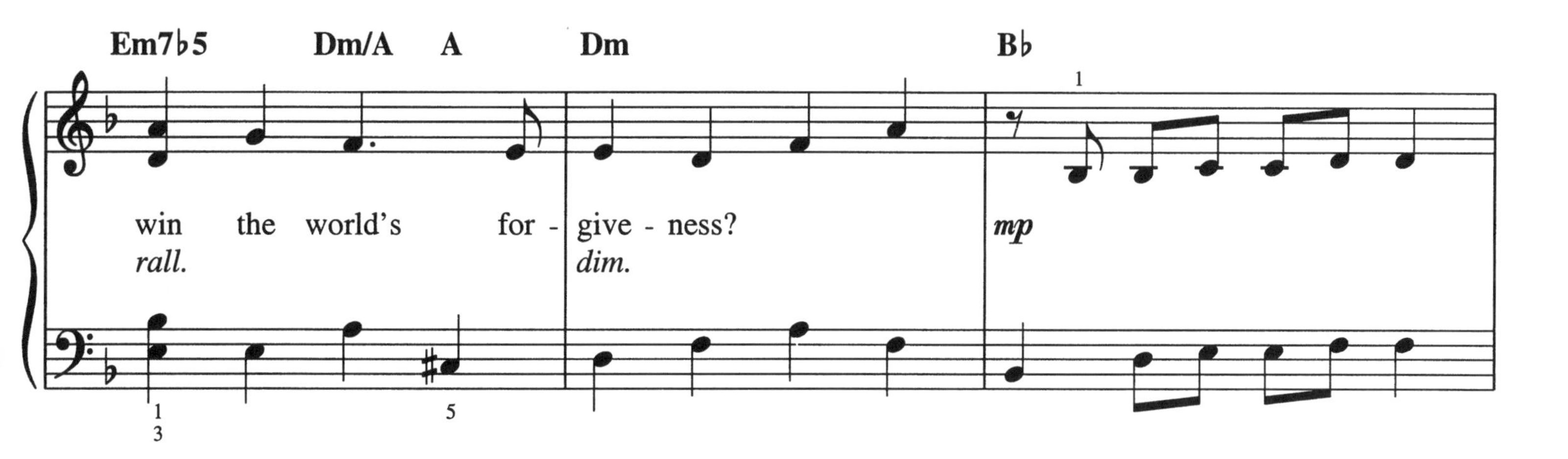
Em7♭5
Dm/A
A
Dm
B♭
win the world's for - give - ness?
rall.
dim.
mp

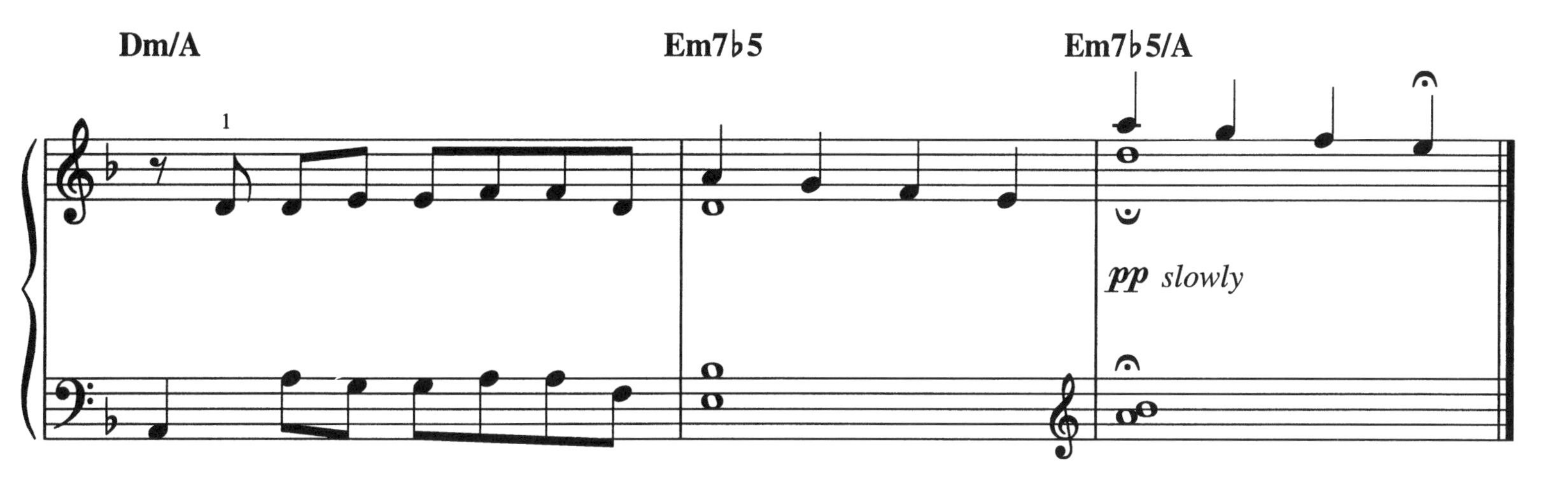
Dm/A
Em7♭5
Em7♭5/A
pp slowly

BE OUR GUEST

Lyrics by HOWARD ASHMAN
Music by ALAN MENKEN

N.C.
G
Gmaj7
your dinner! Be our guest! Be our guest! Put our
a tempo
No pedal

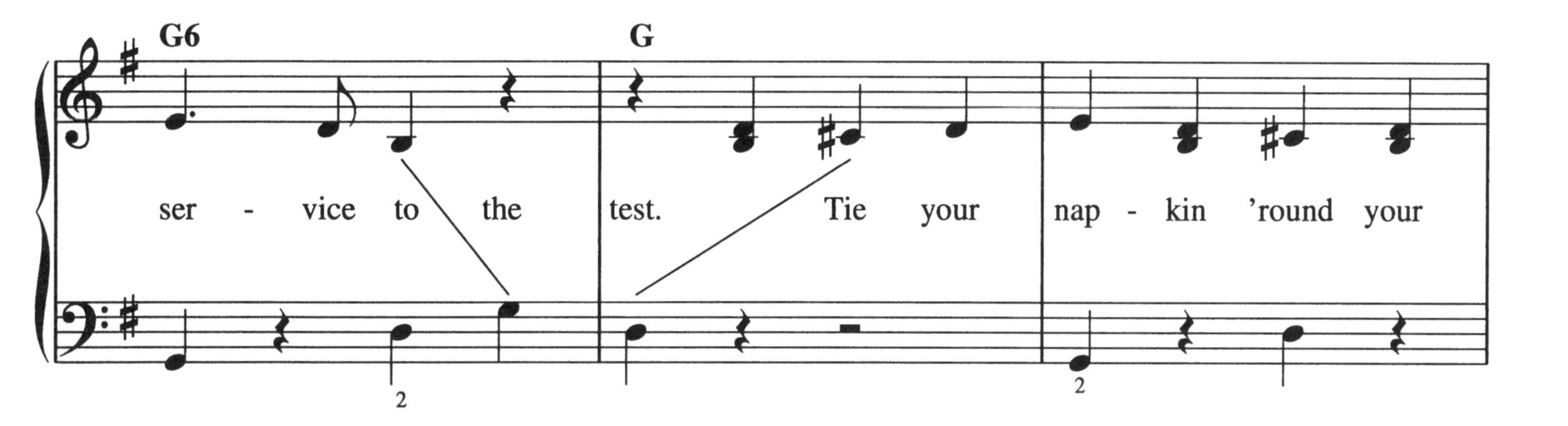
G6
G
ser - vice to the test. Tie your nap - kin 'round your

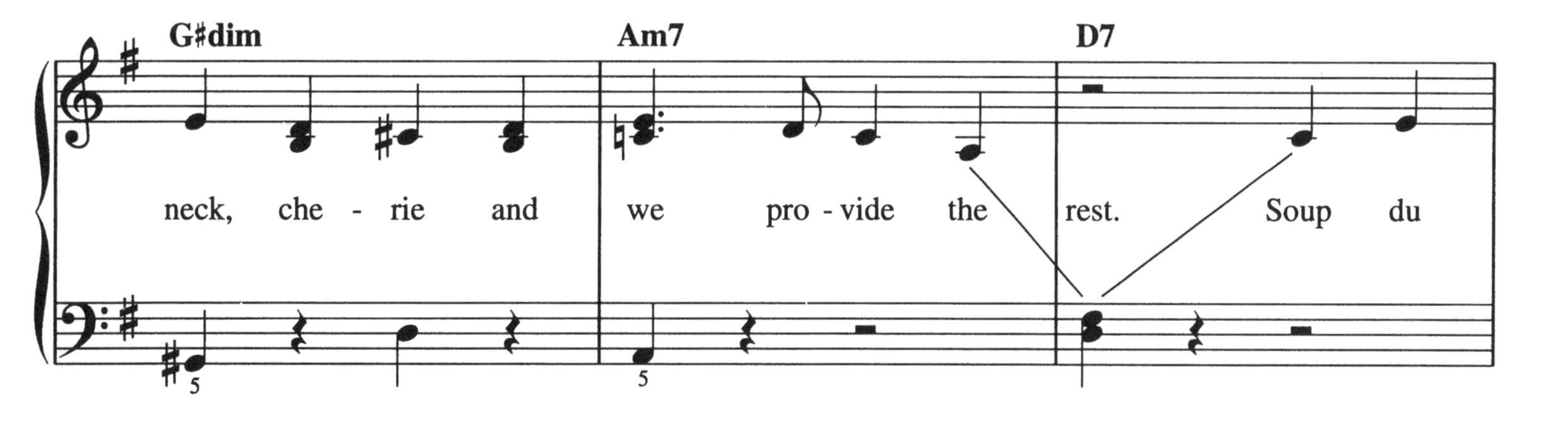
G#dim
Am7
D7
neck, che - rie and we pro - vide the rest. Soup du

Am
Am#7
Am7
jour! Hot hors d'oeuvres! Why, we on - ly live to

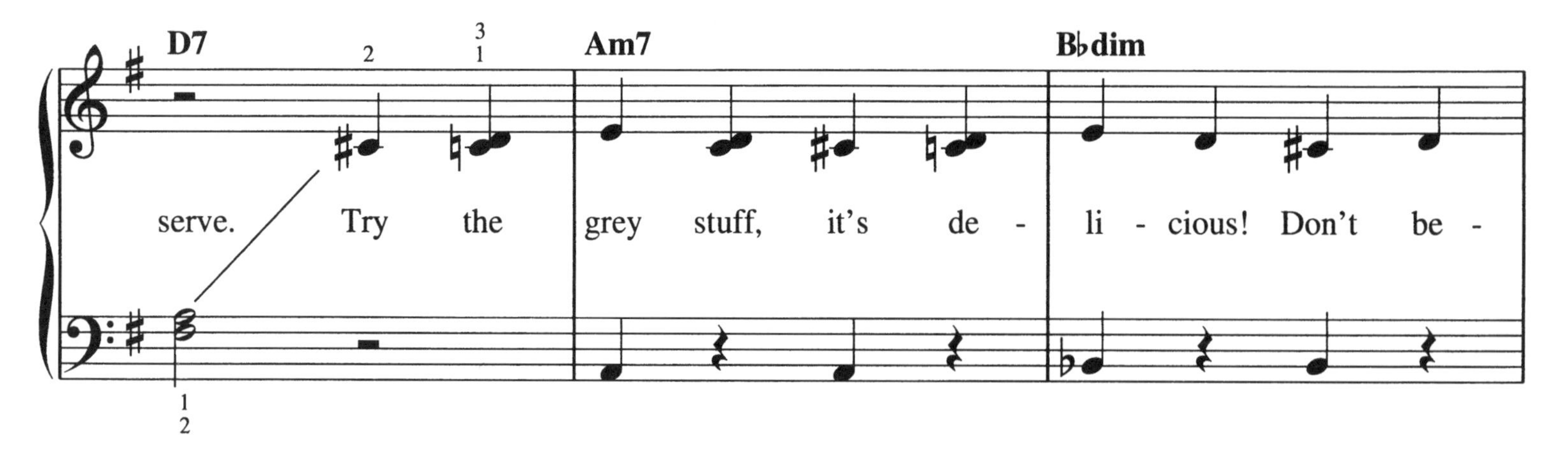
D7
Am7
B♭dim
serve. Try the grey stuff, it's de - li - cious! Don't be -

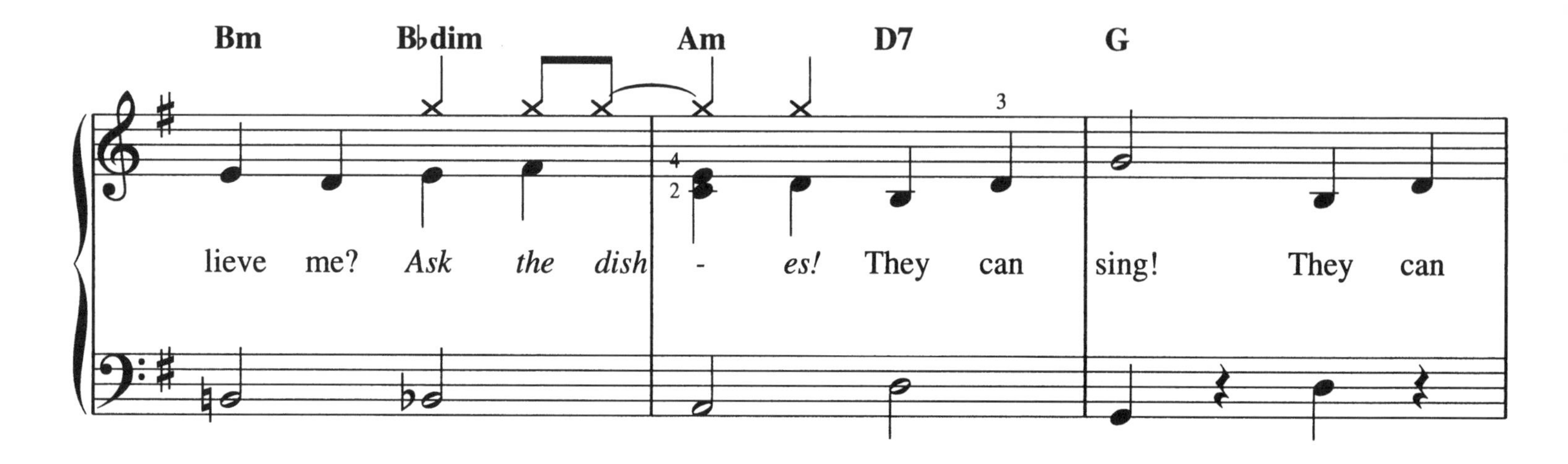
Bm
B♭dim
Am
D7
G
lieve me? Ask the dish - es! They can sing! They can

Gmaj7
G6
G
dance! Af - ter all, Miss, this is France! And a

G7
C6
din - ner here is nev - er sec - ond best.

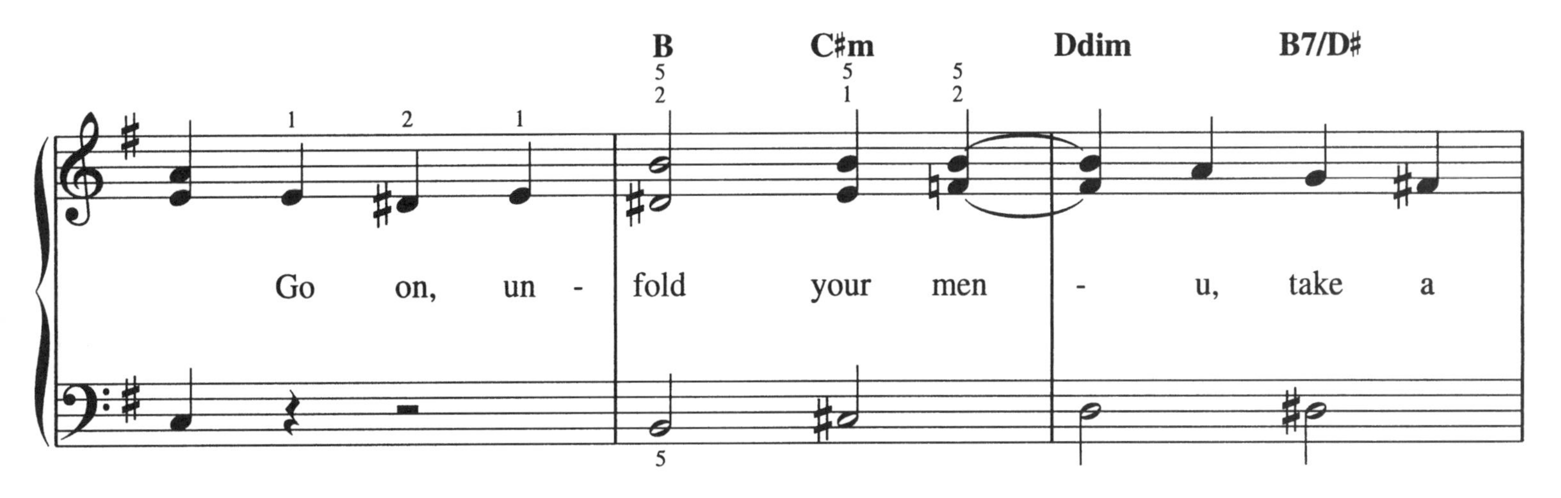
B
C♯m
Ddim
B7/D♯
Go on, un - fold your men - u, take a

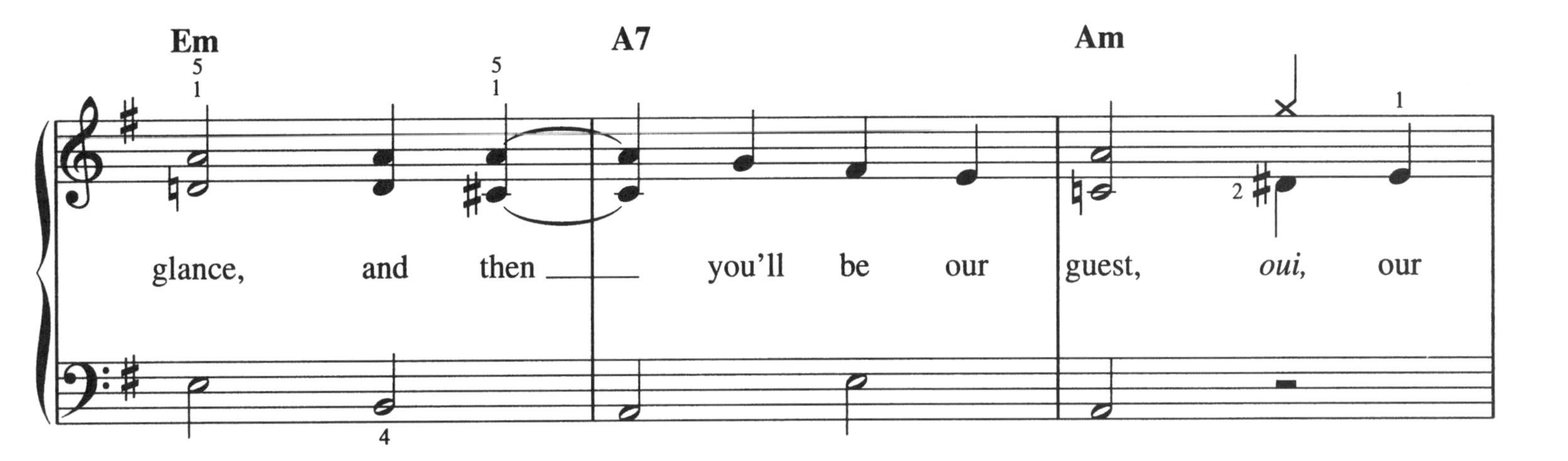
Em
A7
Am
glance, and then you'll be our guest, oui, our

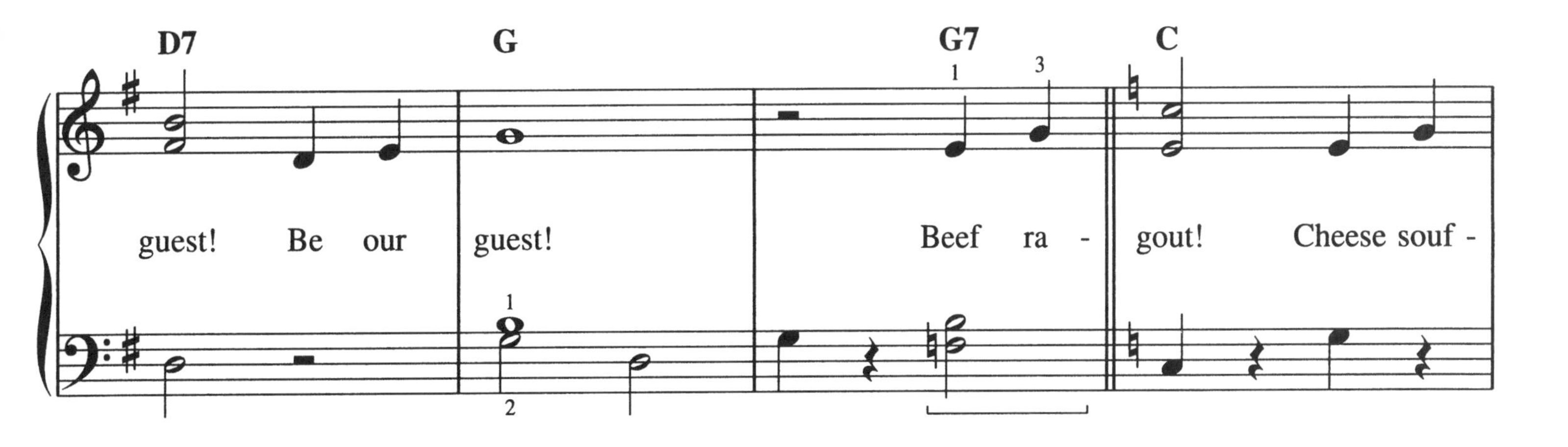
D7
G
G7
C
guest! Be our guest! Beef ra - gout! Cheese souf -

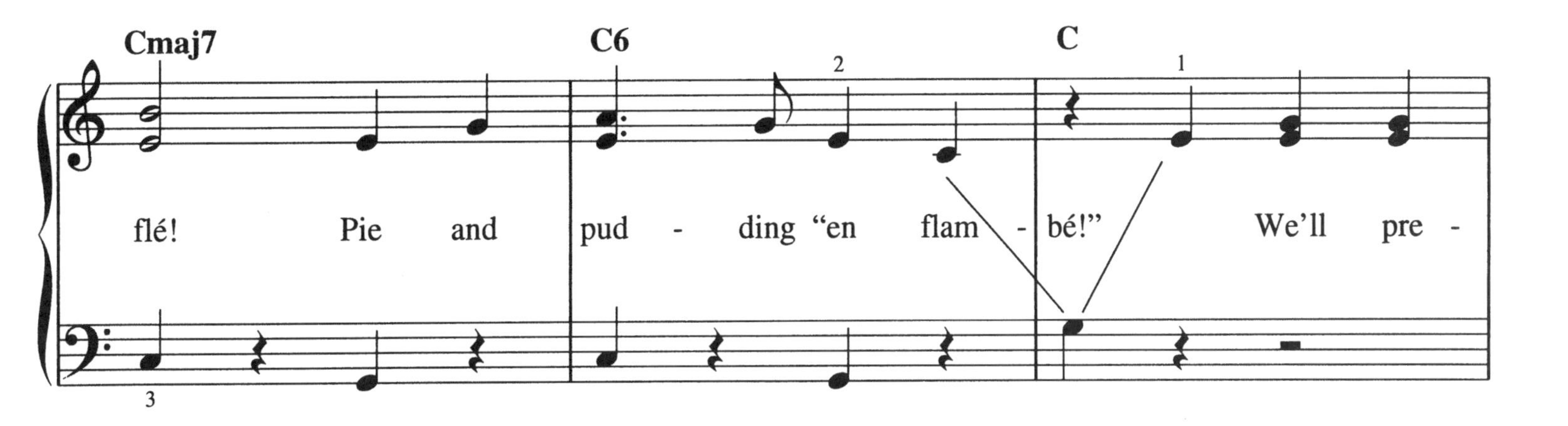
Cmaj7
C6
C
flé! Pie and pud - ding "en flam - bé!" We'll pre -

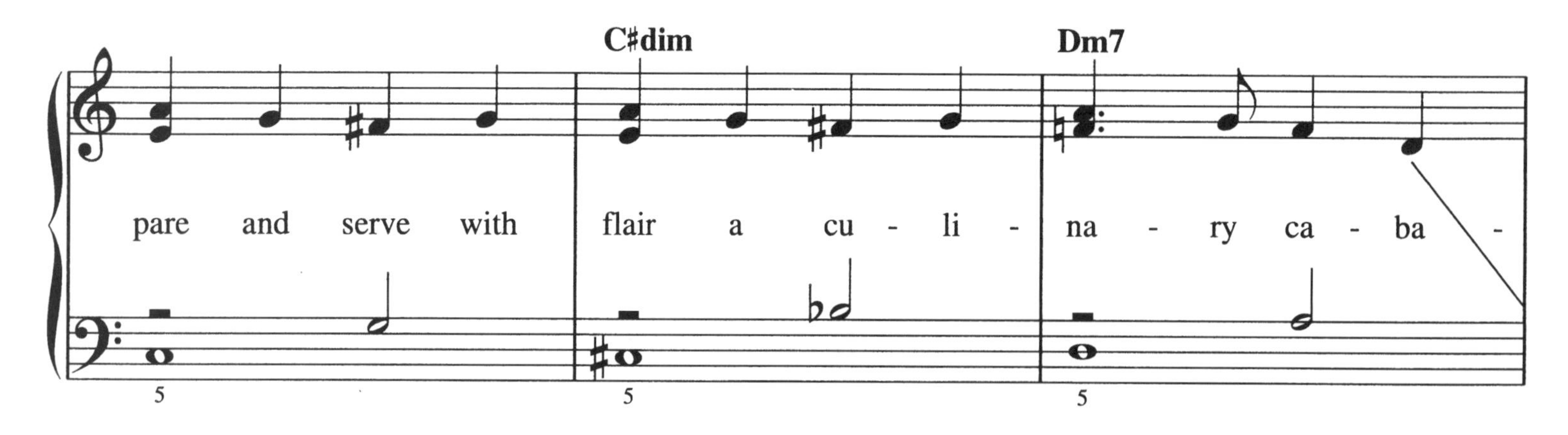
C♯dim
Dm7
pare and serve with flair a cu - li - na - ry ca - ba -

G7
Dm
Dm♯7
ret! You're a - lone and you're scared but the

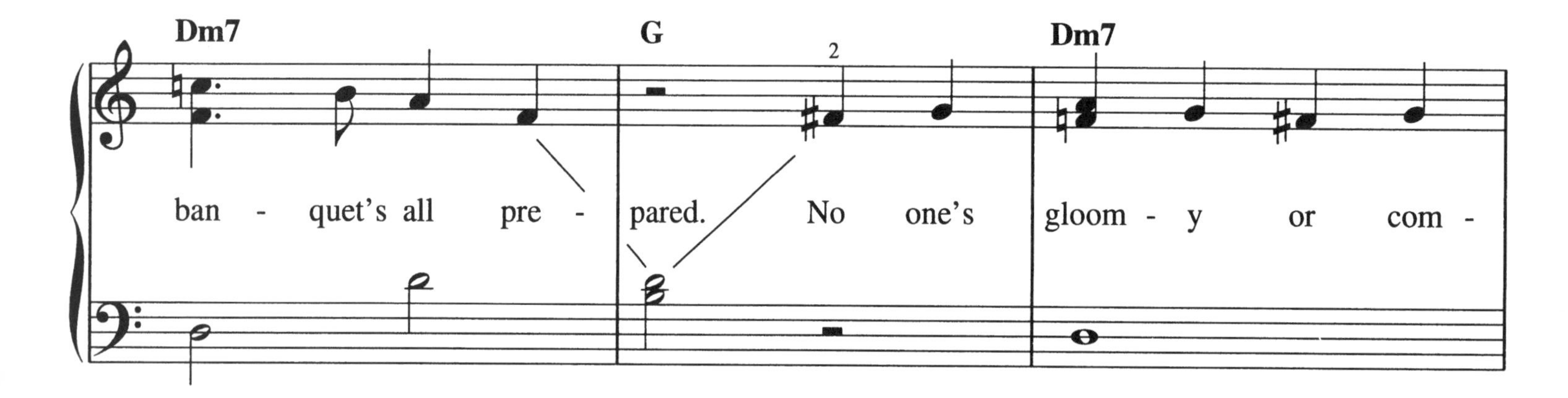
Dm7
G
Dm7
ban - quet's all pre - pared. No one's gloom - y or com -

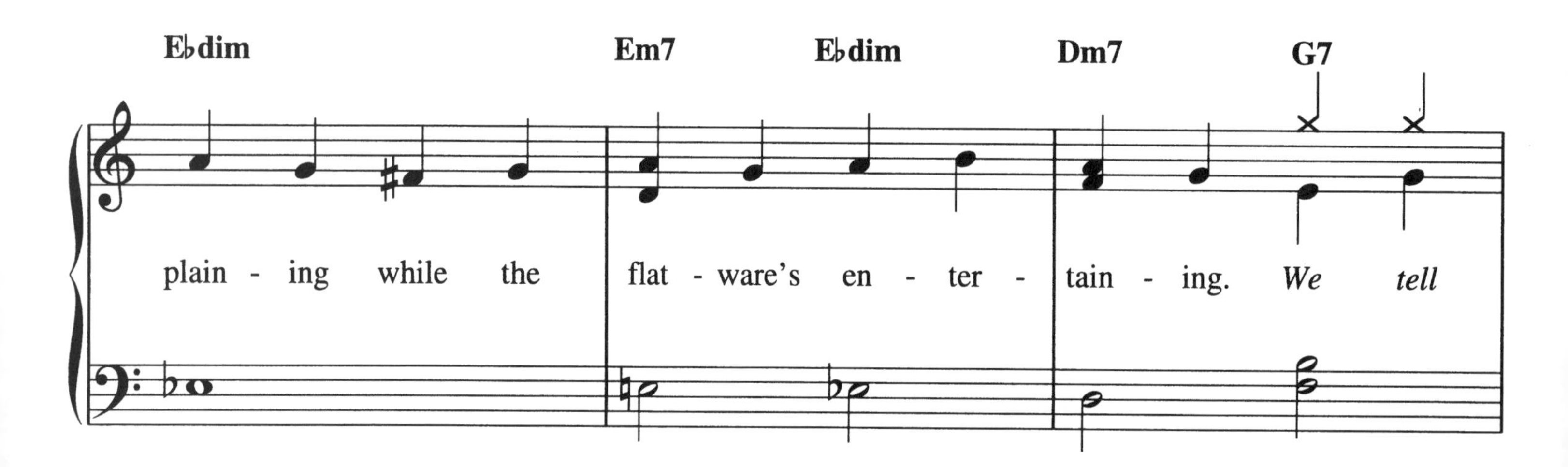
E♭dim
Em7
E♭dim
Dm7
G7
plain - ing while the flat - ware's en - ter - tain - ing. We tell

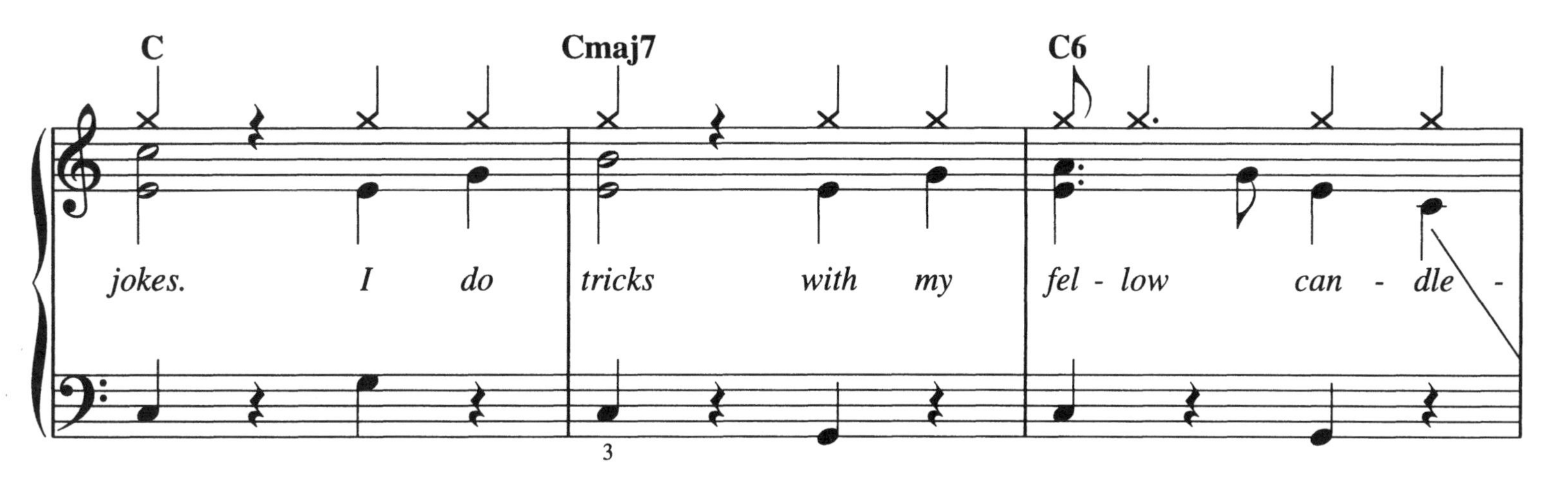
C
Cmaj7
C6
jokes. I do
tricks with my
fel - low can - dle -

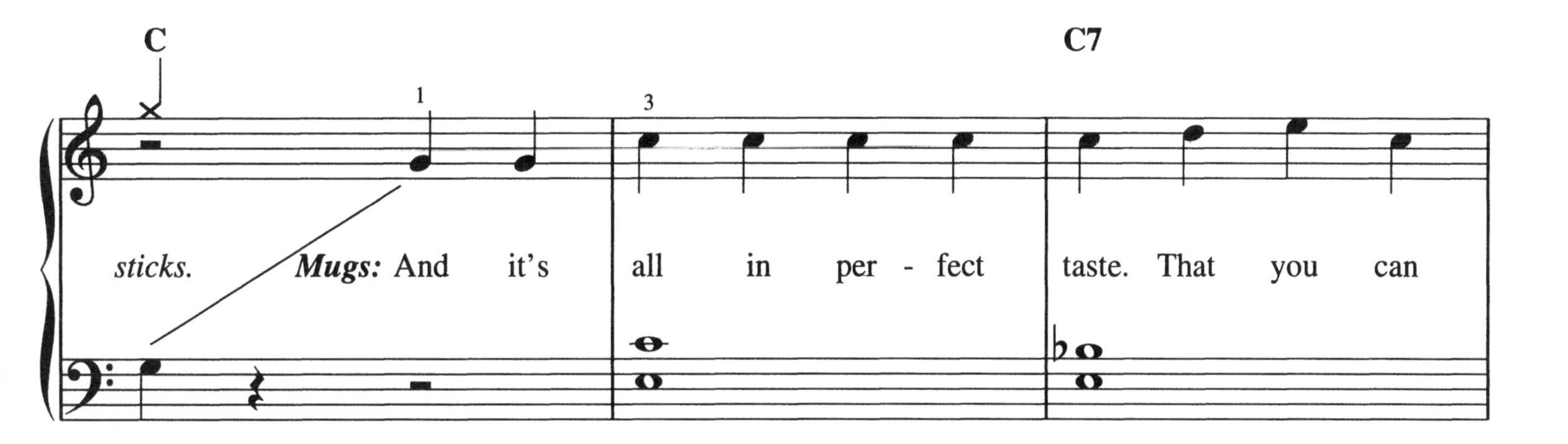
C
C7
sticks. Mugs: And it's
all in per - fect
taste. That you can

F6
E
F♯m7
Gdim
bet!
All: Come on and
lift your glass

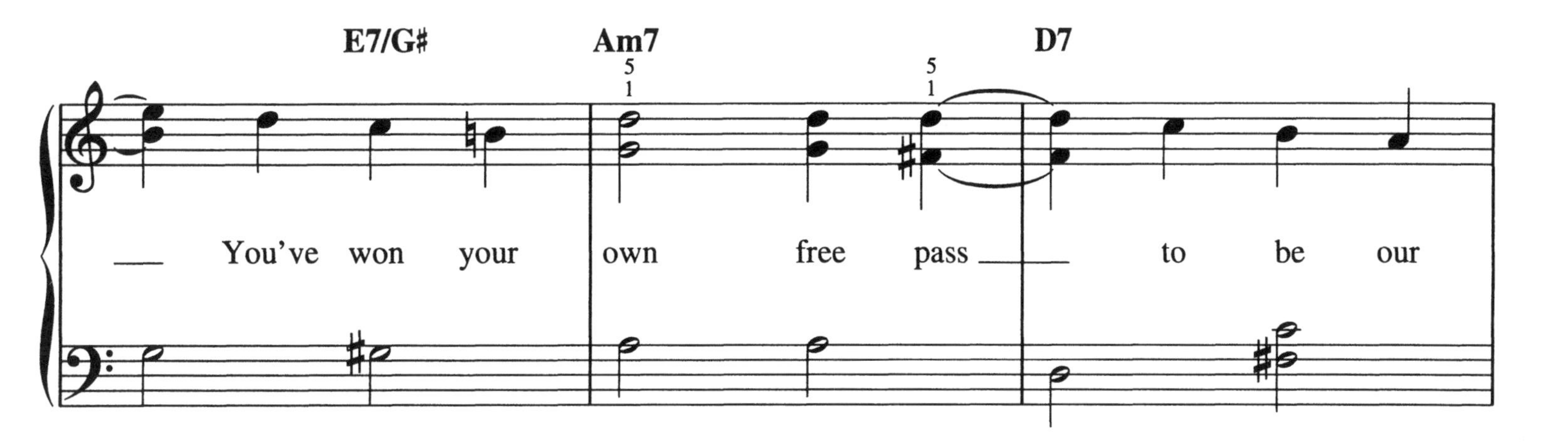
E7/G♯
Am7
D7
You've won your
own free pass
to be our

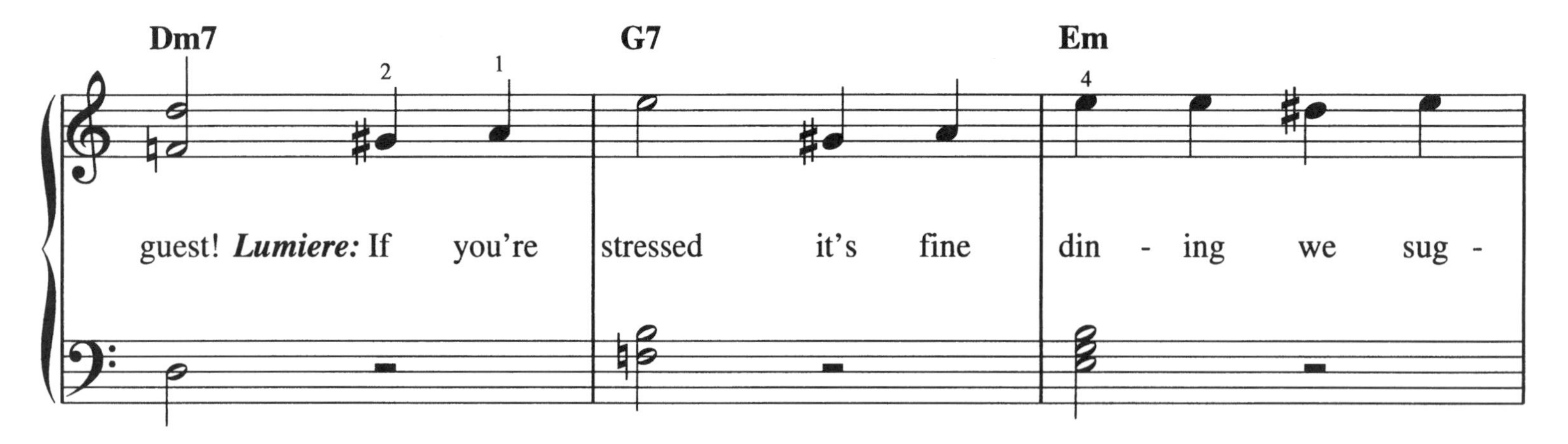
Dm7
G7
Em
guest! Lumiere: If you're stressed it's fine din - ing we sug -

A7♯5
Dm7
G7
C
gest. All: Be our guest! Be our guest! Be our guest!

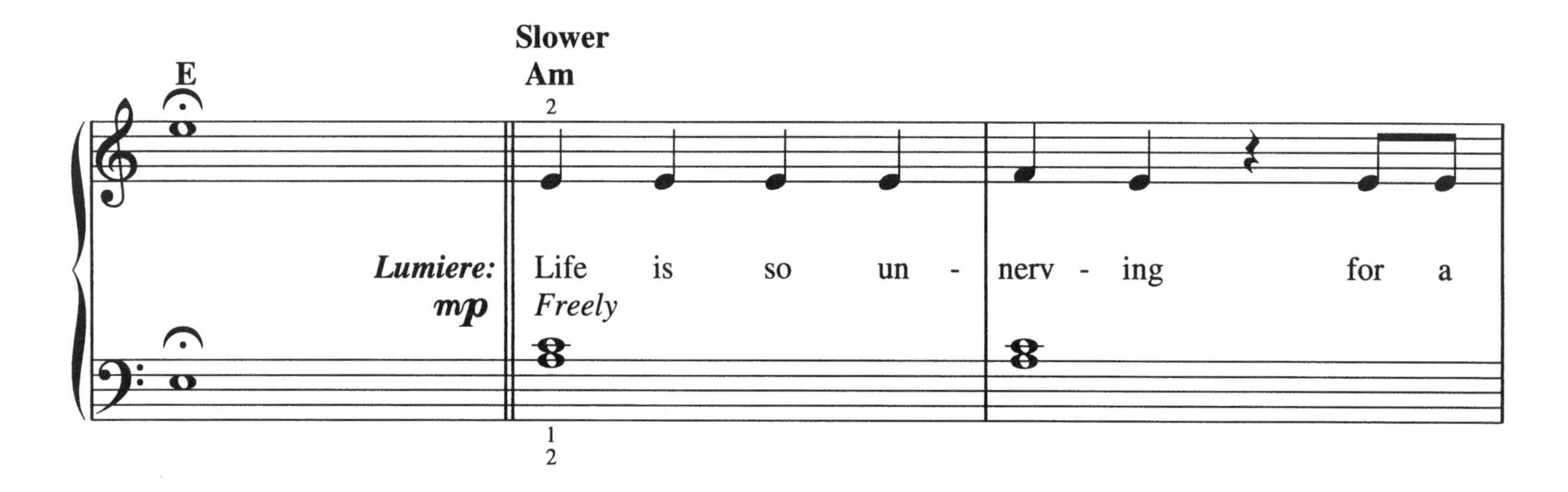
E
Slower
Am
Lumiere:
mp
Freely
Life is so un - nerv - ing for a

E/G♯
Gdim
ser - vant who's not serv - ing. He's not whole with - out a

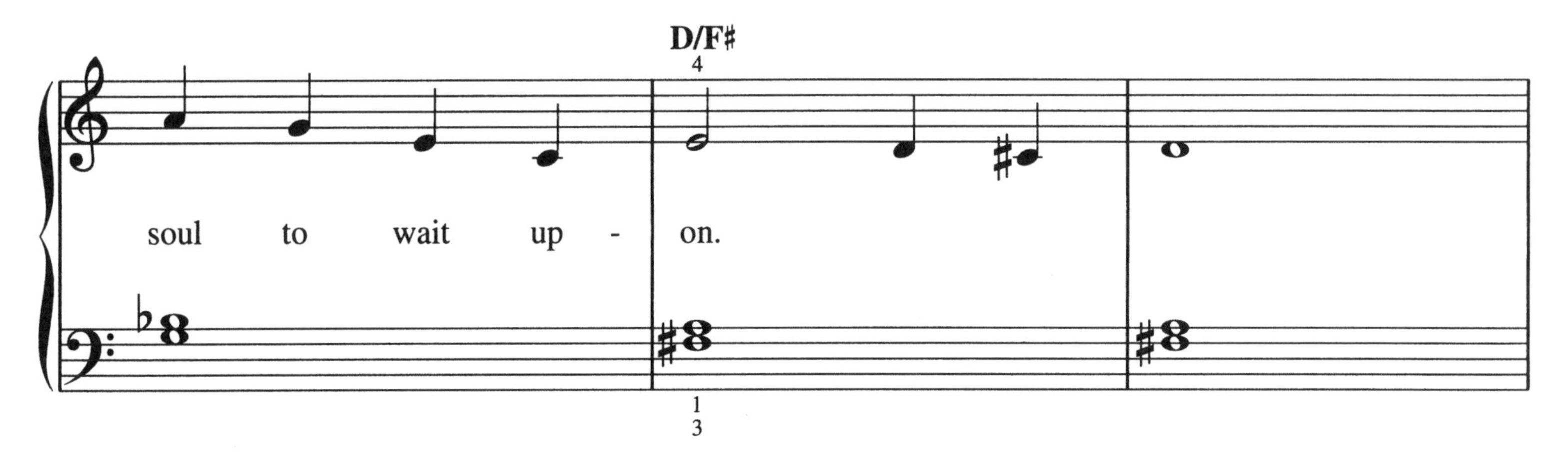
D/F♯
soul to wait up - on.

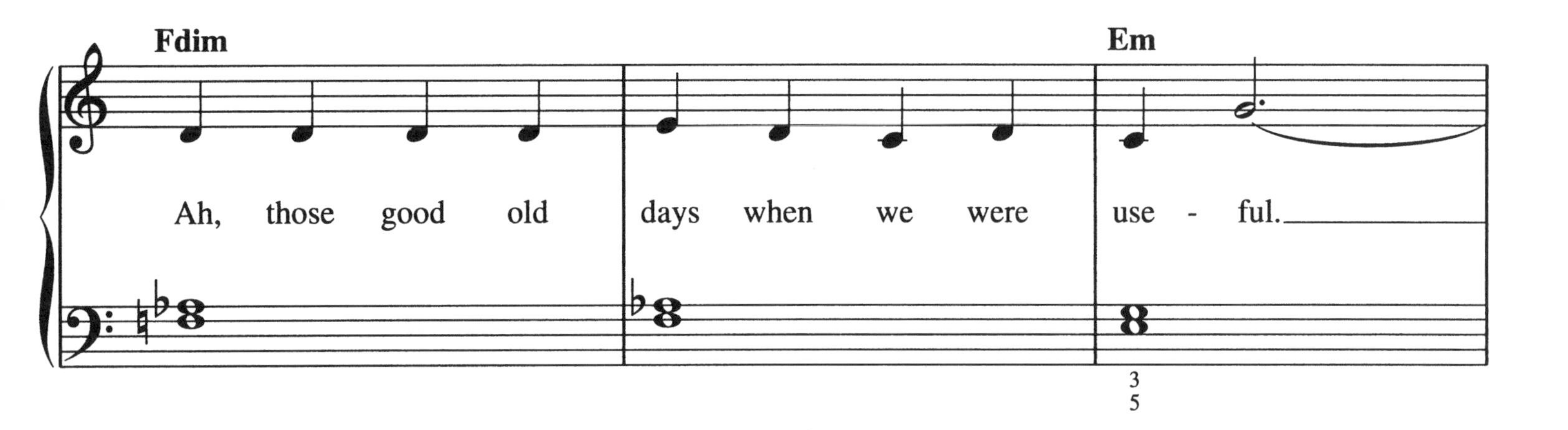
Fdim
Em
Ah, those good old days when we were use - ful.

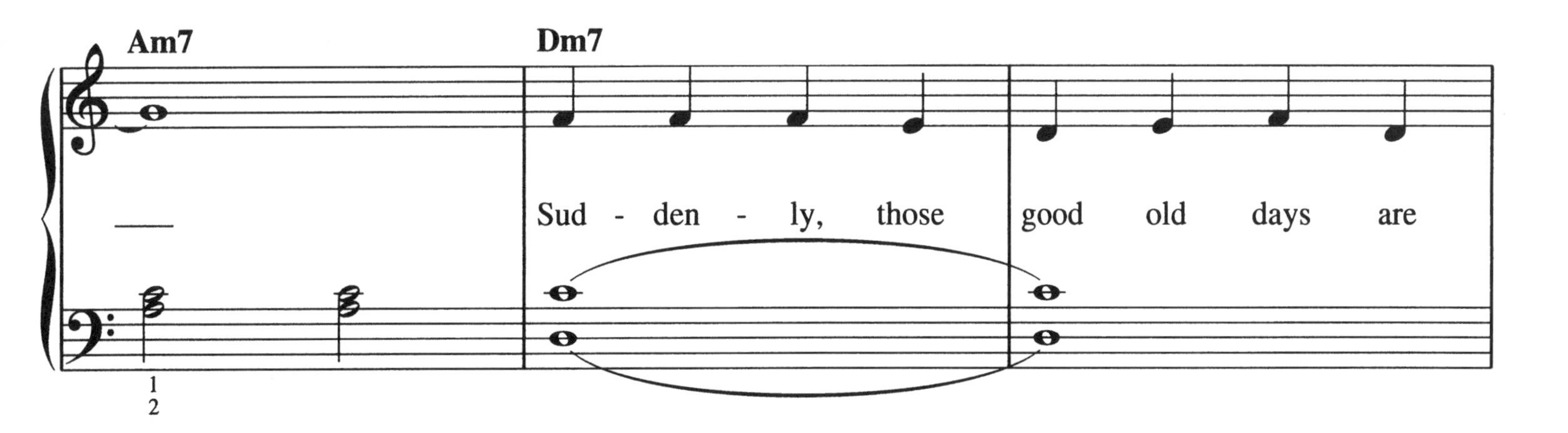
Am7
Dm7
Sud - den - ly, those good old days are

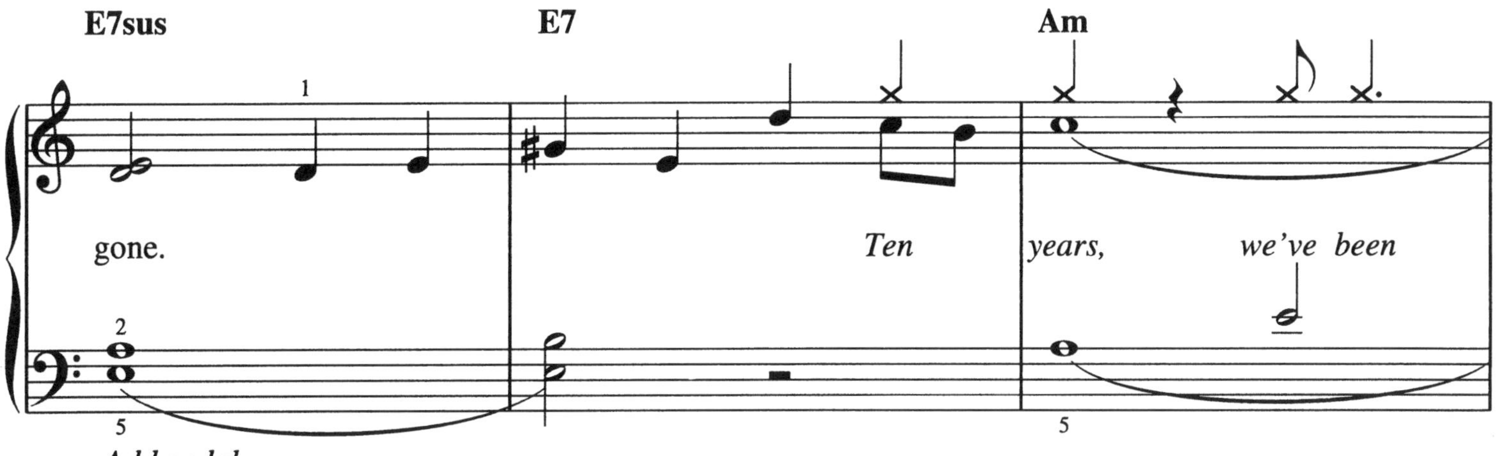
E7sus
E7
Am
gone. Ten years, we've been
Add pedal

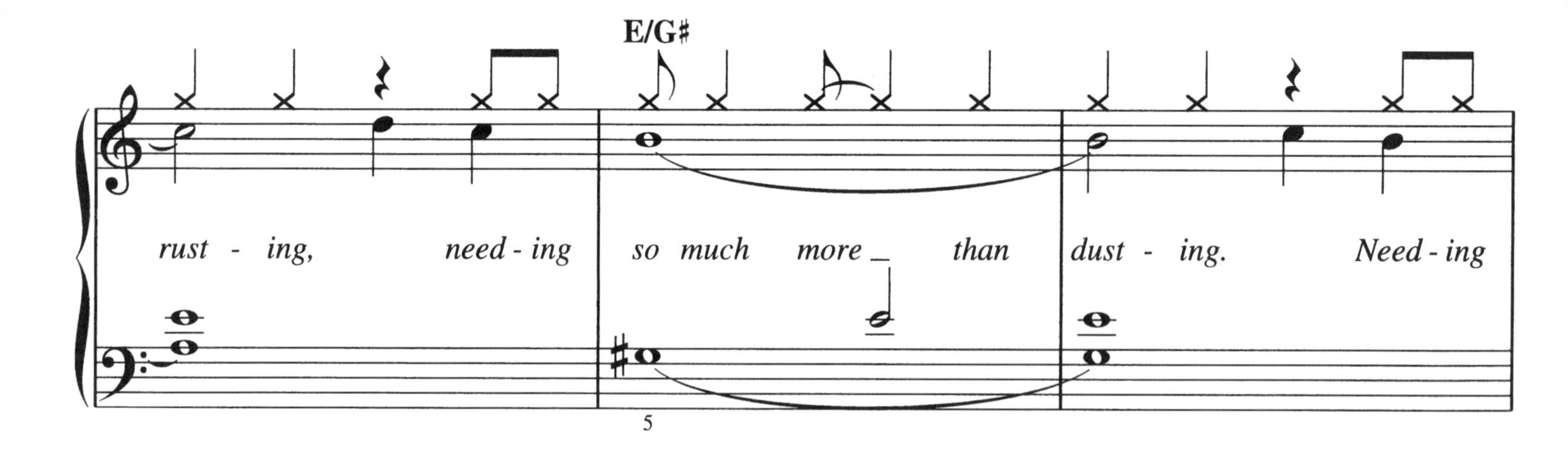
E/G#
rust - ing, need - ing so much more _ than dust - ing. Need - ing
5

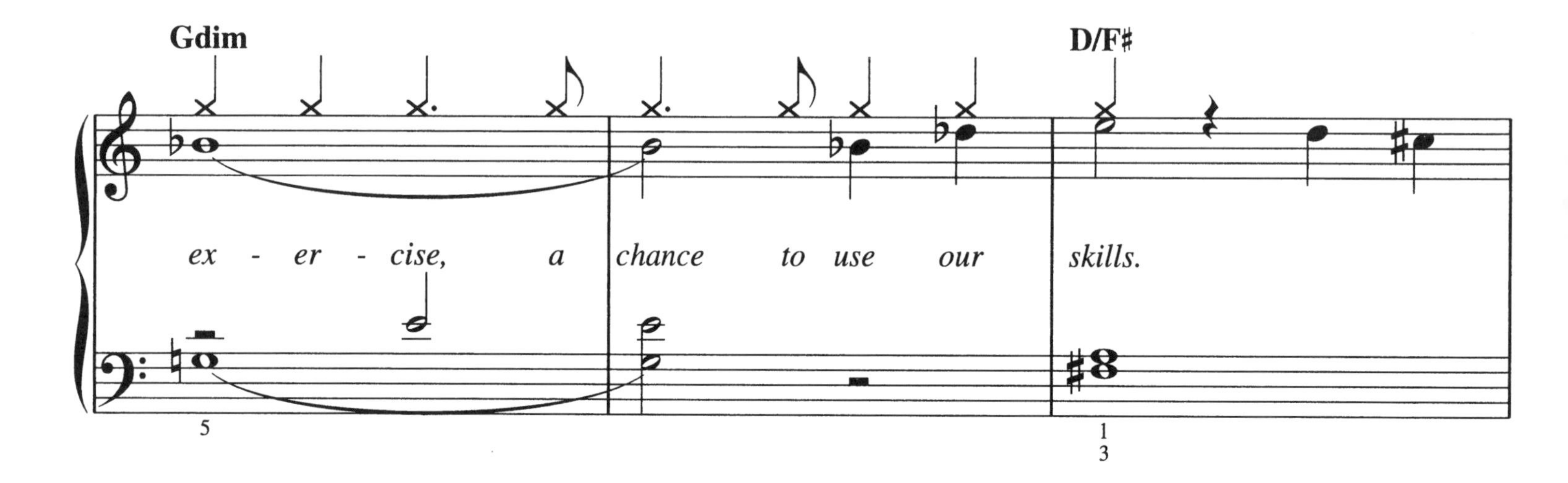
Gdim
D/F#
ex - er - cise, a chance to use our skills.
5
1
3

Fdim
3
Most days, we just lay a - round the

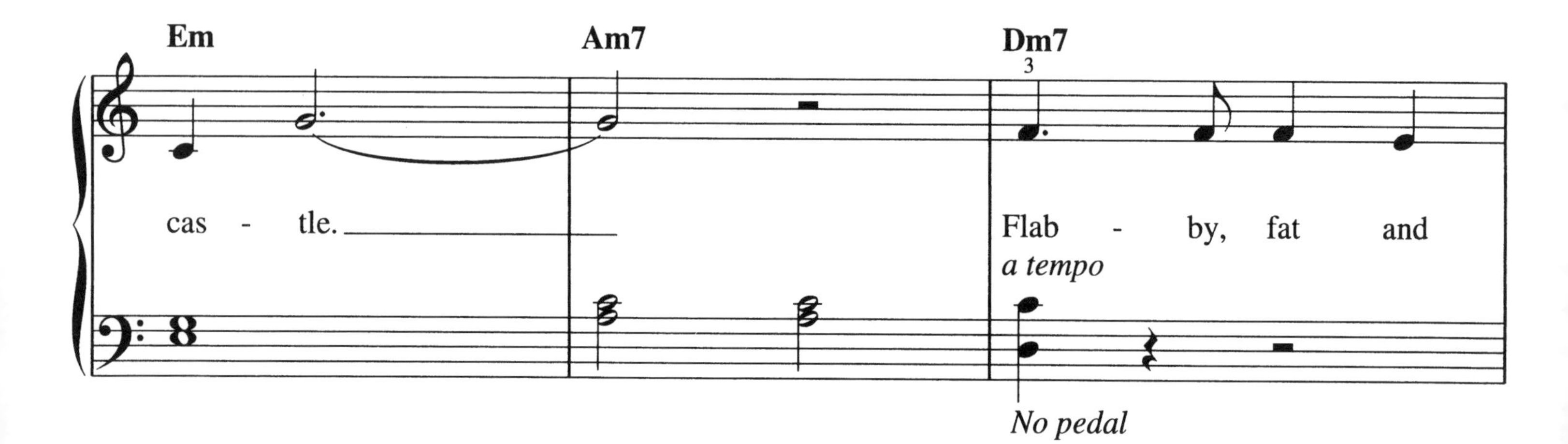
Em
Am7
Dm7
3
cas - tle.
Flab - by, fat and
a tempo
No pedal

G7
la - zy. You walked in and oops - a - dai - sy! Mrs. Potts: It's a

C
Cmaj7
C6
guest! It's a guest! Sakes a - live, well, I'll be
mf

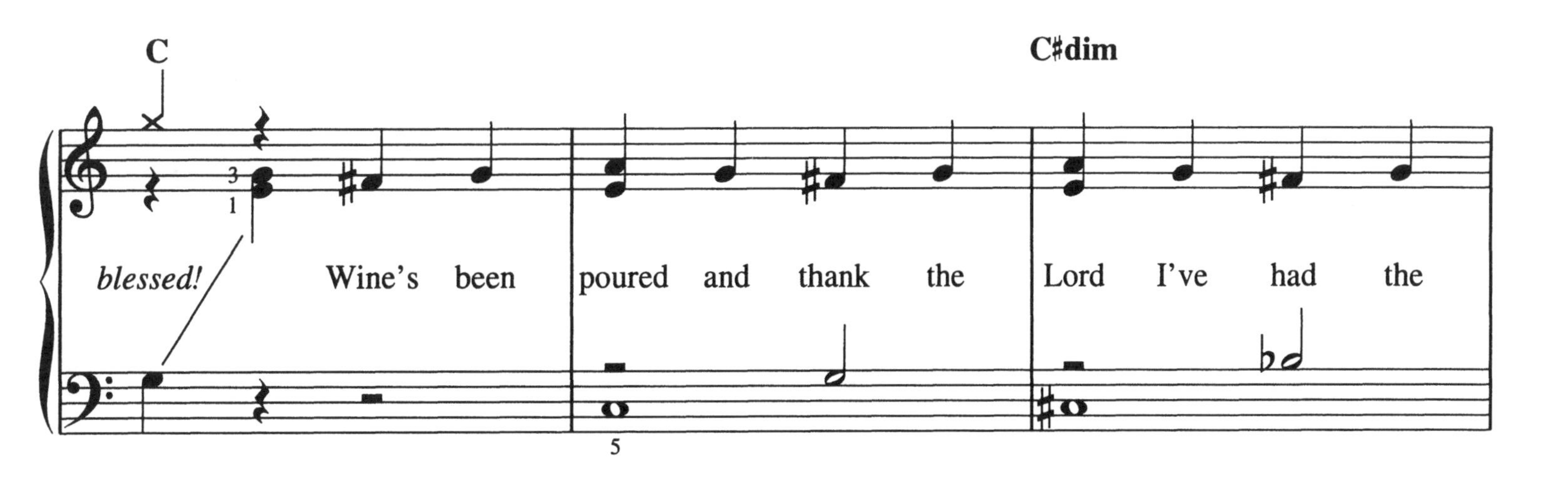
C
C♯dim
blessed! Wine's been poured and thank the Lord I've had the

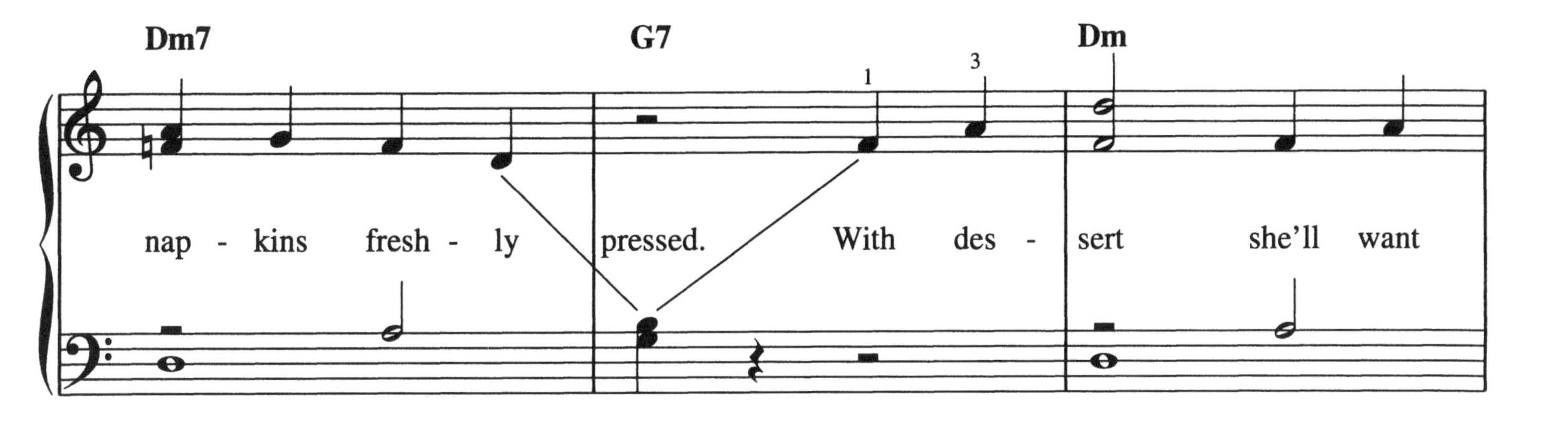
Dm7
G7
Dm
nap - kins fresh - ly pressed. With des - sert she'll want

Dm#7 Dm7 G

tea. *And my dear, that's fine with me.* While the

Dm7
D#dim
Em
E♭dim
cups do their soft shoe - ing, I'll be bub - bling! I'll be

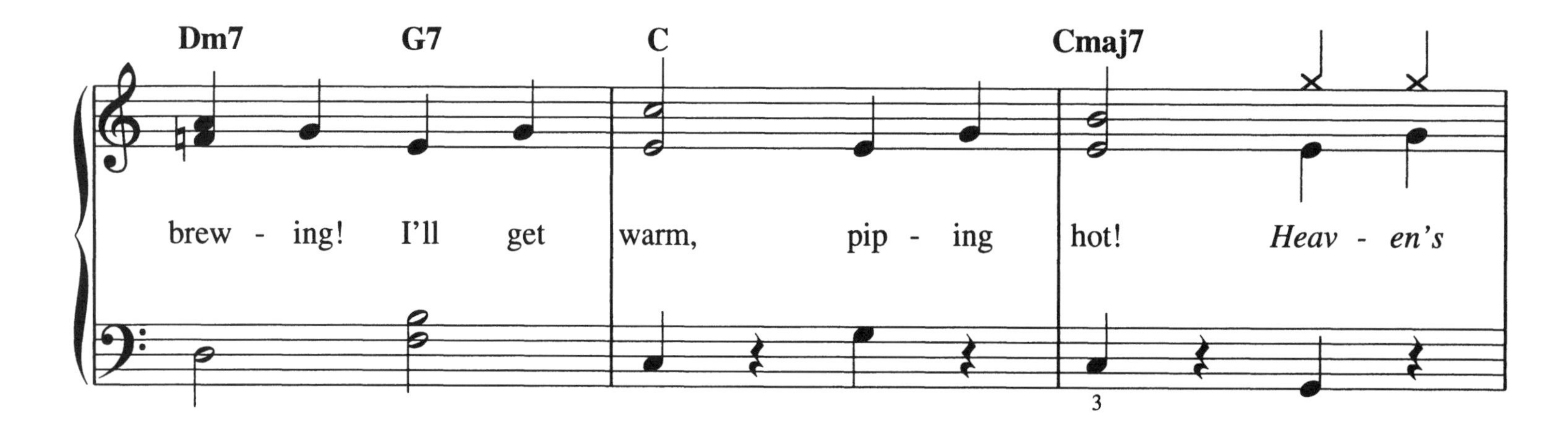

Dm7
G7
C
Cmaj7
brew - ing! I'll get warm, pip - ing hot! Heav - en's

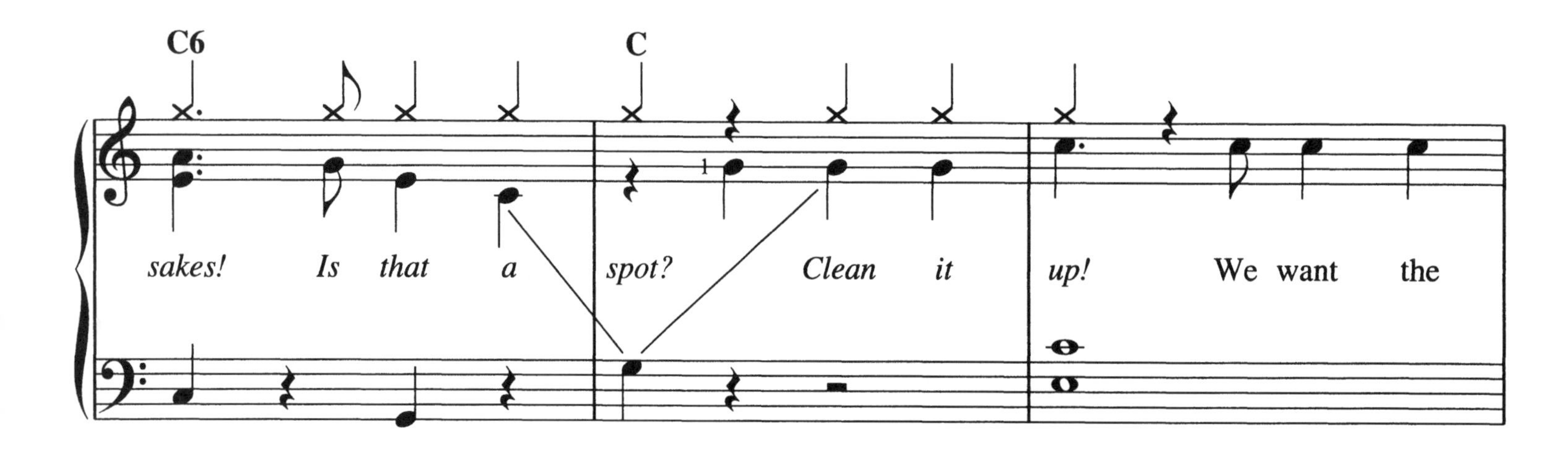

C6
C
sakes! Is that a spot? Clean it up! We want the

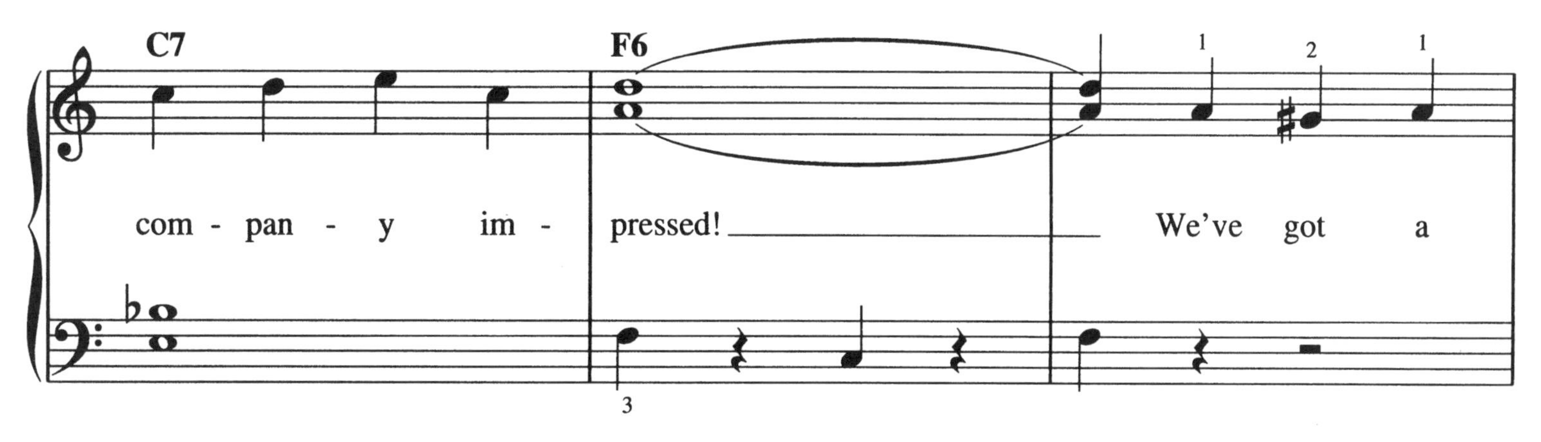
C7
F6
com - pan - y im - pressed!
We've got a

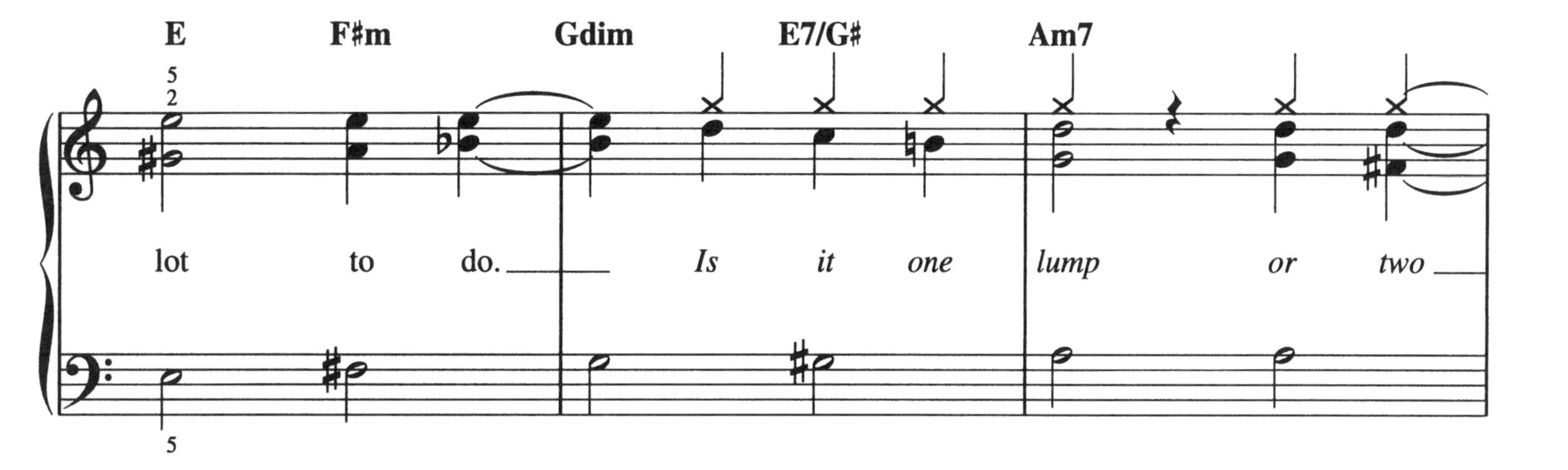
E
F#m
Gdim
E7/G#
Am7
lot to do.
Is it one lump or two

D7
Dm7
G7
for you, our guest? Chorus: She's our
guest! Mrs. Potts: She's our

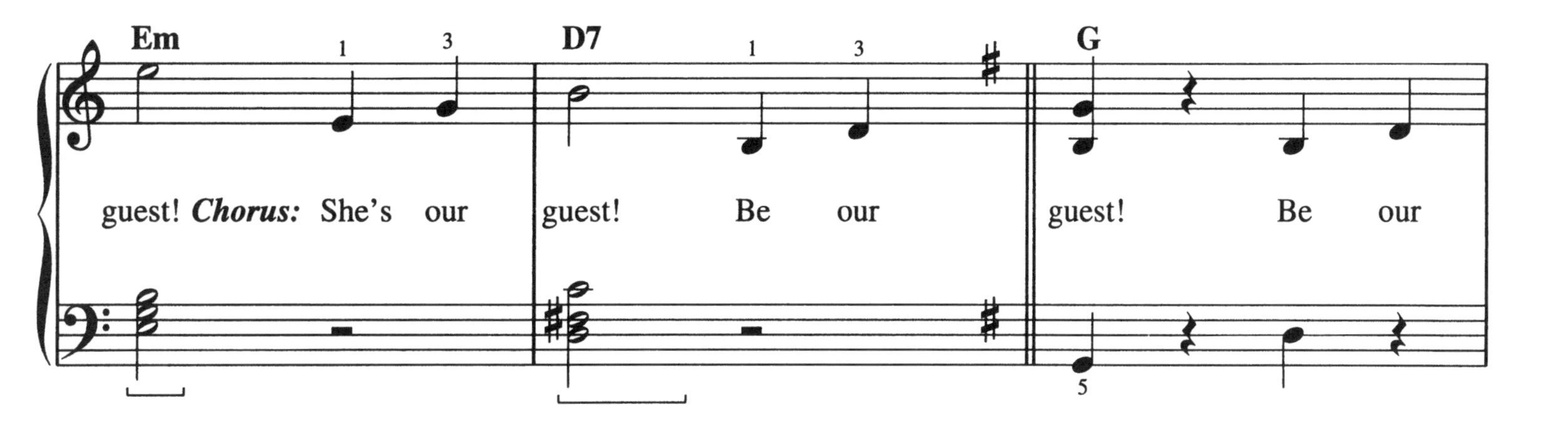
Em
D7
G
guest! Chorus: She's our guest! Be our guest! Be our

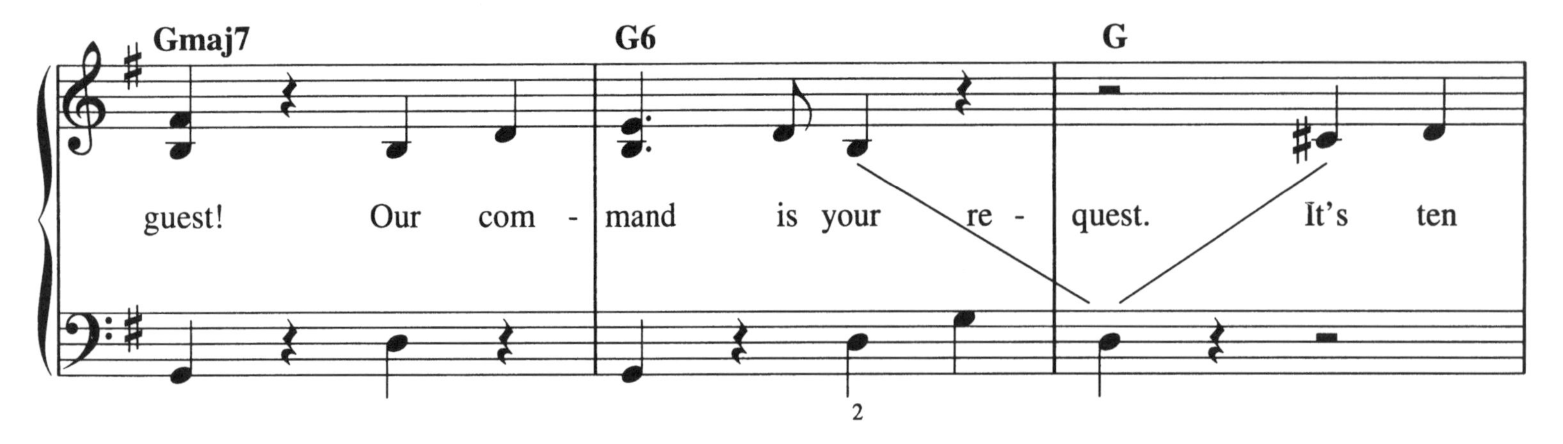
Gmaj7
G6
G
guest! Our com - mand is your re - quest. It's ten
2

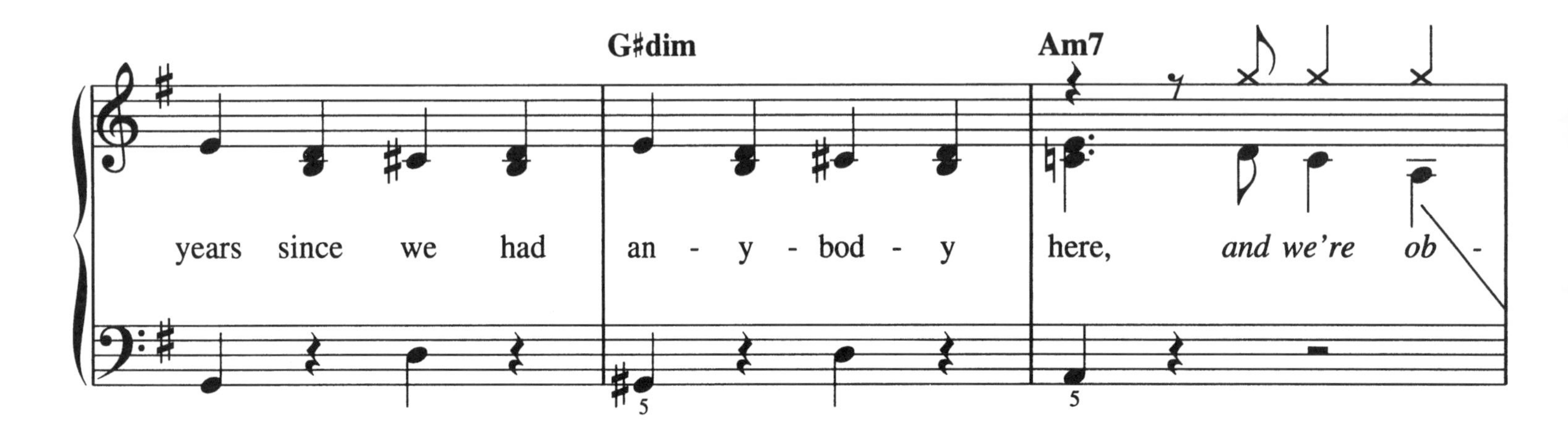
G♯dim
Am7
years since we had an - y - bod - y here, and we're ob -
5
5

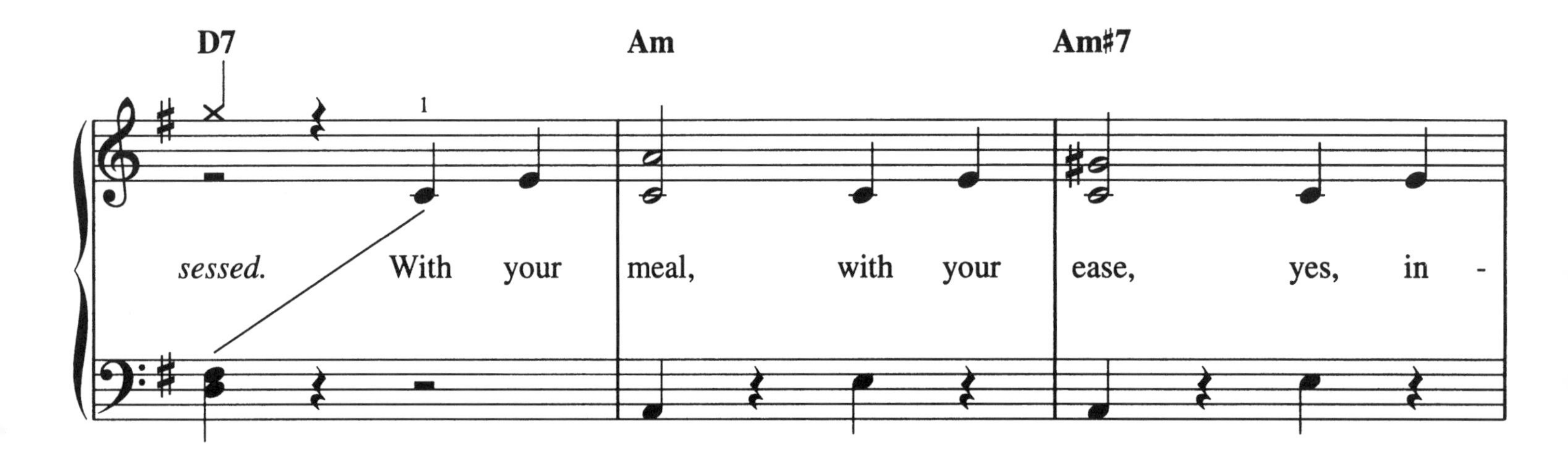
D7
Am
Am♯7
1
sessed. With your meal, with your ease, yes, in -

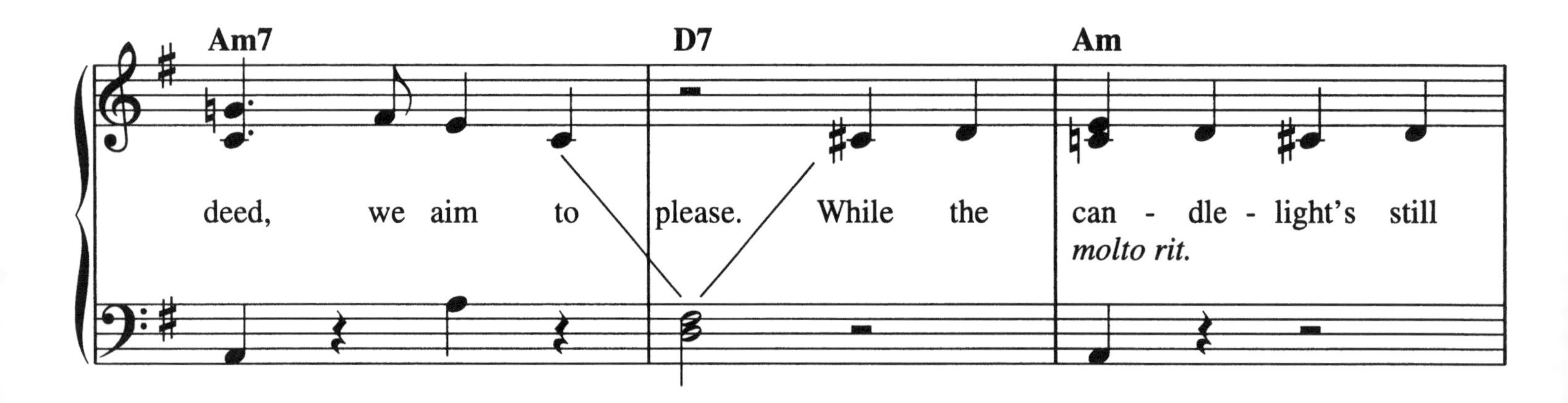
Am7
D7
Am
deed, we aim to please. While the can - dle - light's still
molto rit.

D7
G7
glow - ing let us
help you, we'll keep
go - ing course by
rit.

Much slower
C
Cmaj7
C6
course, one by
one! 'Til you
shout, "E - nough. I'm

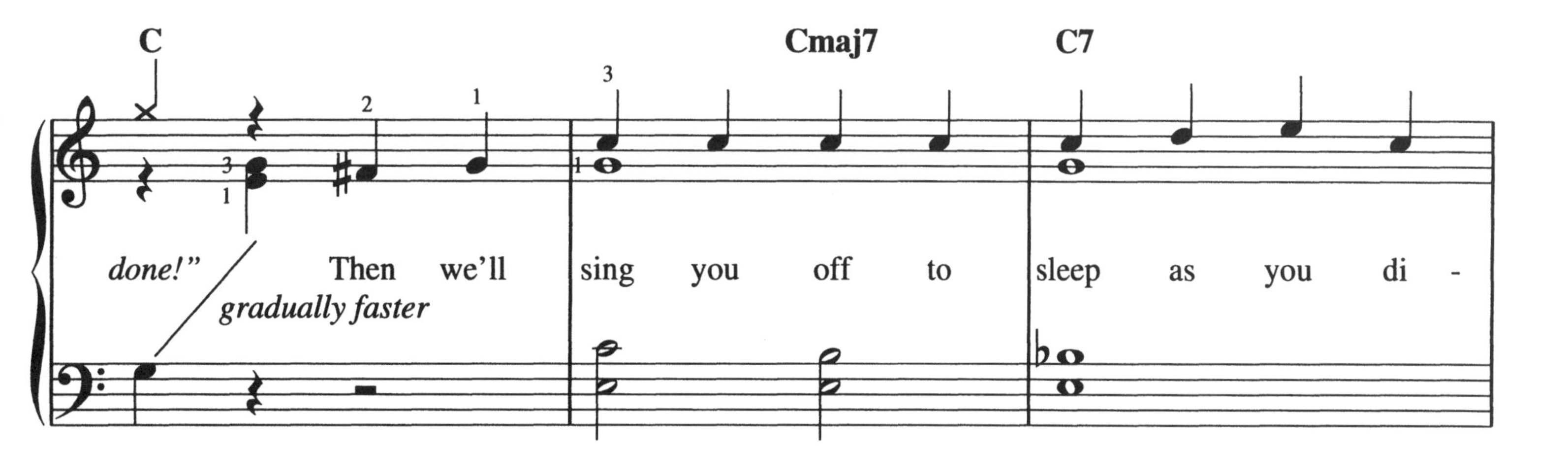
C
Cmaj7
C7
done!" Then we'll
gradually faster
sing you off to
sleep as you di -

F6
E
F#m7
gest.
To - night you'll
prop your feet
a tempo

Gdim
E7/G#
Am7
D7
up! But for now, let's eat up! Be our

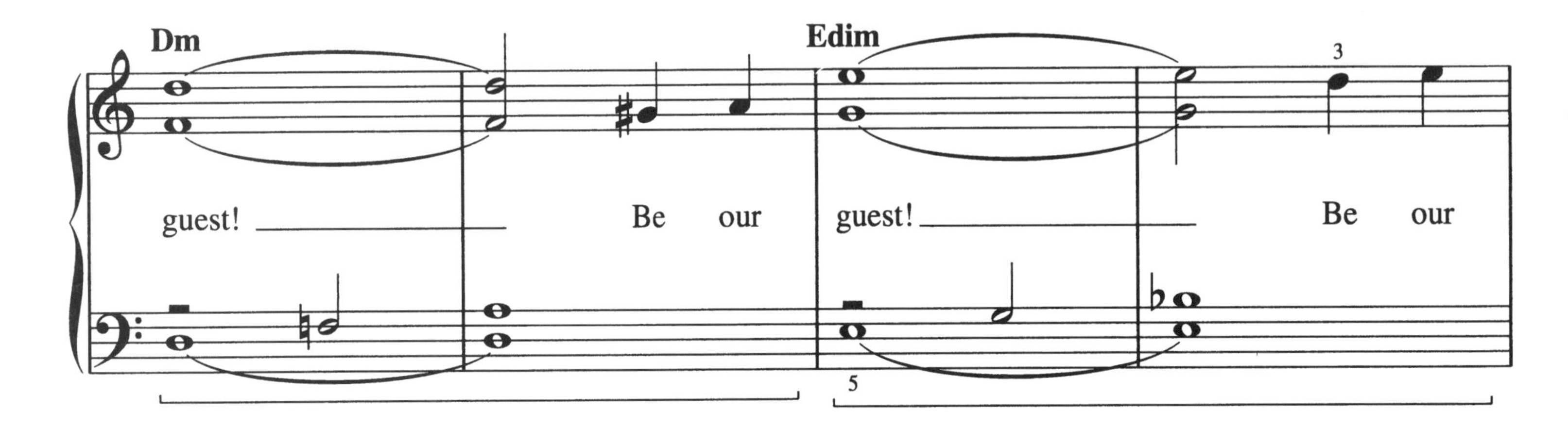
Dm
Edim
guest! Be our guest! Be our

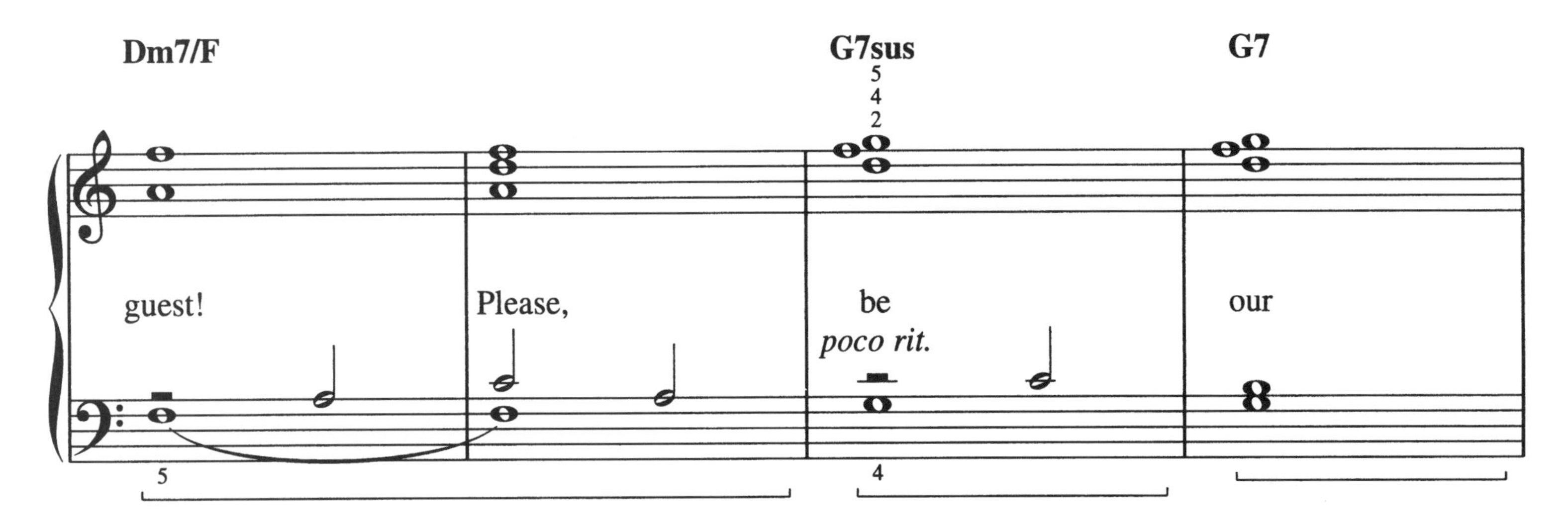
Dm7/F
G7sus
G7
guest! Please, be our
poco rit.

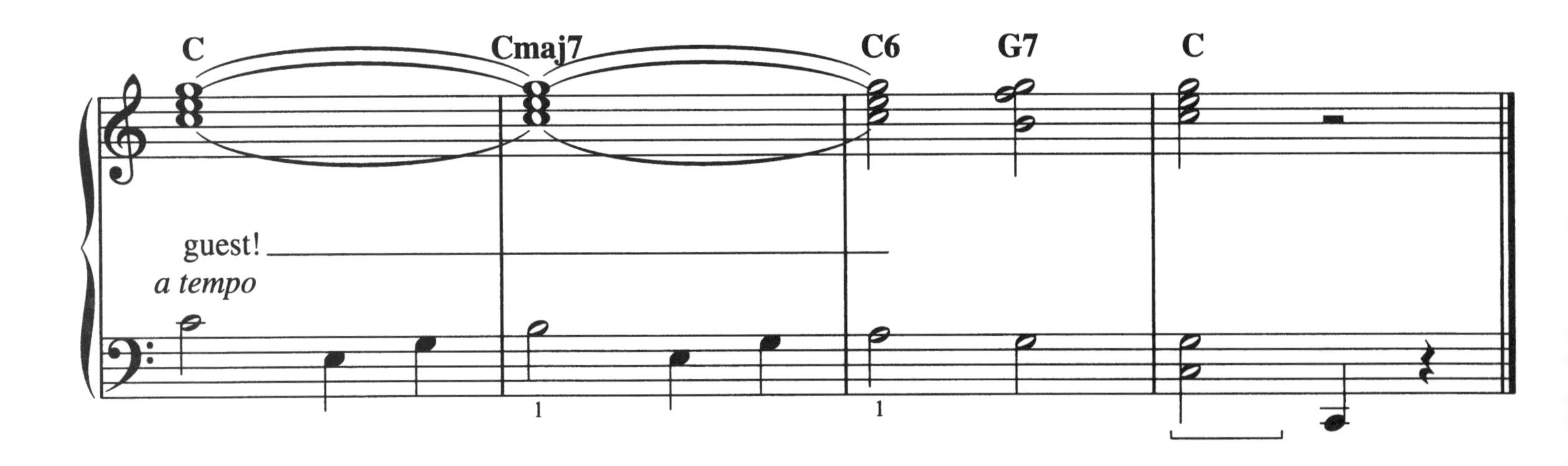
C
Cmaj7
C6
G7
C
guest!
a tempo

IF I CAN'T LOVE HER

Music by ALAN MENKEN
Lyrics by TIM RICE

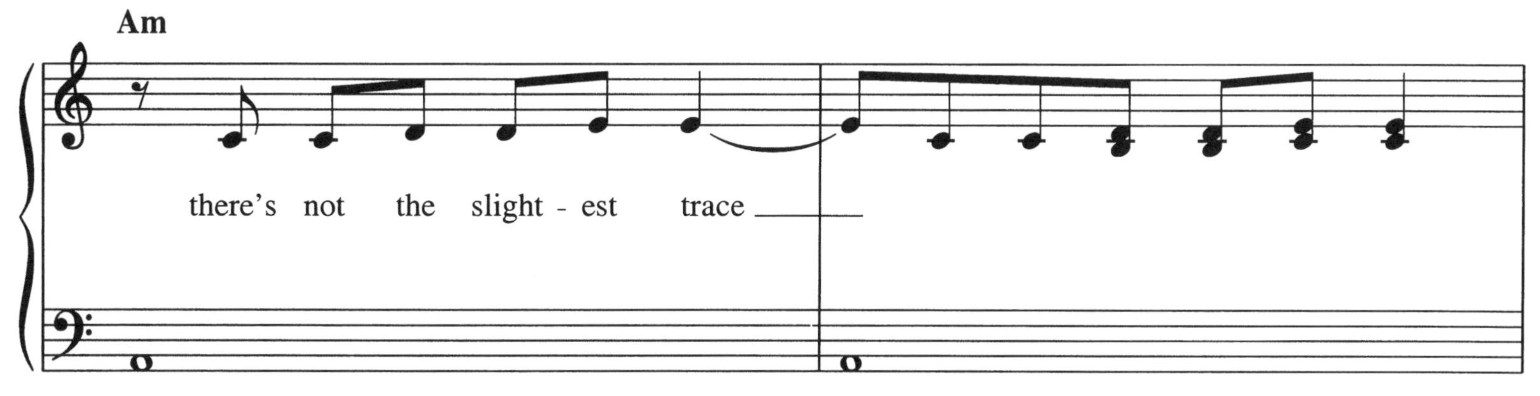

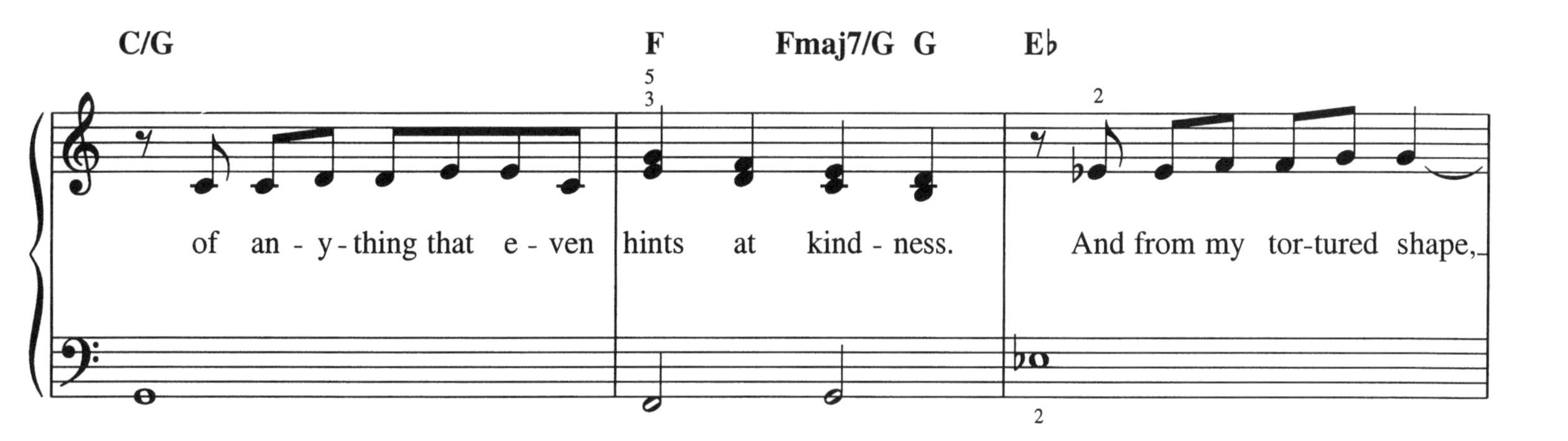

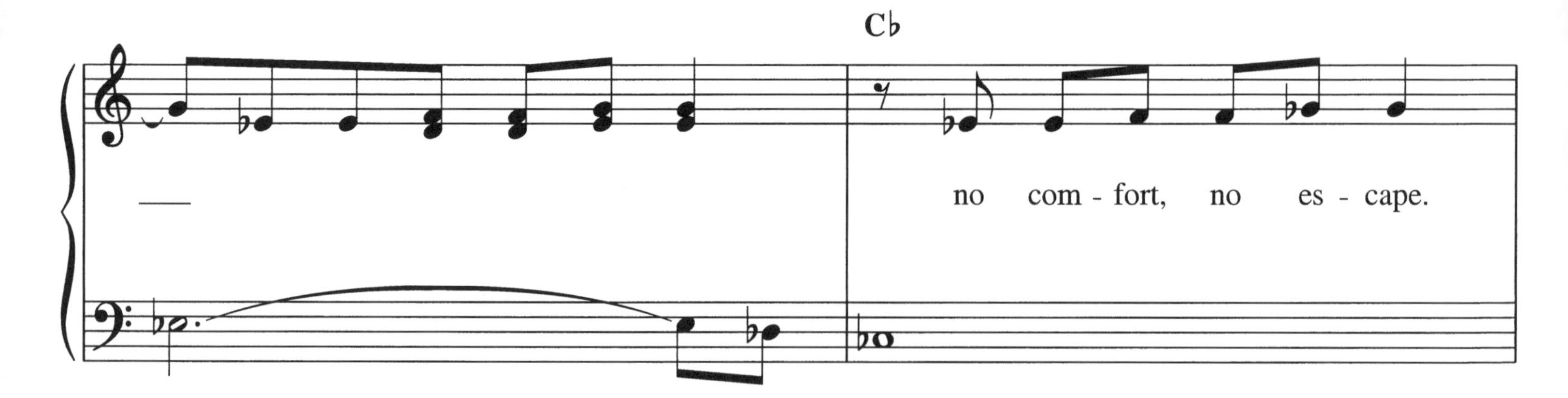
C♭
no com - fort, no es - cape.

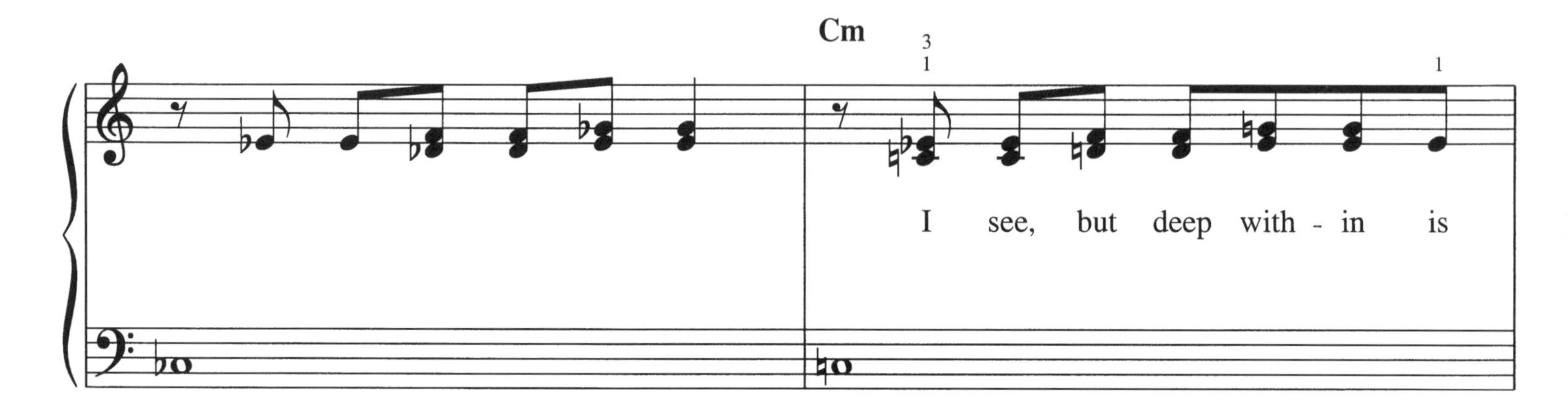
Cm
I see, but deep with - in is

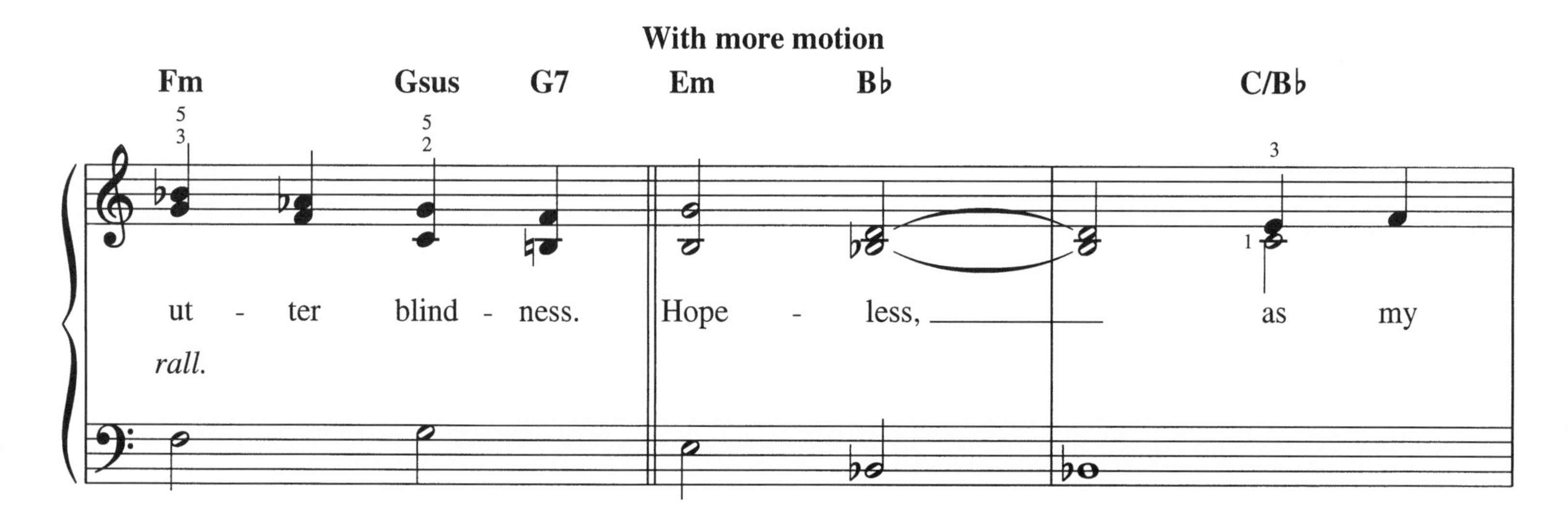
With more motion
Fm Gsus G7 Em B♭ C/B♭
ut - ter blind - ness. Hope - less, as my
rall.

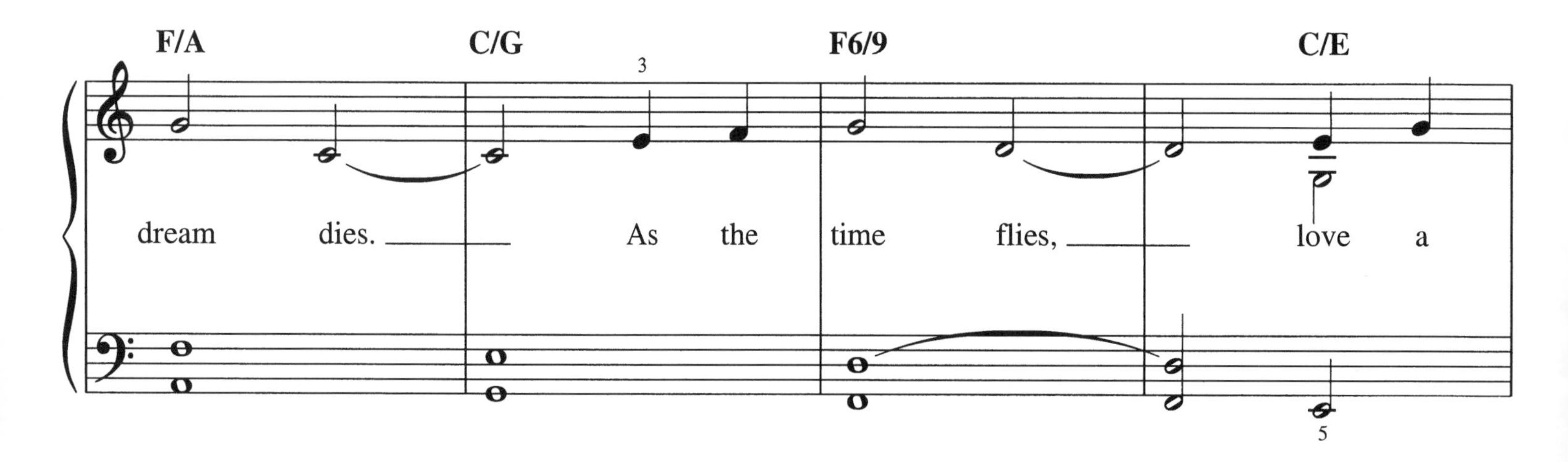
F/A C/G F6/9 C/E
dream dies. As the time flies, love a

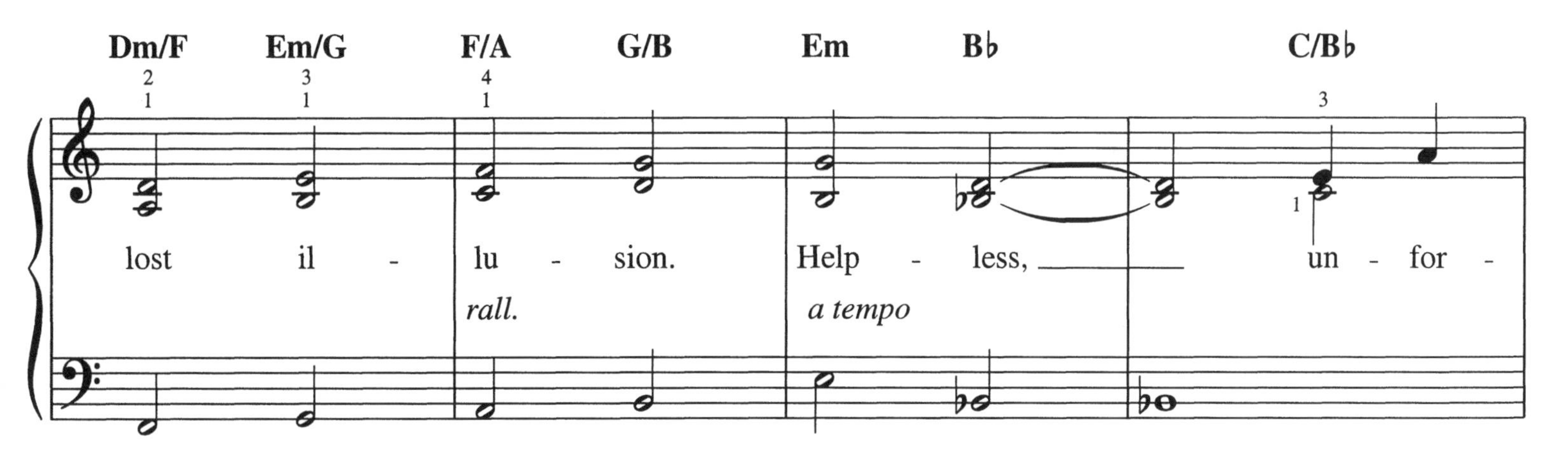
Dm/F Em/G F/A G/B Em B♭ C/B♭
lost il - lu - sion. Help - less, un - for -
rall. a tempo

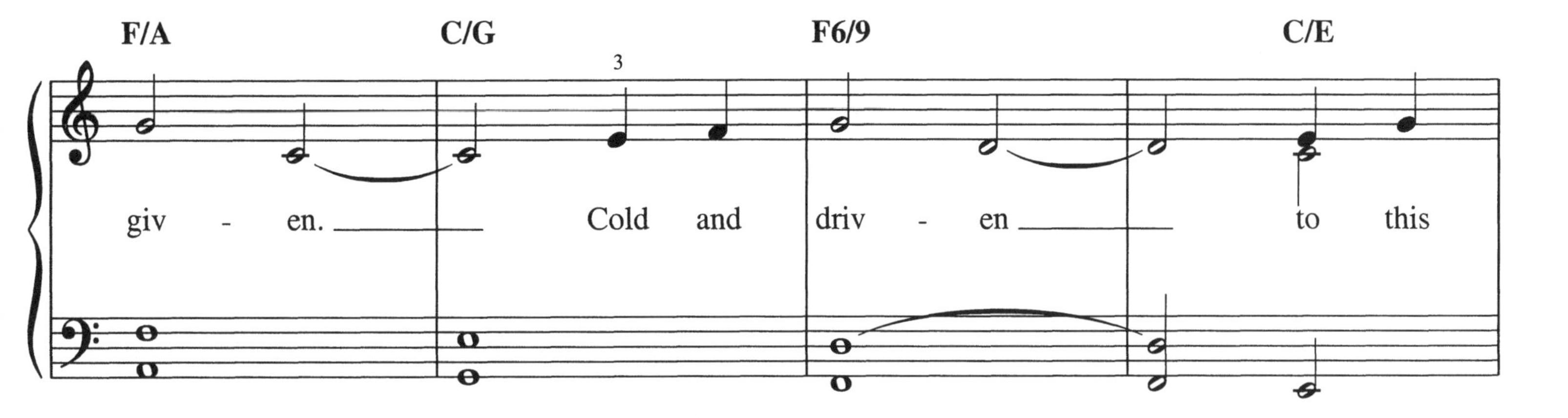
F/A C/G F6/9 C/E
giv - en. Cold and driv - en to this

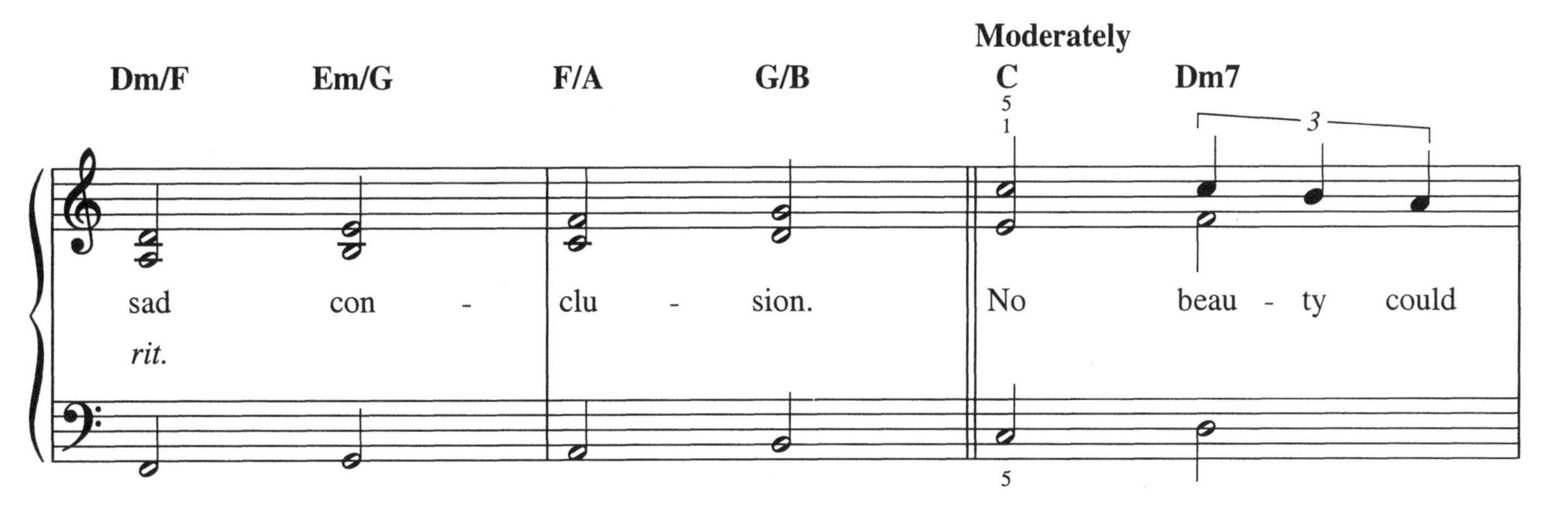
Moderately
Dm/F Em/G F/A G/B C Dm7
sad con - clu - sion. No beau - ty could
rit.

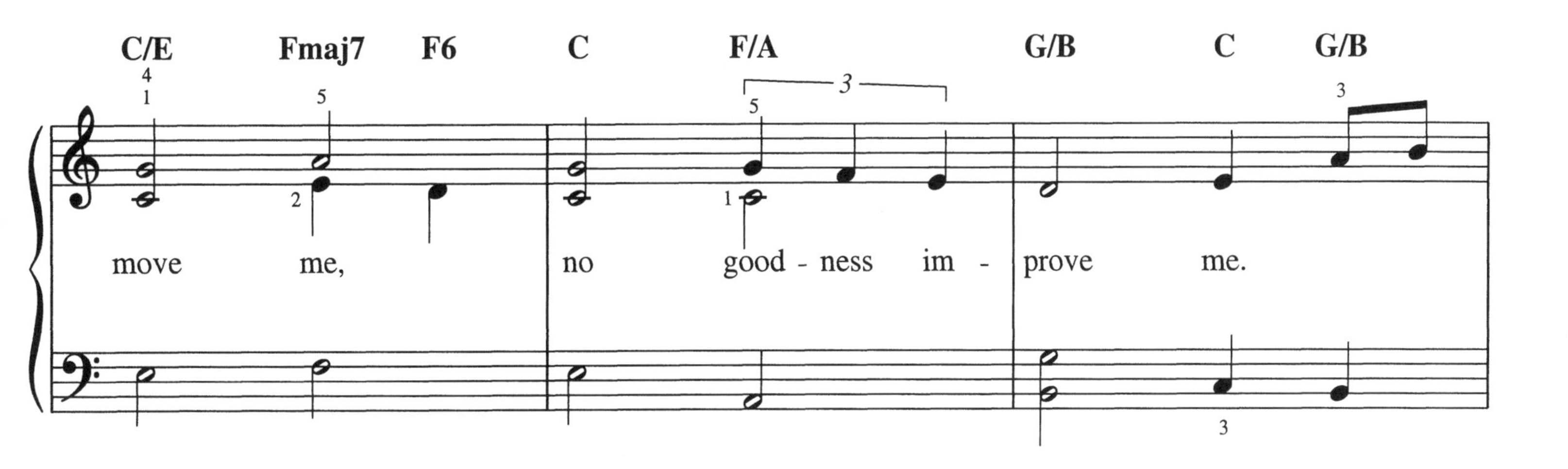
C/E Fmaj7 F6 C F/A G/B C G/B
move me, no good - ness im - prove me.

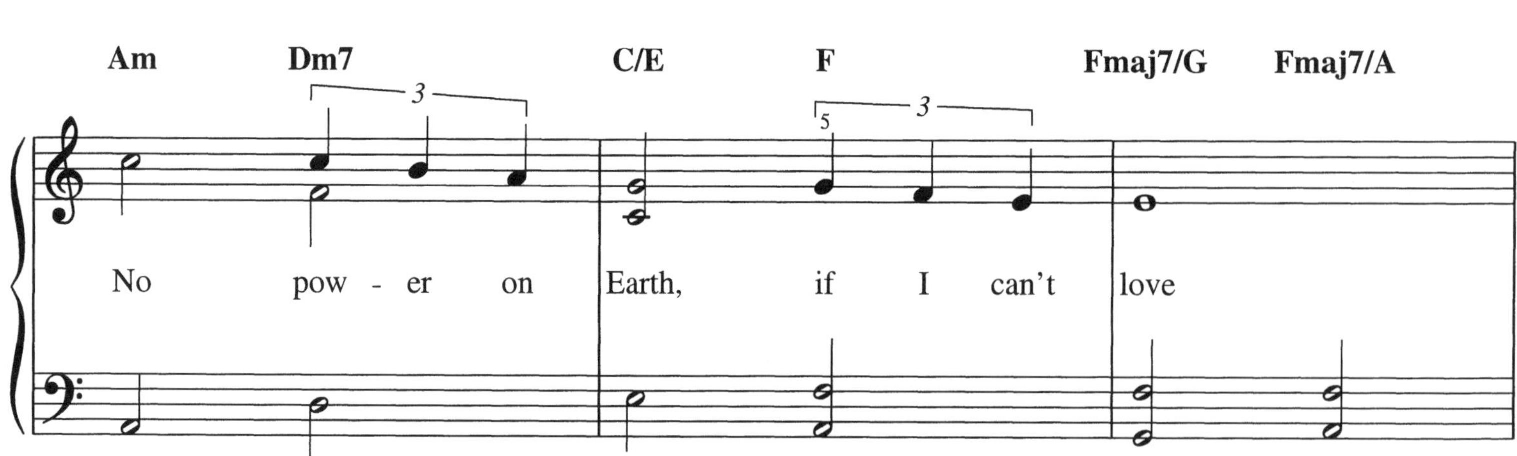
Am Dm7 C/E F Fmaj7/G Fmaj7/A
No pow - er on Earth, if I can't love

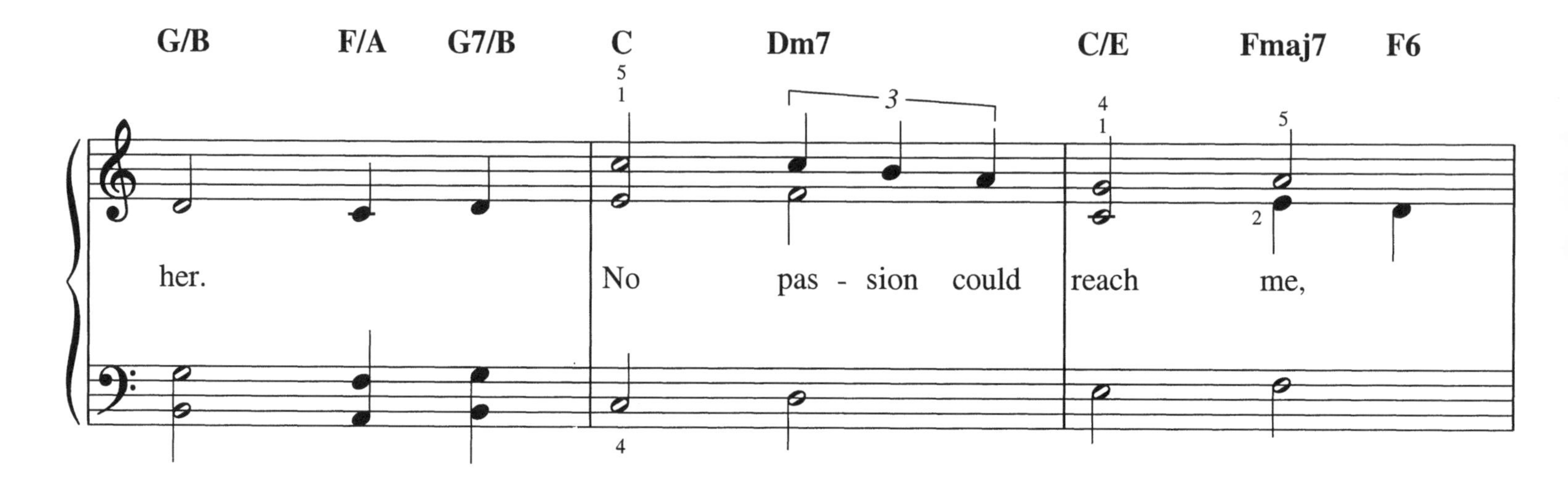
G/B F/A G7/B C Dm7 C/E Fmaj7 F6
her. No pas - sion could reach me,

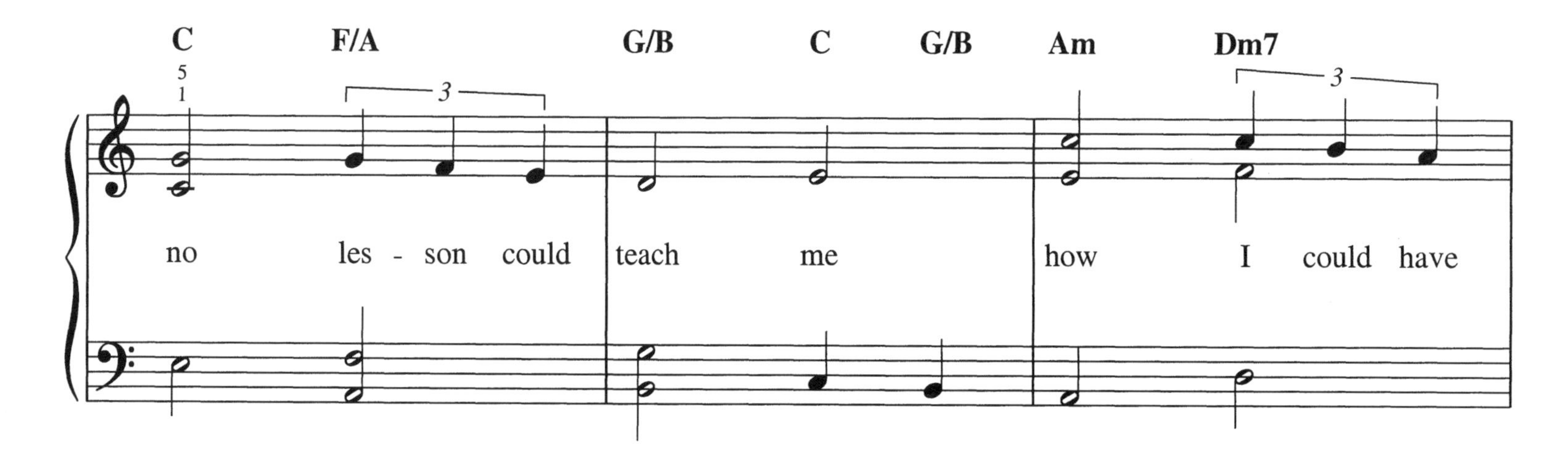
C F/A G/B C G/B Am Dm7
no les - son could teach me how I could have

C/E F Am Em B♭
loved her and make her love me too. If I

Agitated
F/A
Fm/A♭
G7
Am
can't love her, then who?
rit.
f

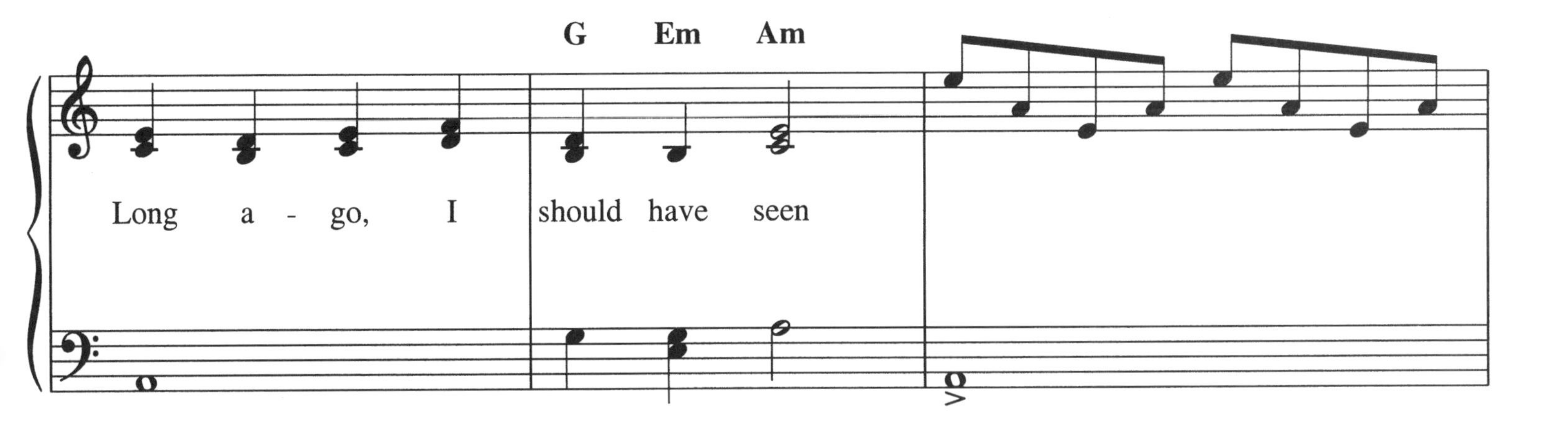
G Em Am
Long a - go, I should have seen

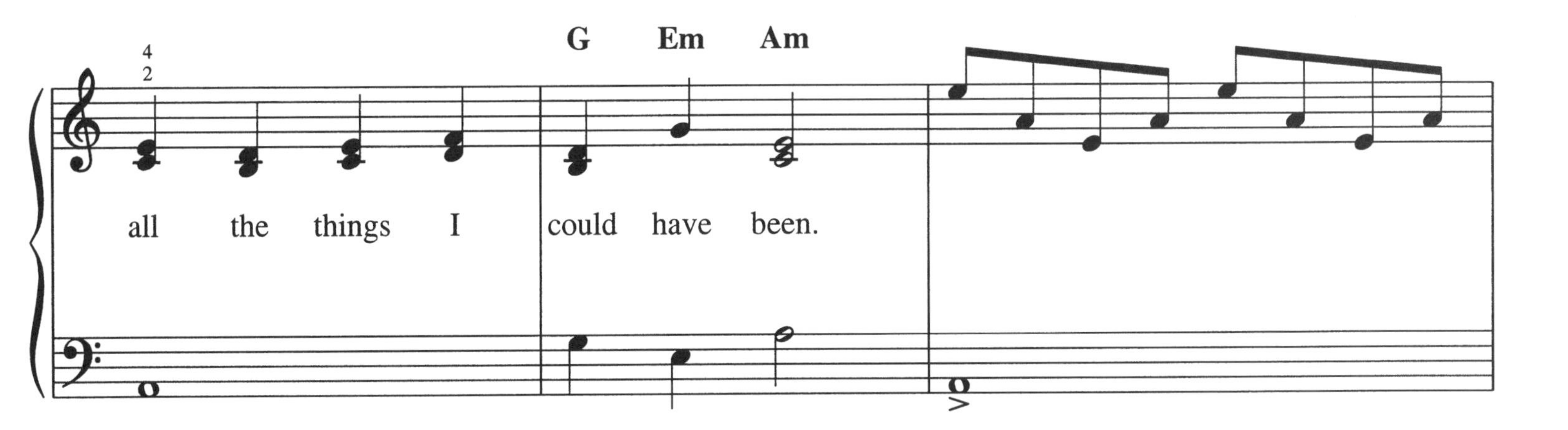
G Em Am
all the things I could have been.

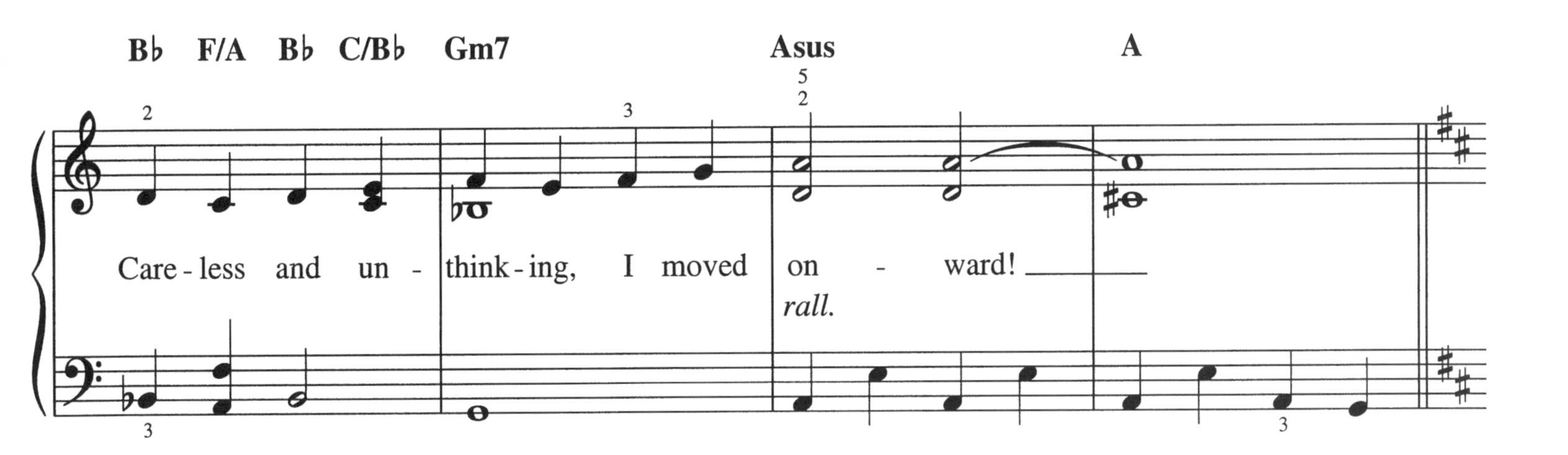
B♭ F/A B♭ C/B♭ Gm7
Asus
A
Care - less and un - think - ing, I moved on - ward!
rall.

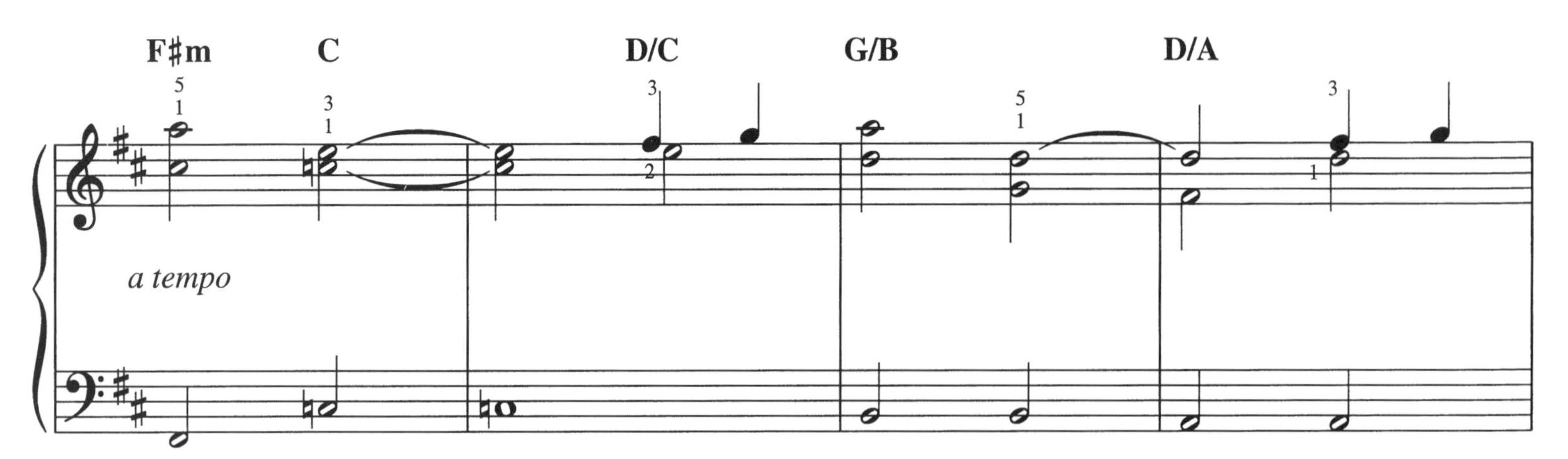
F♯m
C
D/C
G/B
D/A
a tempo

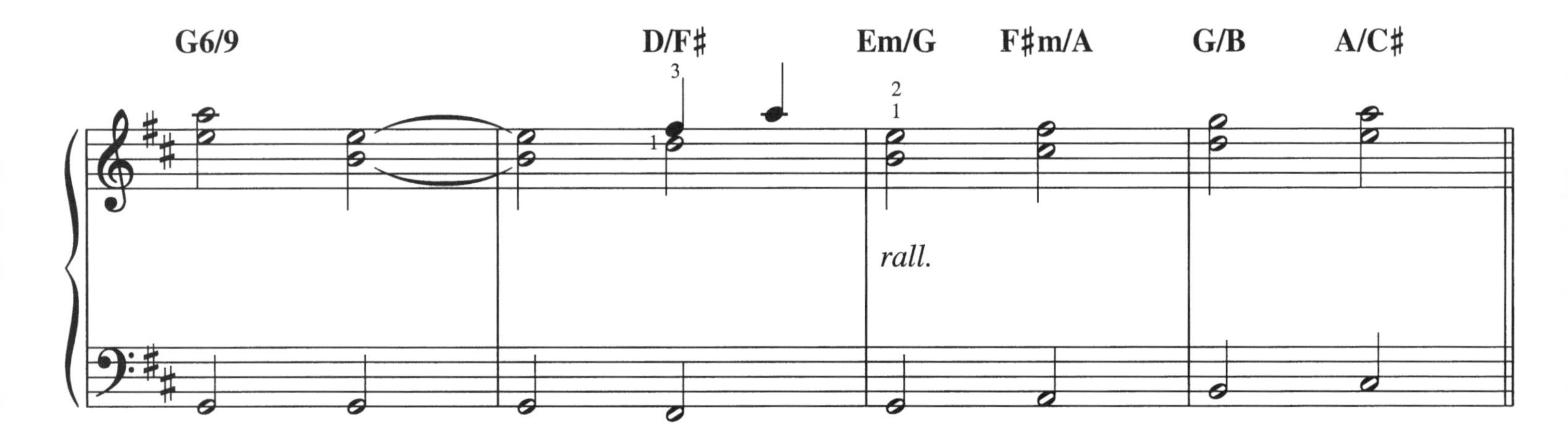
G6/9
D/F♯
Em/G
F♯m/A
G/B
A/C♯
rall.

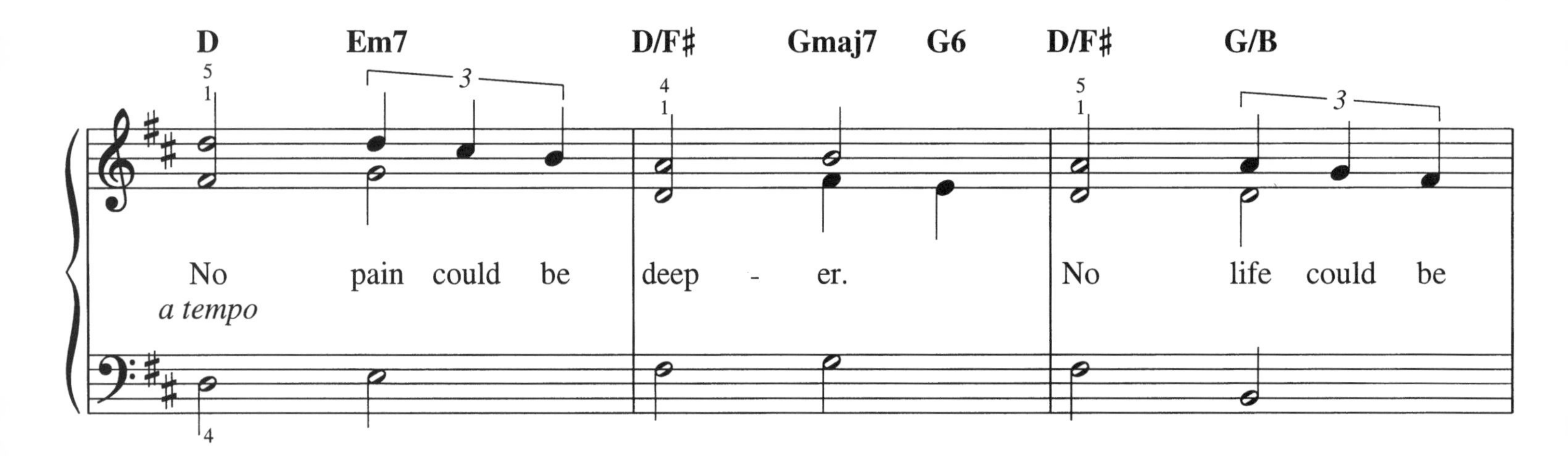
D
Em7
D/F♯
Gmaj7
G6
D/F♯
G/B
No pain could be deep - er. No life could be
a tempo

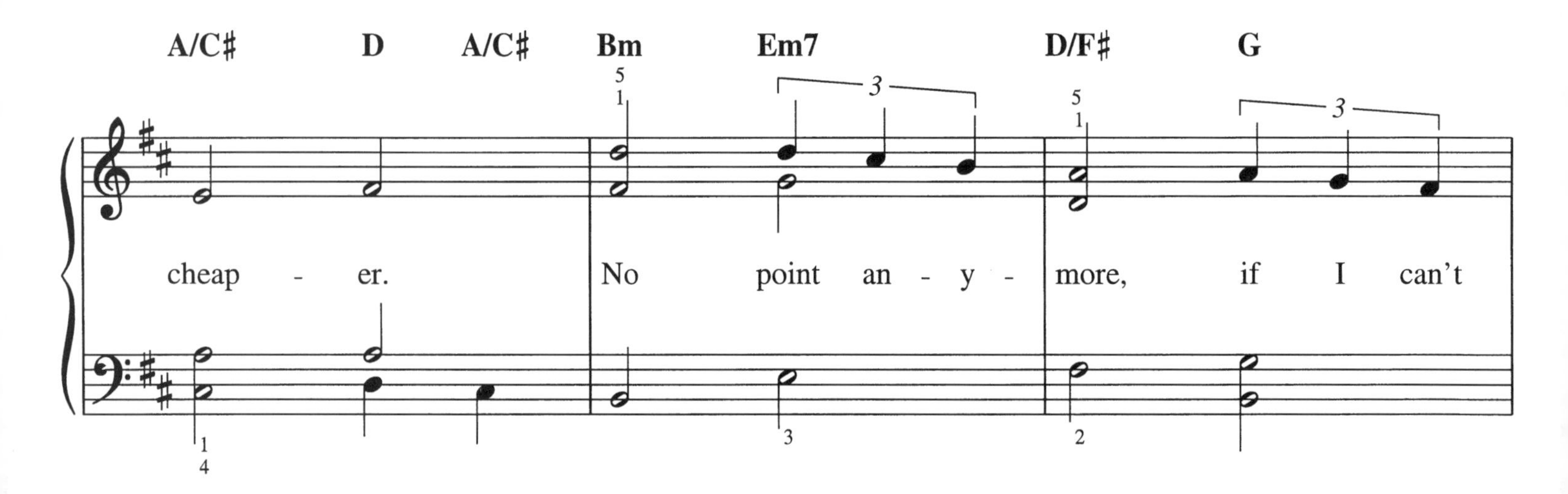
A/C♯
D
A/C♯
Bm
Em7
D/F♯
G
cheap - er. No point an - y - more, if I can't

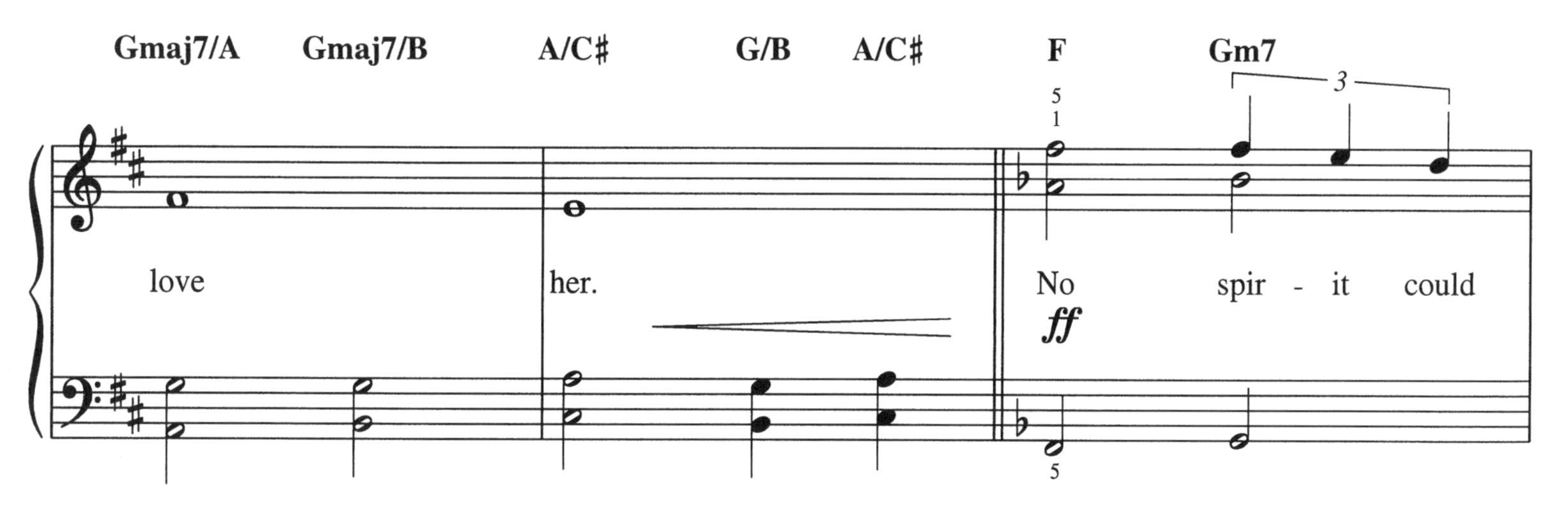
Gmaj7/A
Gmaj7/B
A/C♯
G/B
A/C♯
F
Gm7
love
her.
No spir - it could
ff

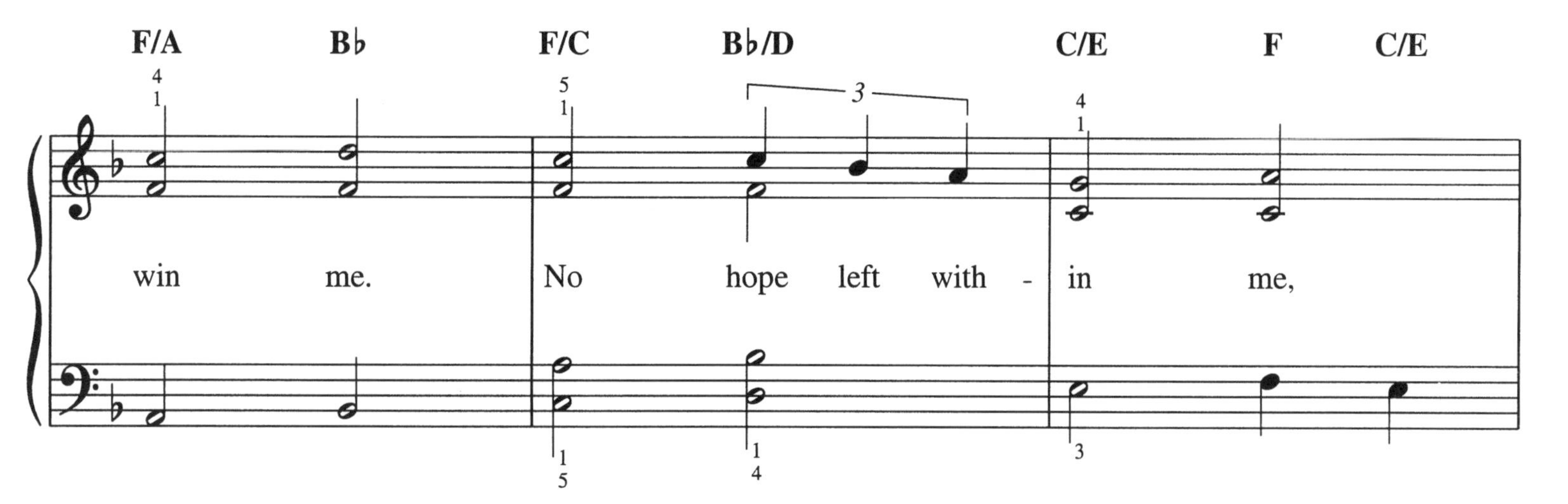
F/A
B♭
F/C
B♭/D
C/E
F
C/E
win me.
No hope left with - in me,

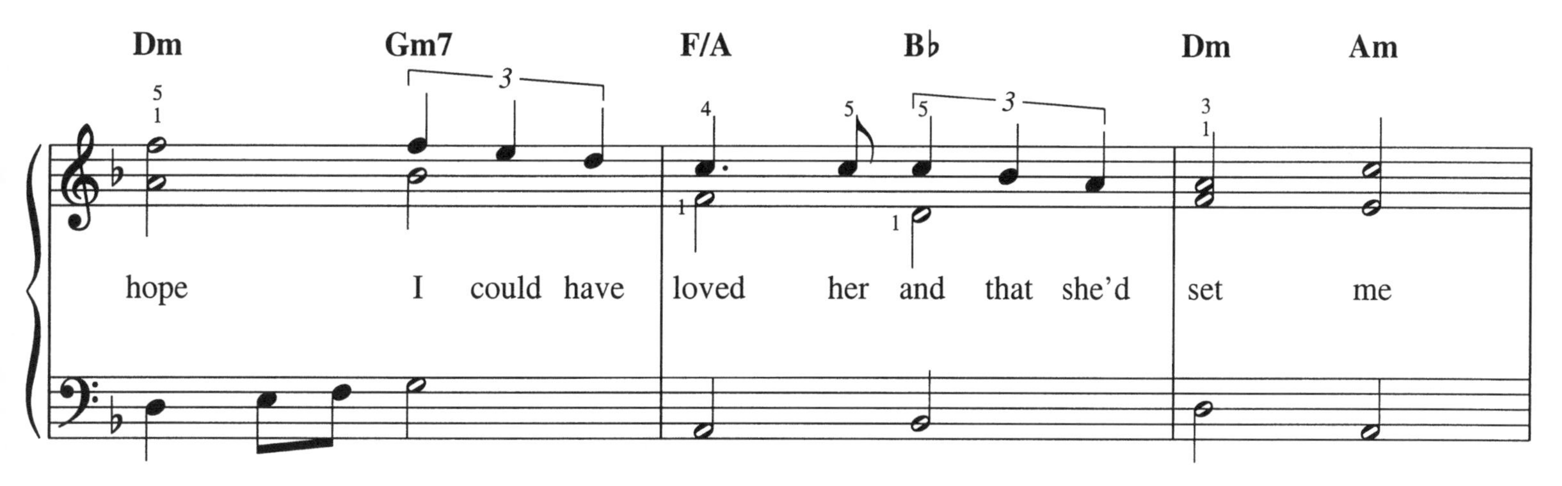
Dm
Gm7
F/A
B♭
Dm
Am
hope I could have loved her and that she'd set me

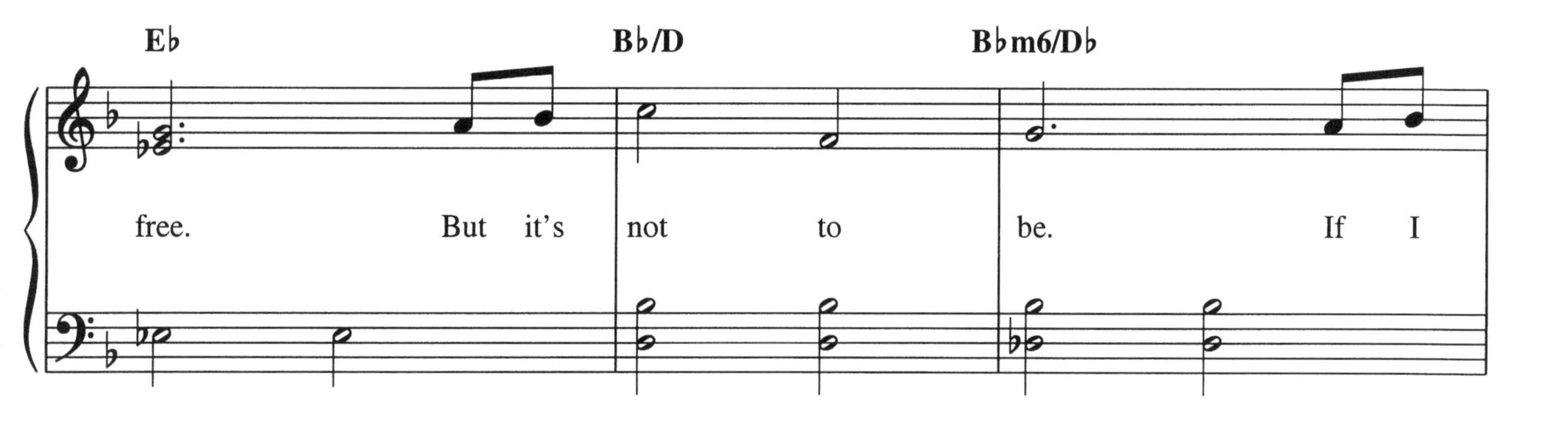
E♭
B♭/D
B♭m6/D♭
free. But it's not to be. If I

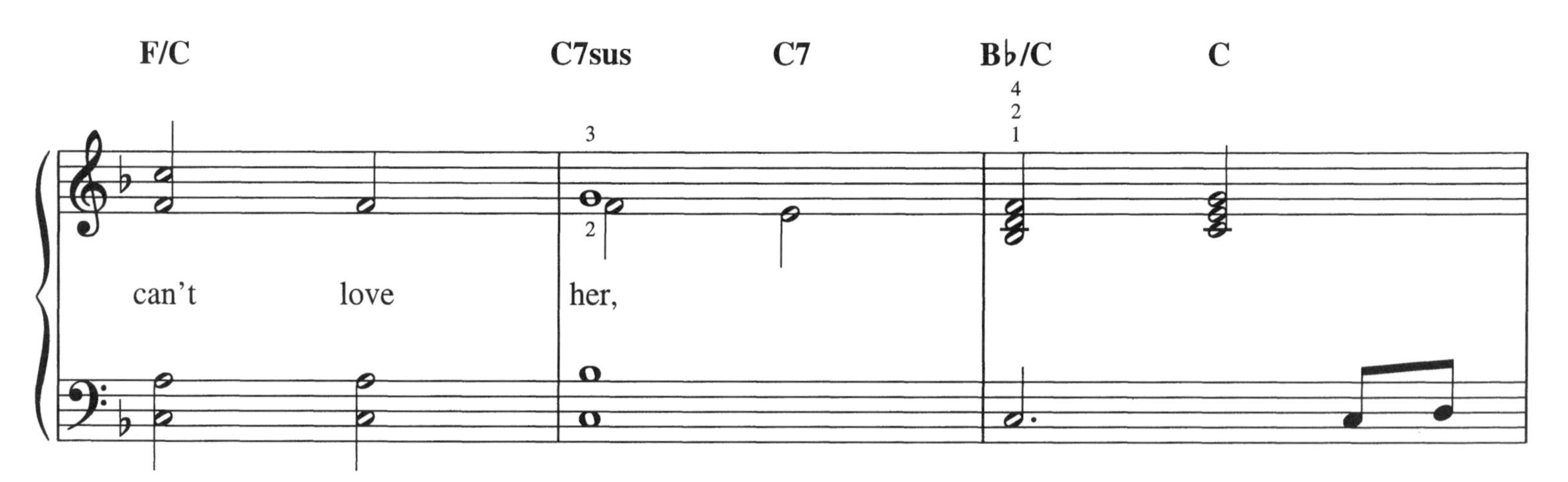
F/C
C7sus
C7
B♭/C
C
can't
love
her,

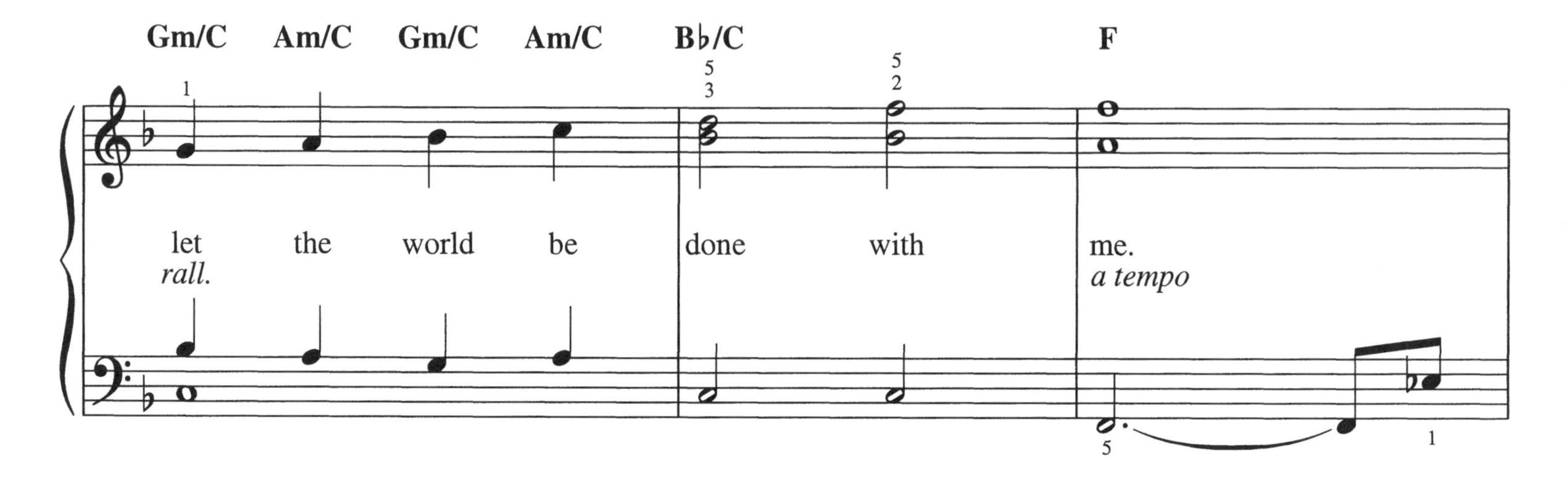
Gm/C
Am/C
Gm/C
Am/C
B♭/C
F
let
the
world
be
done
with
me.
rall.
a tempo

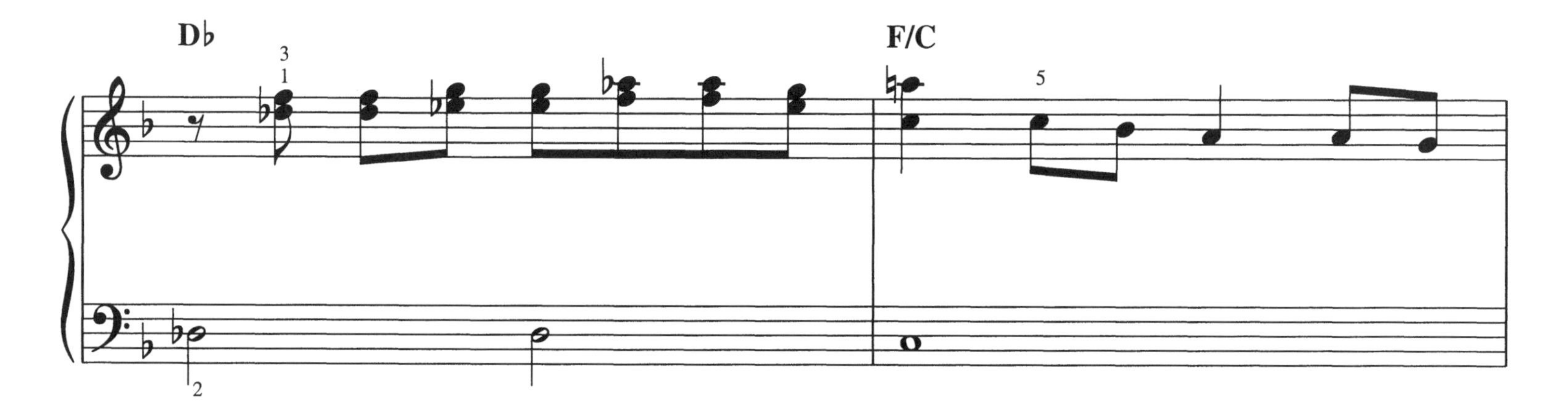
D♭
F/C

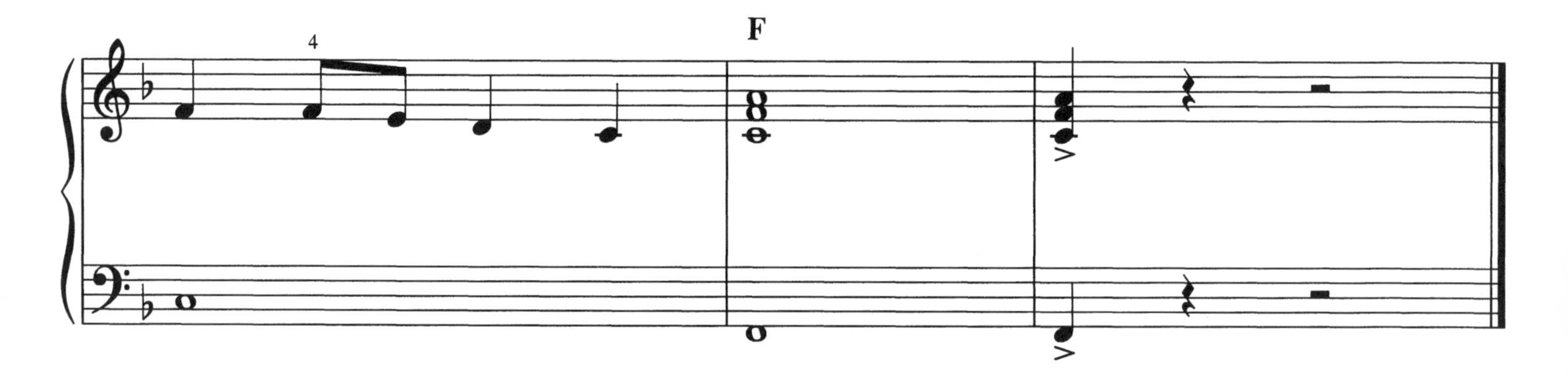
F

SOMETHING THERE

Lyrics by HOWARD ASHMAN
Music by ALAN MENKEN

G7sus
G7
C
G7sus
G7

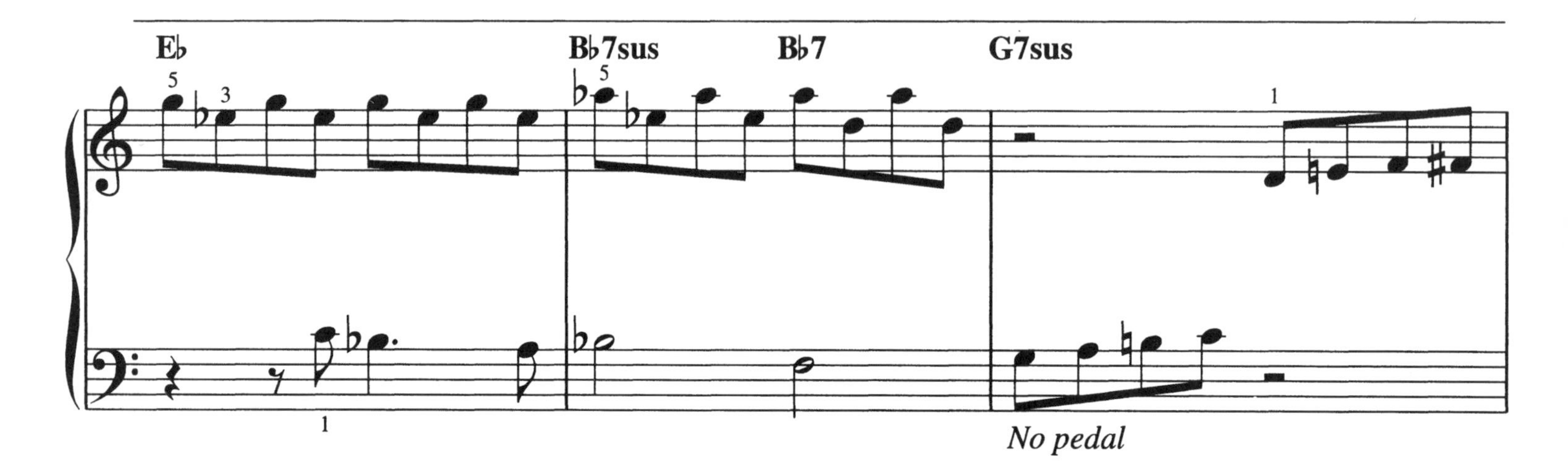
E♭
B♭7sus
B♭7
G7sus
No pedal

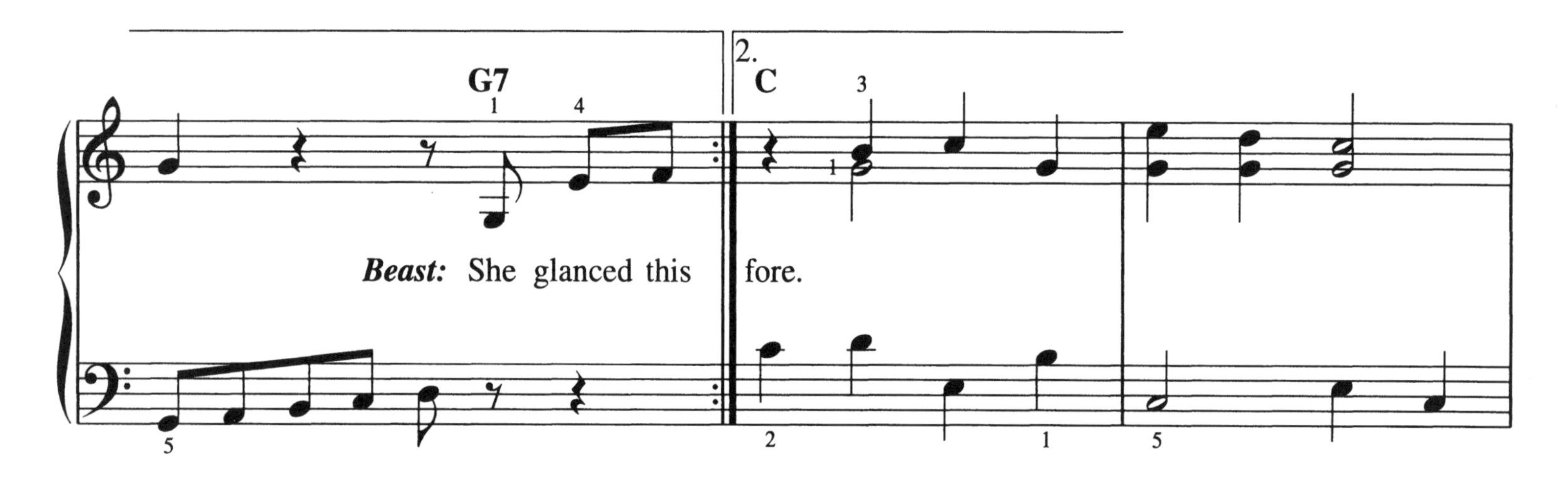
G7
2.
C
Beast: She glanced this
fore.

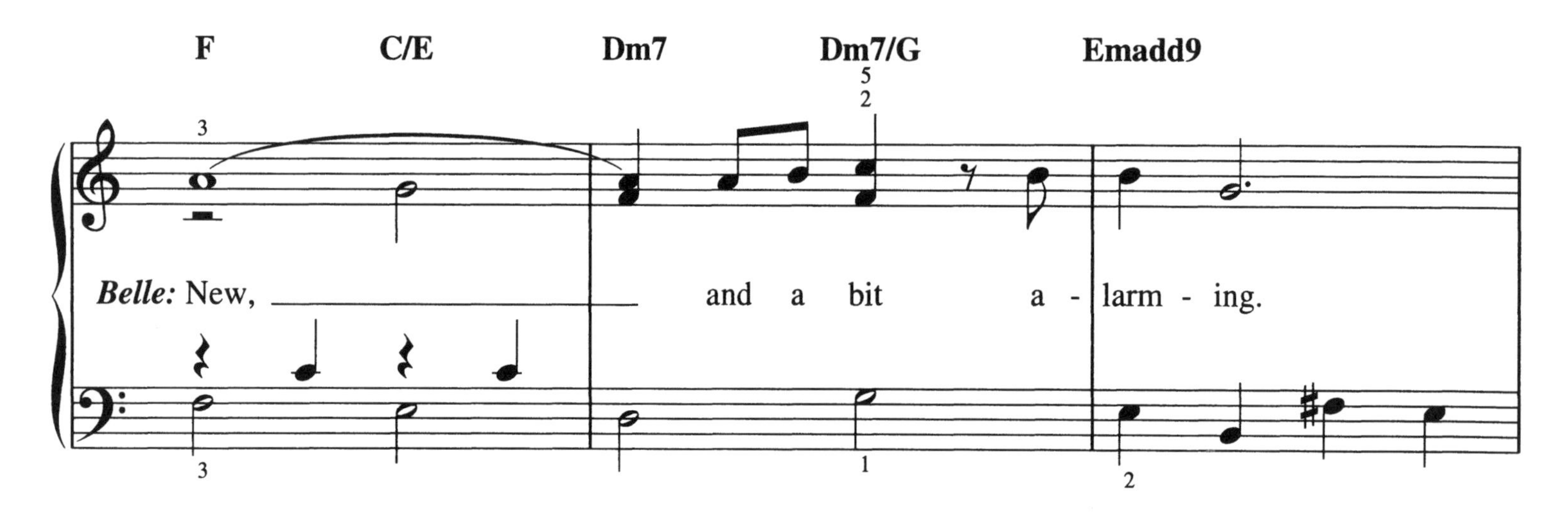
F
C/E
Dm7
Dm7/G
Emadd9
Belle: New,
and a bit a - larm - ing.

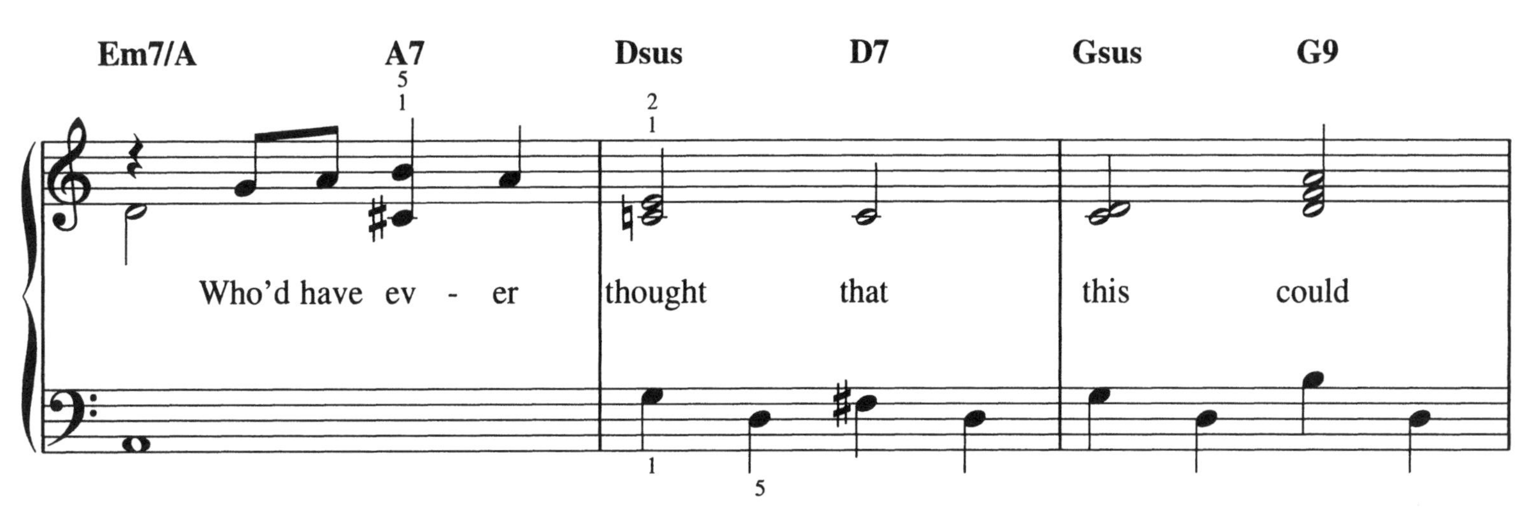
Em7/A
A7
Dsus
D7
Gsus
G9
Who'd have ev - er thought that this could

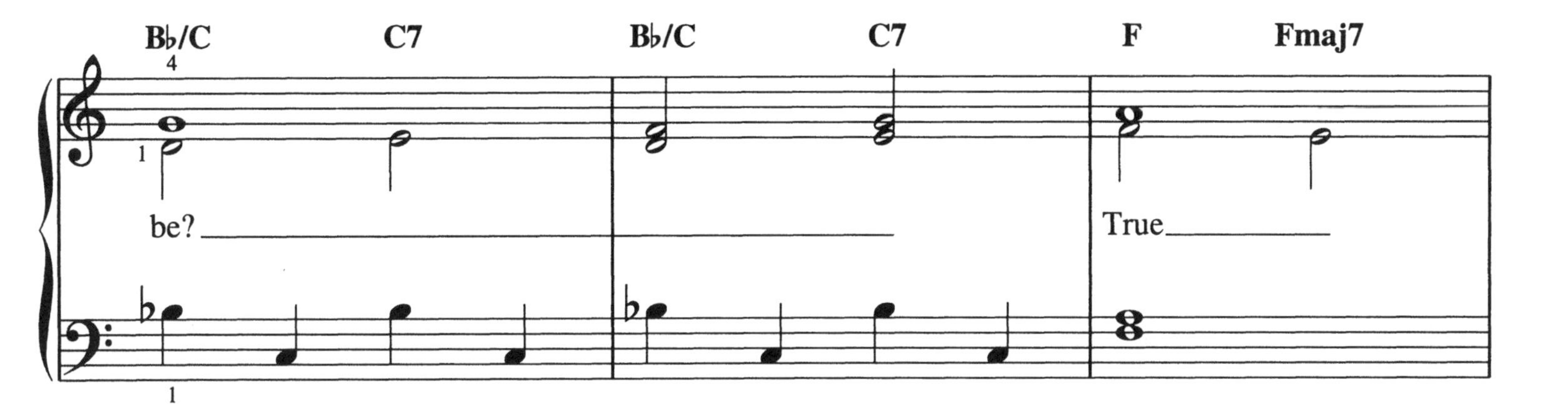
B♭/C
C7
B♭/C
C7
F
Fmaj7
be?
True

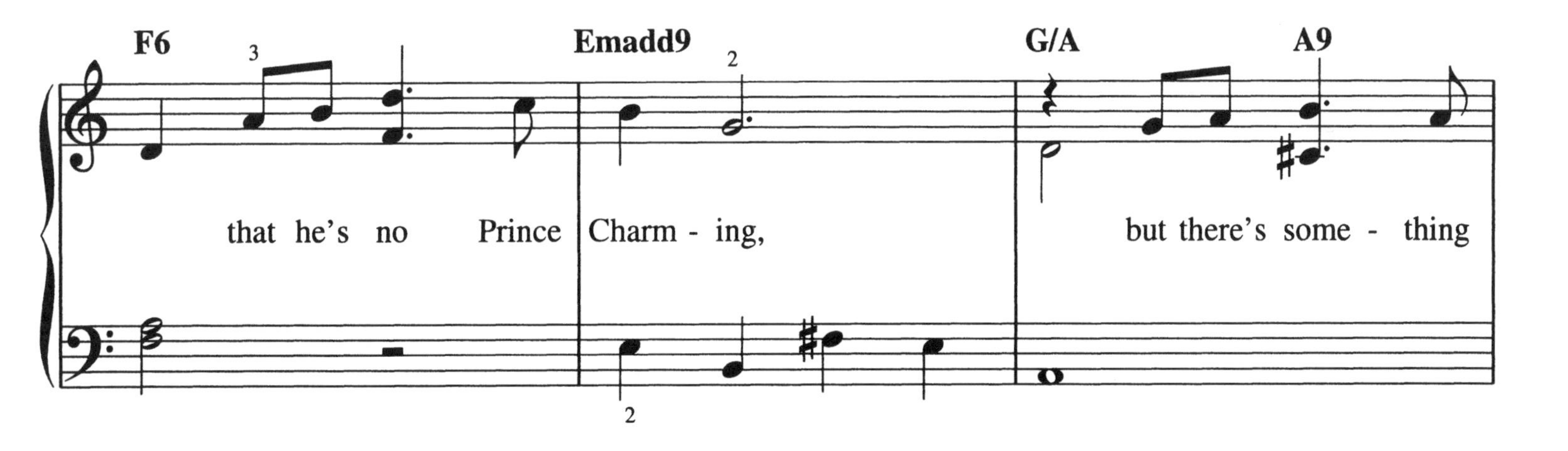
F6
Emadd9
G/A
A9
that he's no Prince Charm - ing, but there's some - thing

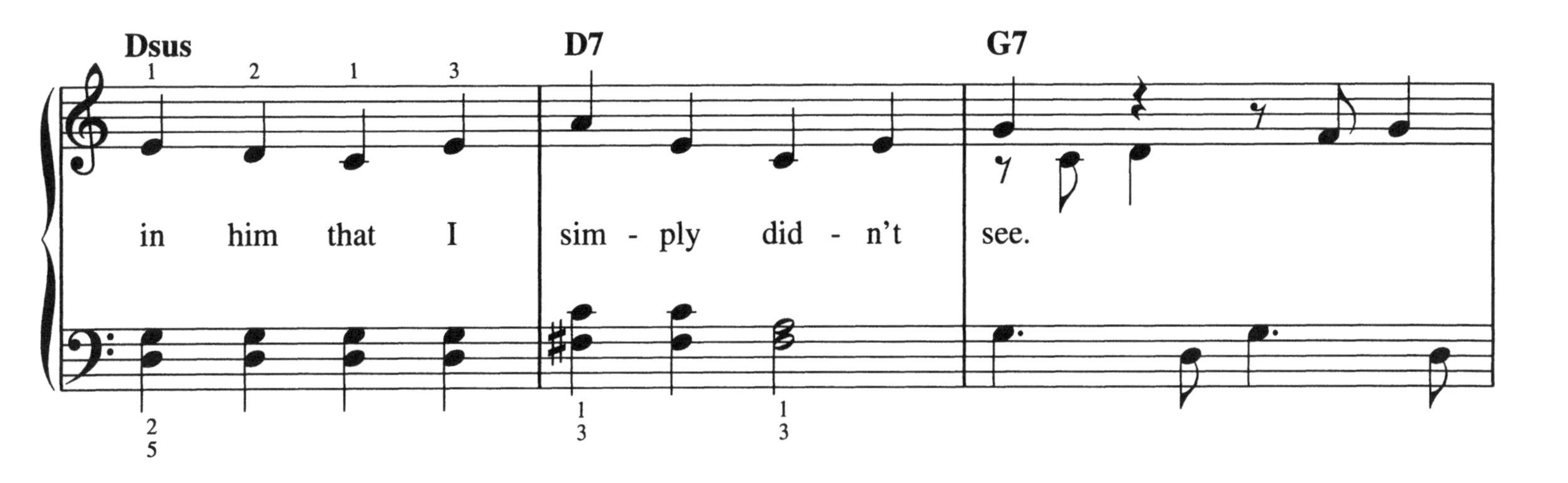
Dsus
D7
G7
in him that I sim - ply did - n't see.

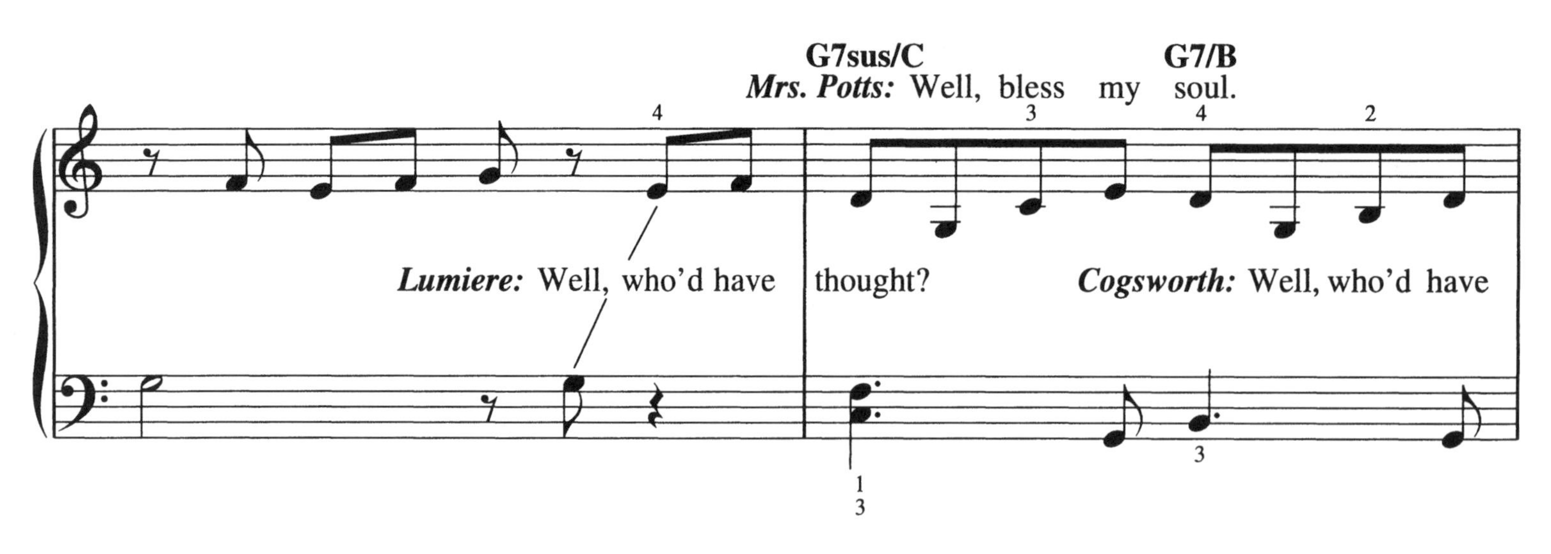
G7sus/C
G7/B
Mrs. Potts: Well, bless my soul.
Lumiere: Well, who'd have thought?
Cogsworth: Well, who'd have

C
Well, who in - deed?
G7sus/C
G7/B
known?
Lumiere: And who'd have
guessed they'd come to - geth - er on their

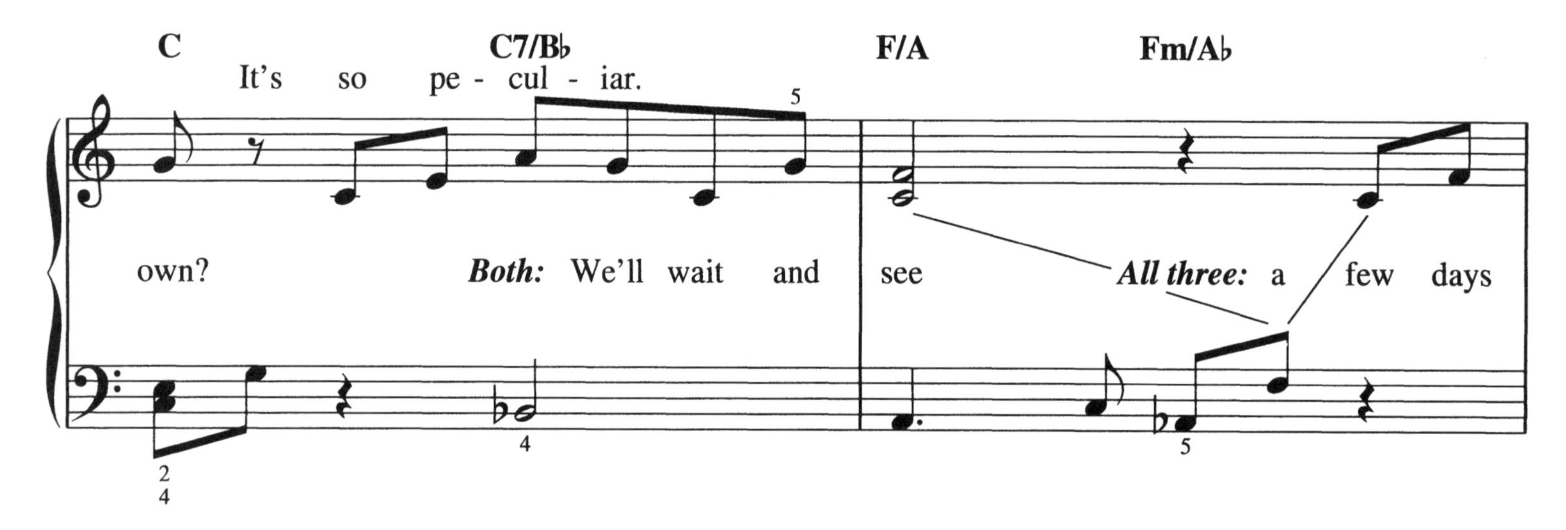
C
C7/B♭
It's so pe - cul - iar.
F/A
Fm/A♭
own?
Both: We'll wait and
see
All three: a few days

E7/G♯
A7/G
Dm7/F
G7
more.
There may be
some - thing there that was - n't there be -

Cadd9
C
G7sus
G7/B
fore. Cogsworth: You know, perhaps there's something there that was-n't there be-

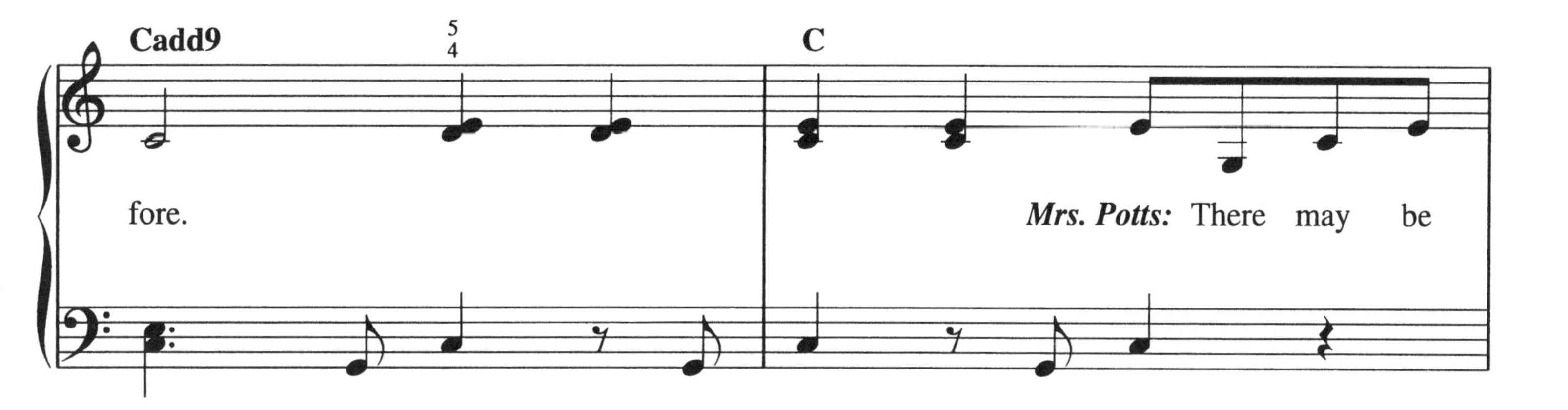
Cadd9
5
4
C
fore.
Mrs. Potts: There may be

G7sus
G7/B
2 3
Cadd9
1
some-thing there that was-n't there be- fore.

rit.

HUMAN AGAIN

Lyrics by HOWARD ASHMAN
Music by ALAN MENKEN

Gentle Parisian Waltz

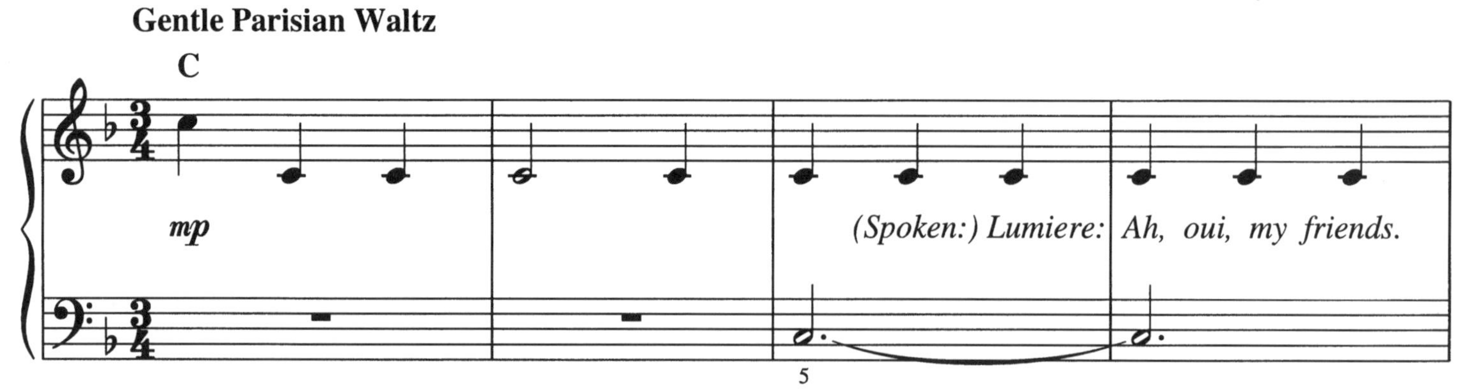
C
mp
(Spoken:) Lumiere: Ah, oui, my friends.
5

B♭/C
Am/C
B♭/C
Am/C
The day we have waited for... may be at hand!
Add light pedal

Fmaj7
Gm7/C
Fmaj7
Gm/C
Mrs. Potts: Oh, if only that were true, Lumiere!
Lumiere: Ah, human again!
1
2

C7sus
2
2
1
Mrs. Potts: Human again...
rit.
Lumiere: Yes...
think what that means!
(Sung:) I'll be
3

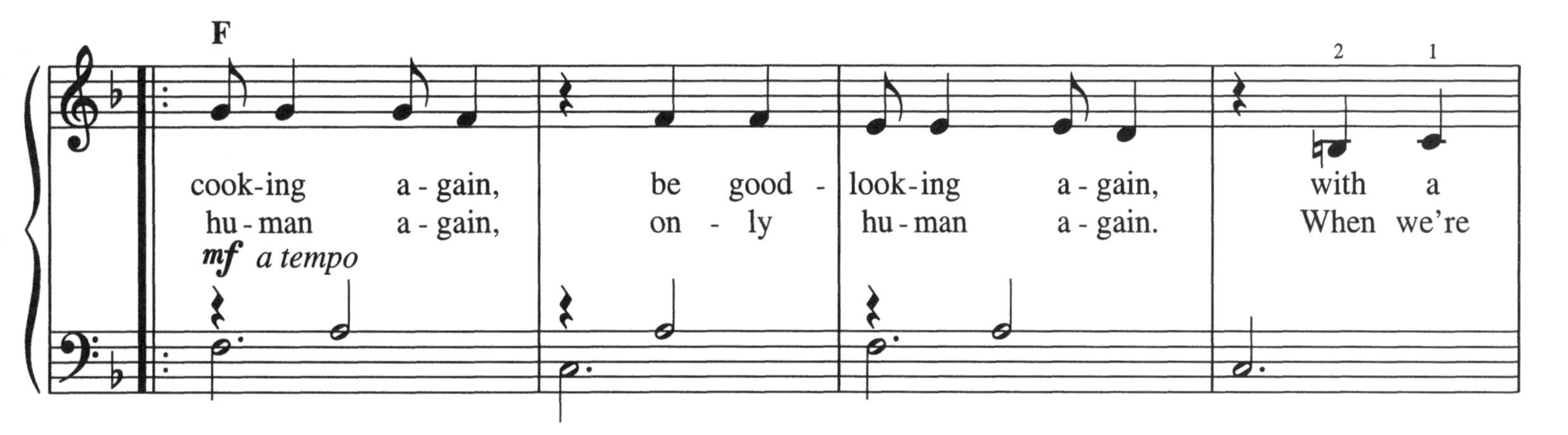
F
cook-ing a-gain, be good-look-ing a-gain, with a
hu-man a-gain, on-ly hu-man a-gain. When we're
mf a tempo

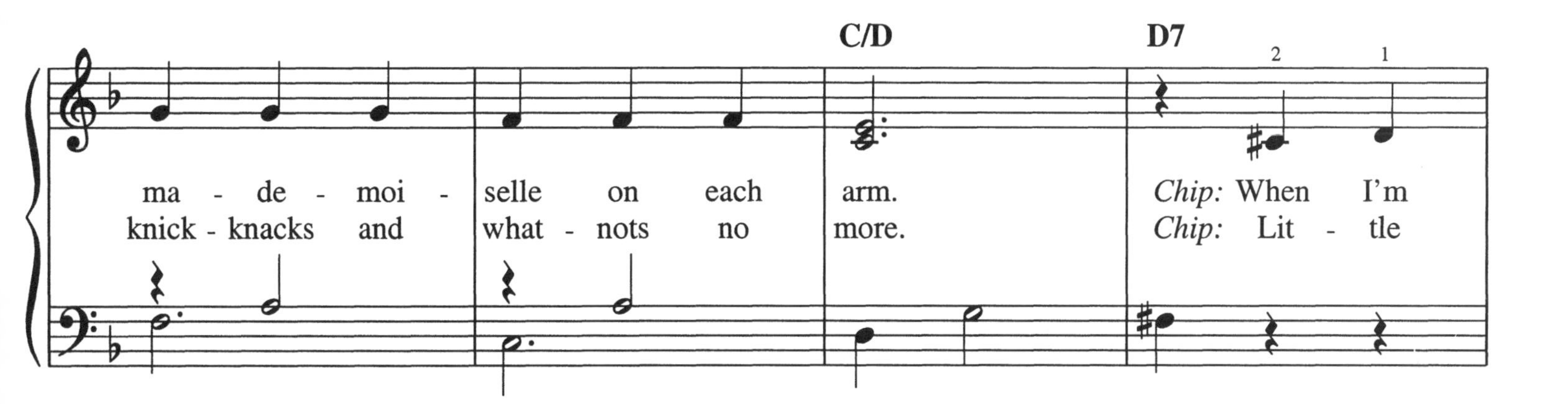
C/D
D7
ma-de-moi-selle on each arm. Chip: When I'm
knick-knacks and what-nots no more. Chip: Lit-tle

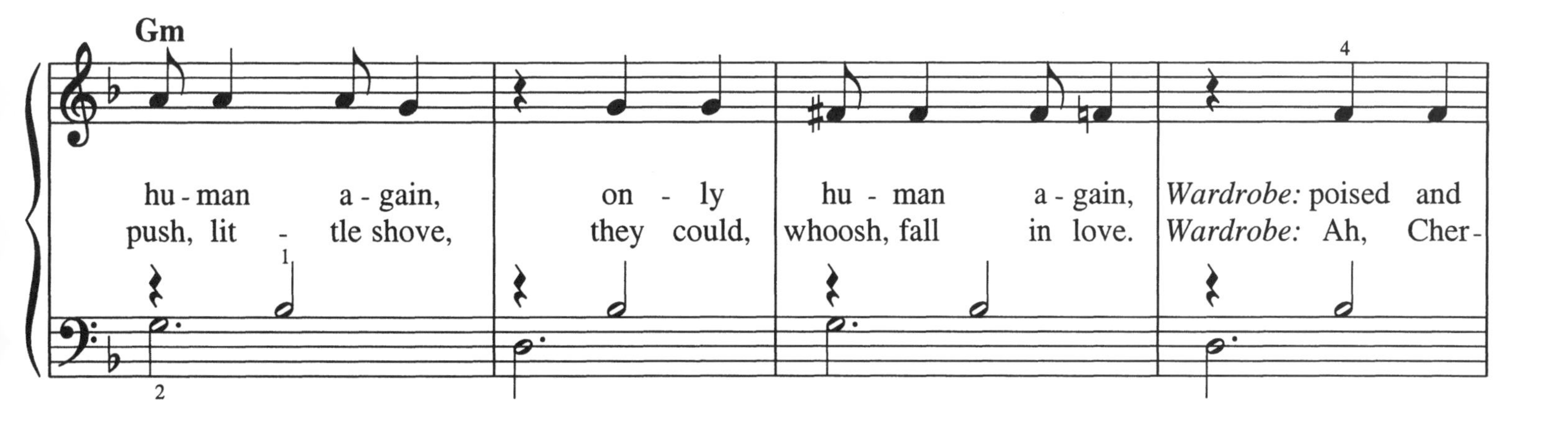
Gm
hu-man a-gain, on-ly hu-man a-gain, Wardrobe: poised and
push, lit-tle shove, they could, whoosh, fall in love. Wardrobe: Ah, Cher-

C7
Gm7
C7
pol-ished and gleam-ing with charm... I'll be
ie, won't it all be top-drawer? I'll wear

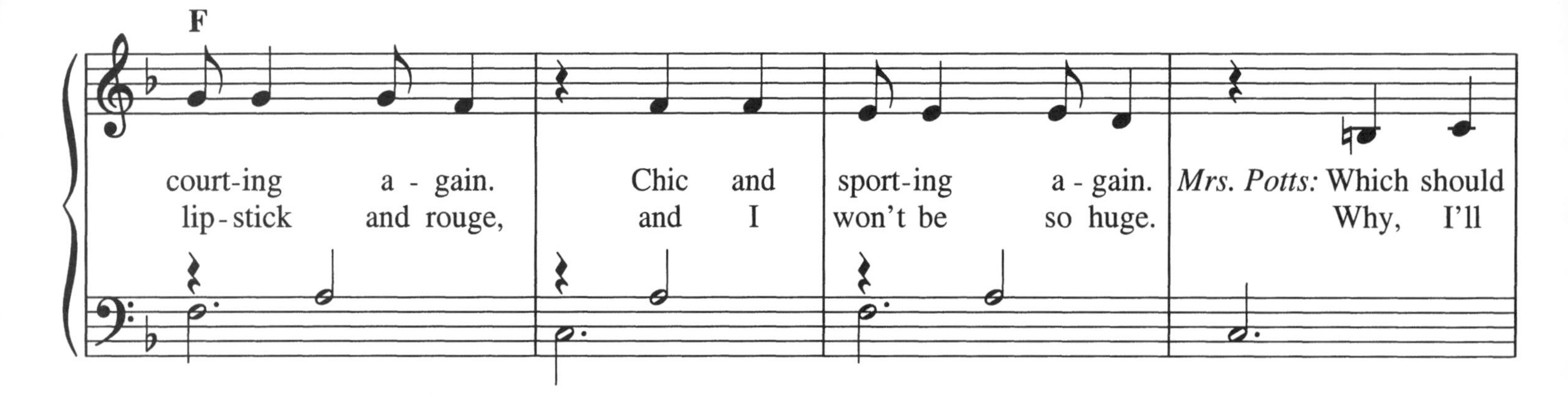
F
court-ing a - gain. Chic and sport-ing a - gain. Mrs. Potts: Which should
lip-stick and rouge, and I won't be so huge. Why, I'll

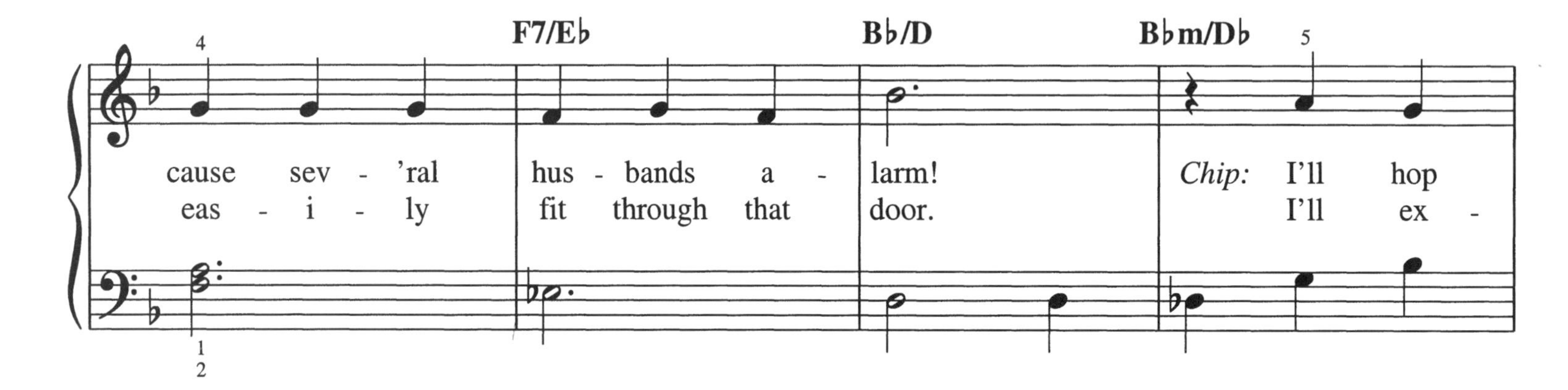
F7/E♭
B♭/D
B♭m/D♭
cause sev - 'ral hus - bands a - larm! Chip: I'll hop
eas - i - ly fit through that door. I'll ex -

F/C
G/B
G7
down off the shelf All 3: and tout suite be my - self Chip: I can't
ude sav - oir faire I'll wear gowns! I'll have hair! It's my

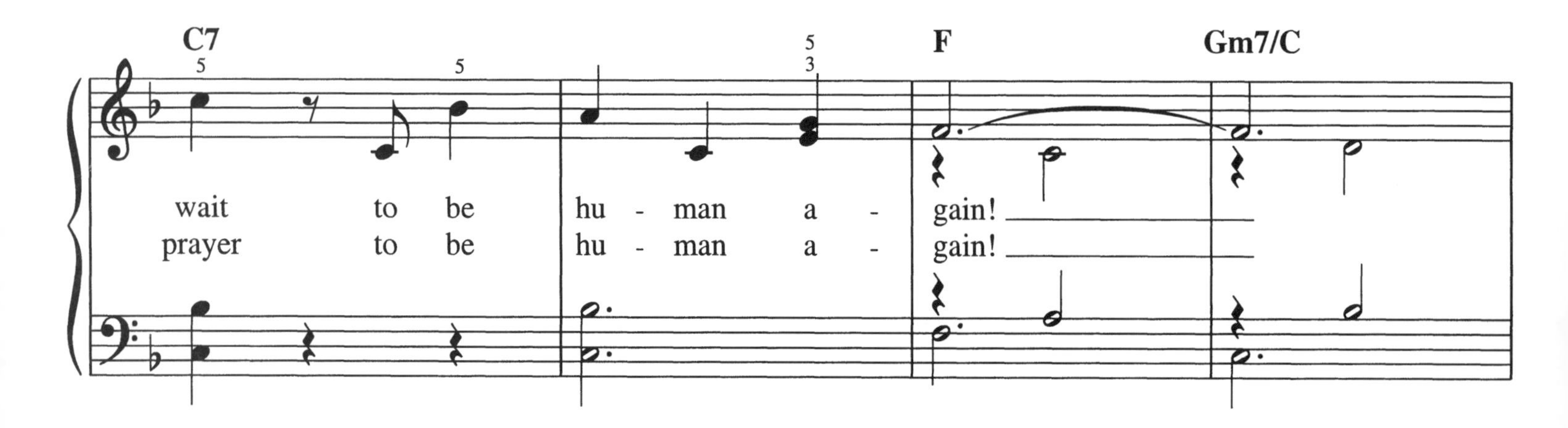
C7
F
Gm7/C
wait to be hu - man a - gain!
prayer to be hu - man a - gain!

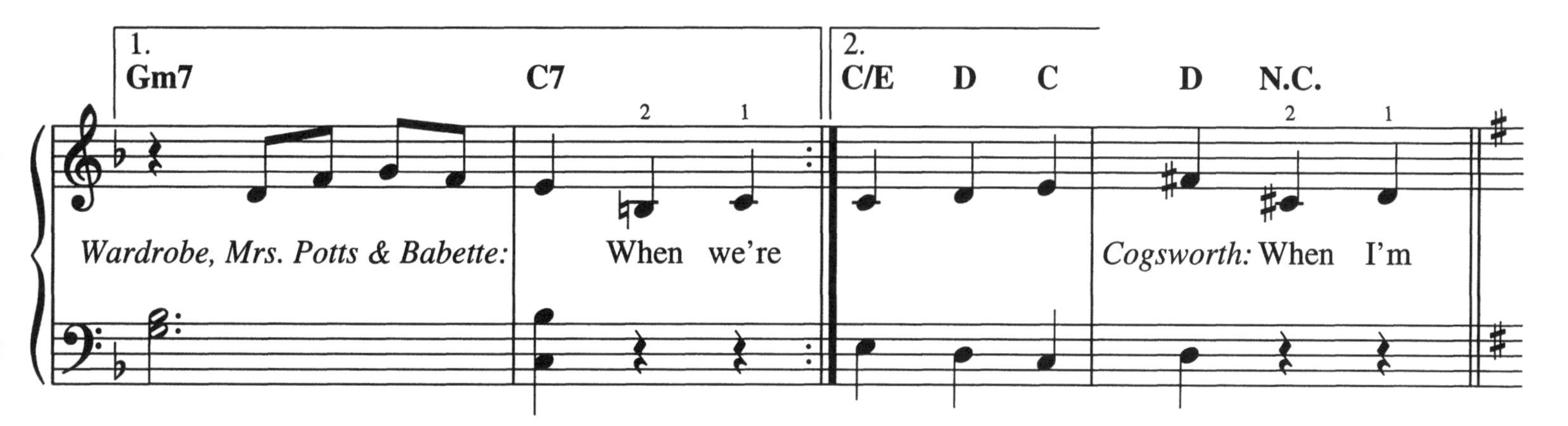
1.
Gm7
C7
2.
C/E D C D N.C.
Wardrobe, Mrs. Potts & Babette: When we're
Cogsworth: When I'm

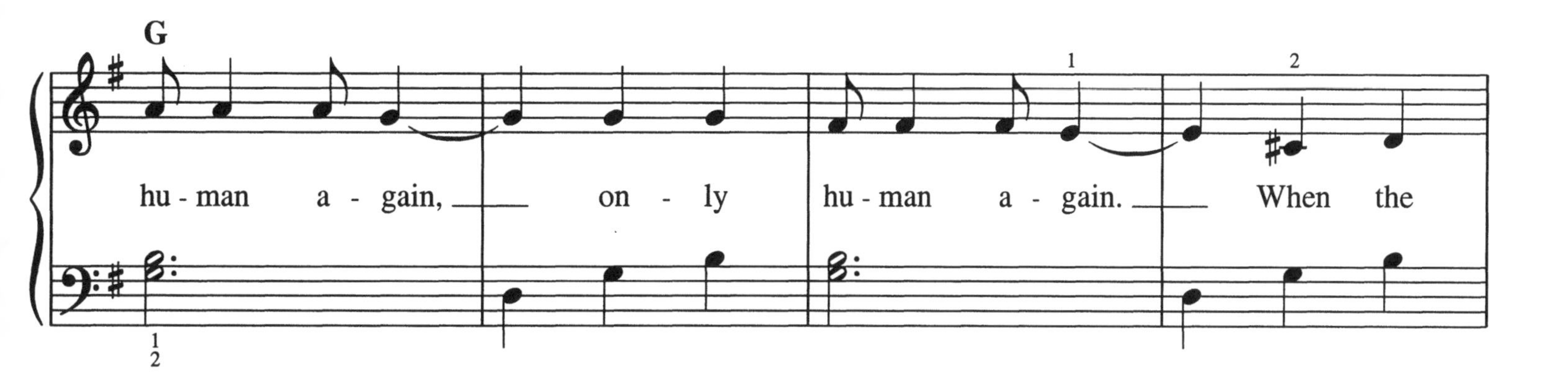
G
hu - man a - gain, on - ly hu - man a - gain. When the

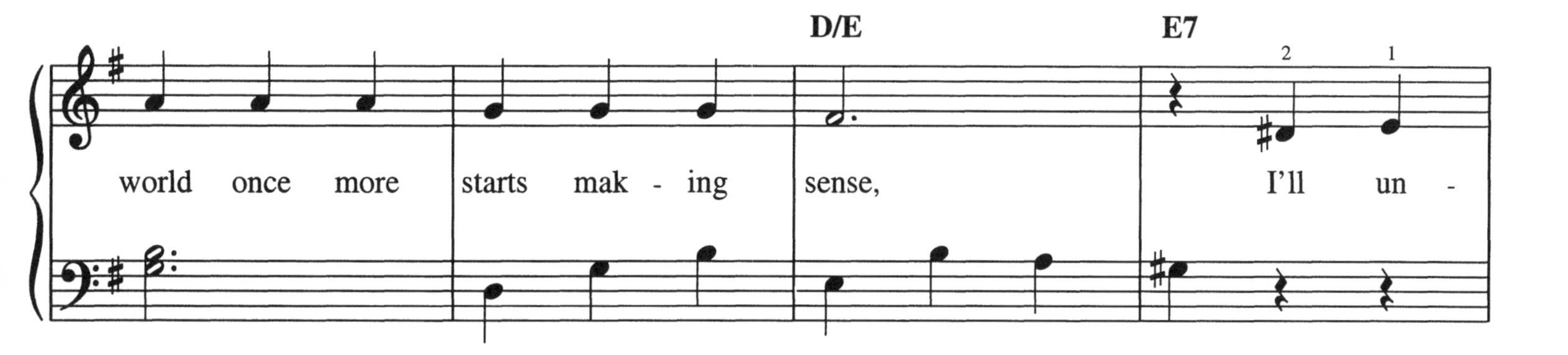
D/E
E7
world once more starts mak - ing sense, I'll un -

Am
wind for a change. Lumiere: Real - ly? That - 'd be strange!
Cogsworth: Can I

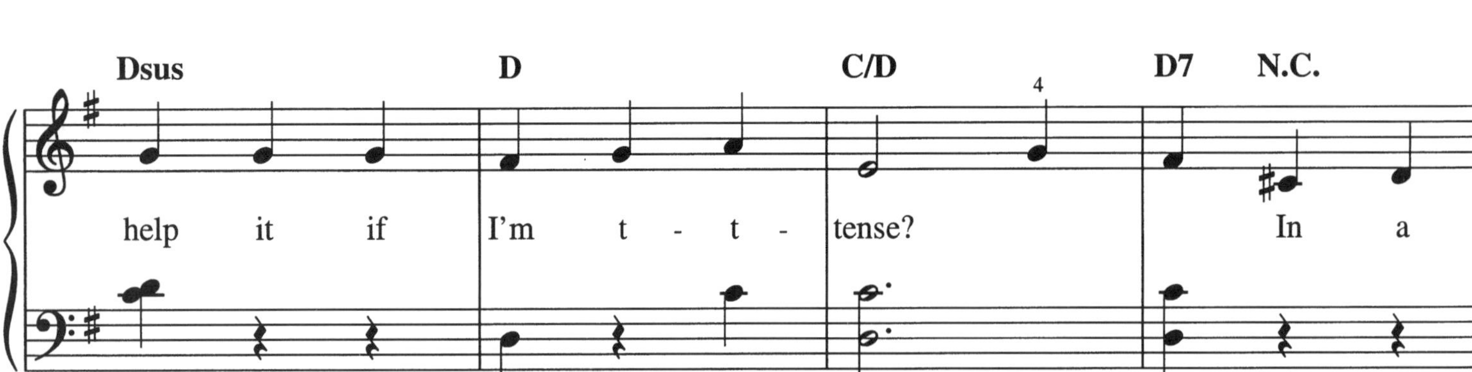
Dsus D C/D D7 N.C.
help it if I'm t - t - tense? In a

G
shack by the sea I'll sit back sip - ping tea, let my

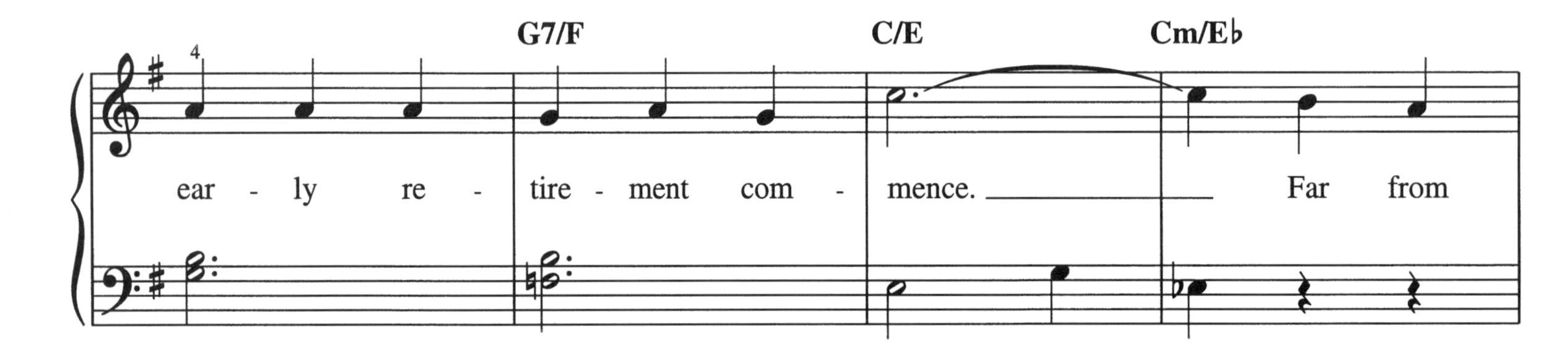
G7/F C/E Cm/E♭
ear - ly re - tire - ment com - mence. Far from

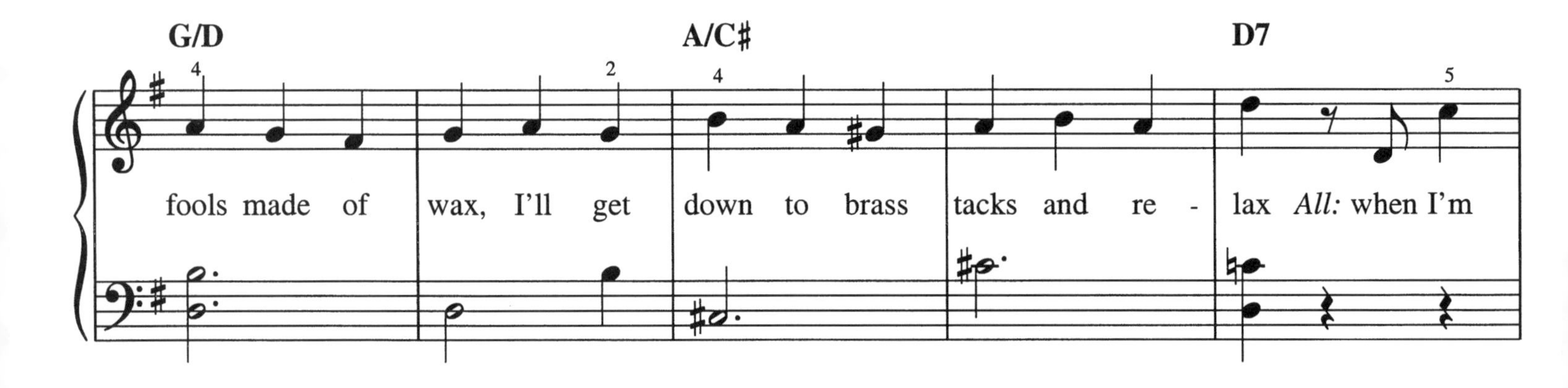
G/D A/C♯ D7
fools made of wax, I'll get down to brass tacks and re - lax All: when I'm

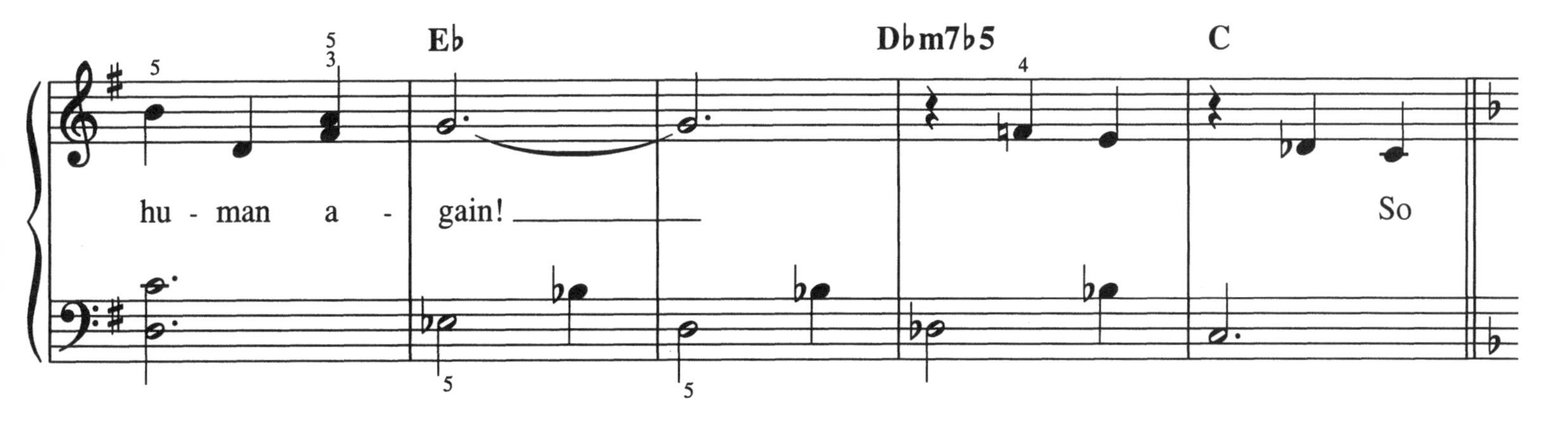
Eb
Dbm7b5
C
hu - man a - gain!
So

Fmaj7
F6
F+
F
Fmaj7
sweep the dust from the floor!
Let's let some
Shine up the brass on the door!
Babette: A - lert the

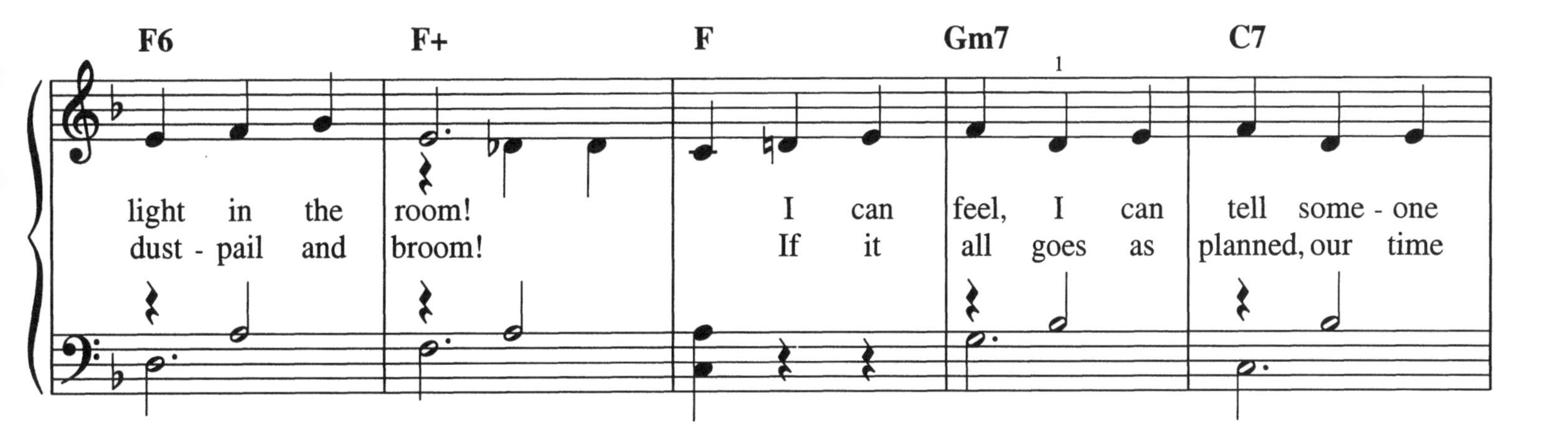
F6
F+
F
Gm7
C7
light in the room!
I can feel, I can tell some - one
dust - pail and broom!
If it all goes as planned, our time

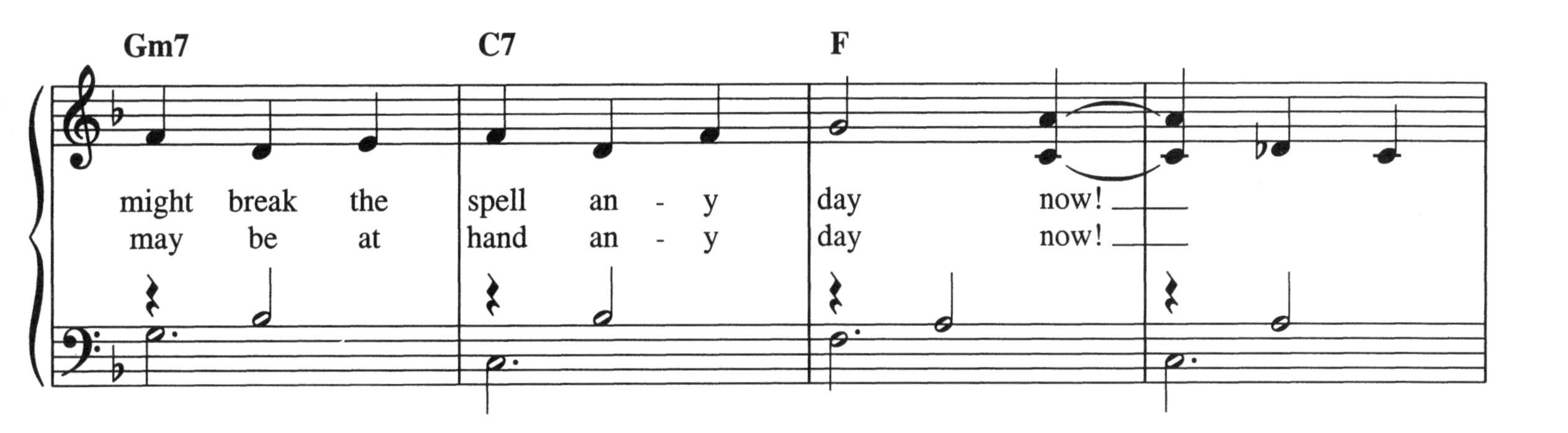
Gm7
C7
F
might break the spell an - y day now!
may be at hand an - y day now!

1.
2.
C7
Lumiere:

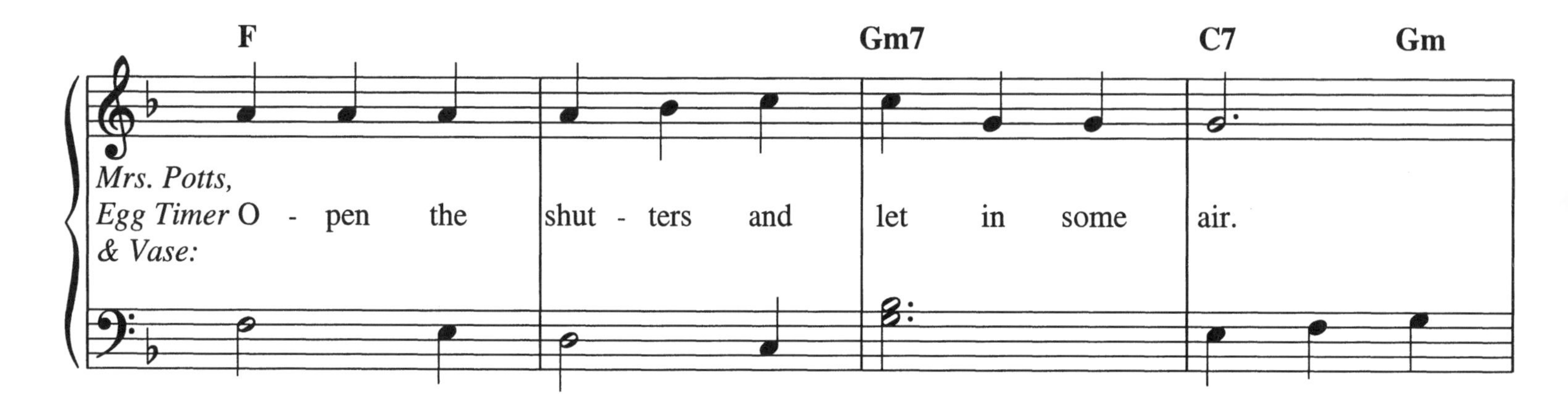
F
Gm7
C7
Gm
Mrs. Potts,
Egg Timer O - pen the shut - ters and let in some air.
& Vase:

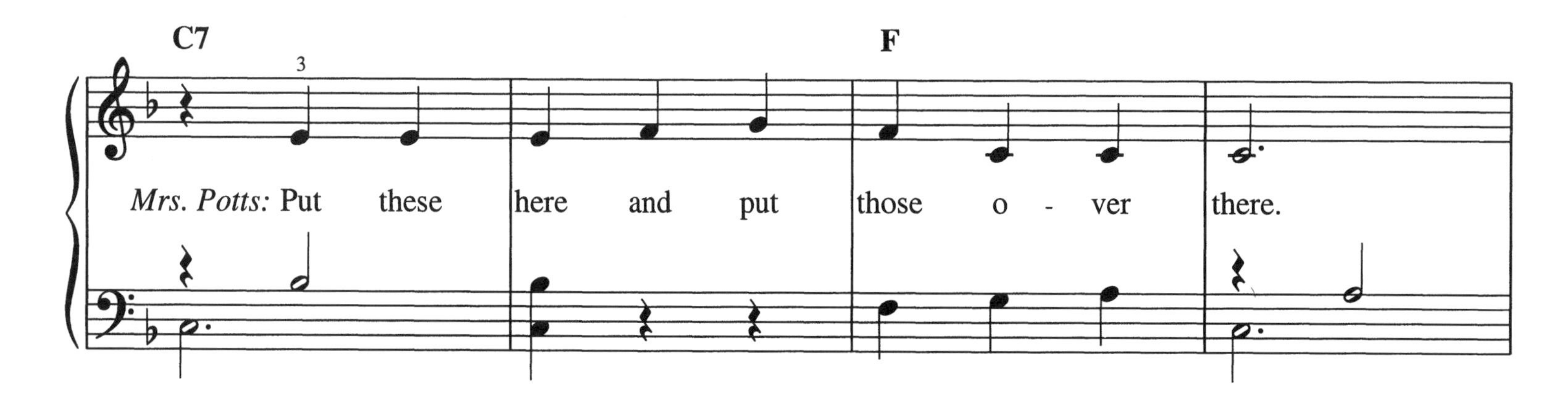
C7
F
Mrs. Potts: Put these here and put those o - ver there.

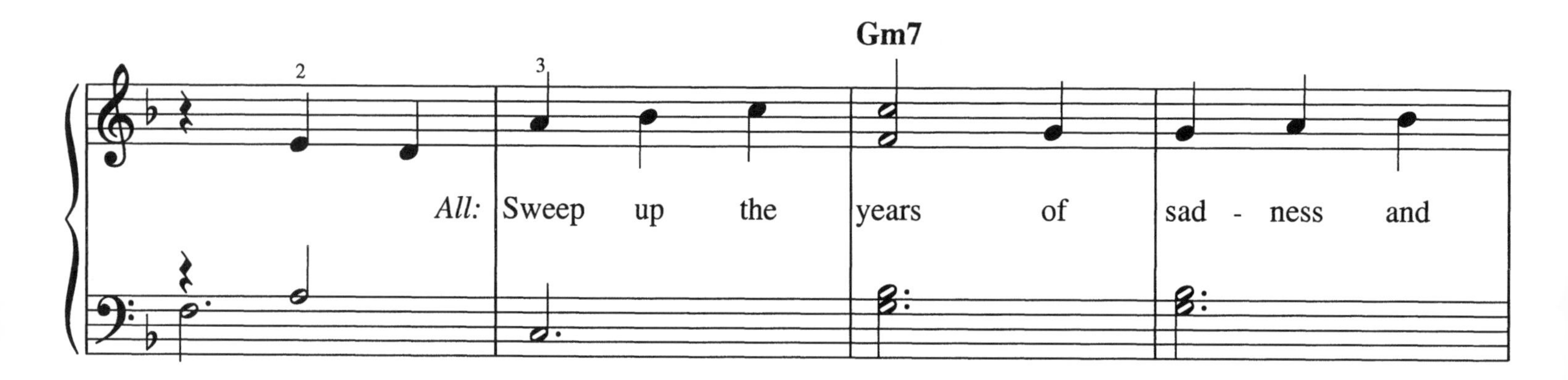
Gm7
All: Sweep up the years of sad - ness and

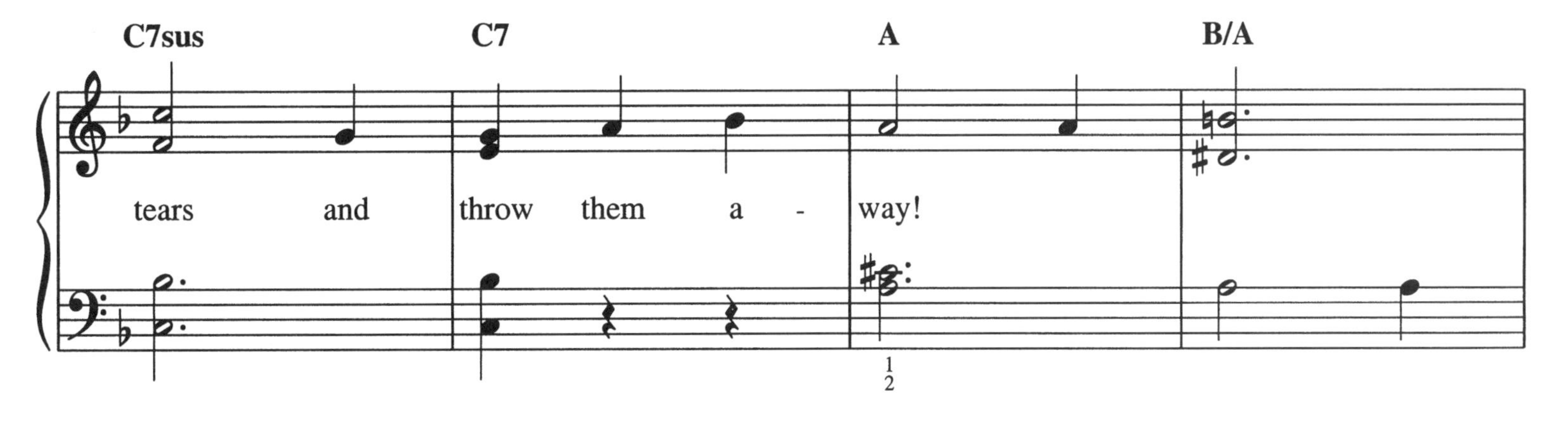
C7sus
C7
A
B/A
tears and throw them a - way!

C/D
D
N.C.
G
When we're hu - man a - gain, on - ly

hu - man a - gain. When the girl fi - n'lly sets us all

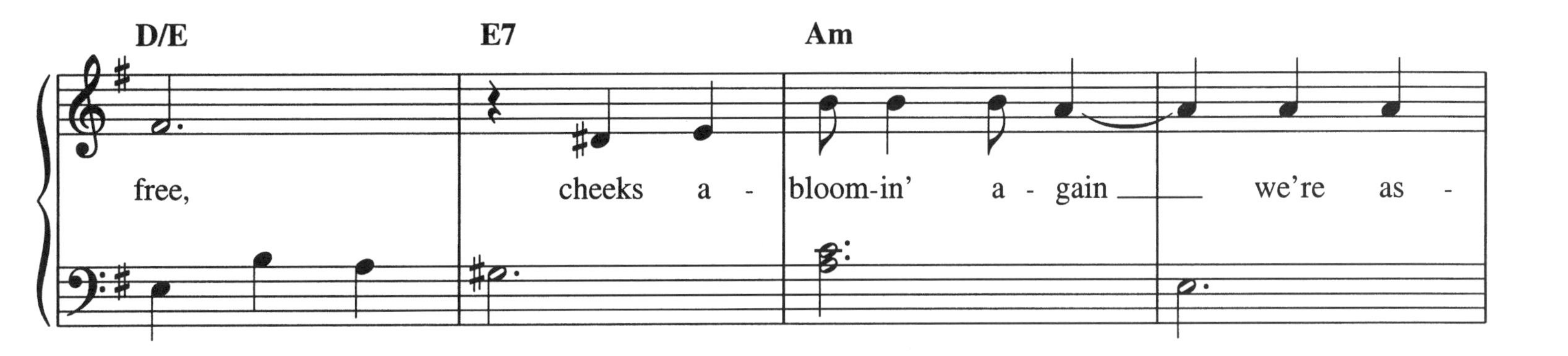
D/E
E7
Am
free, cheeks a - bloom-in' a - gain we're as -

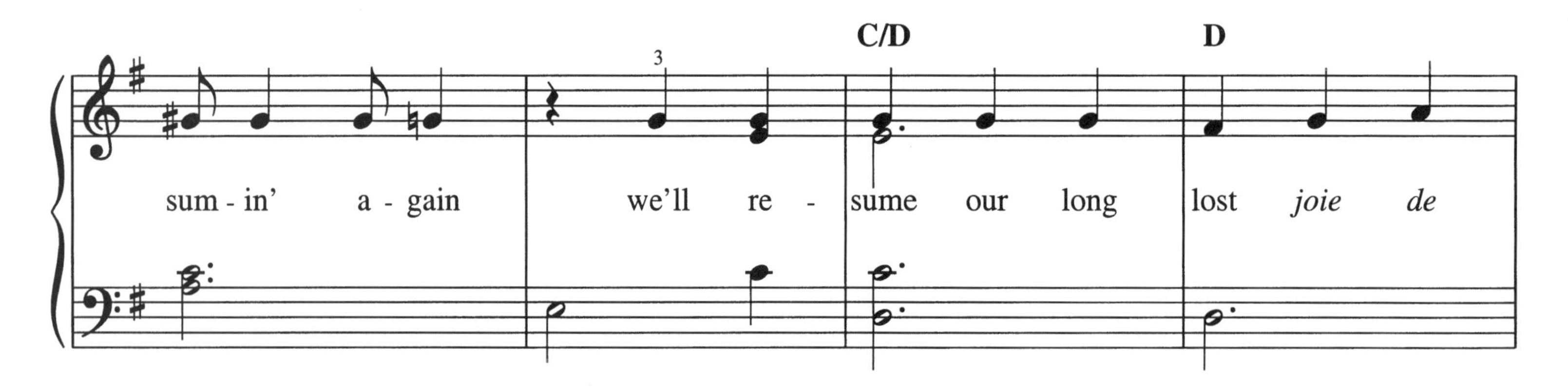
C/D
D
sum - in' a - gain we'll re - sume our long lost *joie de*

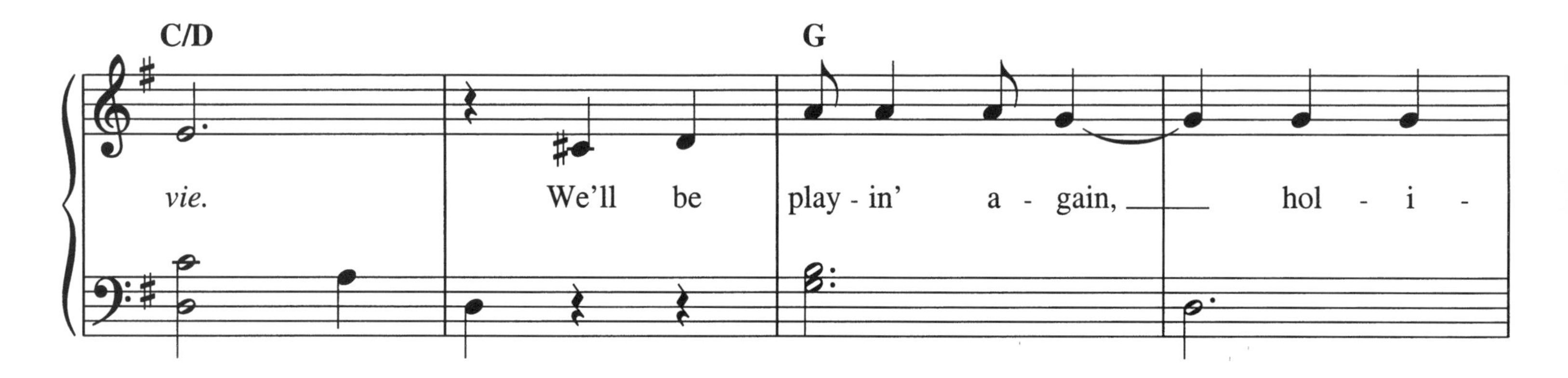
C/D
G
vie. We'll be play - in' a - gain, hol - i -

G7/F
C/E
day - in' a - gain. And we're pray - in' it's A - S - A - P!

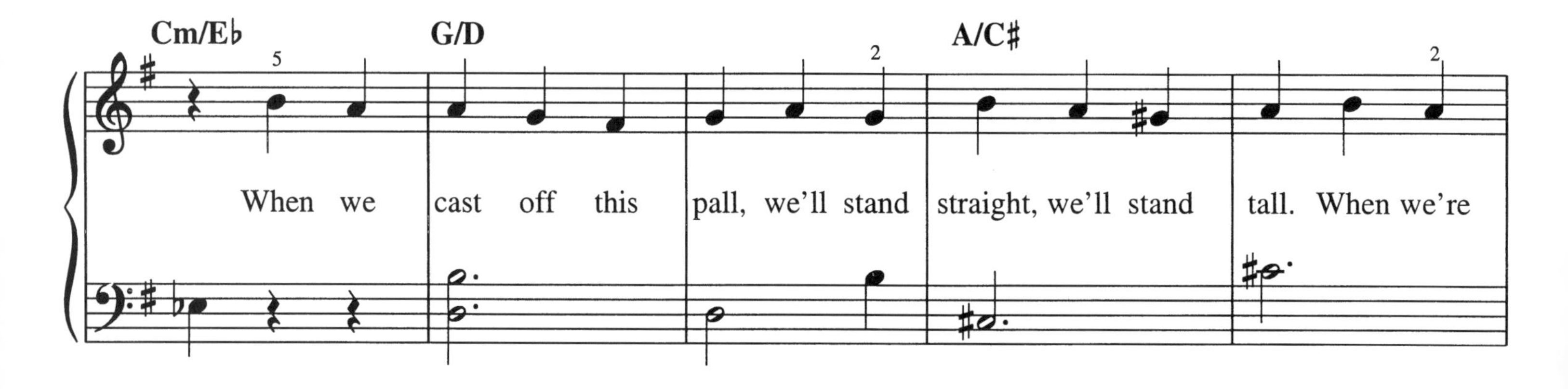
Cm/E♭
G/D
A/C♯
When we cast off this pall, we'll stand straight, we'll stand tall. When we're

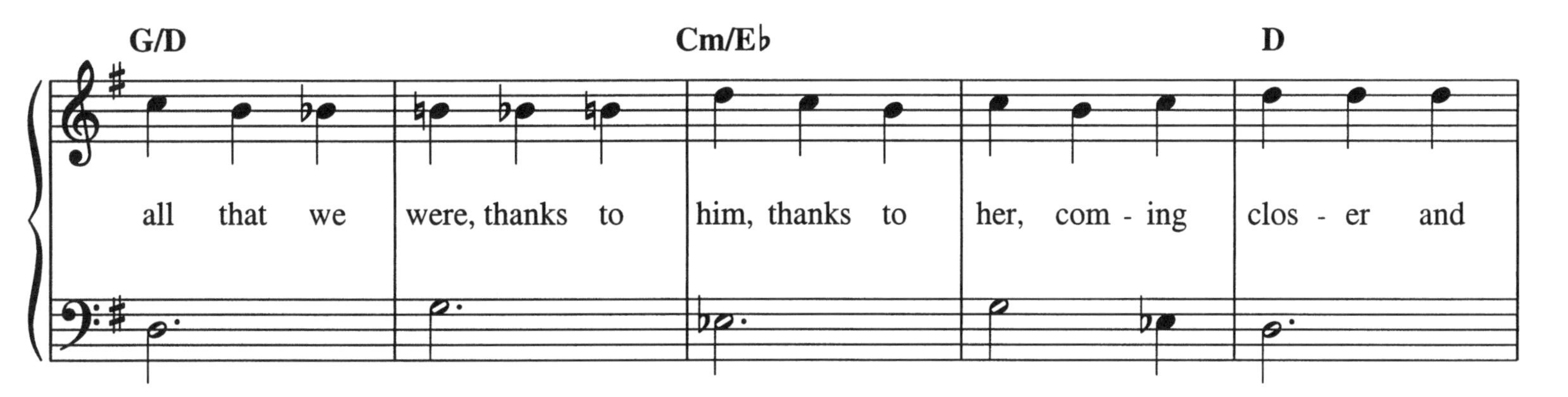
G/D
Cm/E♭
D
all that we were, thanks to him, thanks to her, com - ing clos - er and

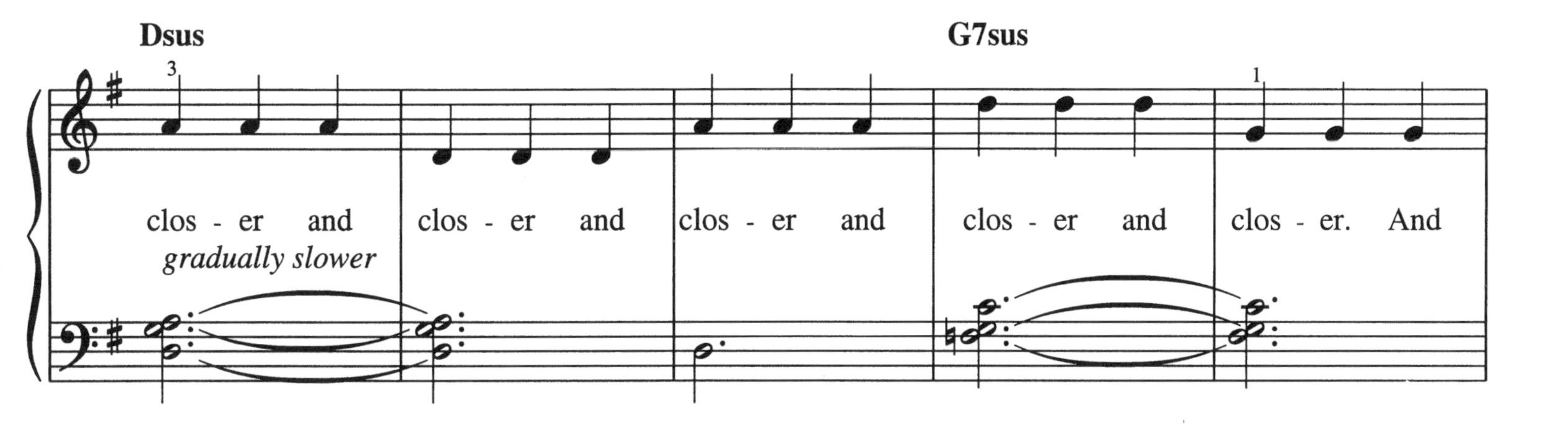
Dsus
G7sus
clos - er and clos - er and clos - er and clos - er and clos - er. And
gradually slower

N.C.
C
we'll be danc-ing a - gain! We'll be twirl-ing a - gain!
f a tempo

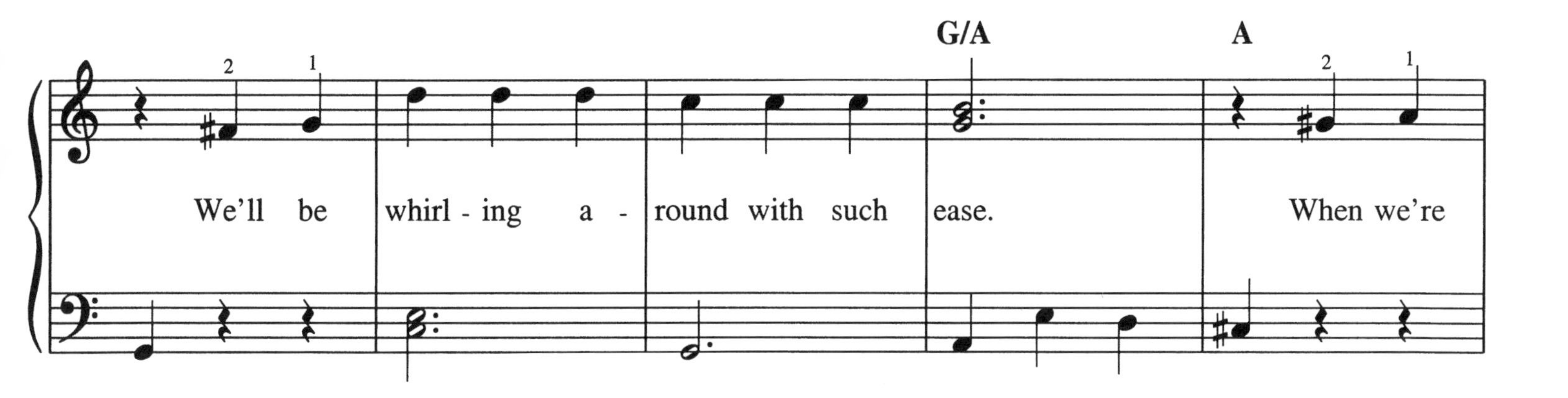
G/A
A
We'll be whirl - ing a - round with such ease. When we're

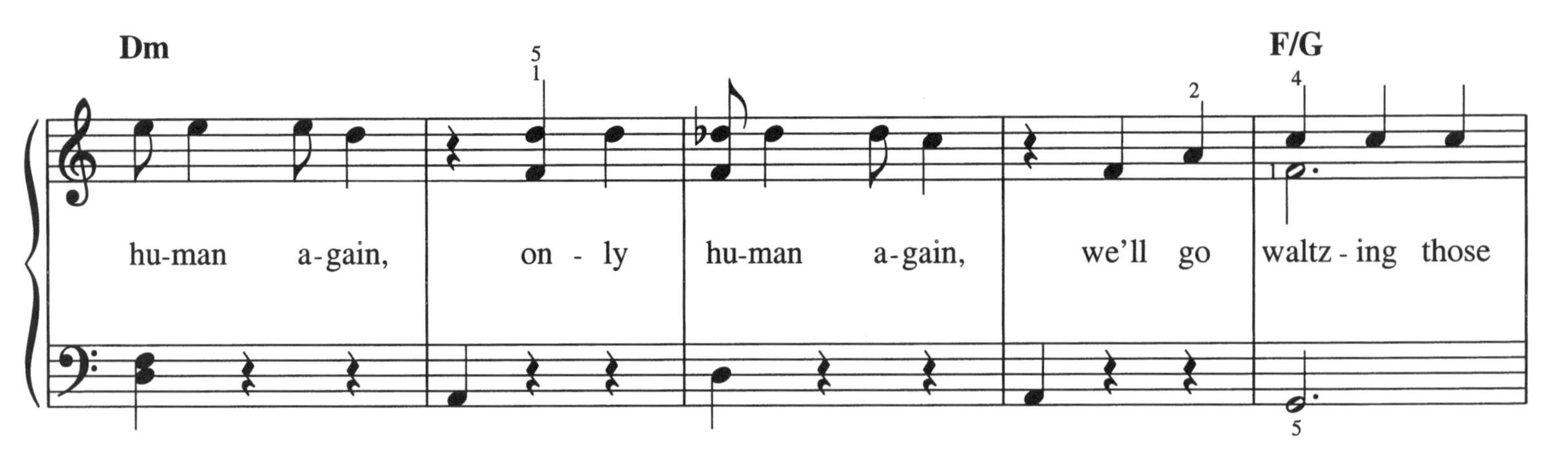
Dm
F/G
hu-man a-gain, on - ly hu-man a-gain, we'll go waltz - ing those

G7
F/G
G7
C
old one - two - threes, We'll be float-ing a-gain! We'll be

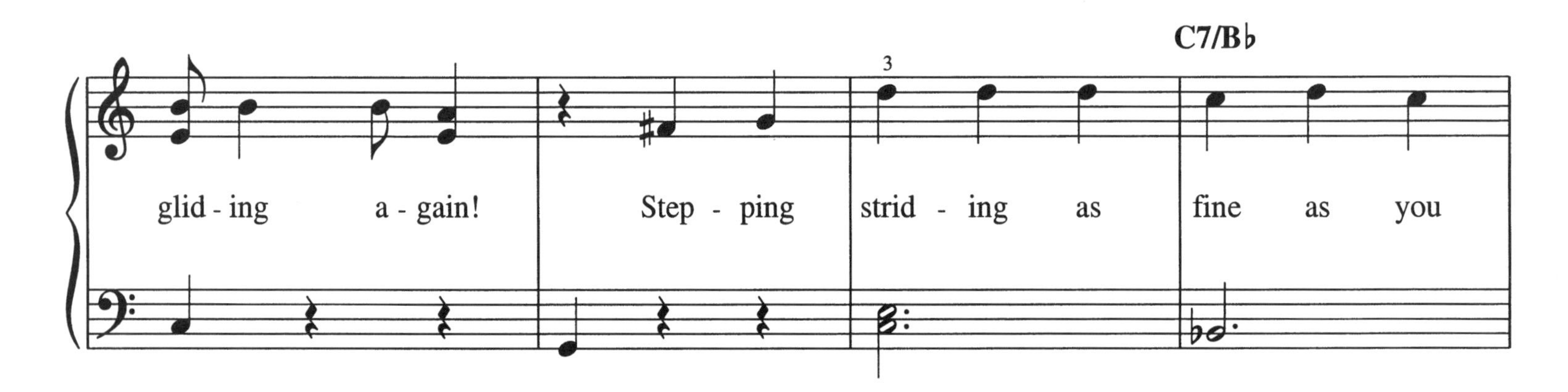
C7/B♭
glid - ing a - gain! Step - ping strid - ing as fine as you

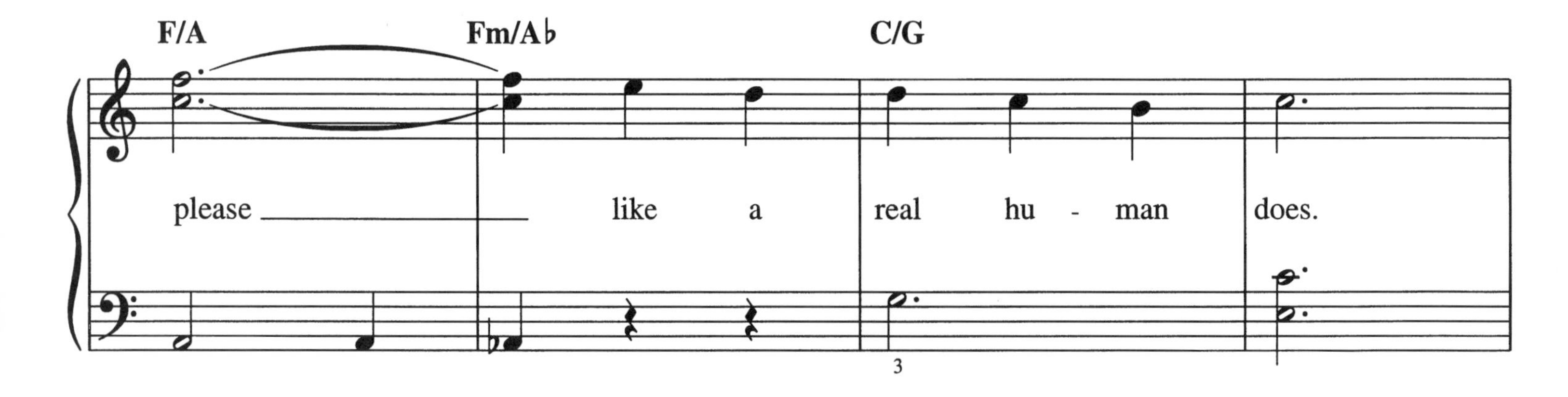
F/A
Fm/A♭
C/G
please like a real hu - man does.

D/F♯
I'll be all that I was

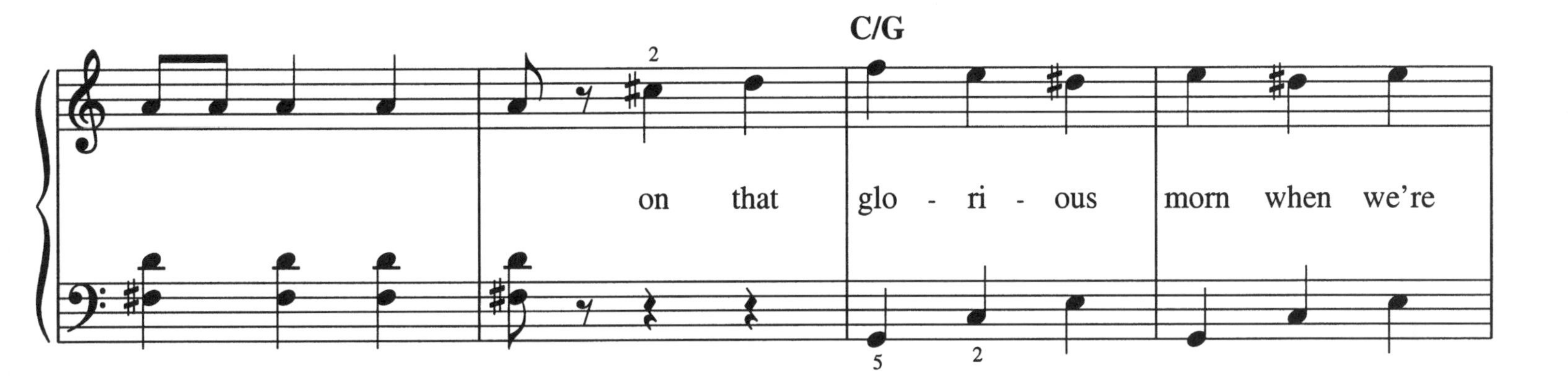
C/G
on that glo - ri - ous morn when we're

Fm/A♭
Faster
G7sus
G7
fi - n'lly re - born and we're all of us hu -

C
man a - gain!

MAISON DES LUNES

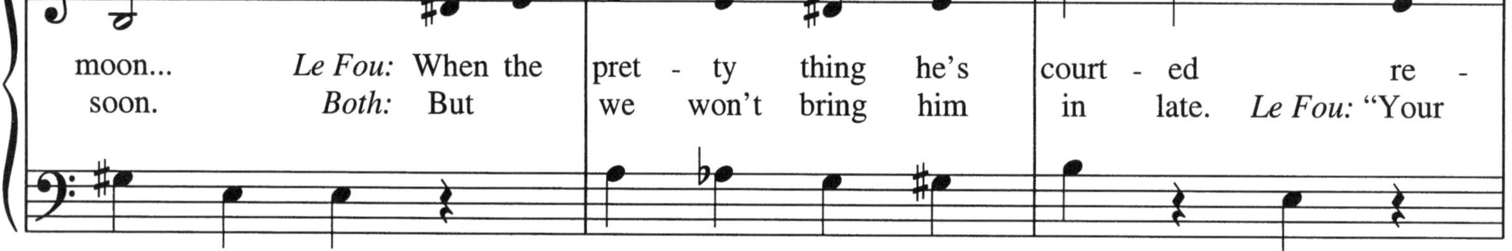

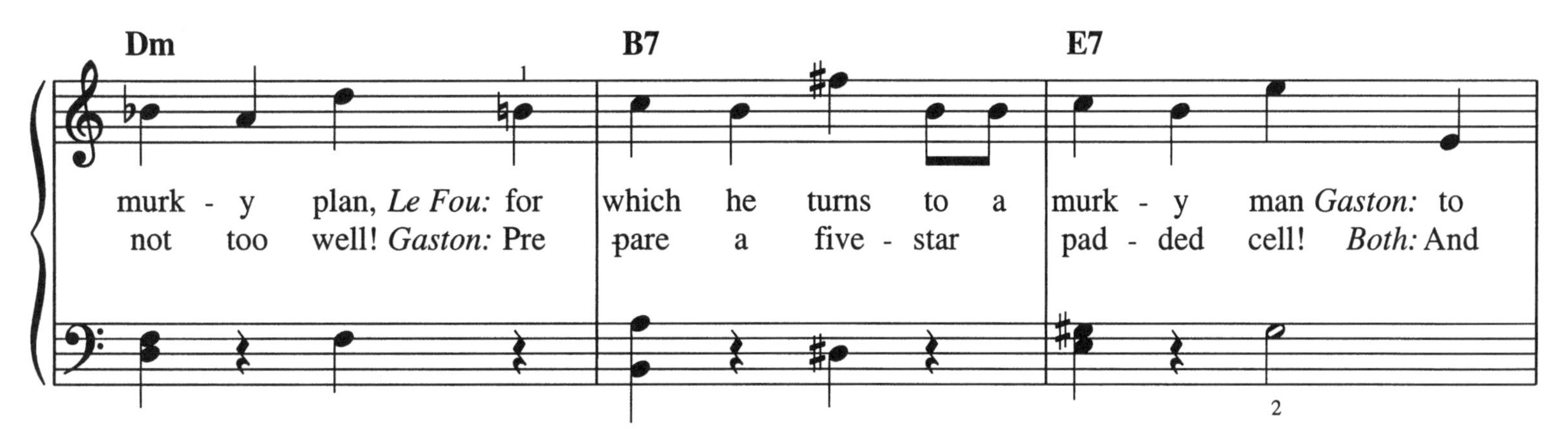
Dm
B7
E7
murk - y plan, Le Fou: for which he turns to a murk - y man Gaston: to
not too well! Gaston: Pre pare a five - star pad - ded cell! Both: And

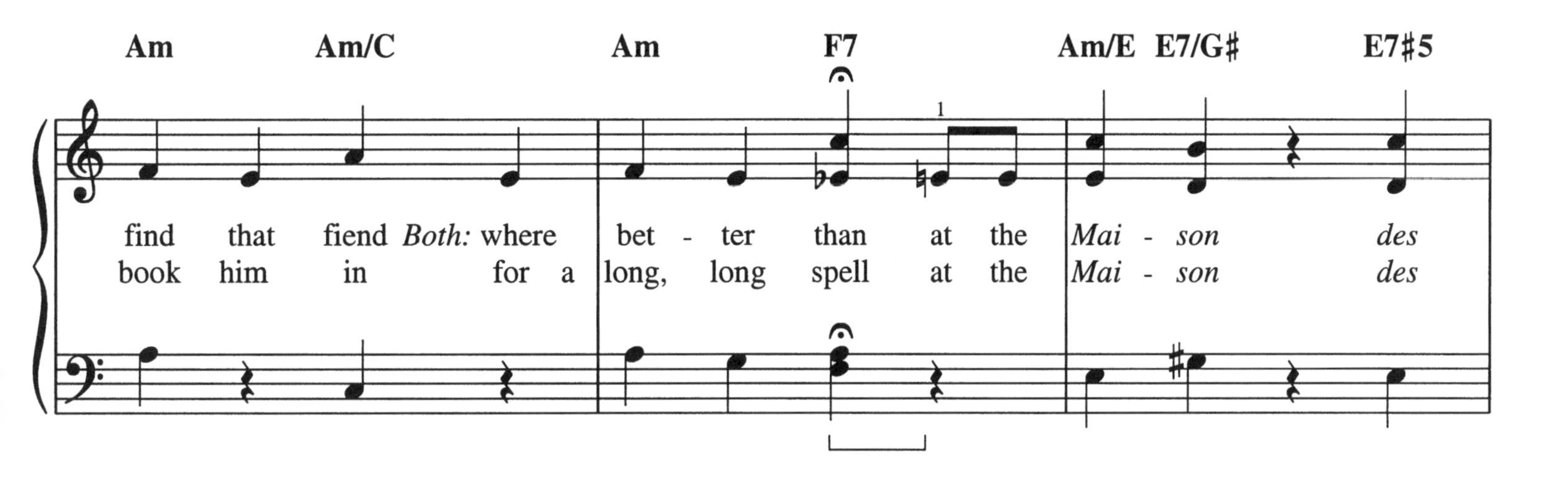
Am
Am/C
Am
F7
Am/E
E7/G♯
E7♯5
find that fiend Both: where bet - ter than at the Mai - son des
book him in for a long, long spell at the Mai - son des

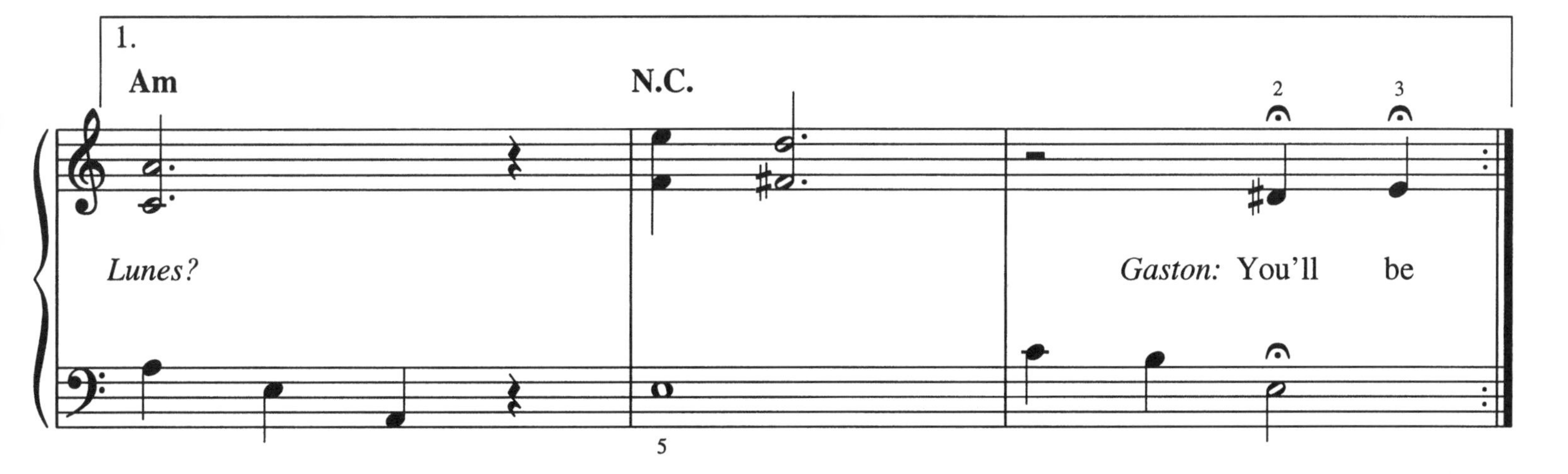
1.
Am
N.C.
Lunes?
Gaston: You'll be

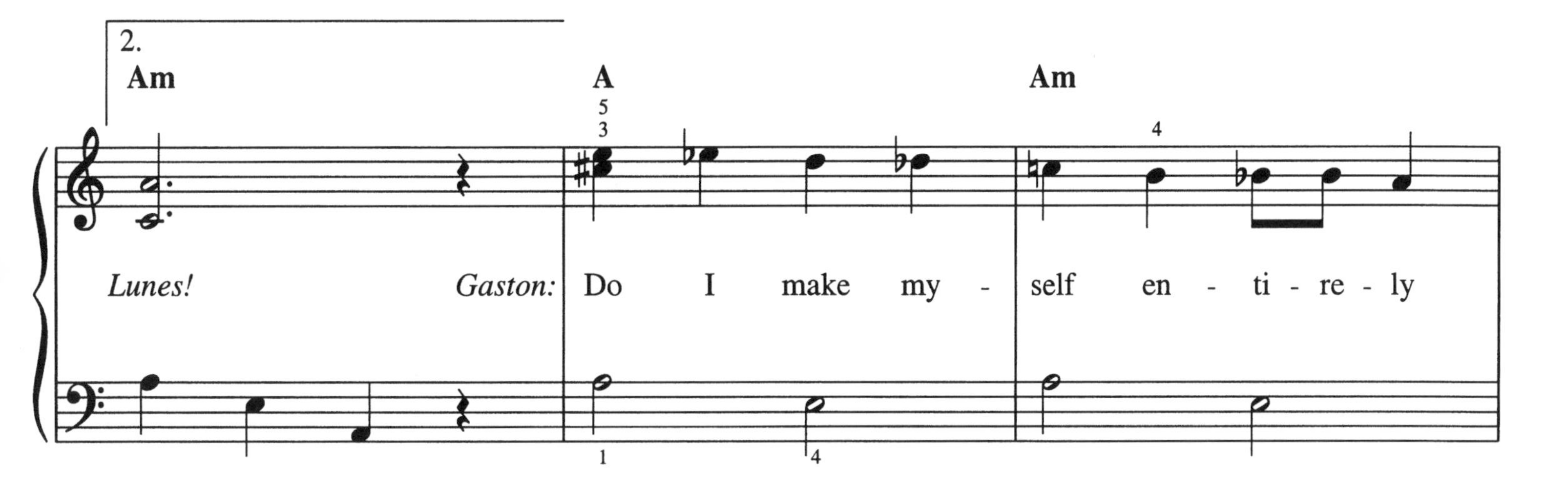
2.
Am
A
Am
Lunes!
Gaston: Do I make my - self en - ti - re - ly

Dm7
E7
A
clear?
Le Fou: It's the
sim - pl - est deal of

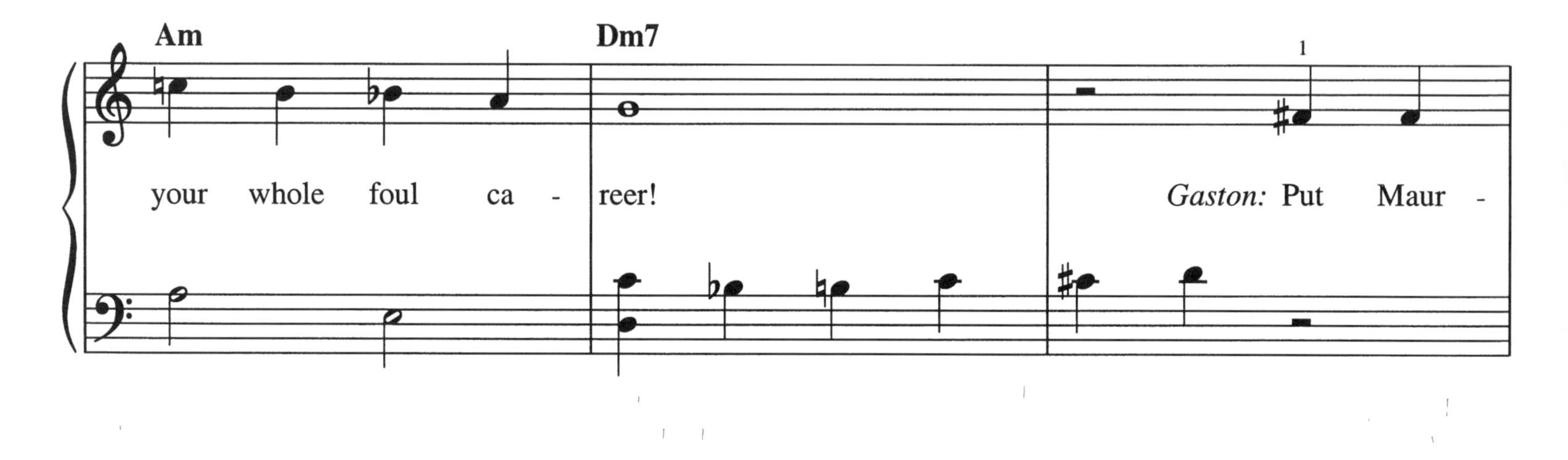
Am
Dm7
your whole foul ca -
reer!
Gaston: Put Maur -

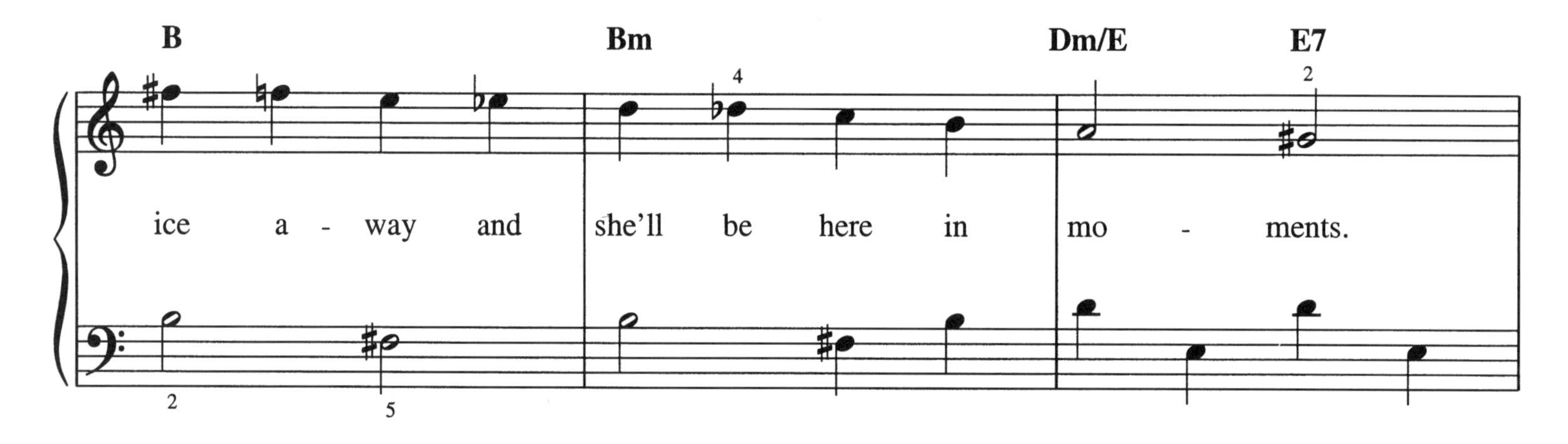
B
Bm
Dm/E
E7
ice a - way and
she'll be here in
mo - ments.

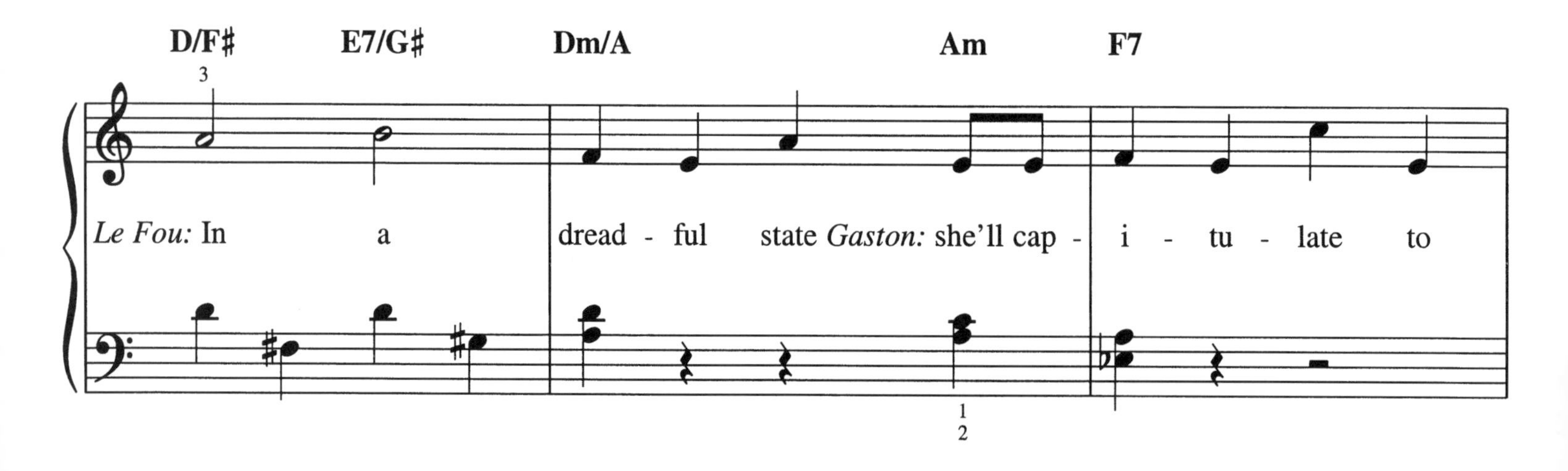
D/F#
E7/G#
Dm/A
Am
F7
Le Fou: In a
dread - ful state Gaston: she'll cap -
i - tu - late to

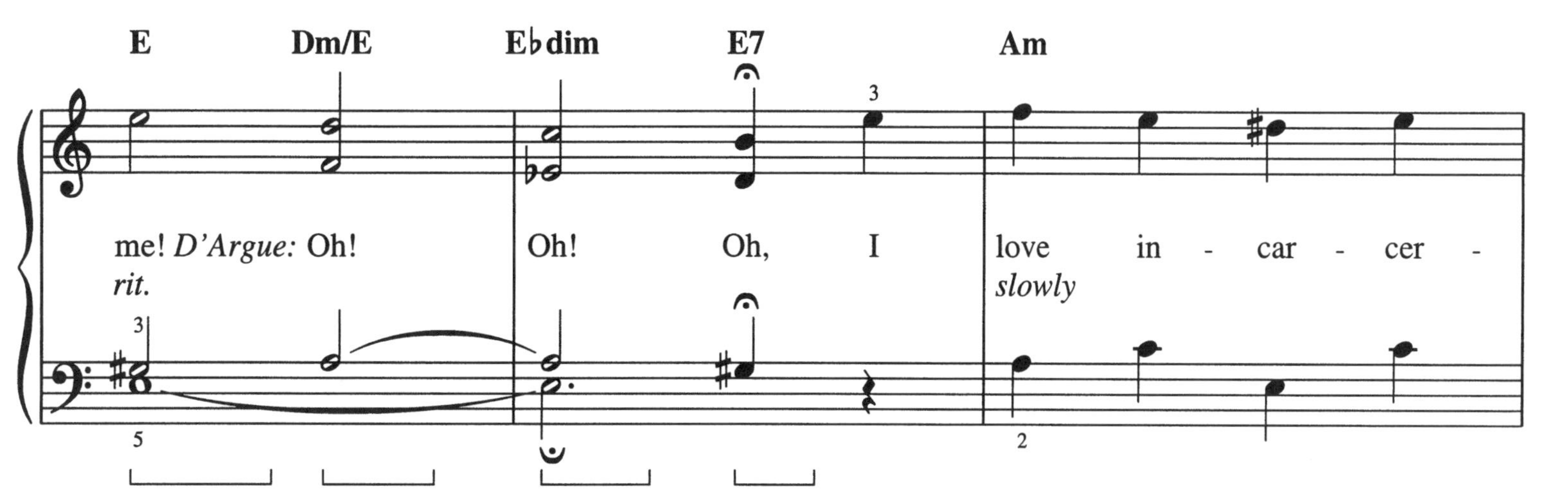
E
Dm/E
E♭dim
E7
Am
me! D'Argue: Oh!
Oh! Oh, I
love in - car - cer -
rit.
slowly

E7
a - tion. I could
lock up a pla -
toon. Gaston & Le Fou: We'll ap -
gradually faster

ply your in - clin -
a - tion to
one old buf -

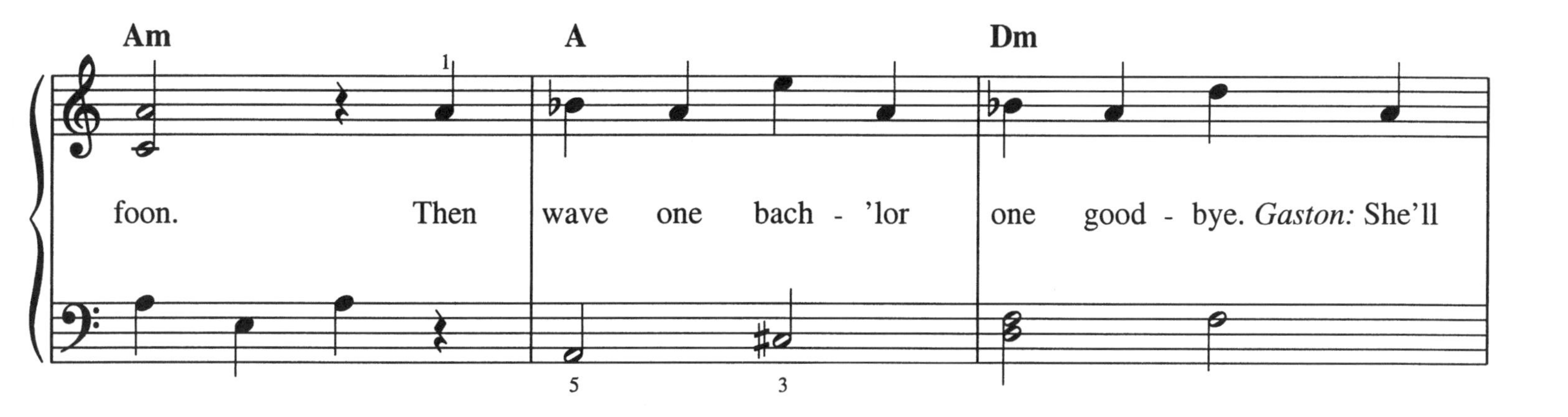
Am
A
Dm
foon. Then
wave one bach - 'lor
one good - bye. Gaston: She'll

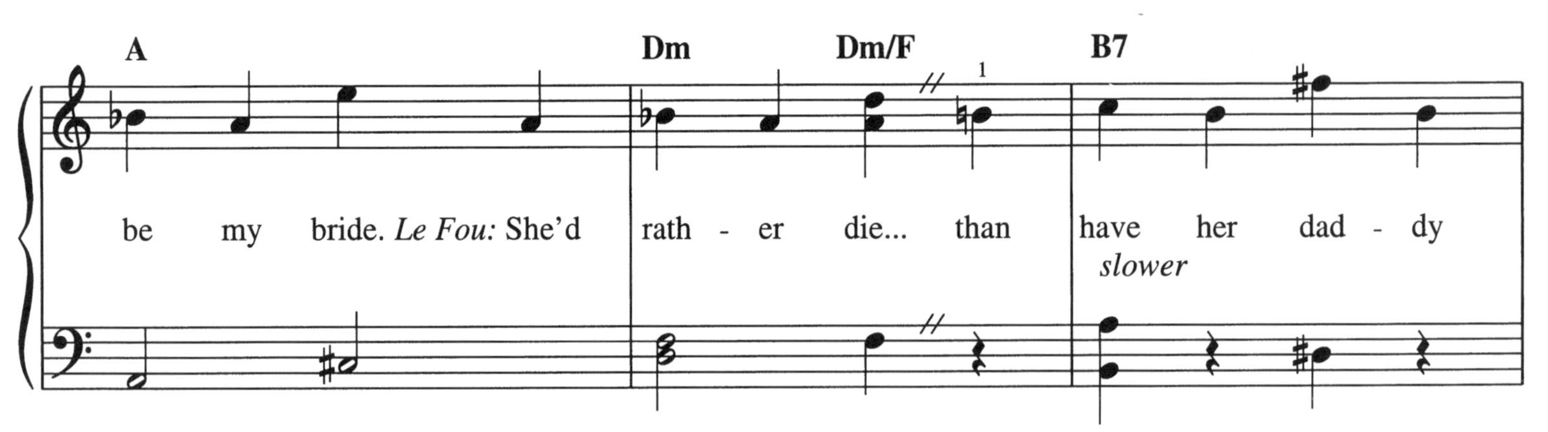
A Dm Dm/F B7
be my bride. *Le Fou:* She'd rath - er die... than have her dad - dy
slower

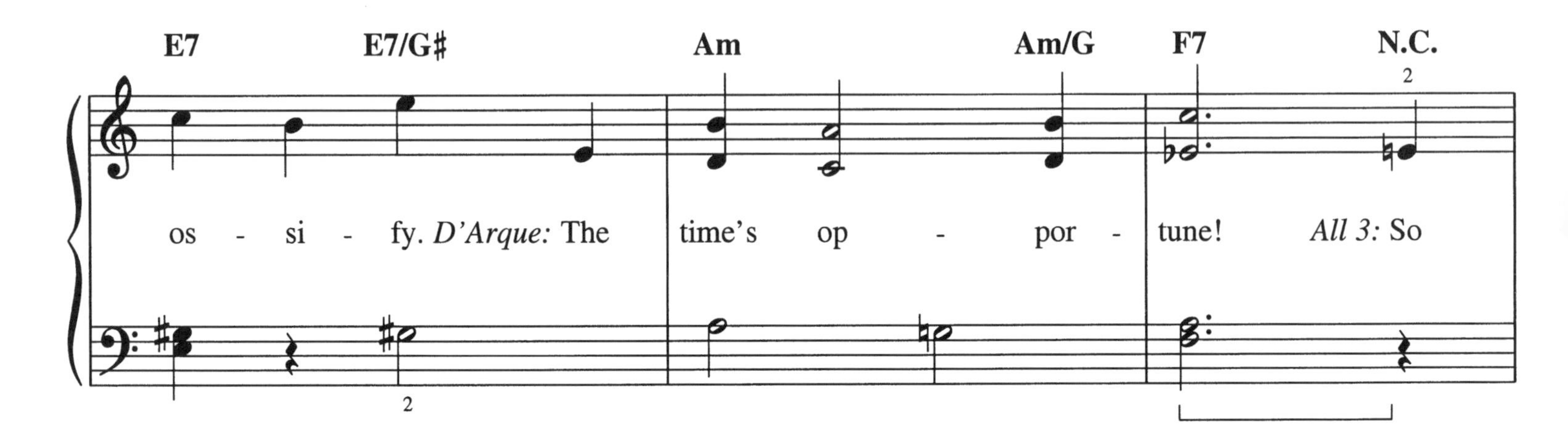
E7 E7/G# Am Am/G F7 N.C.
os - si - fy. *D'Arque:* The time's op - por - tune! *All 3:* So

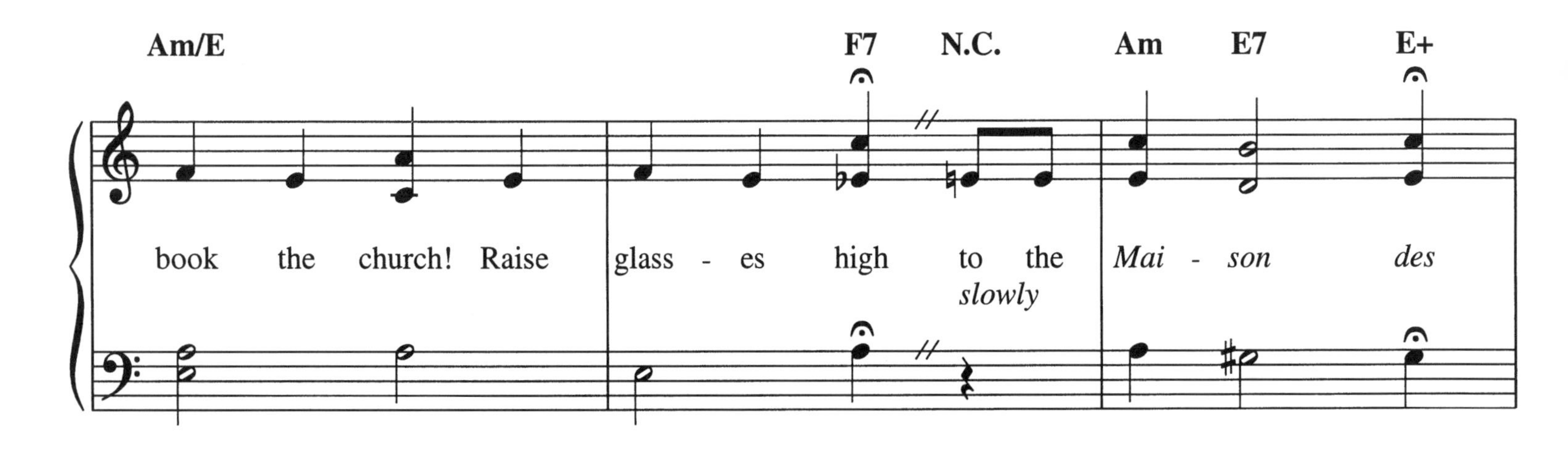
Am/E F7 N.C. Am E7 E+
book the church! Raise glass - es high to the *Mai - son des*
slowly

Am
Lunes!
rit.
sfz

BEAUTY AND THE BEAST

Lyrics by HOWARD ASHMAN
Music by ALAN MENKEN

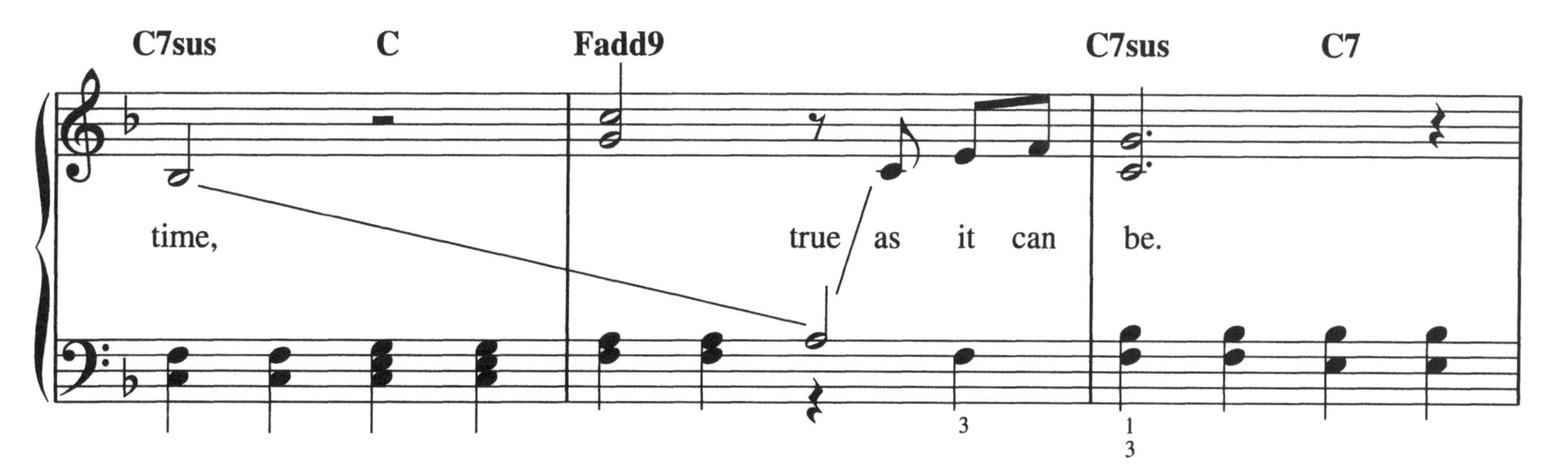

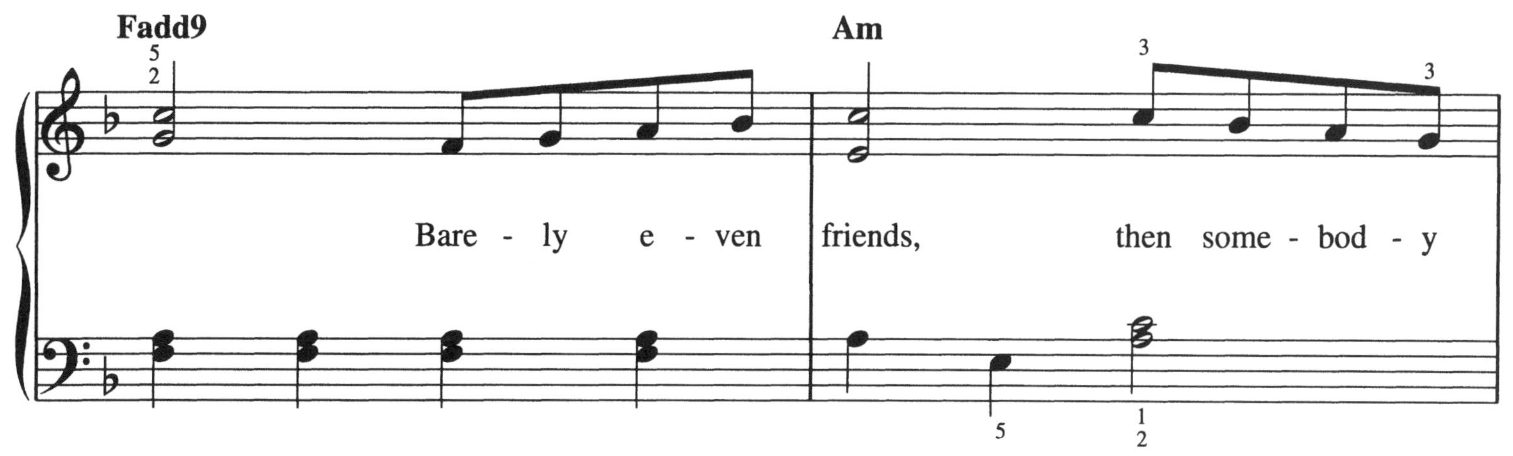

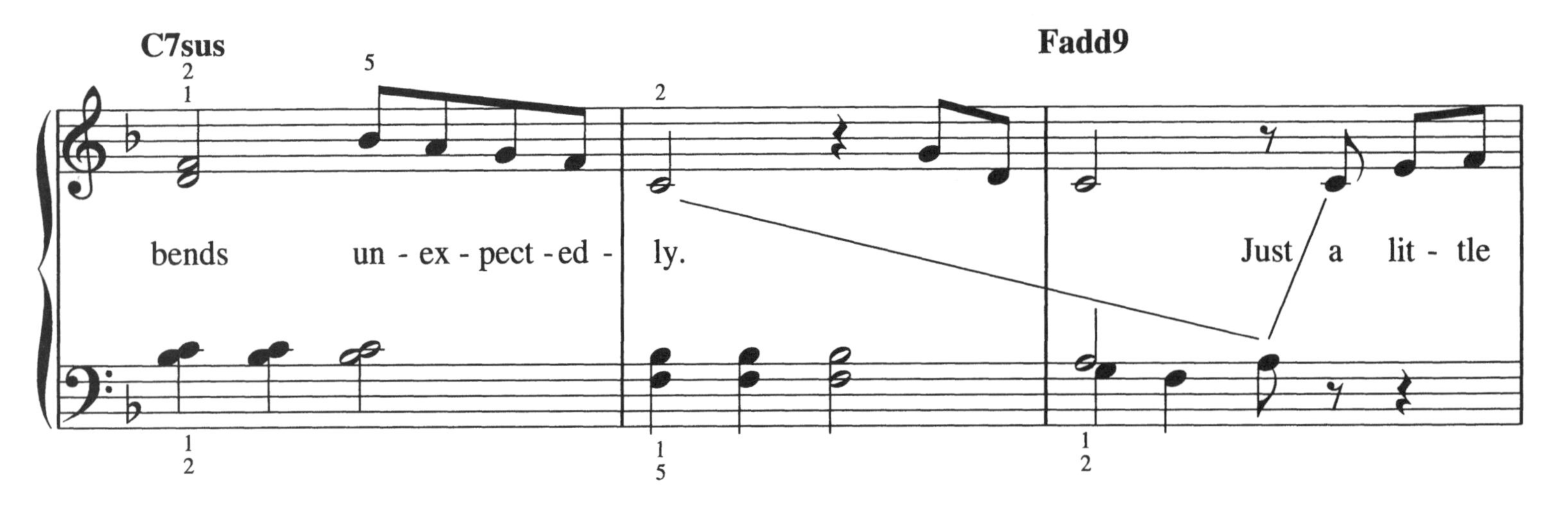
C7sus
Fadd9
bends un - ex - pect - ed - ly. Just a lit - tle

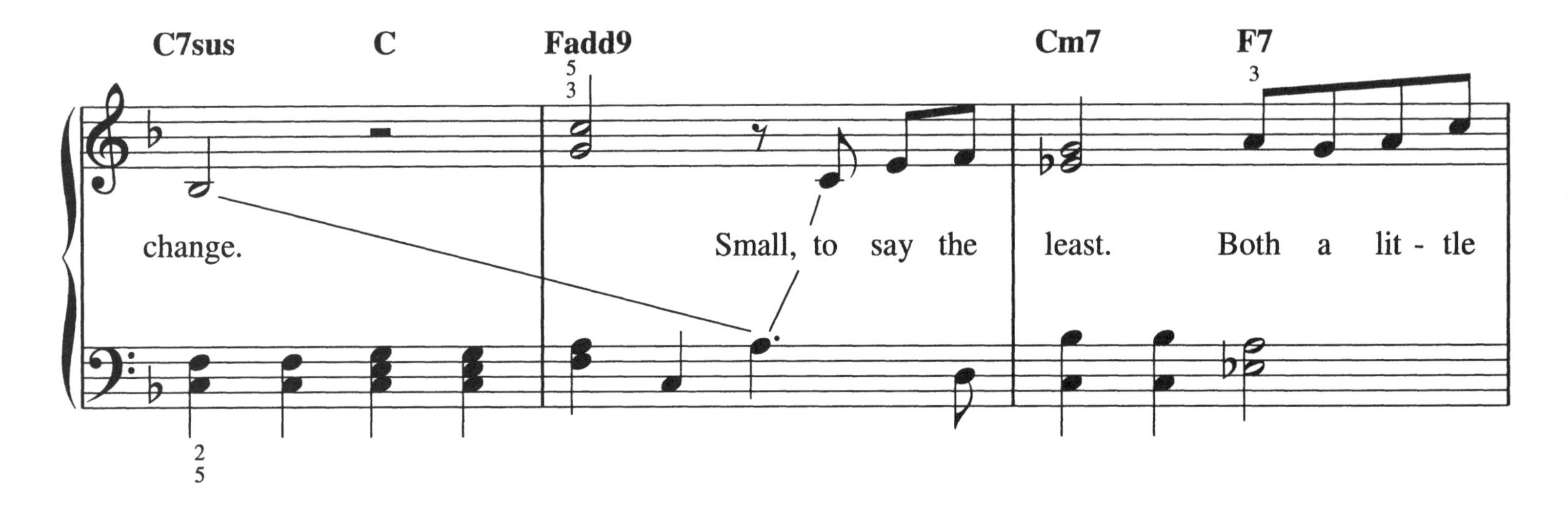
C7sus
C
Fadd9
Cm7
F7
change. Small, to say the least. Both a lit - tle

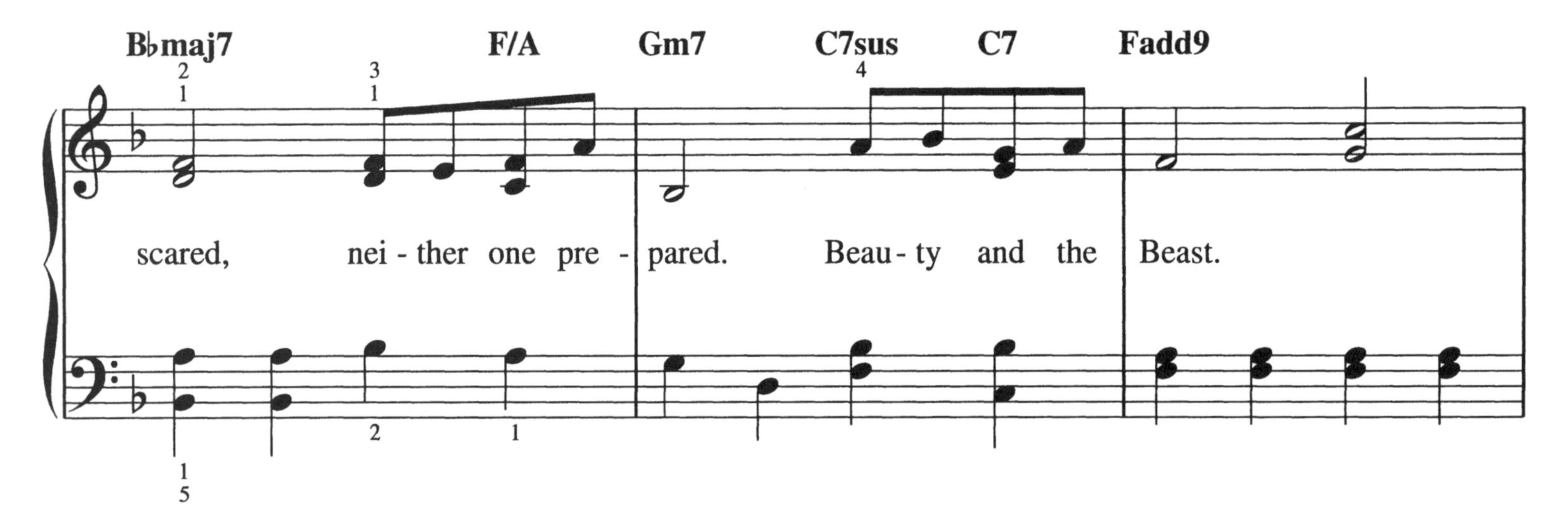
B♭maj7
F/A
Gm7
C7sus
C7
Fadd9
scared, nei - ther one pre - pared. Beau - ty and the Beast.

C7sus
Am
B♭add9
Ev - er just the same. Ev - er a sur -

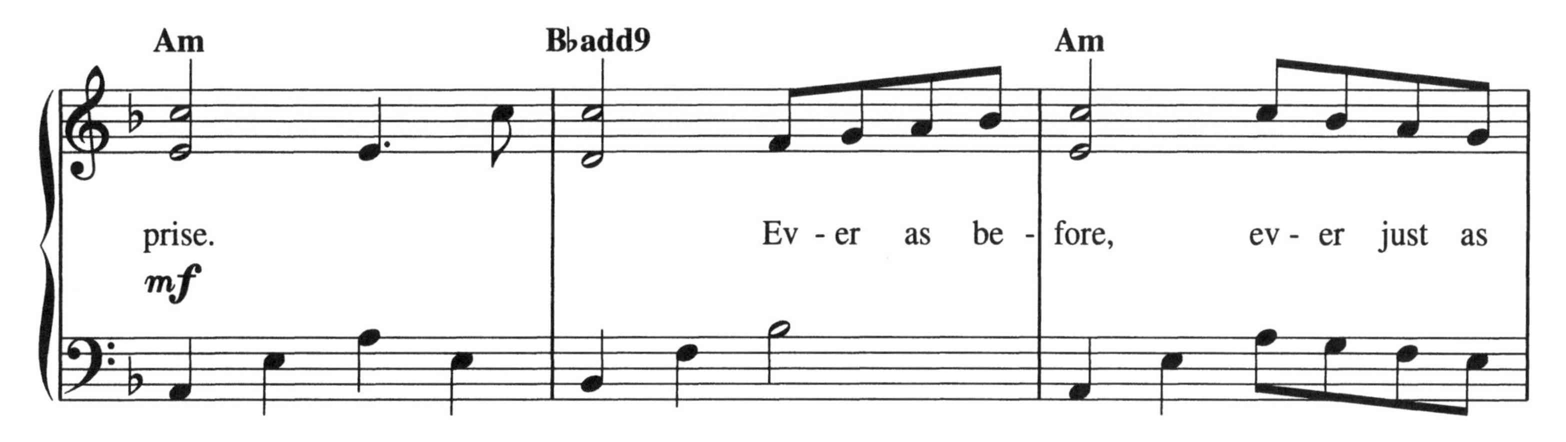

Am
Bbadd9
Am
prise.
mf
Ev - er as be - fore, ev - er just as

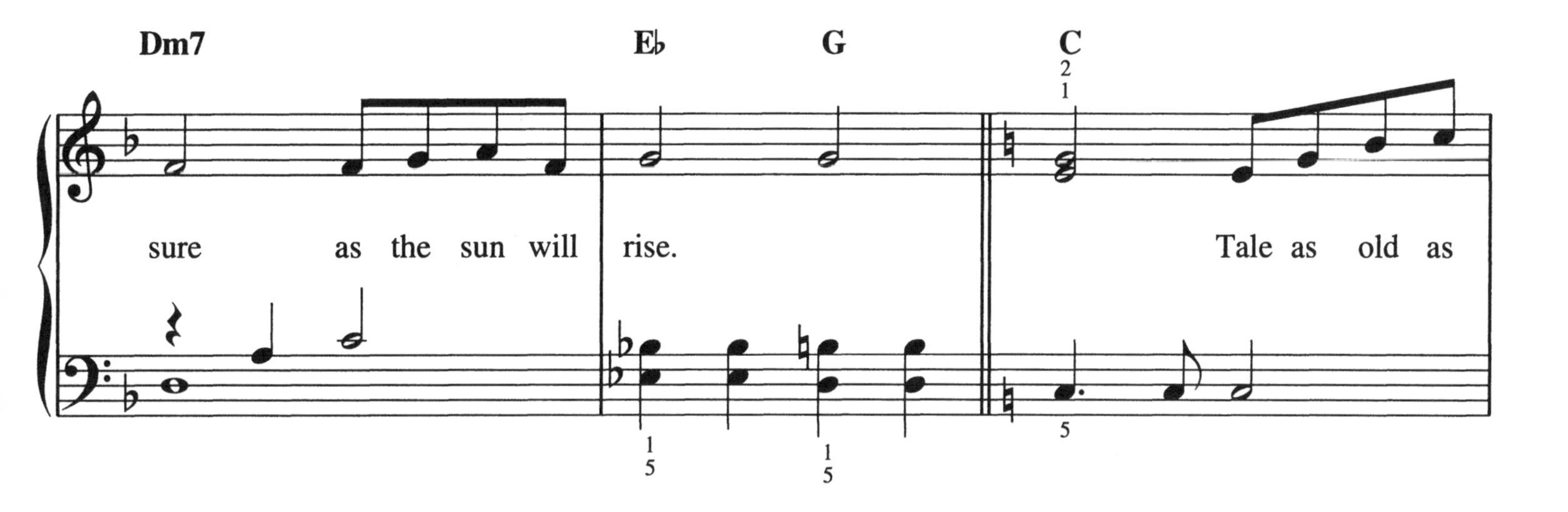

Dm7
Eb
G
C
sure as the sun will rise.
Tale as old as

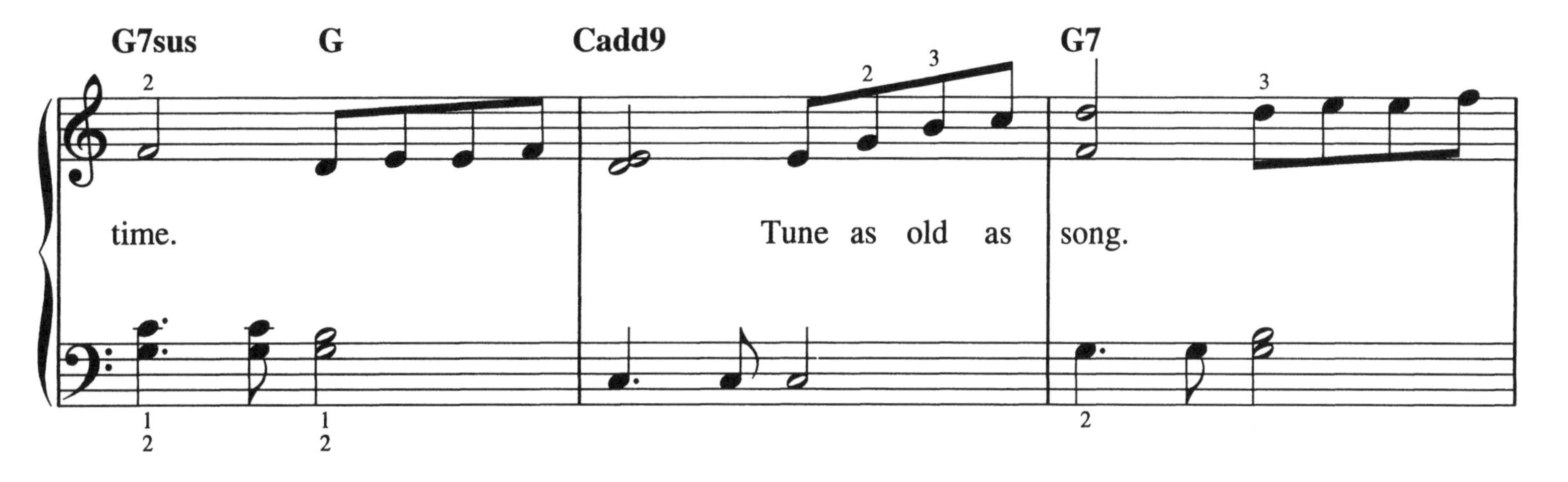

G7sus
G
Cadd9
G7
time.
Tune as old as song.

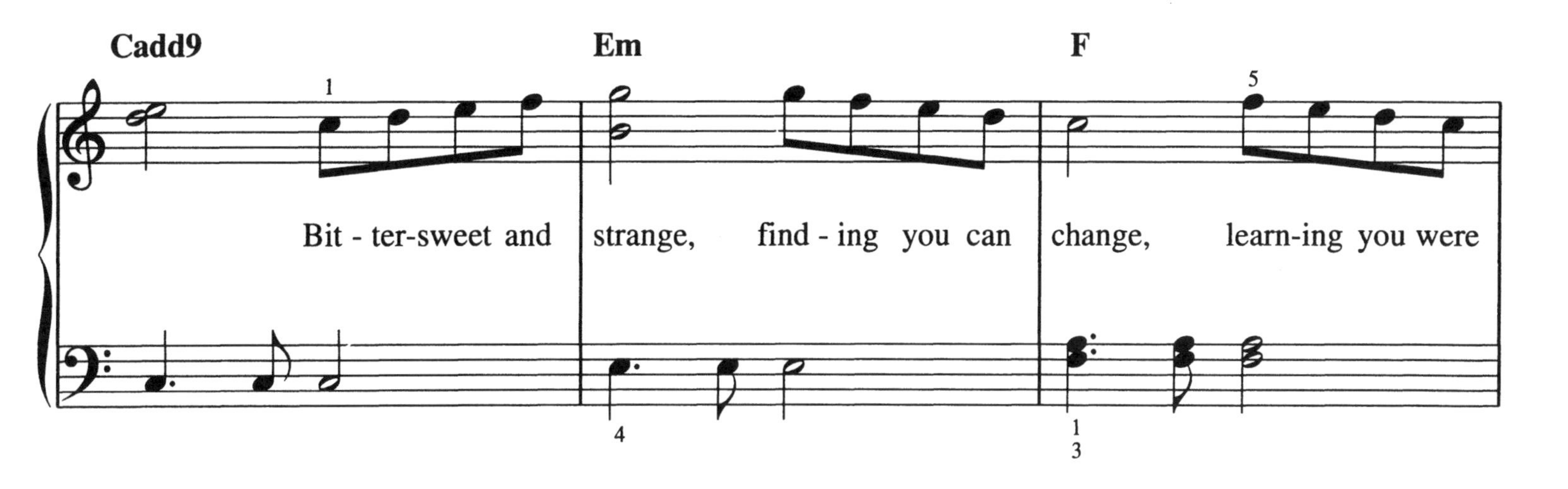

Cadd9
Em
F
Bit - ter-sweet and strange, find - ing you can change, learn-ing you were

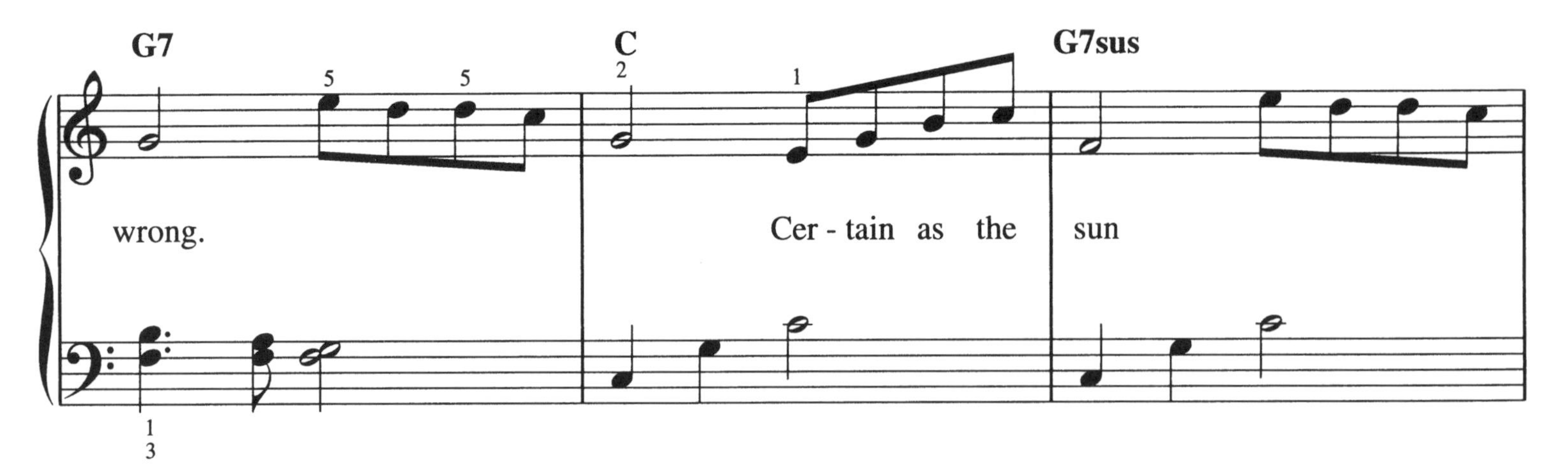
G7
C
G7sus
wrong.
Cer - tain as the
sun

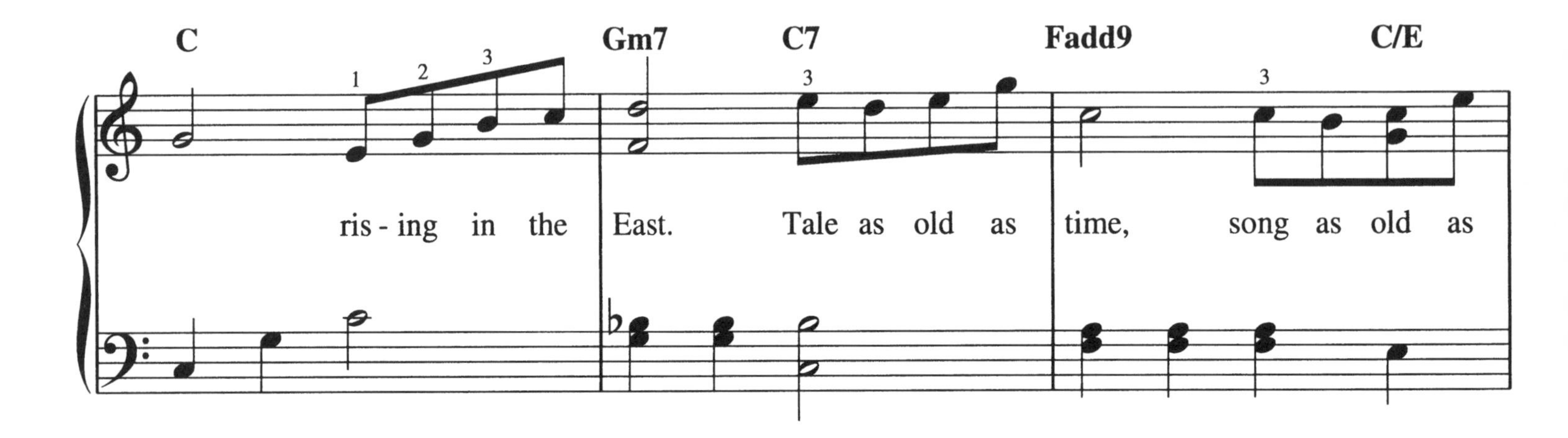
C
Gm7
C7
Fadd9
C/E
ris - ing in the
East.
Tale as old as
time,
song as old as

Dm
G7sus
G
C
rhyme.
Beau - ty and the
Beast.
rit.
a tempo

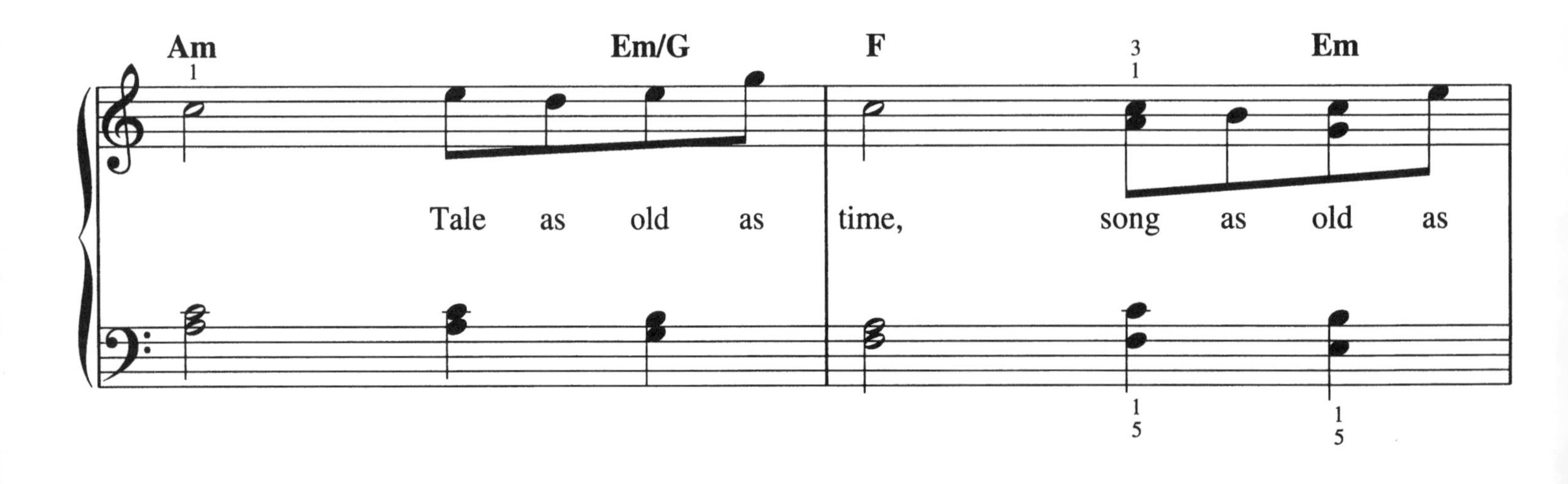
Am
Em/G
F
Em
Tale as old as
time,
song as old as

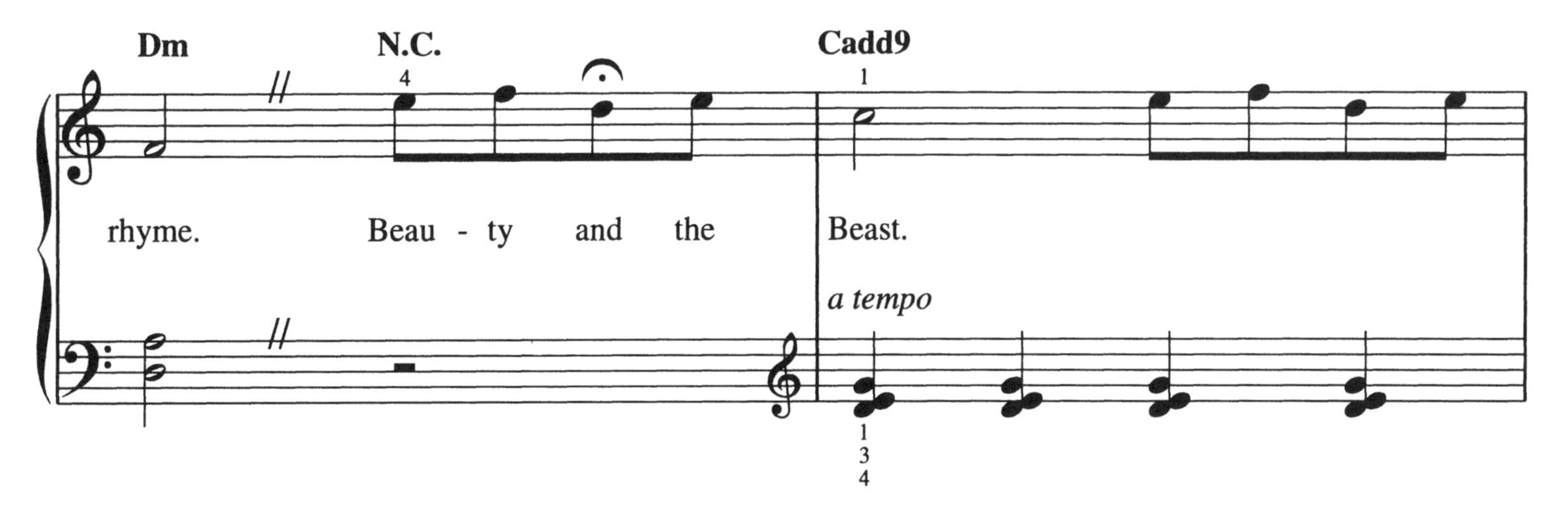
Dm
N.C.
Cadd9
rhyme. Beau - ty and the Beast.
a tempo

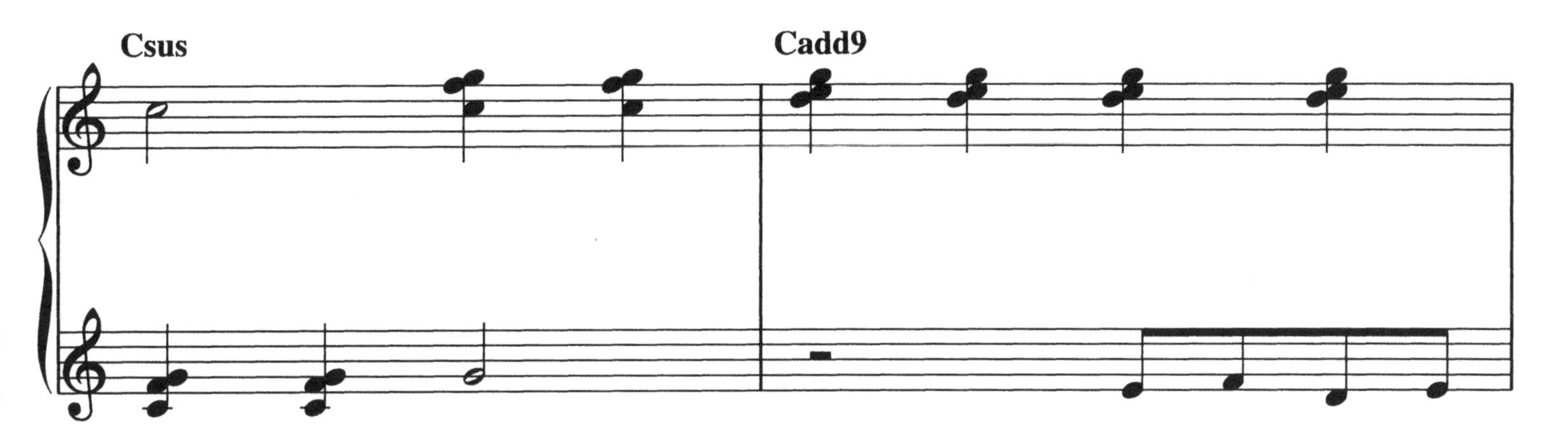
Csus
Cadd9

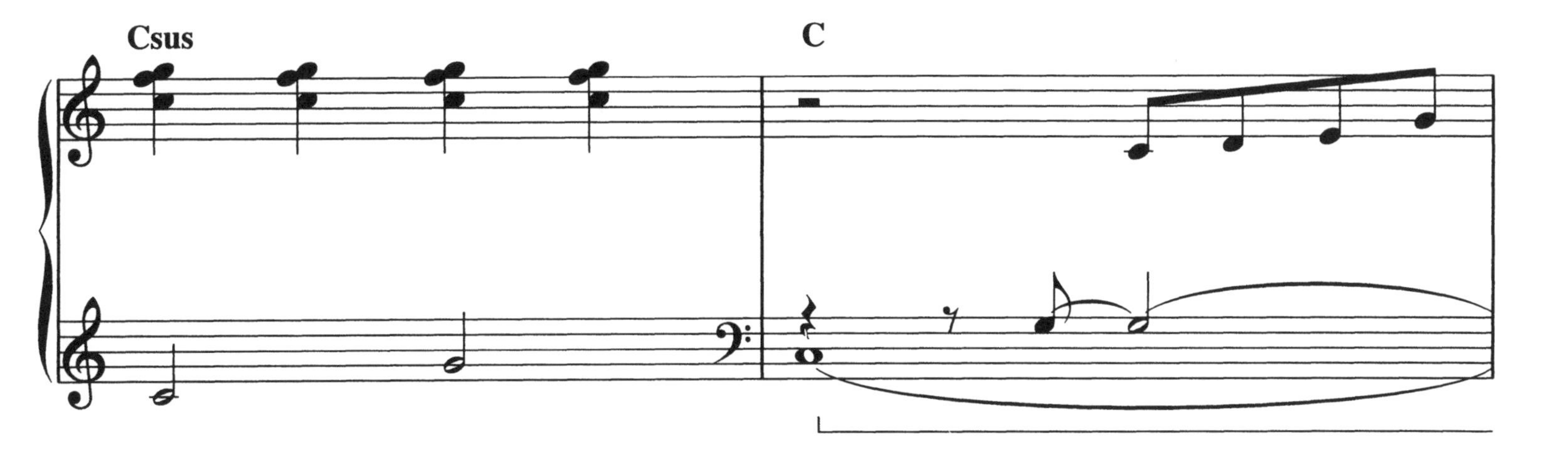
Csus
C

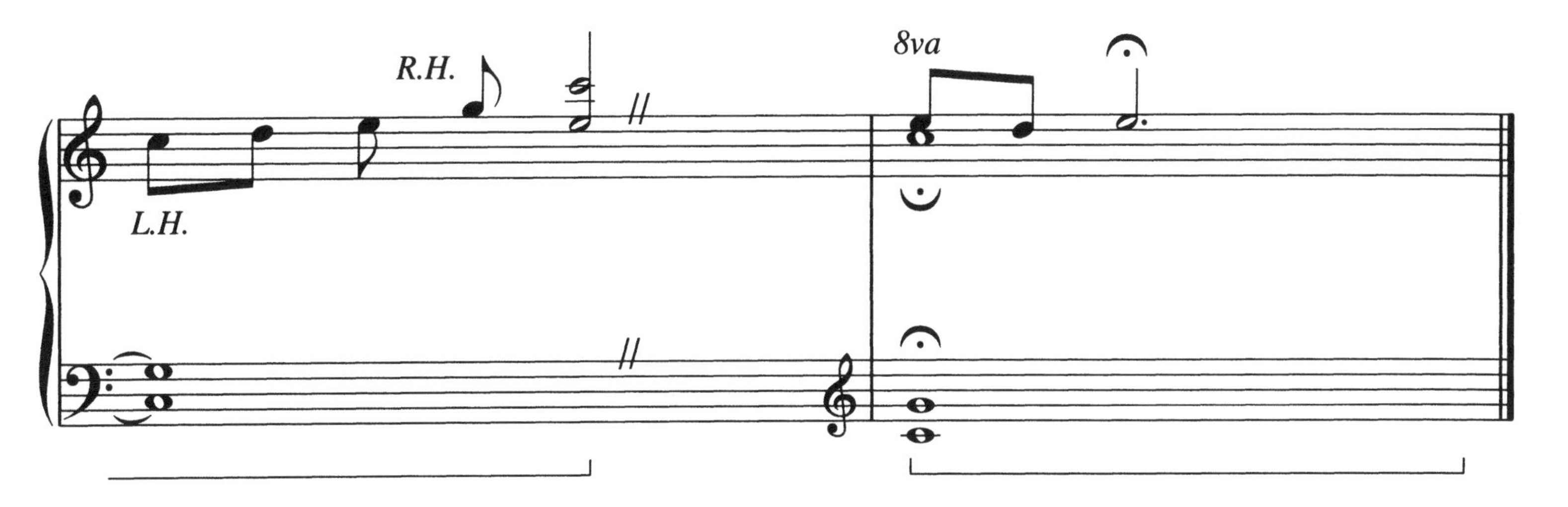
R.H.
L.H.
8va

THE MOB SONG

Lyrics by HOWARD ASHMAN
Music by ALAN MENKEN

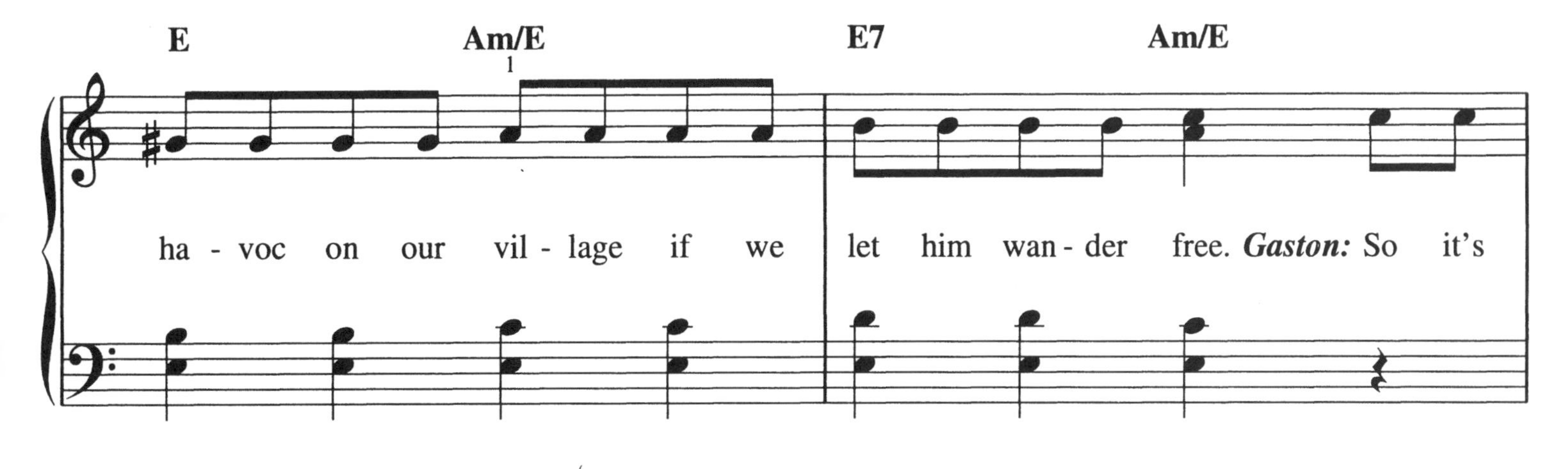
E
Am/E
E7
Am/E
ha - voc on our vil - lage if we
let him wan - der free. Gaston: So it's

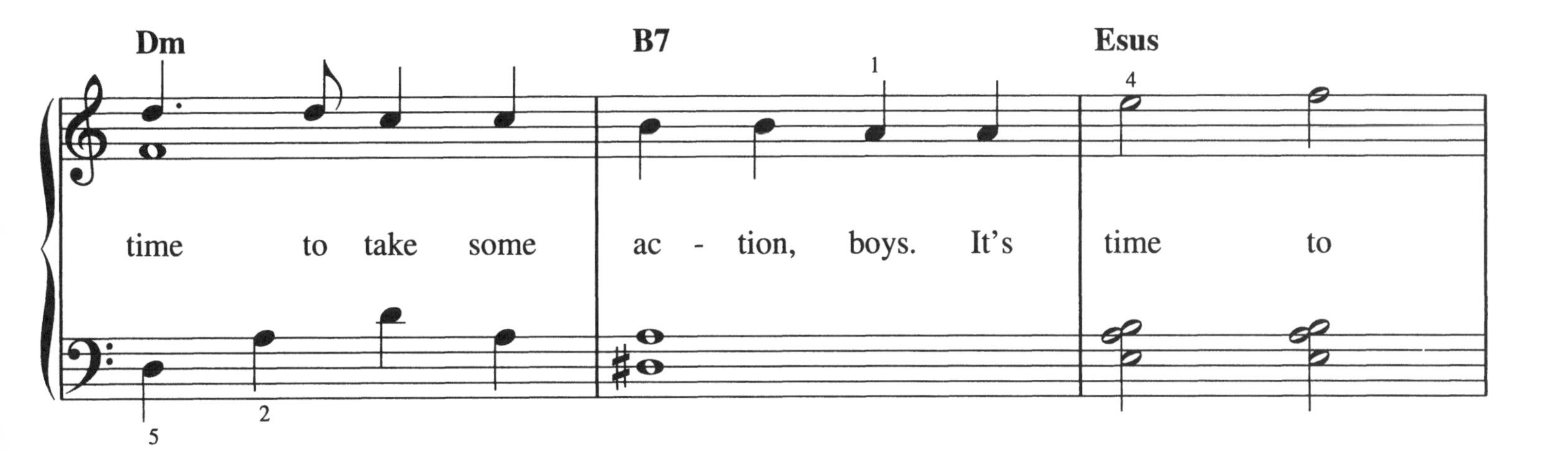
Dm
B7
Esus
time to take some
ac - tion, boys. It's
time to

fol - low
me.
Through the

Am
mist, through the woods, through the
dark- ness and the shad- ows. It's a
torch. Mount your horse. Gaston: Screw your
cour - age to the stick - ingplace! Mob: We're

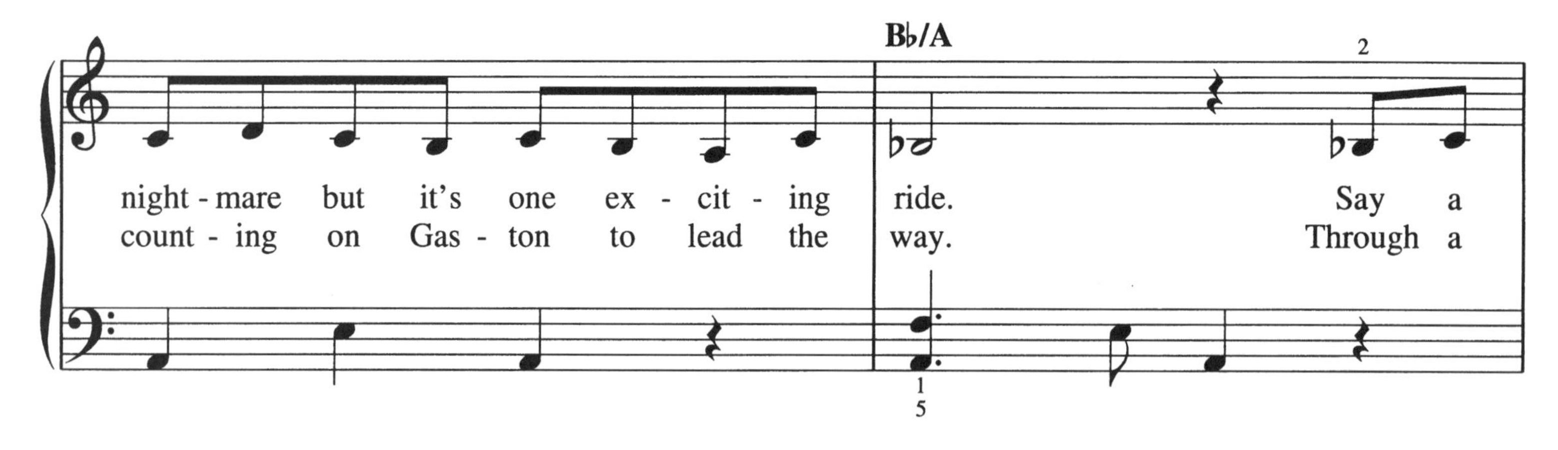
B♭/A
night - mare but it's one ex - cit - ing ride. Say a
count - ing on Gas - ton to lead the way. Through a

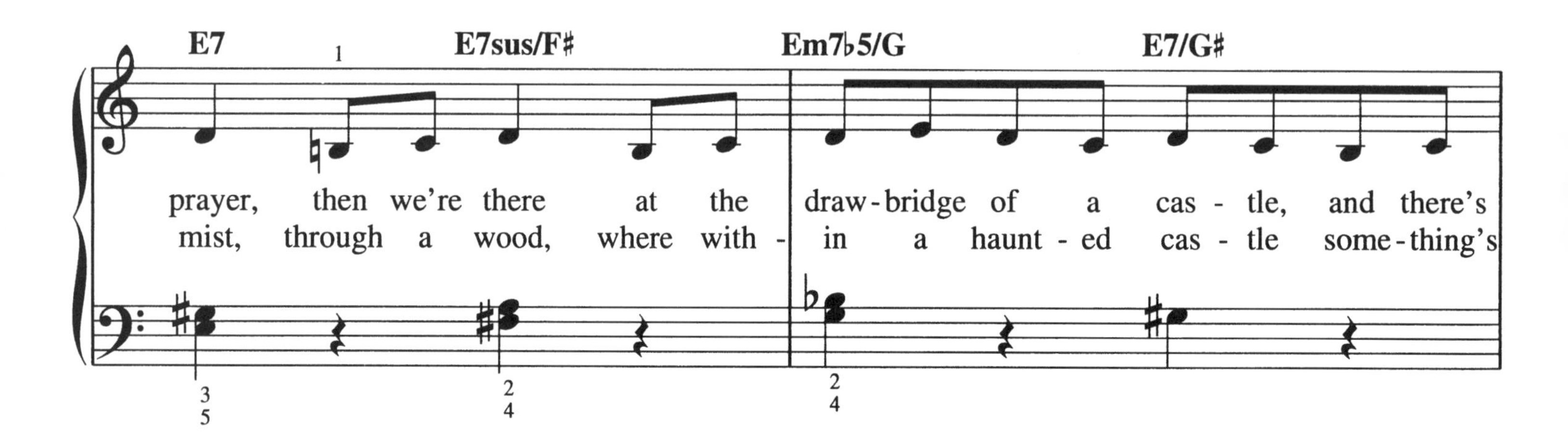
E7
E7sus/F♯
Em7♭5/G
E7/G♯
prayer, then we're there at the draw-bridge of a cas - tle, and there's
mist, through a wood, where with - in a haunt - ed cas - tle some-thing's

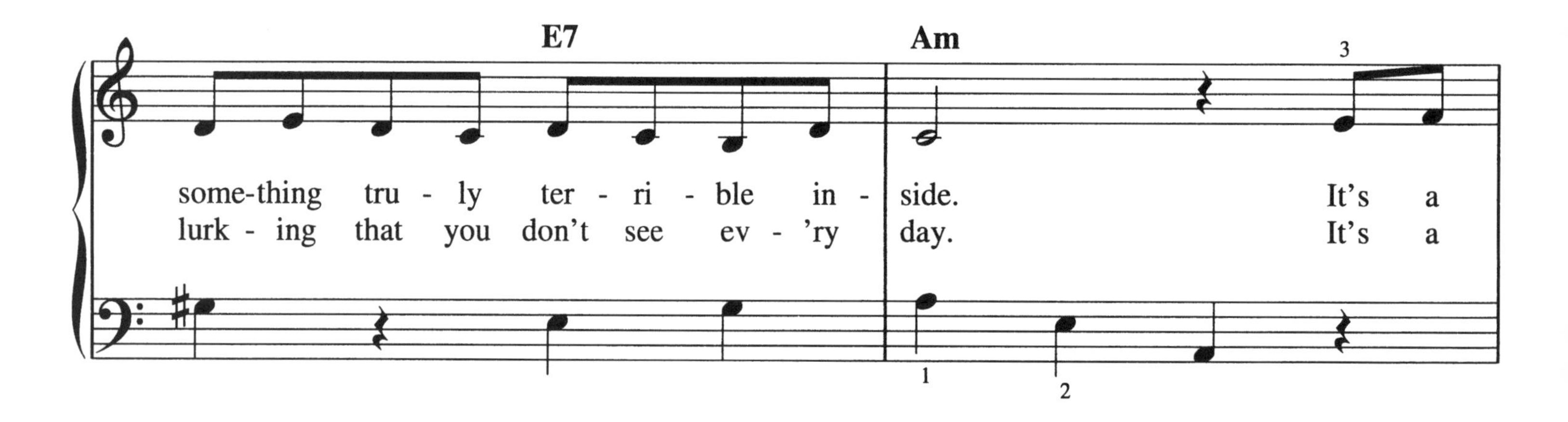
E7
Am
some-thing tru - ly ter - ri - ble in - side. It's a
lurk - ing that you don't see ev - 'ry day. It's a

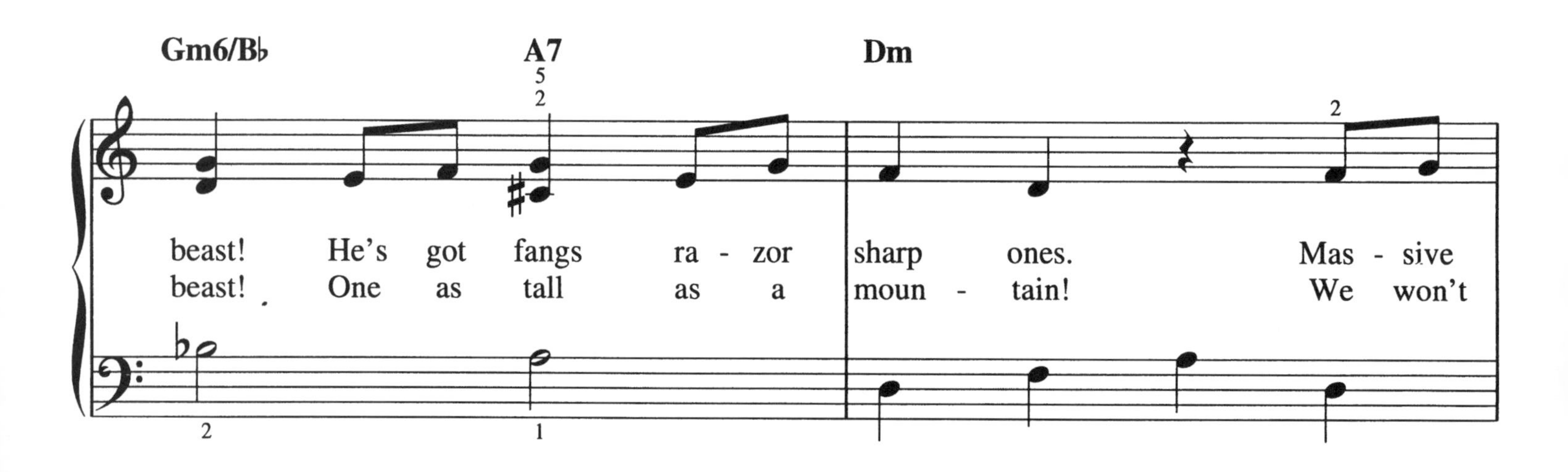
Gm6/B♭
A7
Dm
beast! He's got fangs ra - zor sharp ones. Mas - sive
beast! One as tall as a moun - tain! We won't

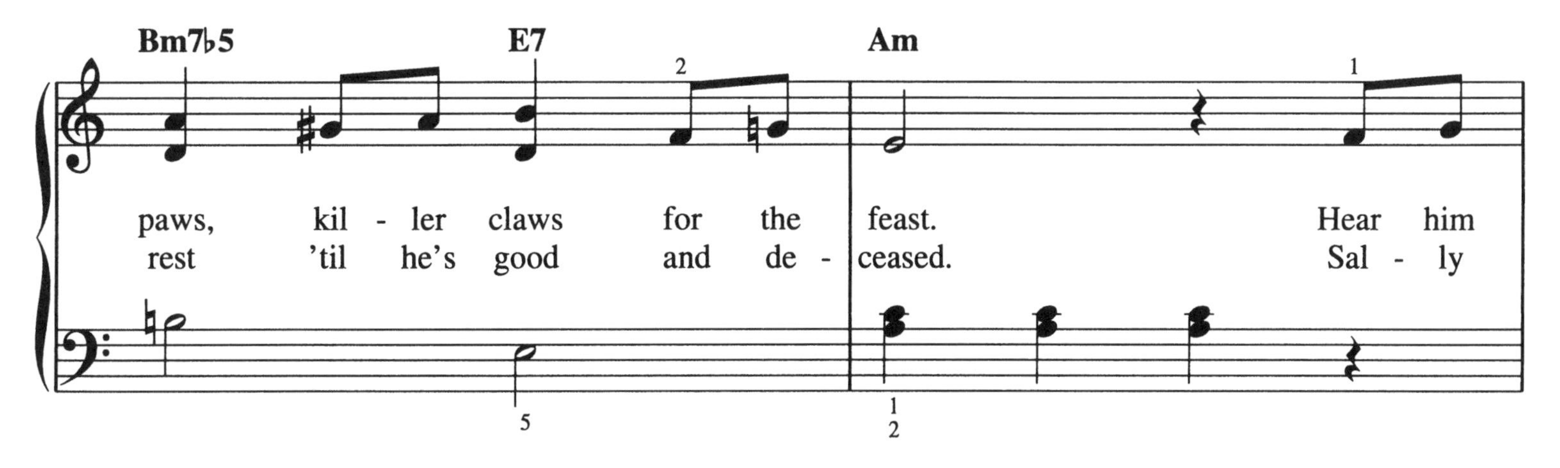

Bm7♭5
E7
Am
paws, kil - ler claws for the feast. Hear him
rest 'til he's good and de - ceased. Sal - ly

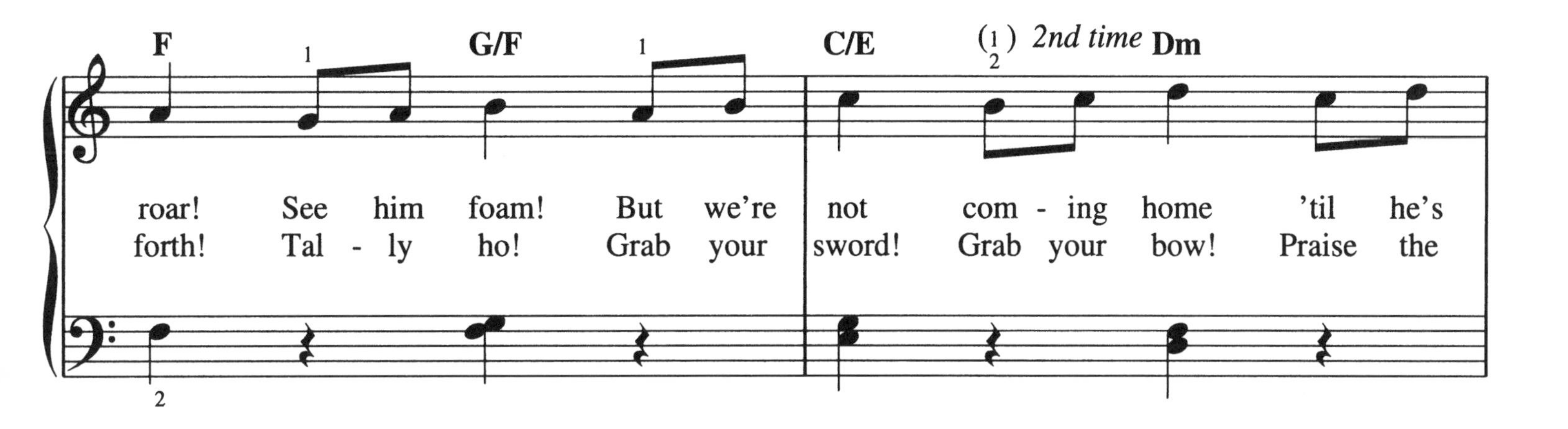

F
G/F
C/E
(1) 2nd time
Dm
roar! See him foam! But we're not com - ing home 'til he's
forth! Tal - ly ho! Grab your sword! Grab your bow! Praise the

1.
Bm7♭5
Esus
E
Am
dead! Good and dead! Kill the Beast! Belle: No! I won't let you
mp
Add pedal

B♭/A
E/A
Am
F/E
B7/E
do this! Gaston: If you're not with us, you're against us. (To the villagers:) Bring the old man!

E
Em7♭5
A
Dm
Maurice: Get your hands off me! Gaston: We can't have them running off to warn the creature! Belle: Let us
Bm7♭5
B7
Esus
out! Gaston: We'll rid the village of this Beast! Who's with me? Mob: I am! I am!
cresc.
Stop pedal
E
2.
Bm7♭5
I am!
f
Light your Lord and here we go! Gaston: We'll lay
Esus
siege to the castle and bring back his head!
mp

F D/F# G Dm/F E
Belle: I have to warn the Beast! This is all my fault! Oh, Papa, what are

Am G/B C7/B♭ F/A
we going to do? Maurice: Now, now, we'll think of something.

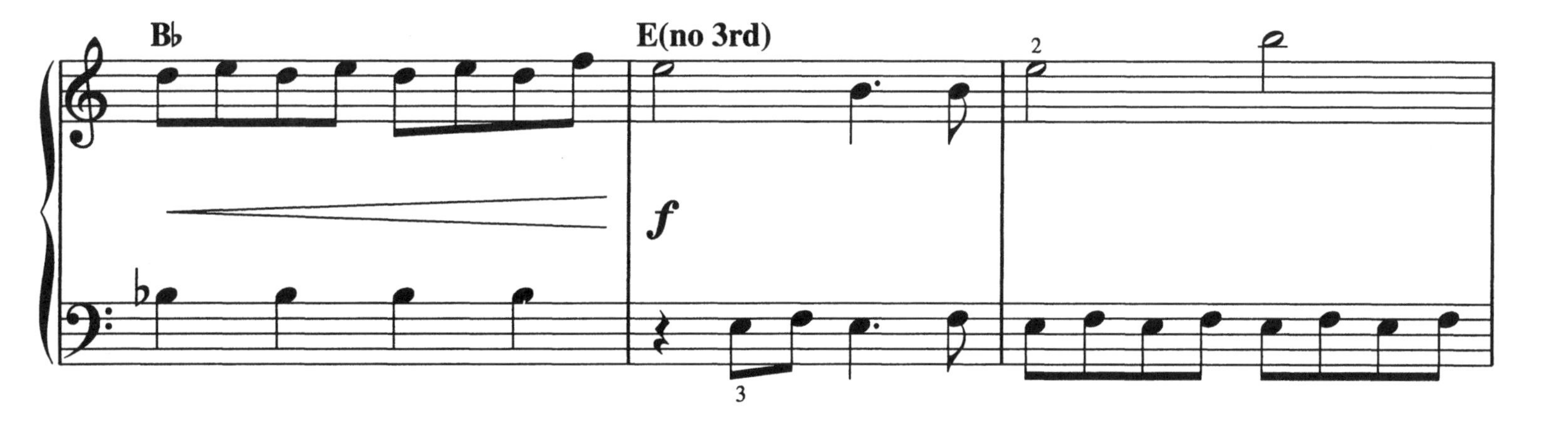
B♭ E(no 3rd)
f

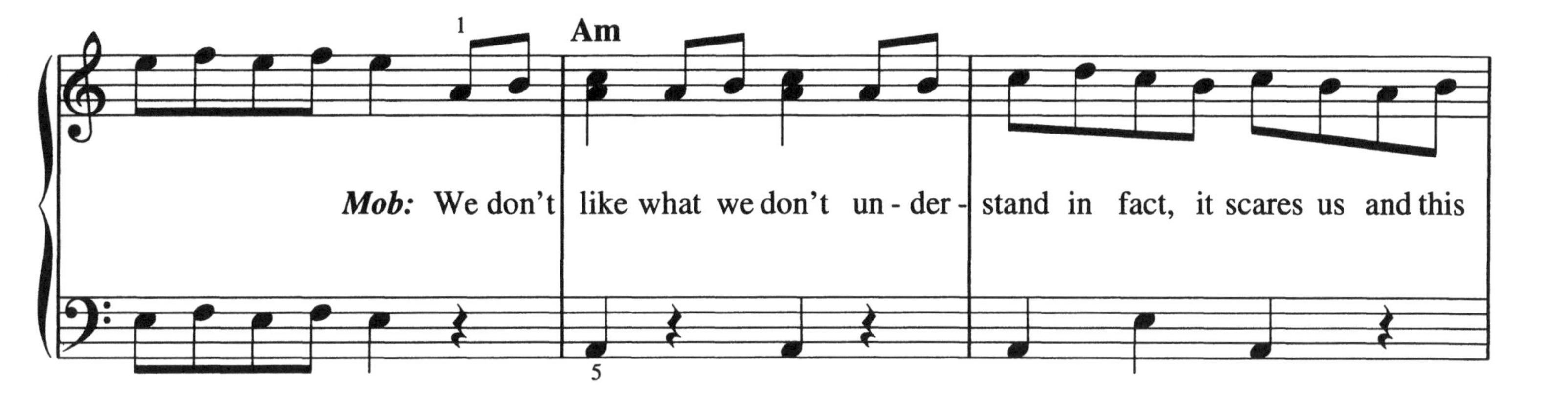
Am
Mob: We don't like what we don't un - der - stand in fact, it scares us and this

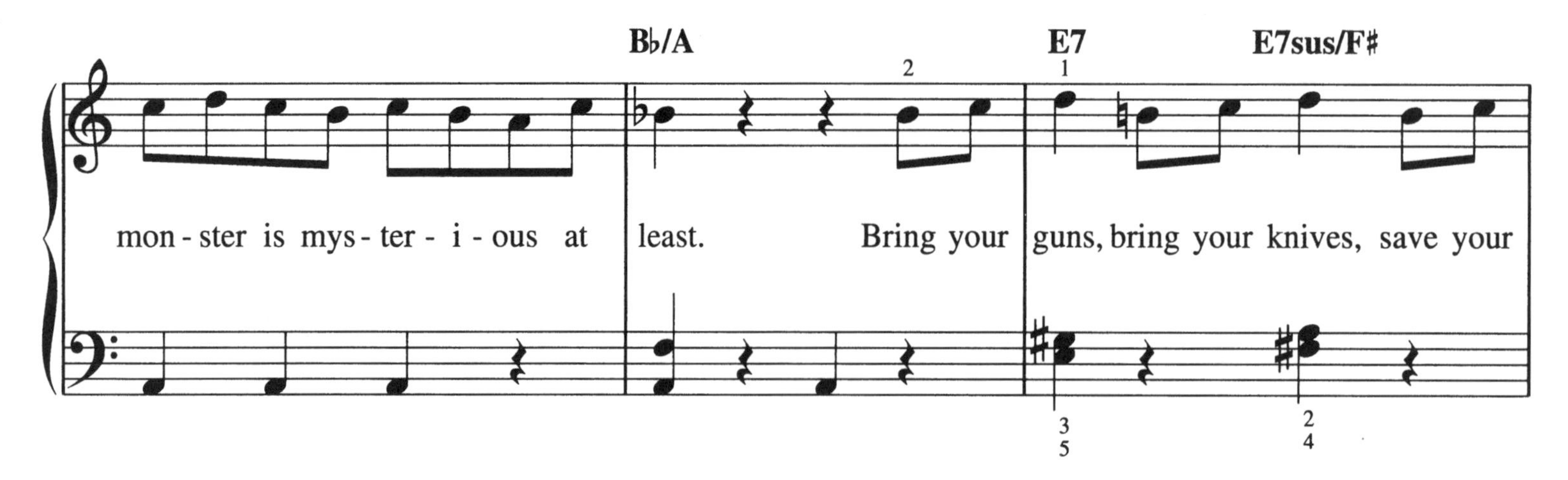

B♭/A
E7
E7sus/F♯
mon - ster is mys - ter - i - ous at
least.
Bring your
guns, bring your knives, save your

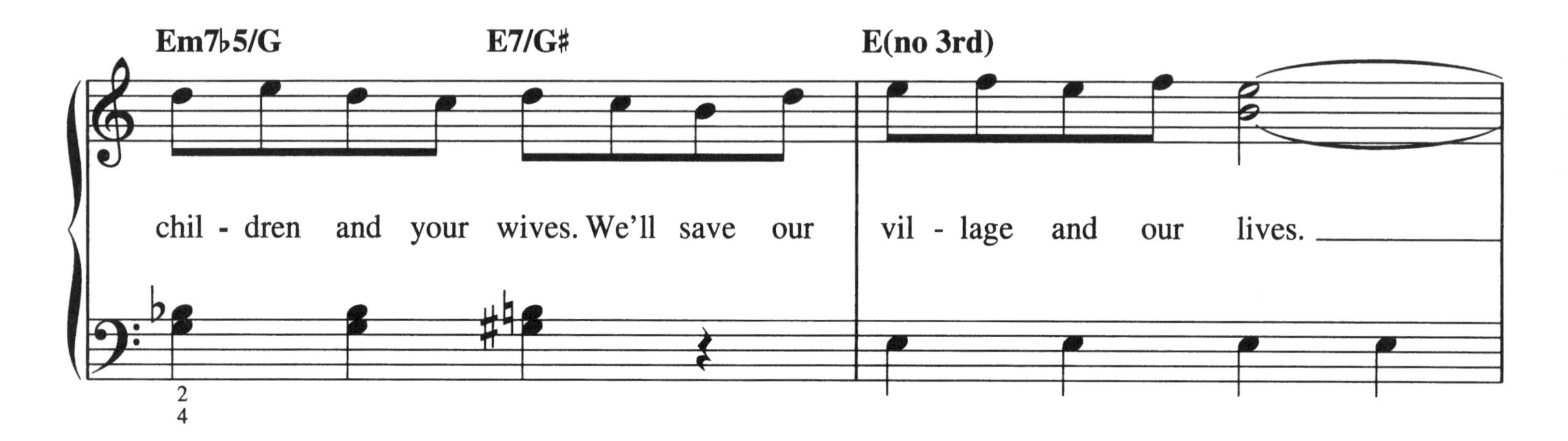

Em7♭5/G
E7/G♯
E(no 3rd)
chil - dren and your wives. We'll save our
vil - lage and our lives.

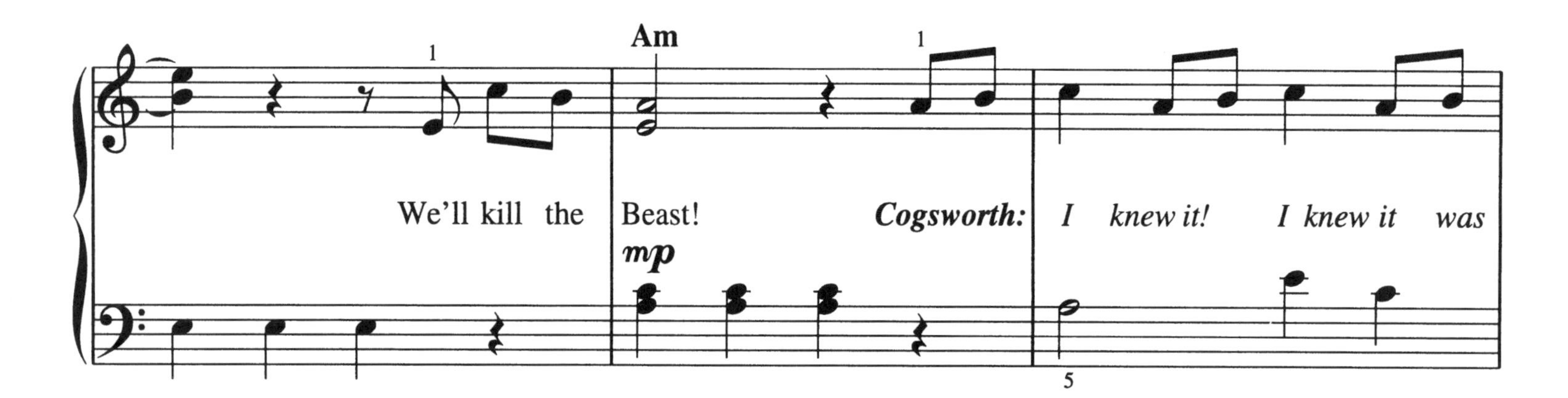

Am
We'll kill the
Beast!
Cogsworth:
I knew it! I knew it was
mp

foolish to get our hopes up.
Lumiere:
Maybe it would have been better if

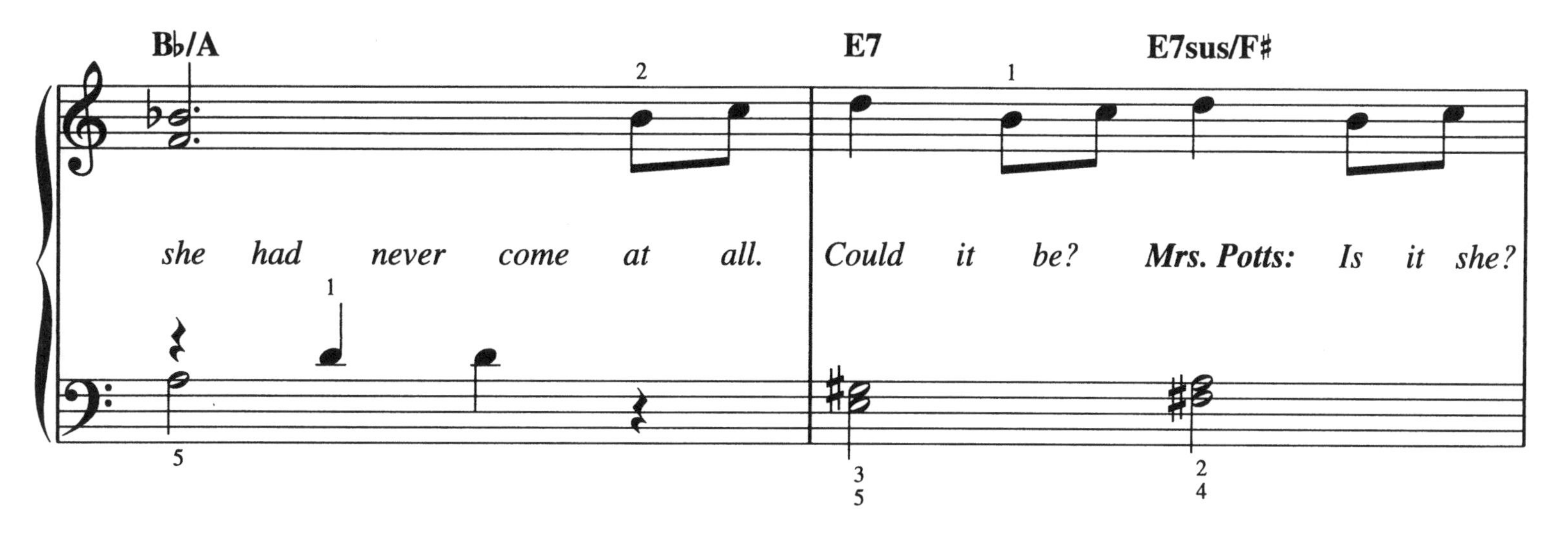
B♭/A
E7
E7sus/F♯
she had never come at all.
Could it be? Mrs. Potts: Is it she?

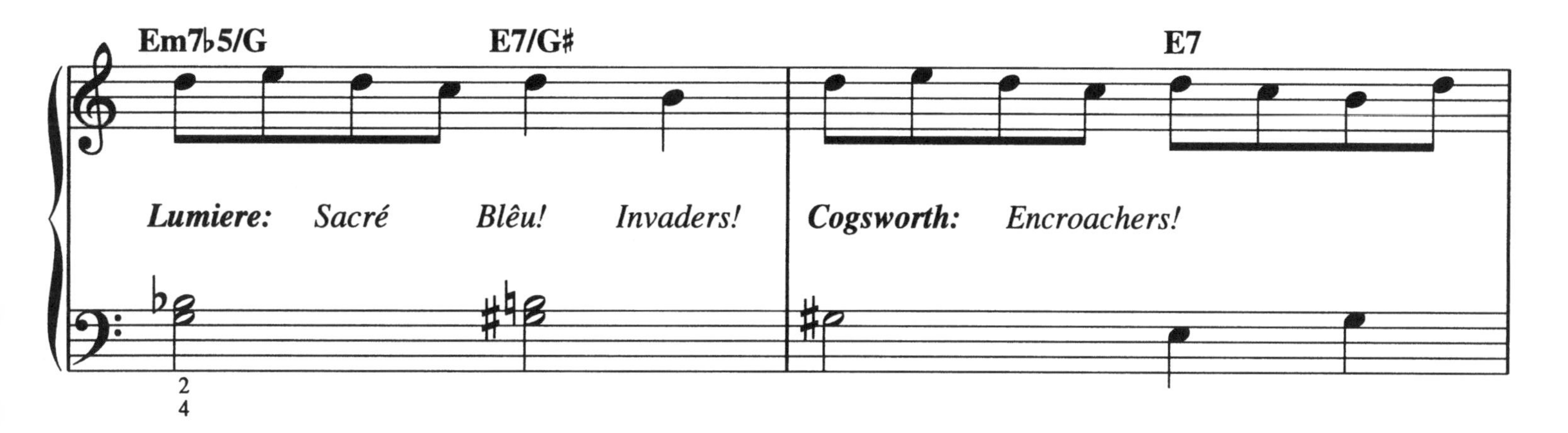
Em7♭5/G
E7/G♯
E7
Lumiere: Sacré Blêu! Invaders!
Cogsworth: Encroachers!

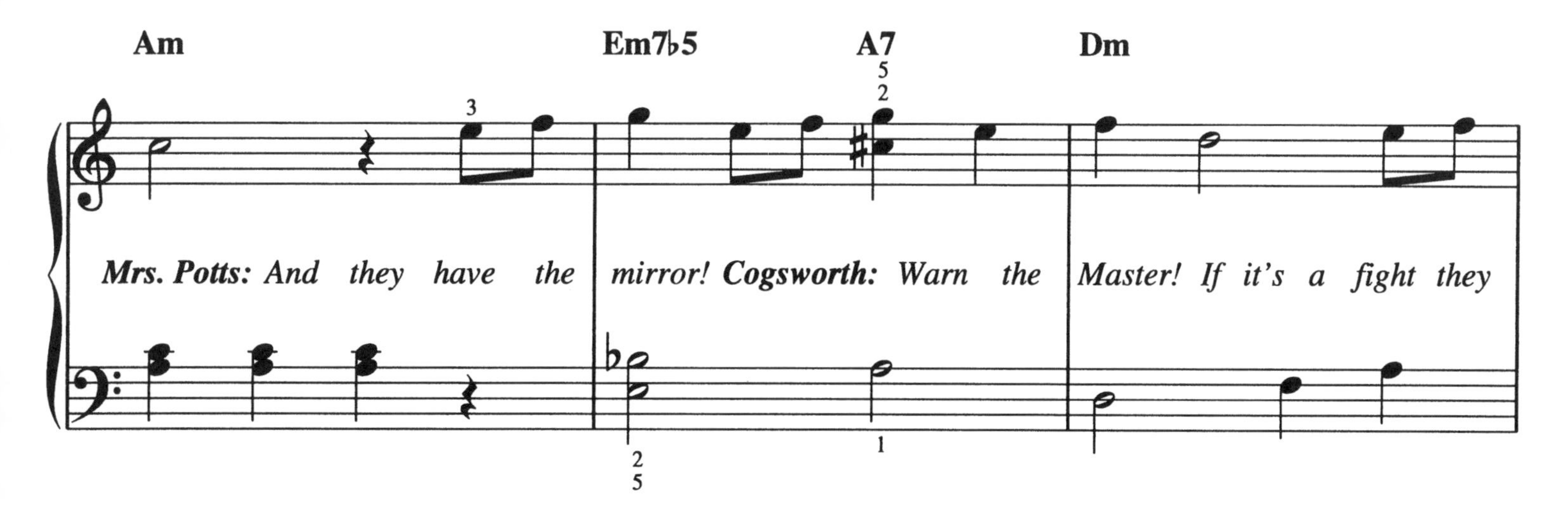
Am
Em7♭5
A7
Dm
Mrs. Potts: And they have the
mirror! Cogsworth: Warn the
Master! If it's a fight they

Em7♭5
A7
Dm
Bm7♭5
E7
want, we'll be ready for them!
Who's with me?
Gaston: Take whatever booty

E(no 3rd)

you can find. But remember, the Beast is mine! ***Objects:*** Hearts a -

f

Am
blaze, ban - ners high, we go marching - ing in - to bat - tle un - a -

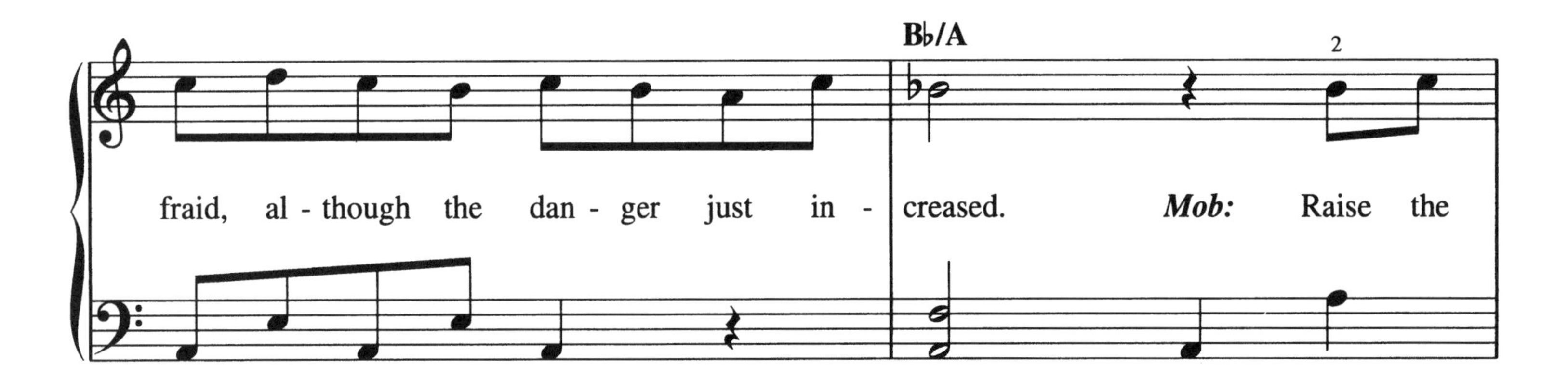
B♭/A
fraid, al - though the dan - ger just in - creased. Mob: Raise the

E7
E7sus/F♯
Em7♭5/G
E7/G♯
flag! Sing the song! Here we come we're fif - ty strong! And fif - ty

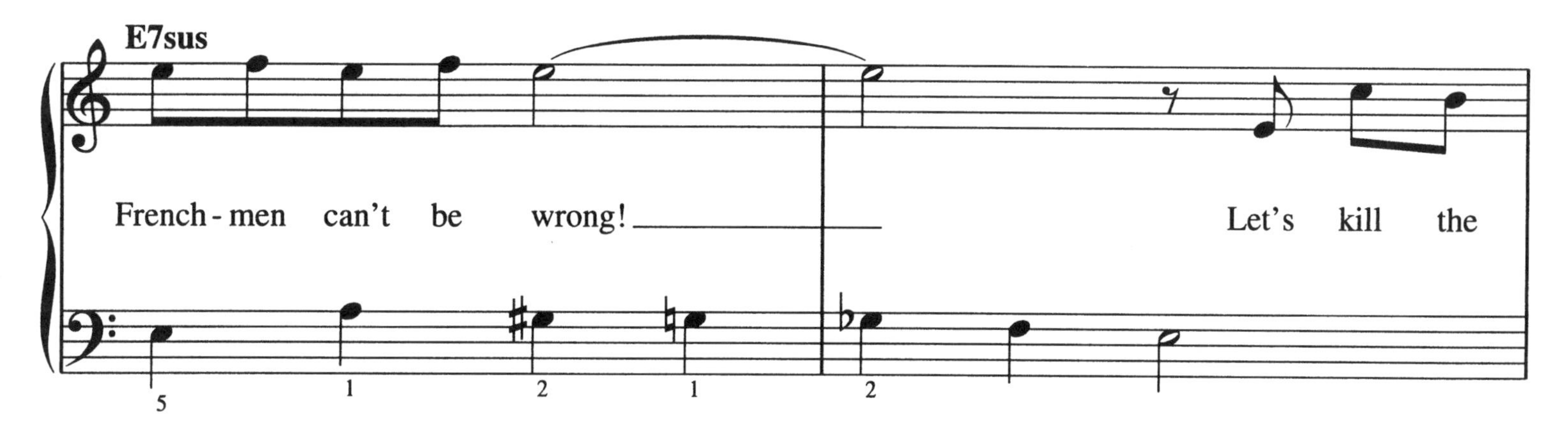
E7sus
French-men can't be wrong!
Let's kill the
5
1
2
1
2

Am
B♭/A
E/A
4
1
Beast!
mp
Mrs. Potts: Pardon me, Master.
Add pedal

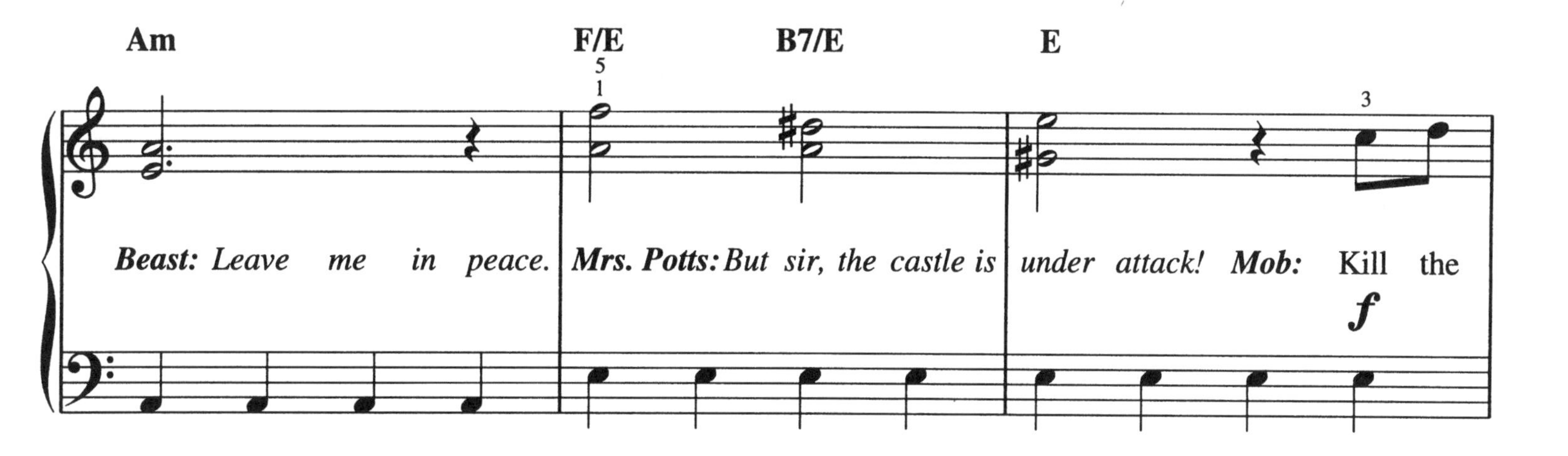
Am
F/E
B7/E
E
5
1
3
Beast: Leave me in peace.
Mrs. Potts: But sir, the castle is under attack!
Mob: Kill the
f

Esus
G♭/F
C7/F
5
1
Beast! Kill the Beast!
Lumiere: This isn't working!
mp
2

F
Ab/G
D7/G
G
3
Feather duster: Oh, Lumiere. We
must do something! Lumiere:
Wait, I know! Mob: Kill the
f

Gsus
Ab/G
D7/G
Beast! Kill the
Beast! Mrs. Potts:
What shall we do, Master?
mp

G
Bb/A
E7/A
A
3
Beast: It doesn't matter
now. Just let them
come. Mob: Kill the
ff
Stop pedal

Asus
Beast! Kill the
Beast! Kill the
Beast!

TRANSFORMATION/ BEAUTY AND THE BEAST (REPRISE)

TRANSFORMATION
Music by ALAN MENKEN
Lyrics by TIM RICE

BEAUTY AND THE BEAST (REPRISE)
Lyrics by HOWARD ASHMAN
Music by ALAN MENKEN

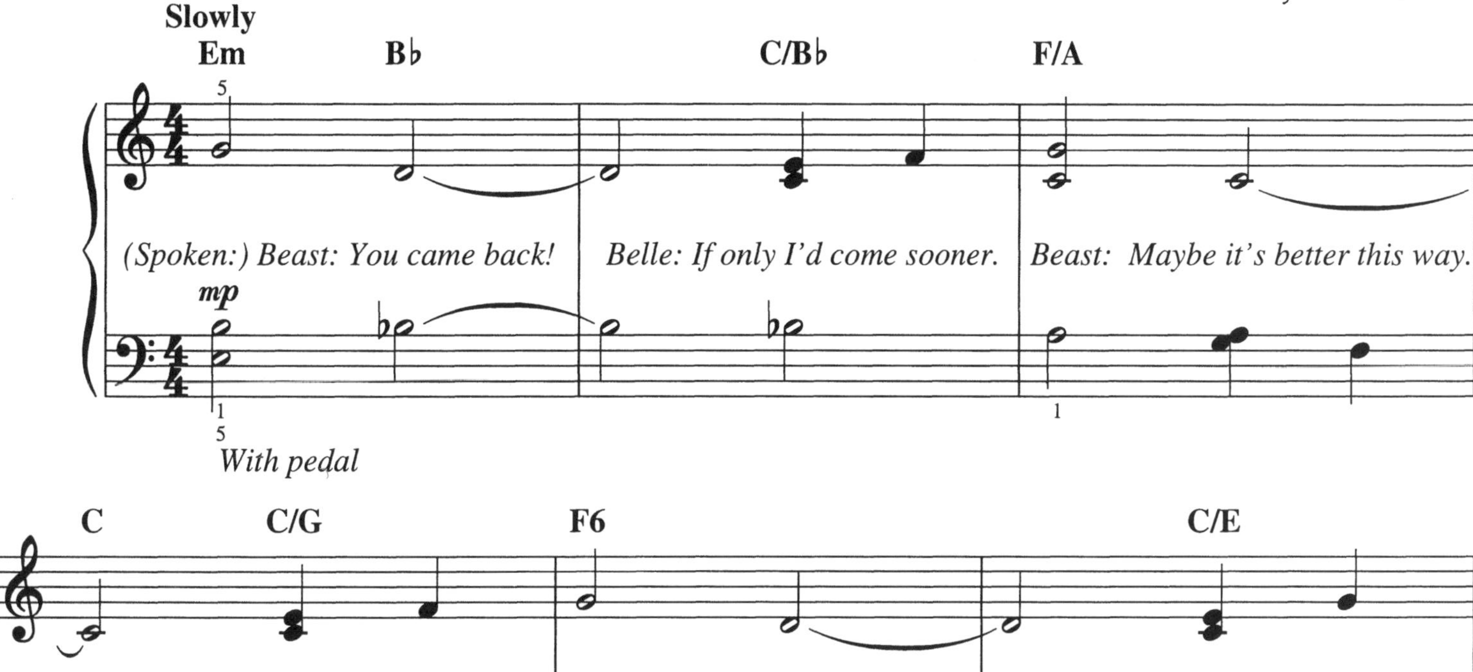

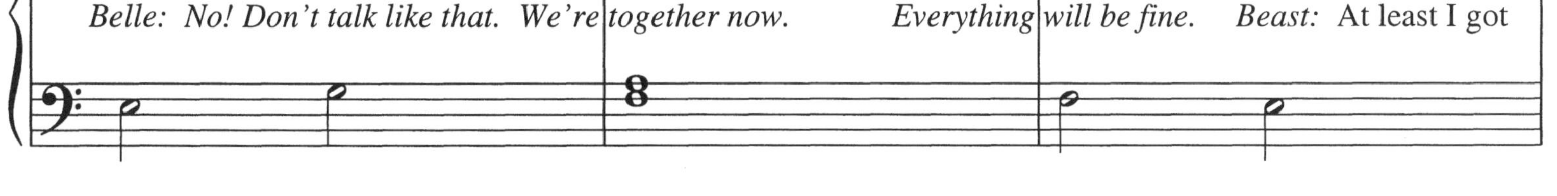

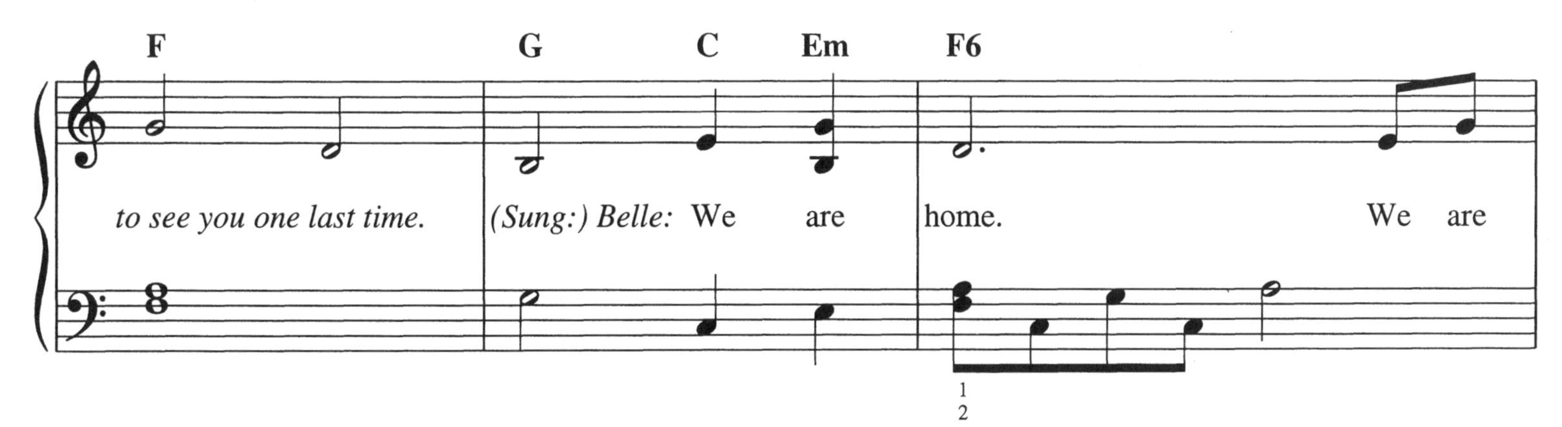

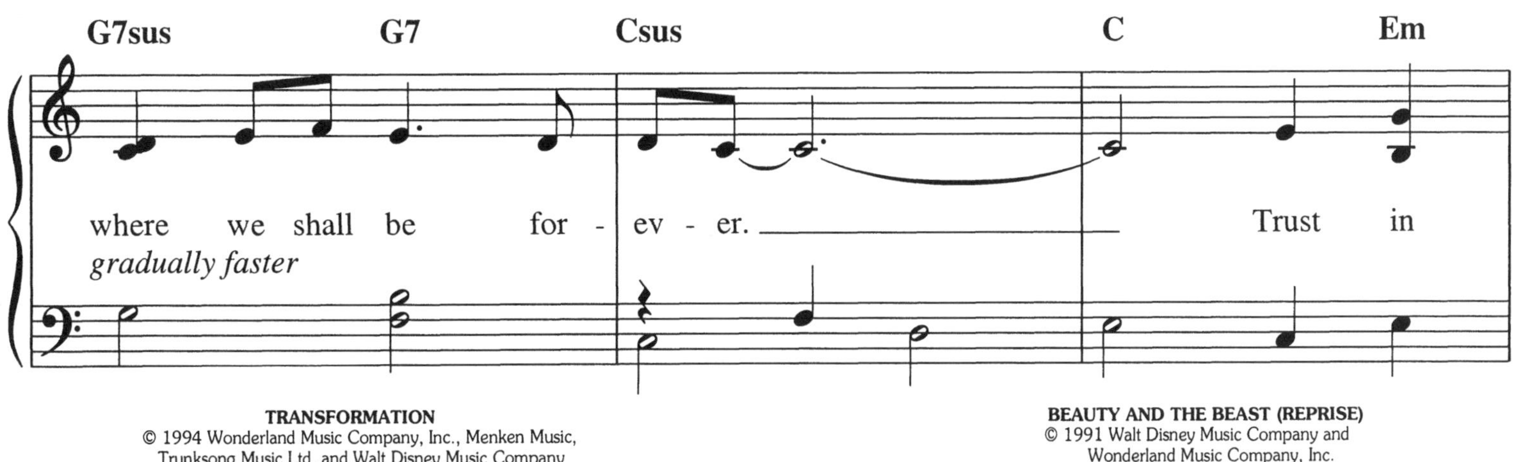

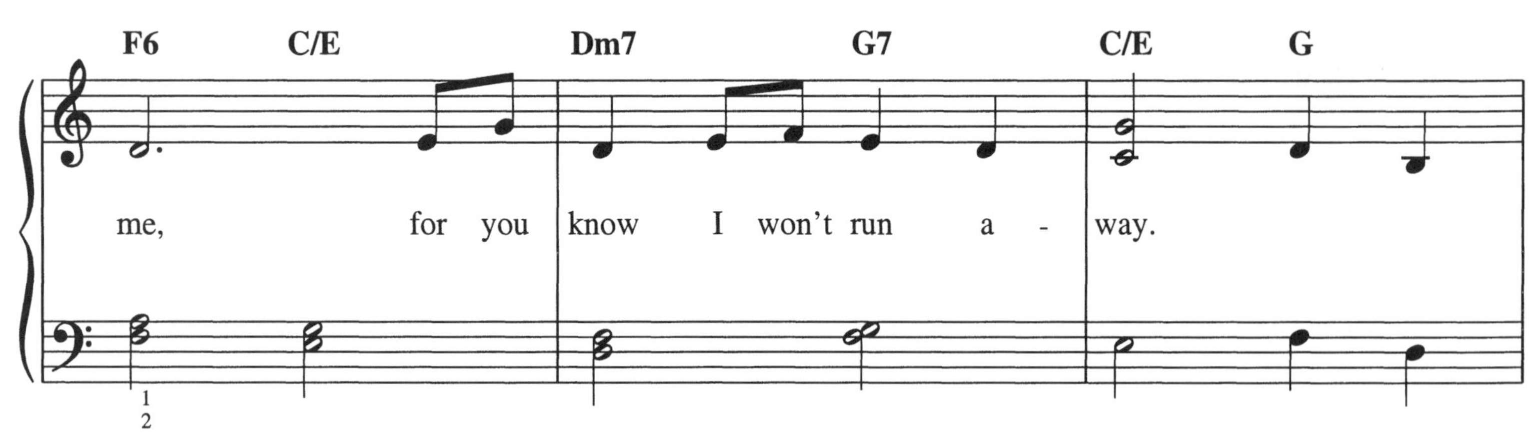
F6 C/E Dm7 G7 C/E G
me, for you know I won't run a - way.

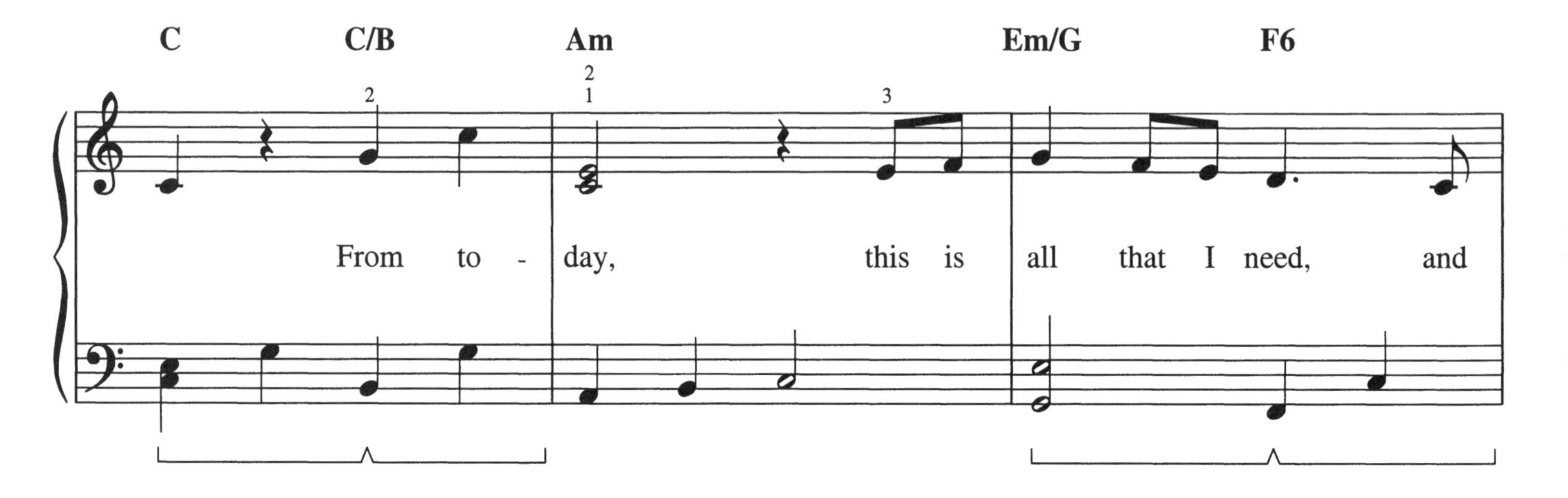
C C/B Am Em/G F6
From to - day, this is all that I need, and

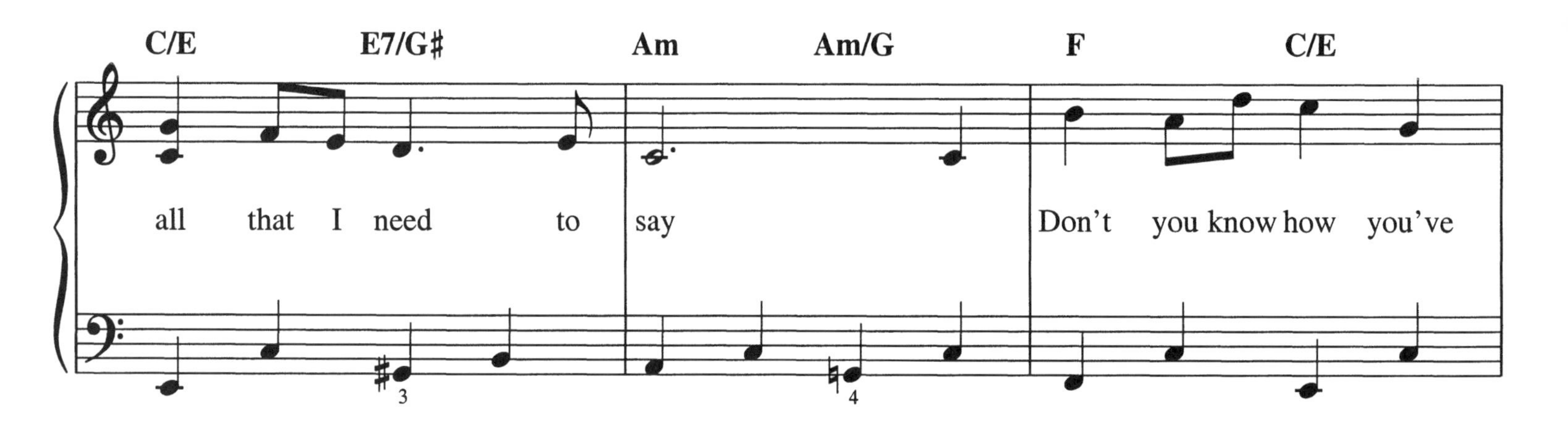
C/E E7/G♯ Am Am/G F C/E
all that I need to say Don't you know how you've

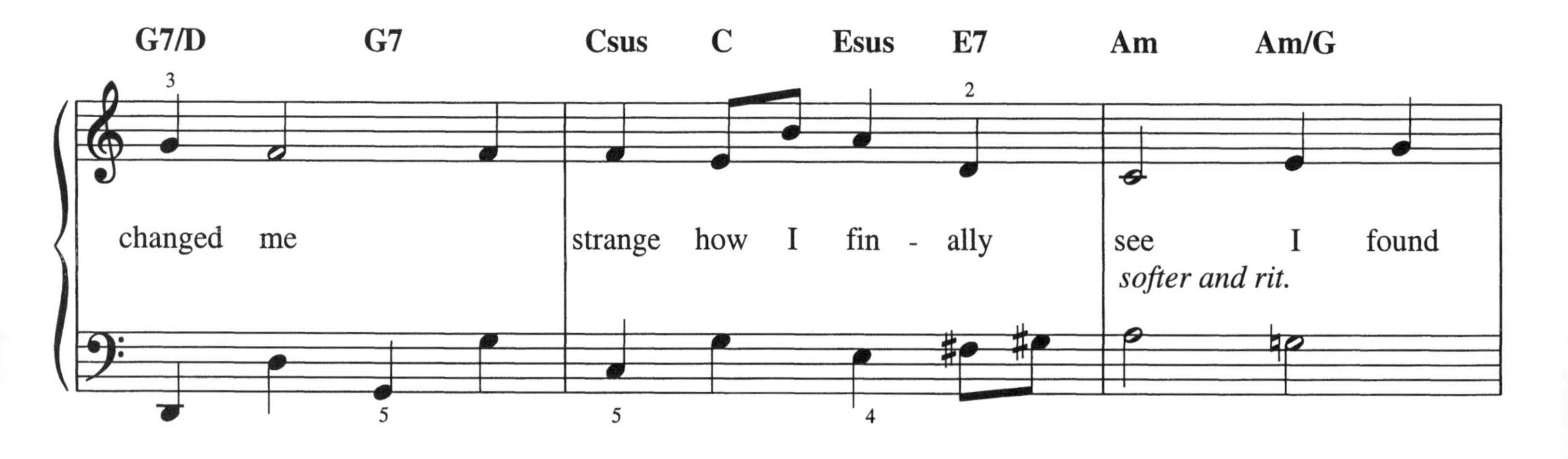
G7/D G7 Csus C Esus E7 Am Am/G
changed me strange how I fin - ally see I found
softer and rit.

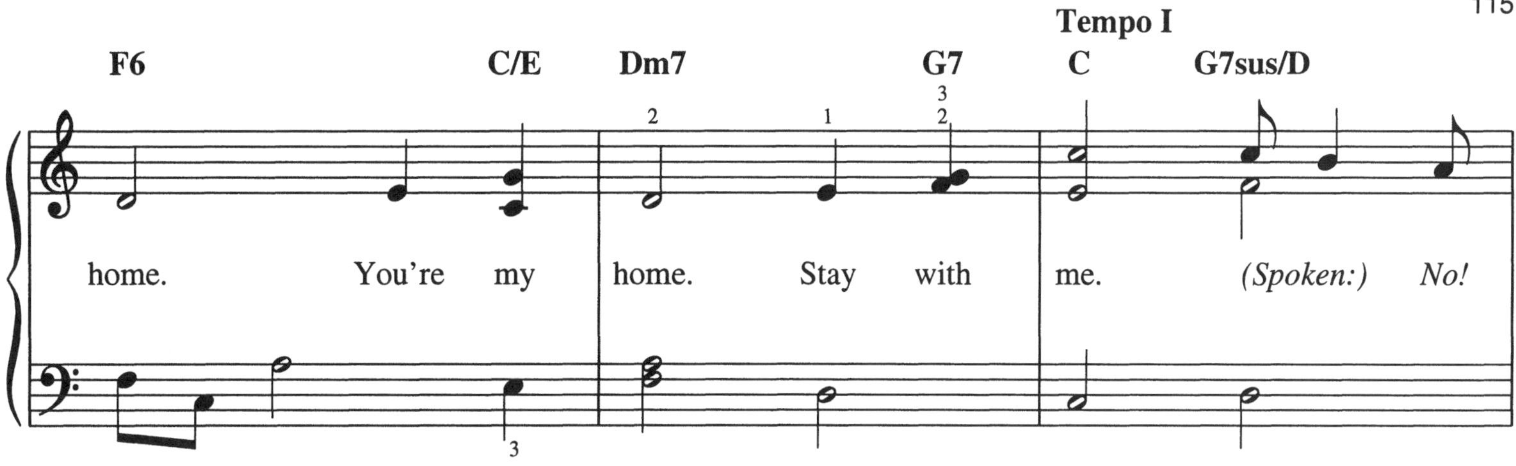
Tempo I
F6
C/E
Dm7
G7
C
G7sus/D
home. You're my home. Stay with me. (Spoken:) No!

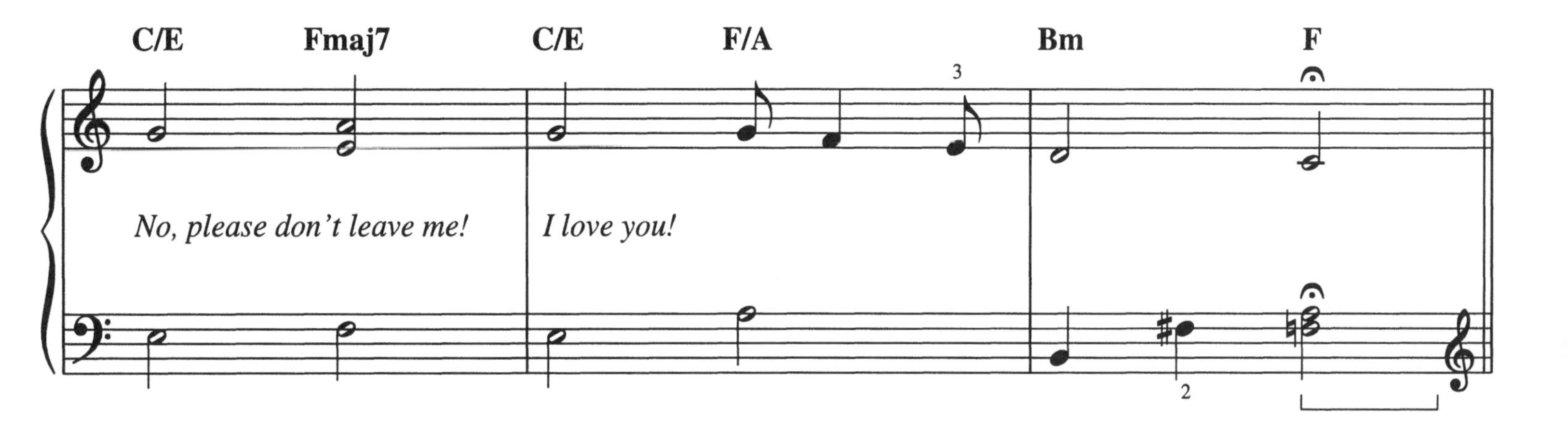
C/E
Fmaj7
C/E
F/A
Bm
F
No, please don't leave me!
I love you!

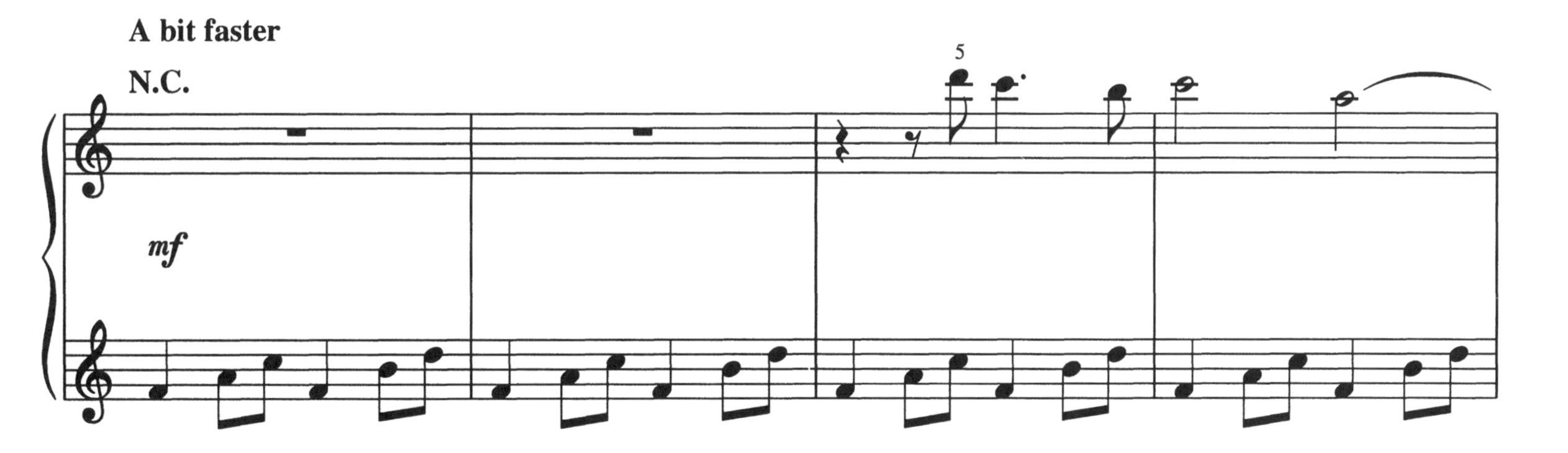
A bit faster
N.C.
mf

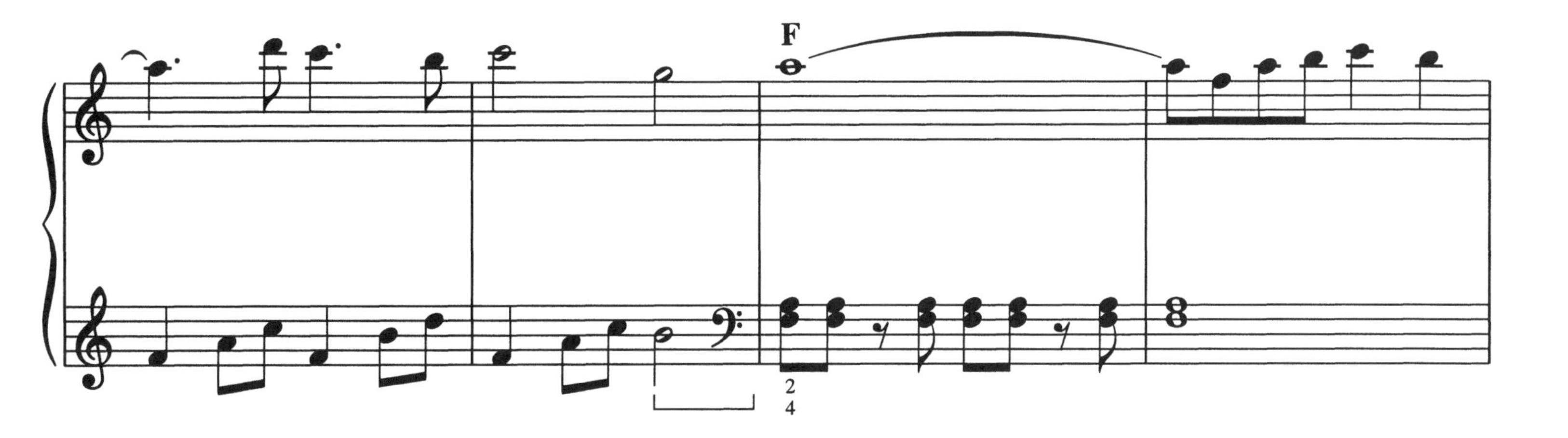
F

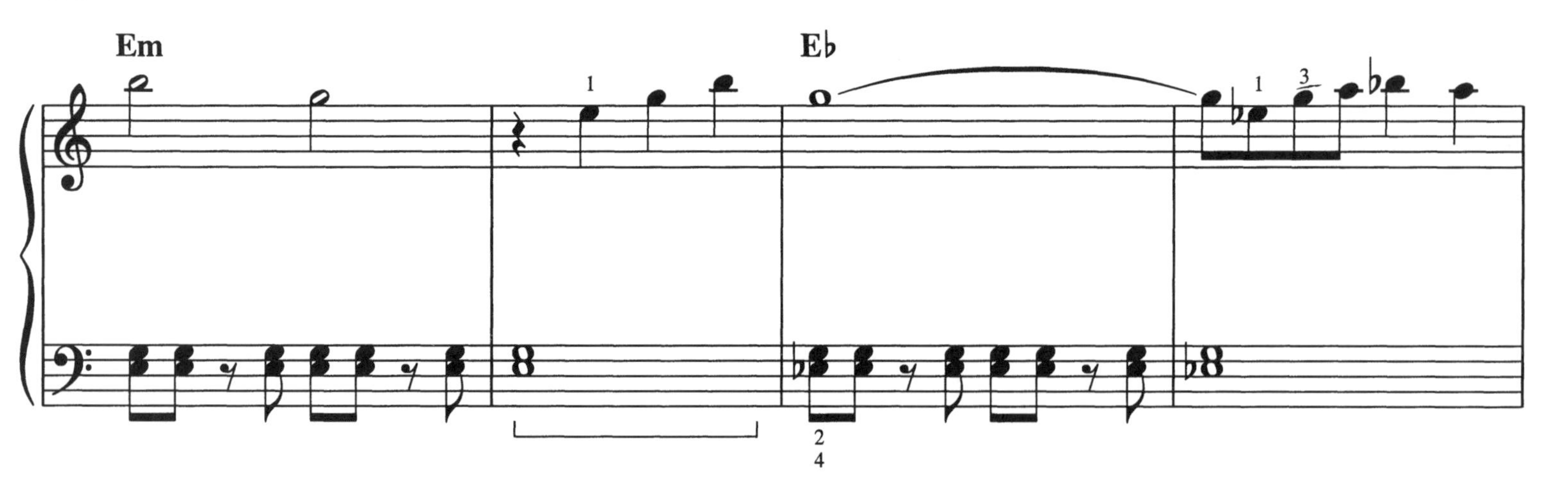
Em
E♭

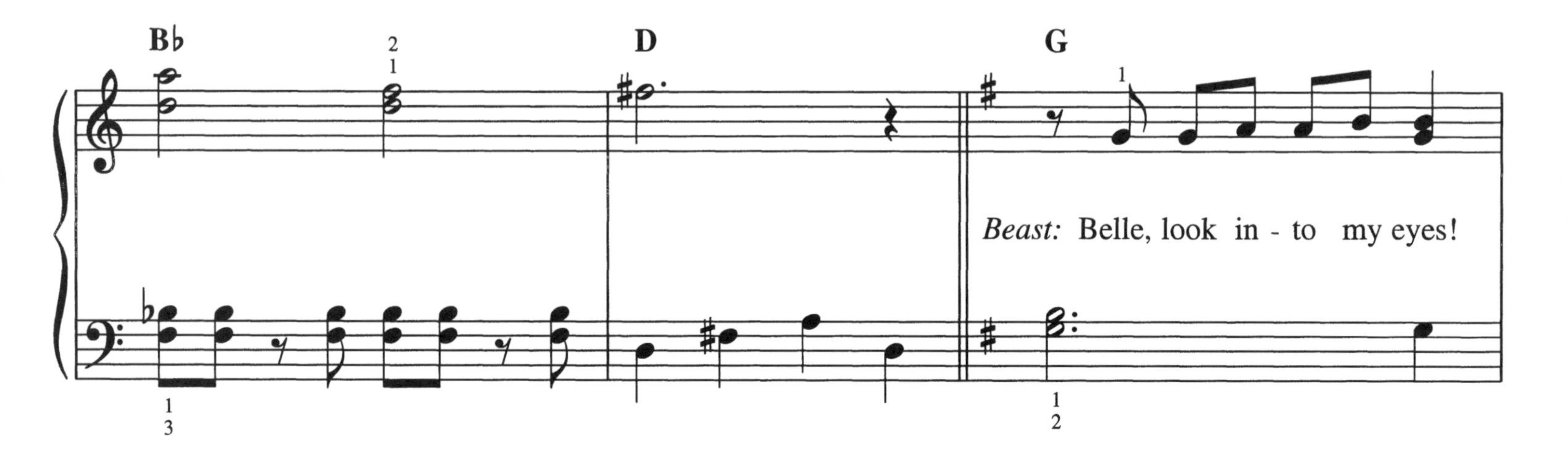
B♭
D
G
Beast: Belle, look in - to my eyes!

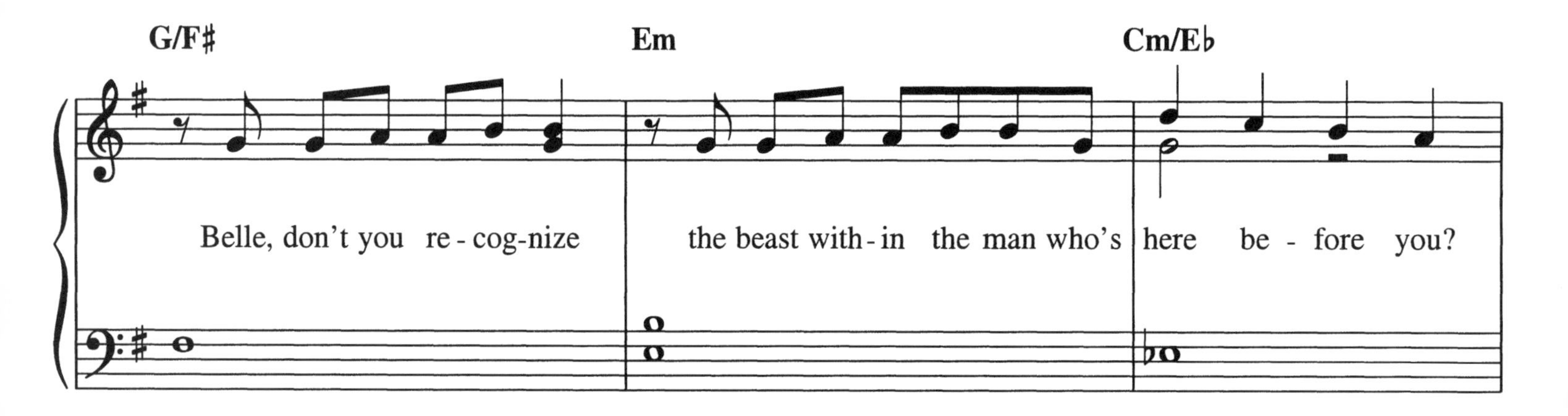
G/F♯
Em
Cm/E♭
Belle, don't you re - cog-nize
the beast with - in the man who's
here be - fore you?

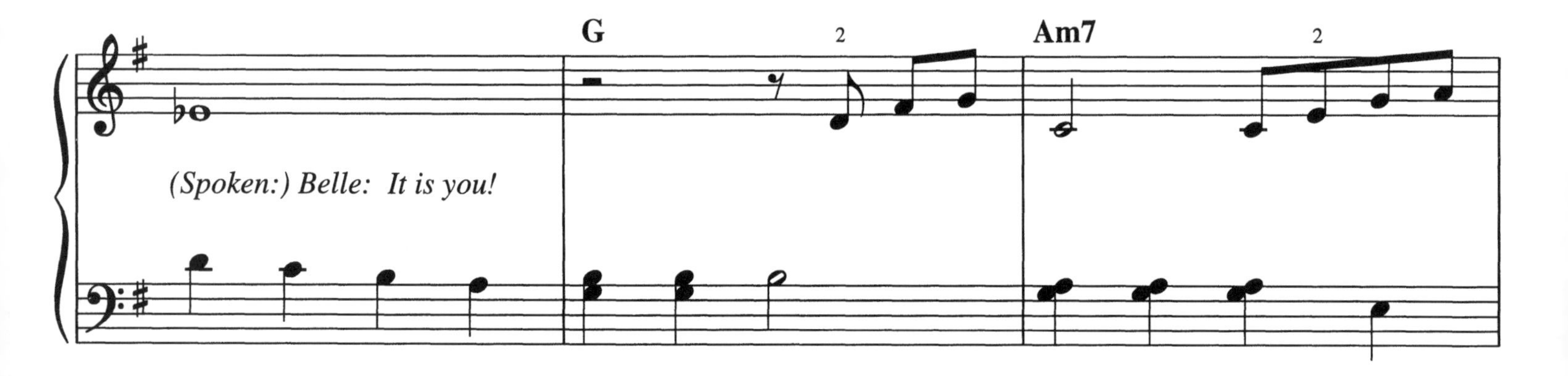
G
Am7
(Spoken:) Belle: It is you!

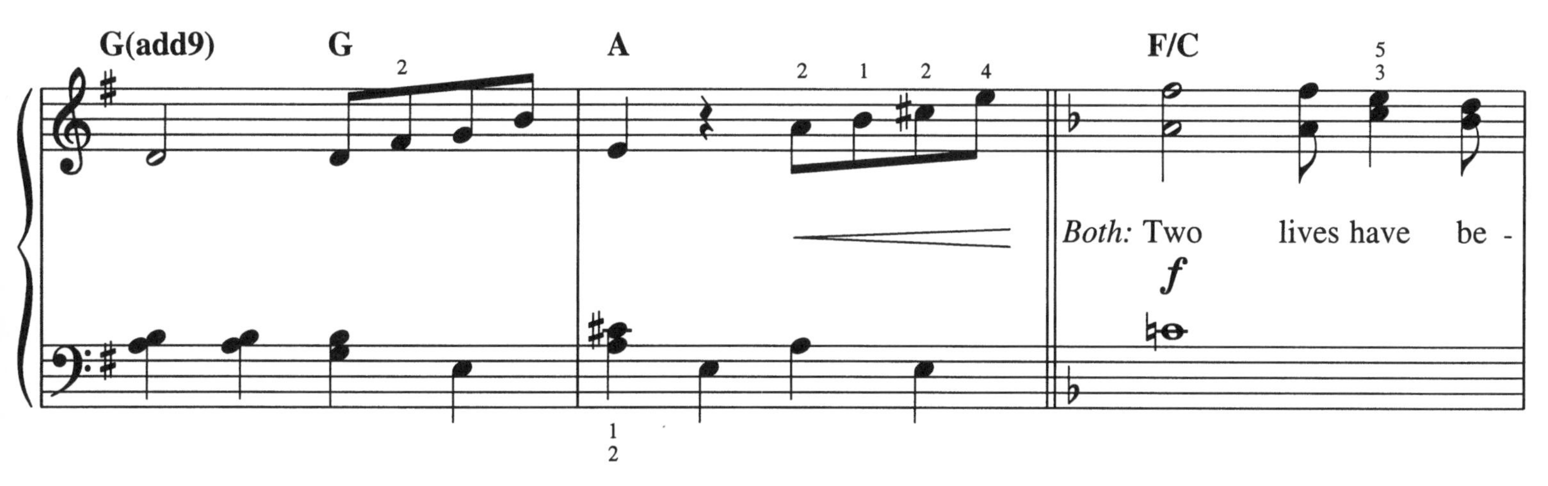
G(add9)
G
A
F/C
Both: Two lives have be -
f

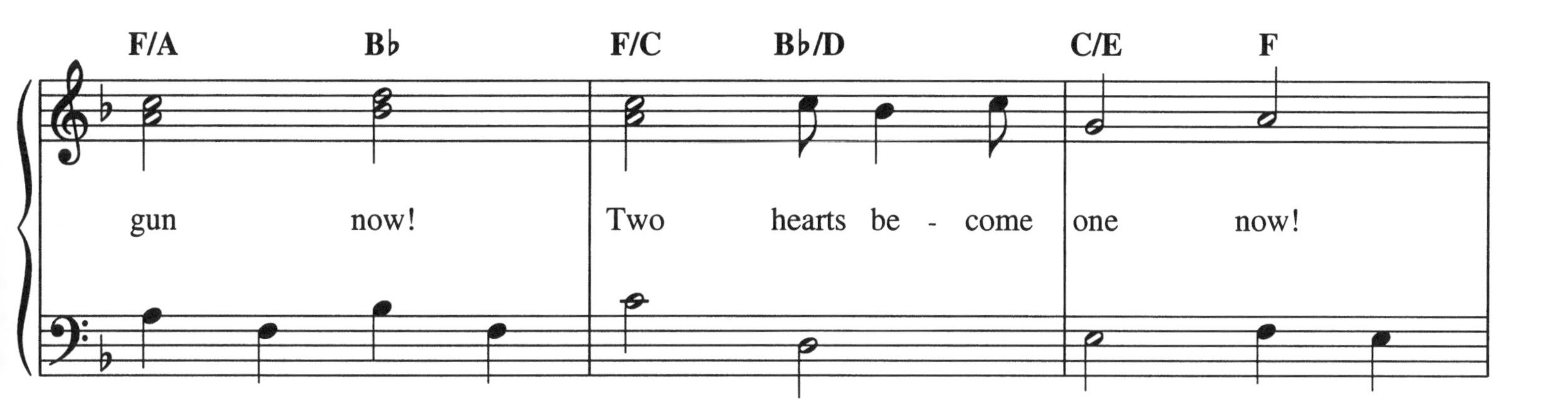
F/A
B♭
F/C
B♭/D
C/E
F
gun now! Two hearts be - come one now!

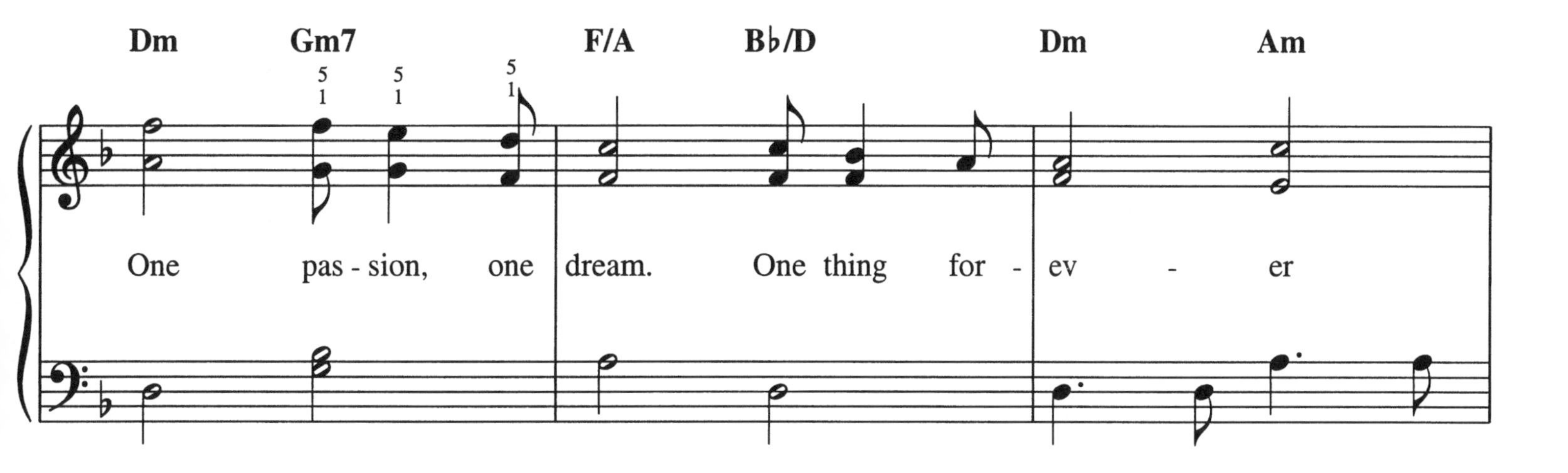
Dm
Gm7
F/A
B♭/D
Dm
Am
One pas - sion, one dream. One thing for - ev - er

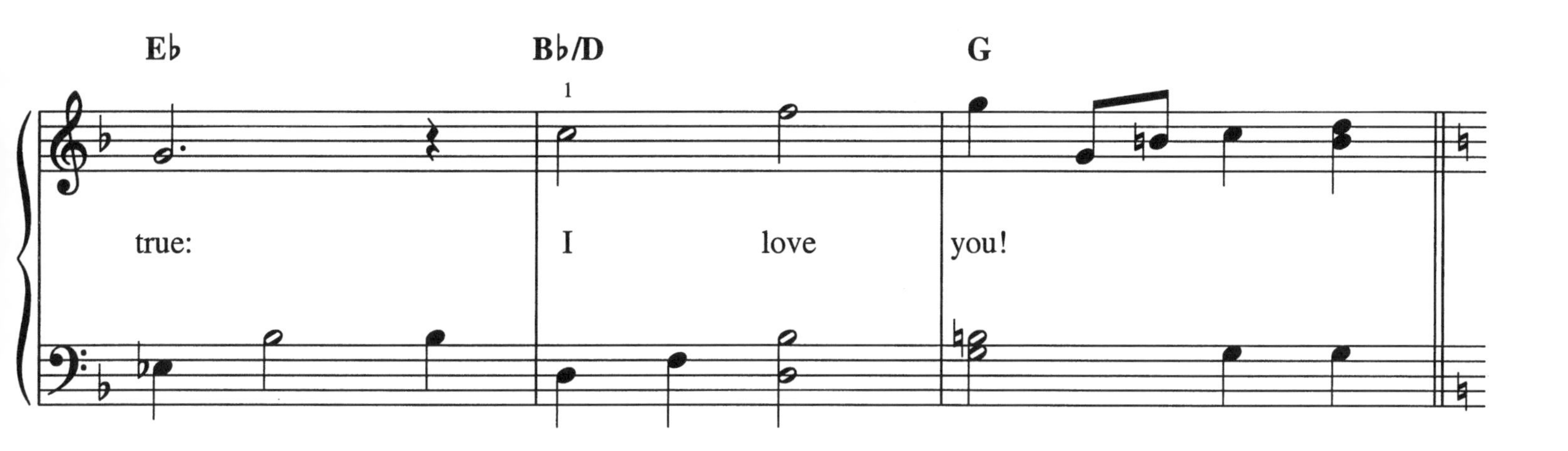
E♭
B♭/D
G
true: I love you!

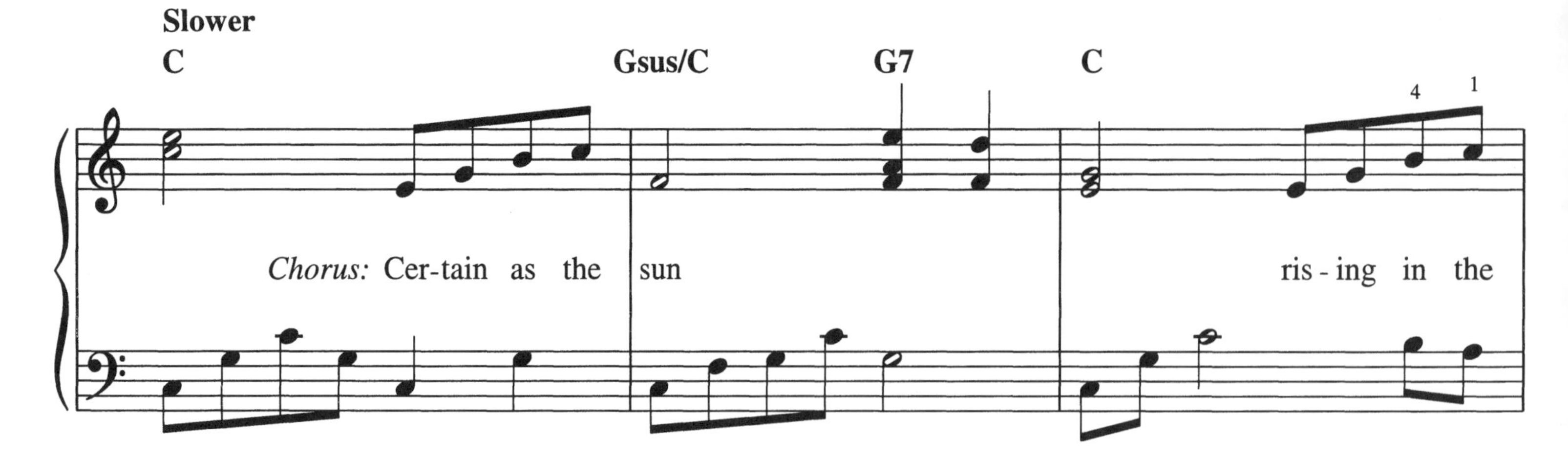
Slower
C
Gsus/C
G7
C
Chorus: Cer-tain as the sun ris - ing in the

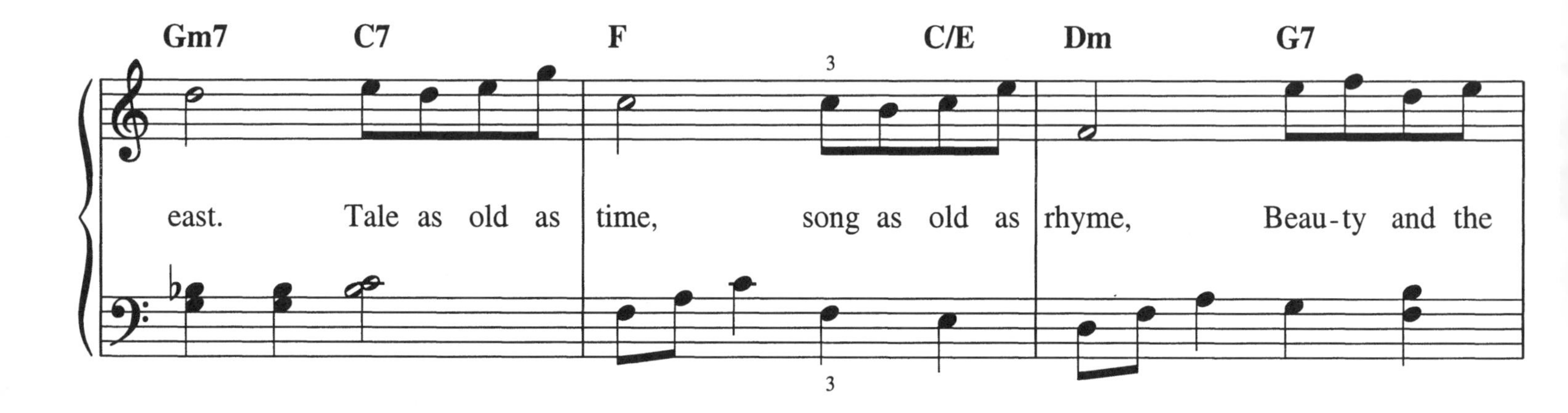
Gm7
C7
F
C/E
Dm
G7
east. Tale as old as time, song as old as rhyme, Beau-ty and the

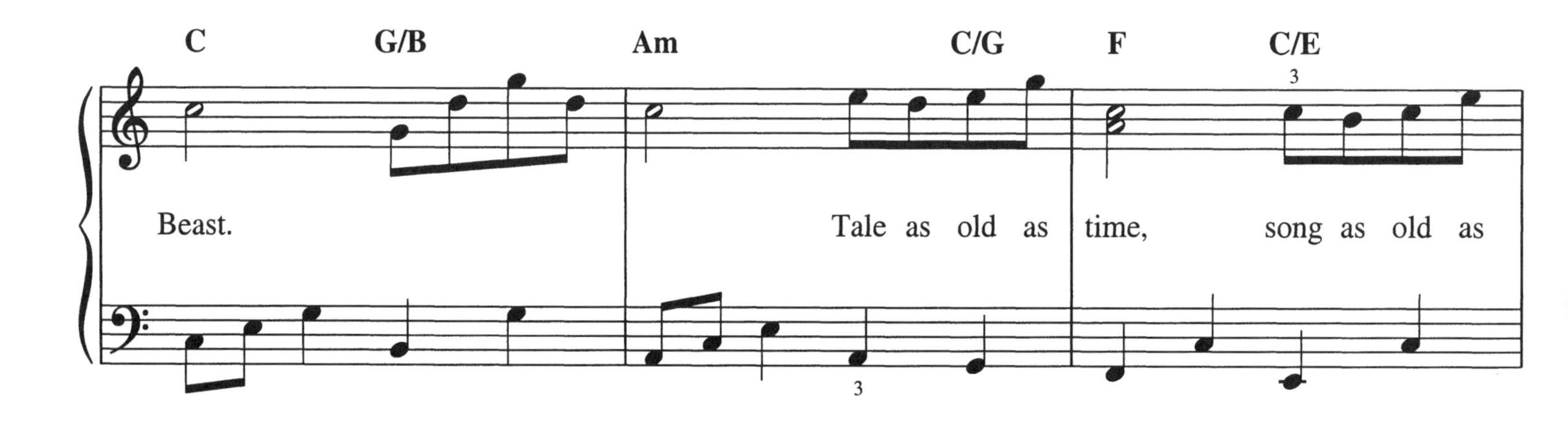
C
G/B
Am
C/G
F
C/E
Beast. Tale as old as time, song as old as

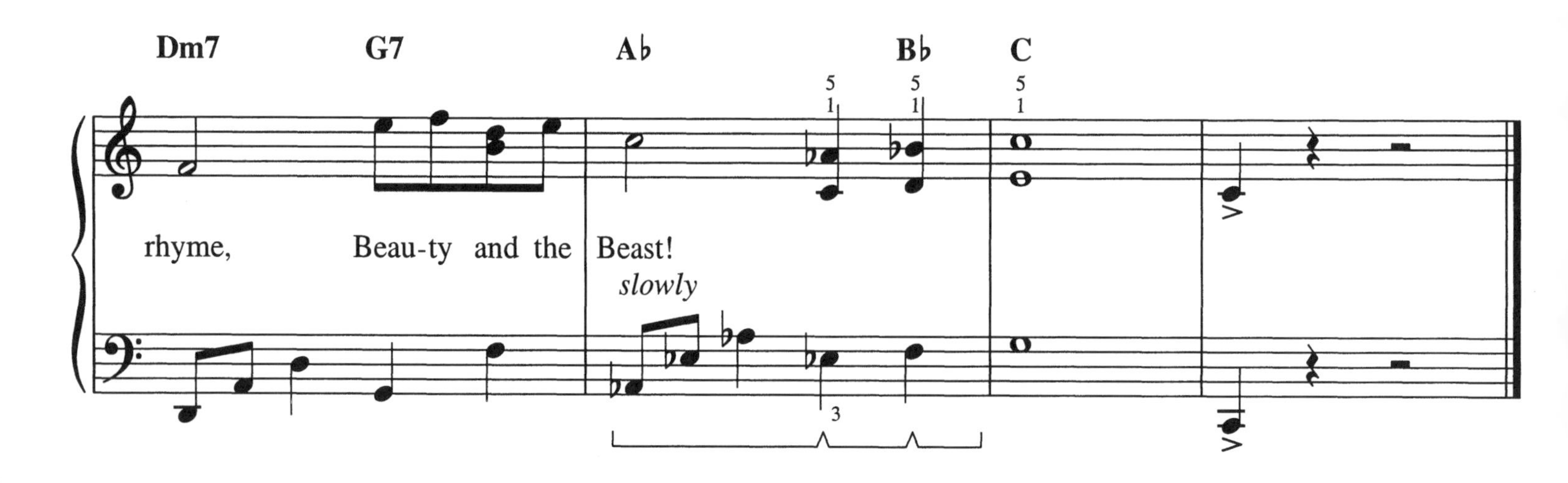
Dm7
G7
A♭
B♭
C
rhyme, Beau-ty and the Beast!
slowly